SOME KIND
OF PARADISE

Recent Titles in
Contributions to the Study of Science Fiction and Fantasy
Series Editor: Marshall Tymn

H. P. Lovecraft: A Critical Study
Donald R. Burleson

A Literary Symbiosis: Science Fiction/Fantasy Mystery
Hazel Beasley Pierce

The Intersection of Science Fiction and Philosophy: Critical Studies
Robert E. Meyers, editor

Clockwork Worlds: Mechanized Environments in SF
Richard D. Erlich and Thomas P. Dunn, editors

Apertures: A Study of the Writings of Brian W. Aldiss
Brian Griffin and David Wingrove

The Dark Barbarian: The Writings of Robert E. Howard
A Critical Anthology
Don Herron, editor

The Scope of the Fantastic—Theory, Technique, Major Authors: Selected
Essays from the First International Conference on the Fantastic in Literature
and Film
Robert A. Collins and Howard D. Pearce, editors

Death and the Serpent: Immortality in Science Fiction and Fantasy
Carl B. Yoke and Donald M. Hassler

The Transcendent Adventure: Studies of Religion in Science Fiction/Fantasy
Robert Reilly, editor

The Return from Avalon: A Study of the Arthurian Legend in Modern Fiction
Raymond H. Thompson

The Comedy of the Fantastic: Ecological Perspectives on the Fantasy Novel
Don D. Elgin

The Scope of the Fantastic—Culture, Biography, Themes, Children's
Literature: Selected Essays from the First International Conference on the
Fantastic in Literature and Film
Robert A. Collins and Howard D. Pearce, editors

SOME KIND OF PARADISE

The Emergence of American Science Fiction

THOMAS D. CLARESON

Contributions to the Study of Science Fiction and Fantasy, Number 16

Greenwood Press
Westport, Connecticut • London, England

Library of Congress Cataloging in Publication Data

Clareson, Thomas D.
  Some kind of paradise.

  (Contributions to the study of science fiction and
fantasy, ISSN 0193-6875 ; no. 16)
  Bibliography: p.
  Includes index.
  1. Science fiction, American—History and criticism.
2. American fiction—20th century—History and criticism.
I. Title. II. Series.
PS374.S35C56   1985   813'.0876   84-29060
ISBN 0-313-23167-2 (lib. bdg.)

PS374
S 35
C 56
1985

Library of Congress Catalog Card Number: 84-29060
ISBN: 0-313-23167-2
ISSN: 0193-6875

First published in 1985

Greenwood Press
A division of Congressional Information Service, Inc.
88 Post Road West
Westport, Connecticut 06881

Printed in the United States of America

10 9 8 7 6 5 4 3 2 1

From the outset, though in different
ways, three individuals have guided my work,
often by their advice and always by their
example. To them I dedicate this present study:

J.O. Bailey
Everett F. Bleiler
Robert E. Spiller

Contents

	Acknowledgments	ix
	Introduction	xi
1	At the Edge of Tomorrow	3
2	The Haunted Men	15
3	"The War to End All Wars"	49
4	"The Machine-Made Millennium"	81
5	Shadows of the Future: Utopia or Catastrophe?	103
6	Journeys to Unknown Lands	157
7	Journeys to Other Worlds	197
	Bibliography	225
	Index	229

Acknowledgments

I think it appropriate to thank my mother, Ruth Dalager Clareson, and Henry Nimitz, who operated Williams Cigar Store in Austin, Minnesota, for introducing me to the pulp magazines of the 1930s. Oudal's Book Store, then at Third Avenue and Marquette in Minneapolis, showed me that there were older magazines as well as used, often out-of-print, books. In those days, one put aside such things when one went to the university. I did—until I needed a dissertation topic. Professor Harold Whitehall and others at Indiana University encouraged my early suggestions for a topic, but it was such teachers as Robert Spiller, Thomas Haviland, Maurice Johnson, and Allen Chester who conducted the final oral examination in 1955.

I must acknowledge a great indebtedness to the members of the Philadelphia Science Fiction Society (PSFS), especially during the early 1950s. They proved that fan, professional writer, and student can work together. Elsewhere I have singled out Ossie Train, who always let me borrow his rarest books. From the first, Sam Moskowitz shared his knowledge of the little-known magazines. Robert Lowndes, then editor of *Science Fiction Quarterly*, accepted my first article on the history of the field for the August 1953 issue. Somewhere along the line the word American got left out of the title, "The Evolution of Science Fiction"; the letter columns of the October issue steamed. L. Sprague de Camp and, later, Catherine Crook de Camp, helped me to see the ties between the fiction and the fact. Jim Williams, Milt Rothman—and many others. All of them have always made me feel at home in fandom.

I have been fortunate enough to work with such scholars as Mark Hillegas and Patrick G. Hogan, Jr., who helped make possible the Modern Language Association (MLA) Seminar on Science Fiction in the 1960s and 1970s. Later, the group widened as it became the Science Fiction Research Association (SFRA). From the early 1970s onward, members of the Popular Culture Association (PCA) added fresh perspectives. The exchange of ideas proved invaluable. Not all of them were Americans: for example, Susan Wood, Brian Aldiss, and I. F. Clarke.

I could again enumerate the libraries and librarians who have helped me. John Newman of Colorado State University and Robert A. Tibbetts of Ohio State University rank high among them. But this time around I should like particularly to thank those reference librarians who have come to my aid at odd hours when some detail demanded attention: Glenna Morris, Alice Roberts Finley, Ange Hurd, and Amy Hagelin of the Wayne County Public Library; L. W. Coolidge, William Weiss, and Michael Freeman of The College of Wooster. At the College Professors Vivian Holliday, the Dean of the Faculty, and Donald Harward, Vice President for Academic Affairs, have given me their unquestioning support. Nor should I forget Dr. James T. Sabin, Robert Hagelstein, Margaret Brezicki, and Carole Bronson of Greenwood Press.

In terms of producing the manuscript, Merilyn Drumm has combined high tech, love of science fiction itself, and her considerable editorial skill. My thanks to Thomas F. R. Clareson for his editorial assistance, especially with the index. And, finally, as always, there is Alice. Her questions remain the hardest and the best; her patience, the greatest.

A NOTE ON THE TEXT

Because a number of these novels and stories are little known, I have at times given more detail regarding plot action than I normally would. More importantly, the page references cited in the text are to the first editions unless otherwise indicated.

Introduction

When I began my formal study of the emergence of American science fiction at the University of Pennsylvania under Professor Robert E. Spiller, the major published work surveying the field as a whole was J. O. Bailey's *Pilgrims Through Space and Time* (1947), while the essential bibliography was Everett F. Bleiler's far-reaching *The Checklist of Fantastic Literature* (1948). Yet Bailey's book grew out of his own dissertation which had focused on the fiction of H. G. Wells and which had been written some ten years earlier before the outbreak of World War II, while Bleiler's *Checklist* made no distinction between science fiction and fantasy. Although the issuing of both works within a year of one another does emphasize the role World War II played in bringing attention to the field, a few earlier critics had glanced at the field. Probably the most distinguished appraisal had occurred a generation earlier when Dorothy Scarborough devoted a chapter to ''Supernatural Science'' in *The Supernatural in Modern English Fiction* (1917); she accepted ''the scientific romance'' as an established form but seemed somewhat uncomfortable with the stories of Wells and his contemporaries. In 1930, Edward Shanks, himself the author of the novel *The People of the Ruins* (1920), thought the field worthy of study, but in 1936 Clemence Dane, the creator of several fantasies, dismissed science fiction as ''nothing in the world but America's fairy stories,'' while in 1939 Bernard DeVoto downgraded it because of what he regarded as its uniformly pessimistic view of the future. Nearly thirty years later at a meeting in 1968, Lester del Rey seemed to echo DeVoto when he denounced the effects of the British-inspired ''New Wave'' on the sf of the 1960s, declaring that the portrayal of man as a ''degraded and indecent animal, doomed to failure'' measured the intrusion of a pessimistic literary naturalism into the field.[1] Ironically, perhaps the widest acceptance of science fiction, especially among academic critics, has resulted from a concentration upon that type of story which J. B. Priestley found and praised in the fiction of Ray Bradbury as early as 1953: the ''future nightmare.''

But this is to jump ahead too quickly. Between them, Bailey and Bleiler laid the groundwork for the serious study of the field. Other works, like those of Marjorie Nicolson, Philip Babcock Gove, and Edith Birkhead, could be cited, but without exception they dealt either with a specific phase of the general field— the imaginary voyage, the journey to the moon, or the tale of terror—or with British contributions, focusing upon a period no later than that of the Gothic novel. Edgar Allan Poe, Charles Brockden Brown, and Fitz-James O'Brien had received some attention, of course, but important as they were to the subsequent development of the field in America, they provided merely the tip of the iceberg. Because writers of all periods made use of the literary forms which they had inherited—the utopia and imaginary voyage, for example—it is difficult, if not impossible, to assert that the field of science fiction came into being at a specific date. Some would see it appear full-blown with the works of Jules Verne; others, with H. G. Wells. Many would delay its birth until after the appearance of Hugo Gernsback's pulp magazine *Amazing Stories* (1926), although both Gernsback himself and the Munsey magazines published sf earlier. One can argue for the early 1870s when the "future-war" motif flourished after Sir George Tomkyns Chesney's *The Battle of Dorking* was issued first in *Blackwood's Magazine* and then as a pamphlet—so ably documented by I. F. Clarke. Perhaps it is sufficient to say here that cumulatively—and diversely—the writers of fiction in the nineteenth century reflected the impact of scientific discoveries and theories which transformed the old order into the modern world. Yet such a statement does not really begin to indicate the complexity of what occurred. In 1971 I suggested that science fiction and literary naturalism were twin/mirror responses to the impact of nineteenth-century science and technology.

What any attempt to establish a precise beginning to science fiction fails to take into account is the view that such critics as Harry Levin have stressed: the entire body of literature forms a continuum which the writers of each generation "manipulate in their own idiom and manner to reflect those ideas and focus upon those areas of human experience which most concern them."[2] Thus, for example, although a variety of prose narratives exist from earlier dates, critics say that the "modern" novel originated in the works of certain writers during the eighteenth century, and one must add that despite similarities, both in content and form, eighteenth-century fiction constantly surprises and pleases by its variety. So it is with science fiction.

In the present comprehensive view of science fiction in America from the beginnings until the 1930s (that is, before World War II), I have deliberately omitted any discussion of authors and stories appearing only in the specialist magazines which came into being after 1926. I have included, however, a sampling of authors and stories originally printed in the Munsey magazines and sometimes later reissued in such magazines as *Famous Fantastic Mysteries* and *Fantastic Novels*. What I hope to show is that even during the 1930s science fiction existed outside of the so-called ghetto of the specialist pulps. Beyond that restriction, there are several matters which I suggest as points of departure. Perhaps in reality they form only one principle, because they originate in my reluctance to divide fiction into a "mainstream"—certainly an elitist concept whose source, I believe, can be shown—and a number of subliterary backwaters and swamps. I would suggest instead that throughout Western history all fiction can be divided into two equally important streams: the first examined closely the everyday world of the individual and society; the second, perhaps most often using the voyage as a narrative structure, took its characters into the unknown, often into exotic corners of the world. (Notice, incidentally—and I think of Poe, Ambrose Bierce, Wilkie Collins, M. R. James, Algernon Blackwood, and Henry James—that the supernatural or terrible can become a part of either stream of fiction.) Secondly, for too long, many critics have written disparagingly of popular fiction. I think of those famous Victorian novelists who published in various magazines when I say this. Moreover, "popular fiction" may be a label dreamed up out of frustration and envy by persons who never succeeded in selling a work. Perhaps it is simply an elitist's denial of the mass market which developed in the late nineteenth and early twentieth centuries.

Beyond this I would say only that I do not intend to offer a rigid definition of science fiction. No matter how catholic the definition, it can only be exclusive. I prefer to suggest that in this volume both author and reader should examine the characteristics of a body of fiction whose authors were responding to the ideas and theories—awe and wonder, if you will—of science during the last two centuries. For convenience, I will call that body of literature science fiction. Perhaps I should call it fantasy as Brian Aldiss does in *Science Fiction Art* (1975).[3] I am no longer so certain of the distinction between science fiction and fantasy as some critics are. Indeed, particularly in a wide historical context, I am not certain whether "science fiction" is so narrow and distinct, either in content or in form, that it makes up a separate and distinct genre. To look at this problem from a somewhat different perspective: at what point does what was once regarded as science become fantasy because of new theories? All of us live in a post-Newtonian world. Does that realization now make all Newtonian physics—and stories based on that physics—fantasy? A second example may suffice. When Hiram Bingham discovered the ruins of the Incan city Machu Picchu in 1911, was that discovery a matter of hard science or not? Again one encounters the problem of definition. I cannot but recall a discussion some years ago at an MLA meeting which attempted to define the novel. One highly regarded scholar insisted that a novel is a novel is a novel only if it presents a deep study of character. I am not sure that that debate has been permanently decided.

The present volume is a companion and complement to the annotated bibliography *Science Fiction in America, 1870s–1930s*, published by Greenwood Press in 1984. Neither that volume nor this should be regarded as definitive, because even in the brief interval between preparing the two books for publication, I have turned up several short stories not included in any other bibliography past or present. We simply do not yet know, exhaustively, what is in the old magazines. In a sense, as a reference book, *Science Fiction in America* is complete within itself; in another sense it has provided much of the data for this overview. But unlike that annotated bibliography, *Some Kind of Paradise* includes works from the period before 1870 and does not necessarily limit itself to works which saw hardback publication. A second contrast occurs because in this volume I emphasize the contribution of American writers to the field. Granting the influence of Verne, Wells, and Sir H. Rider Haggard, are there certain characteristics which set American writers apart from their British and Continental contemporaries? My concern here, then, is primarily with American science fiction—not with science fiction in America. As I write this, I recall Donald A. Wollheim's discussion of how such writers as Isaac Asimov and Robert A. Heinlein created a future history covering some 2 million years (at least) into which an author or a reader can enter. The more the writer or reader has experienced that future history through various stories, the more the individual is able to understand and to create. Looking backward, then, and working within a much more limited timespan, I hope that in a small way *Some Kind of Paradise* will help us to understand the manner in which writers have made use of materials which they regarded *at the time they wrote* as having a basis in science. Perhaps as we search for patterns in what they wrote, we will gain an insight uniting us in our common humanity despite distances in space and time.

NOTES

1. Edward Shanks, "Other Worlds Than Ours," *The New Statesman*, June 14, 1930, pp. 305–306; Clemence Dane, "American Fairy Tale" *North American Review*, 242 (Autumn 1936), 143–152; Bernard DeVoto, "Doom Beyond Jupiter," *Harpers*, 179 (September 1939), 445–448; "The MLA Forum: Science Fiction: The New Mythology," *Extrapolation*, 10 (May 1969), 102.

2. Harry Levin, as cited in Thomas D. Clareson, "The Other Side of Realism," in *The Other Side of Realism* (Bowling Green, Ohio: Bowling Green University Popular Press, 1971), p. 3.

3. Brian Aldiss, *Science Fiction Art: The Fantasies of SF* (London: New English Library, 1975), p. 3.

SOME KIND
OF PARADISE

1

At the Edge of Tomorrow

Certainly no one will disagree with Brian Aldiss's assertion in *Billion Year Spree* (1973) that the terror and mystery of the Gothic novel remain popular with a large audience and make up an important element of contemporary science fiction[1]; nor will one argue with the importance which he assigns to Mary Shelley's *Frankenstein* (1818) as a cornerstone in the development of the field. He notes in passing that in *The Last Man* (1826), published anonymously, Shelley refers to Charles Brockden Brown's *Arthur Mervyn* (1799–1800), a tale of the yellow plague.[2] For whatever reasons, however, Aldiss neglects to mention that in her "Preface" to *Frankenstein* she explicitly emphasizes her indebtedness to the scientific speculations of the late eighteenth and early nineteenth centuries when she remarks, "The event on which this fiction is founded has been supposed, by Dr. [Erasmus] Darwin, and some of the physiological writers in Germany, as not of impossible occurrence. . . . I have not considered myself as merely weaving a series of supernatural terrors. The event on which the interest of the story depends is exempt from the disadvantages of a mere tale of spectres or enchantments."[3] In recent decades, most studies of the work of Charles Brockden Brown have ignored or minimized his reputation both in Britain and America in the years following his death, nor have they tied him to Mary Shelley.[4] Yet in *The Tale of Terror: A Study of the Gothic Romance* (1921), Edith Birkhead points out that between 1814 and 1816 Mary Shelley "patiently unravelled the 'mystery' novels" of Brown, while in a series of articles devoted to American writers in *Blackwood's Magazine* in 1824, an anonymous critic judges him to be the foremost American novelist.[5]

In an attempt to establish a secure place for science fiction in Western literary tradition, most scholars have gone back past the Gothic. Some would find its beginnings in Lucian and Plato; others would stop with Sir Thomas More's *Utopia* (1516, 1551) and Sir Francis Bacon's unfinished *The New Atlantis* (1627), as well as such imaginary voyages as Francis Godwin's *The Man in the Moone* (1638), Ludwig Holberg's *A Journey to the World Under-Ground* (1741, 1742),

Johannes Kepler's *Somnium* (1634) and Jonathan Swift's *Gulliver's Travels* (1726). I. F. Clarke has named Samuel Madden's *The Memoirs of the Twentieth Century* (1733) and the anonymous *The Reign of George VI, 1900–1925* (1763) among the first important forecasts portraying a future world.[6] Whatever the specific literary origins, however, general consensus agrees that *quantitatively* sf did not emerge as a separately identifiable form of fiction—a separate genre?— until the last decades of the nineteenth century.

Because the public of the 1980s has been so inundated by the impact of high technology—from personal computers to the INTELSTAT satellites which gave perhaps 2 billion people in some 170 countries the opportunity to view some portion of the Olympic Games in Los Angeles[7]—the complex transformations marking the late nineteenth century and giving rise not only to literary realism and naturalism but also to a recognizable science fiction may have faded from the popular memory.

Fundamental to the late nineteenth century was a fresh awareness of change itself. Not since the idealism which had shaped American transcendentalism in the 1840s "had there been such a ferment in the intellectual world. . . . The neat, orderly universe of the Enlightenment—a universe governed by laws whose nature could be discovered by man—was disintegrating under the blows of Darwinian evolution."[8] One has only to turn to the magazines to find how widely and variously the issues were examined. As early as the second issue of *The Popular Science Monthly* (June 1872), "Darwinism and Divinity" suggested that "whatever the ultimate verdict" as to the "soundness" of the theory of evolution, "Darwinists are not necessarily hoofed and horned monsters. . . . Room may be made for their tenets alongside of the Thirty-nine Articles, by a little judicious crowding and rearrangement."[9] From its first issue, *The Popular Science Monthly* provided Herbert Spencer with a lectern. In 1873 an anxious Henry Lake could ask, "Is Electricity Life?" while as late as 1889, in *The Atlantic Monthly*, W. G. A. Bonwill carefully explained "Why I Deny Evolution."[10] *The Atlantic* became a forum for Louis Agassiz and John Fiske, who held widely opposing views regarding Darwinism. In one spin-off of the debate, innumerable articles turned to prehistory, some of them attempting to discover evidence of man in the Americas as early as the Pliocene or Miocene. In questioning whether or not mankind made up a single species, A. De Quatrefages began with "the principle that, so far as the body is concerned, man is an animal—nothing more, nothing less."[11] By September 10, 1911, addressing the First International Congress of Monists at Hamburg, Germany, regarding "The Mechanistic Conception of Life," Jacques Loeb, of the Rockefeller Institute of Medical Research, could defend the premise that biologists fully explain life in terms of physico-chemical analysis.[12] Henry Steele Commager suggests that Theodore Dreiser knew the article.[13] A generation earlier in 1874, the well-known theologian Charles Hodge had condemned Darwinism, asserting that "a more incredible theory was never propounded for acceptance among men"; in the same year, in *Cosmic Philosophy*, John Fiske had announced that throughout the universe a divinely guided parallel evolution had as its end "that last consummate specimen of God's handiwork, the Human Soul."[14]

In short, the new ideas demanded, at least, the modification of traditional concepts of mankind. At the extreme, man became a product of his environment and—especially after the advent of genetics—his heredity. That assumption, in turn, led to the reexamination of the basic tenets of Christianity which had so long governed Western thought. (Although for the most part the questions may now be phrased with more sophistication, many of the same issues disturb the 1980s. One tie, for example, occurs in the insistence by a few that the concept of Creationism be given equal hearing in the schools.) Surely one does not need to rehearse again the increasing despair felt by such men as Mark Twain, William Dean Howells, and Henry Adams in the face of a pessimistic determinism which implied meaninglessness—Ernst Haeckel's blank universe.

The importance of their reaction in terms of fiction reveals itself in Howell's essay "Novel-Writing and Novel-Reading" (1899), in which he asserted that "the business of the novelist is to make you understand the real world through his faithful effigy of it."[15] In the same essay he insisted, "If I do not find that [the novel] is like life, then it does not exist for me as art." Along this line of reasoning he equated life with truth: "The truth which I mean, the truth which is the only beauty, is truth to human experience."[16] In this view lay the authority, the rationale, for that replication of the external world giving rise to literary realism and naturalism. In short, fiction could deal meaningfully with life only when it was as "like life" as possible. In this way, supposedly, the writers could capture reality. It is as though, being deprived of a divine and absolute moral world, they followed the lead of contemporary science and turned to an absolute material world. An early article in *The Popular Science Monthly*, "Epidemic Delusions" (1872), catches something of the pathos of their position. After admitting "the difficulty of arriving at absolute truth upon any historical subject," the writer remarks, "Now, we do hope and believe that there is absolute truth in science, which, if not at present in our possession, is within our reach."[17]

Historical perspective indicates that their anguish and their rationalizations came during a cumulative shift in perspective. The psychological empiricists questioned what man could know; Lyell expanded the geological timespan; Darwin's premise showed that the species were mutable; the new physics of Niels Bohr, Max Planck, Albert Einstein, and Pierre and Marie Curie cut away the solidity of the material universe. By the 1980s, many persons believe that man has been reduced to another animal in an absurd universe beyond comprehension; so complex is modern physics, for example, that perhaps only specialists can speak meaningfully of its theories. The existential confrontation, by and large, is the child of this continually changing shift in perspective regarding man's place in the universe.

Despite the many articles in the magazines, the despair felt by Howells and his contemporaries remained confined, largely, to intellectual circles. The majority of Americans concerned themselves with the changes which they saw taking place around them. While a historian of Cleveland, Ohio, could retrospectively celebrate the growth of that city resulting from "The Industrial Age" beginning in the 1870s,[18] Mark Sullivan could observe that in 1900 "America presented to the eye the picture of a country that was still mostly frontier of one sort or another, the torn edges of civilization's first contact with nature, man in his invasion of the primeval. . . . Only the Eastern seaboard had the appearance of civilization having really established itself and attained permanence. From the Alleghenies to the Pacific Coast, the picture was mainly of a country still a frontier and a people still in flux."[19]

"Still a frontier . . . still in flux": the image of the footloose cowpoke undertaking deeds of derring-do and drifting between the Rio Grande and the high plateaus of Wyoming and Montana has become so deeply embedded in the myth of the Western frontier and has so encompassed his predecessors—except, perhaps, for the wagon trains seeking new lands of promise—that one too easily forgets that, historically, the cowboy rode trail only briefly after the Civil War during those same years when such forces as the railroads, steam, and electricity began to accelerate the transformation of the United States into the modern nation that it now is.

By 1900 some 40 percent of Americans—that is, approximately 30 million of a total population just over 76 million—already lived in cities, although Oklahoma, New Mexico, and Arizona had not yet achieved statehood. The other 60 percent lived "on farms or in communities with less than 2,500 inhabitants," villages whose very existence often depended upon whether or not they touched the route of a railroad so that they were "needed to service the panting locomotives, which had to take on water every 40 miles or so."[20] Thus, as Allan B. Forbes has pointed out, as early as the 1880s and 1890s "the process of industrialization which the Civil War did so much to accelerate first reached such large dimensions as to be the greatest single determining factor in all phases of American life."[21] By 1915, as suggested elsewhere, the basic urbanization and industrialization necessary to change the United States into a society dependent upon technology had been completed, as the process had been finished in Great Britain more than a half century earlier by the time of the Great Exhibition of 1851. It thus seems appropriate that the Chicago World's Columbian Exposition (1893) and the St. Louis World's Fair (1904) should herald "a vision of a new age of power and enlightenment,"[22] even though in the mushrooming cities, including those in the East, "unfinished streets push[ed] out to the fields" of an open, seemingly empty countryside.[23] (So swiftly did the transition from wilderness to urban civilization take place that Henry Steele Commager asserts, "By the end of the century the nostalgic stories of Owen Wister and the romantic drawings of Frederic Remington were thrilling thousands of cityfolk to whom the Wild West was as distant and exotic as Salem witchcraft."[24])

What had occurred resulted from the swiftness of transition. One might argue that two cultures existed cheek by jowl: the expanding city and the seemingly empty countryside. The city was where the action was. The dichotomy created—with its belief in the good country people and the evil city, an inheritance from Romanticism—may not yet have vanished completely from the American imagination. Moreover, the basic cause of the dichotomy primarily affected the cities.

Almost too casually in *The Big Change* (1952), Frederick Lewis Allen notes that a "remarkable series of inventions and technological improvements" had sparked the progress and rapid growth of industrialism.[25] Had these not been developed, the transition from an agrarian society would have been slowed; with them, it could only accelerate exponentially. Again, the magazines and newspapers of the period reflect the impact that the new technology had upon the public imagination. Even before World War I, pioneers of science fiction, like Hugo Gernsback, with their predictions of machines-to-come, made these "gadgets" the earliest focal point of what has come to be known as "hard" science fiction.

A cursory listing of these achievements would be overwhelming. Yet if one arbitrarily ignores the medical and theoretical discoveries, for example, and concentrates primarily upon what the bystander would have observed, one can find certain patterns illustrating the manner and thoroughness with which these inventions transformed the potential of American life.

1868. On June 23, C. Latham Sholes and several associates patented the typewriter. Although Sholes obtained further patents during the following decade, he could not produce and market his machine. On March 1, 1873, for $12,000 he sold his rights to the Remington Arms Company, which immediately introduced the model as the Remington typewriter. (Some historians, like Commager, writing in the mid-twentieth century, applauded the manner in which the typewriter "emancipated" young women from the farm and the home.[26])

1870. Although the steam engine on elevated tracks on 9th Street in New York would have been more visible, on January 10 in Cleveland, Ohio, under the leadership of John D. Rockefeller, the Standard Oil Company of Ohio was incorporated, its capital given as $1 million.

1873. Andrew Carnegie began construction of a mill in Pittsburgh to produce steel by the Bessemer method. In 1873, cable cars appeared in San Francisco.

1874. In the same year that barbed wire assured the end of the open range, F. W. Woolworth opened his first store in Lancaster, Pennsylvania. On July 4, with proper ceremony, the Eads Bridge across the Mississippi at St. Louis was opened to traffic. Its designer, Captain James Buchanan Eads, had insisted on Bessemer steel. Carnegie fretted over his demand for quality.

1876. On February 14, the Bell telephone was patented almost a month before Bell himself actually sent a spoken message over the wire. Later that summer, the first long-distance call—eight miles—was made, while in 1877 the first phone in New York City was installed. By 1900, some 19,000 operators and more than 1.3 million phones were busy. Although Boston and New York had been connected by phone as early as 1884, not until 1915 was there a line between New York and San Francisco.

1877. Having moved to Menlo Park and set up an extensive laboratory, Thomas Edison invented the phonograph. After contributing to the development of the phone, he developed the incandescent bulb in 1879. Perhaps because his work varied so widely, Edison became a public symbol of the inventor. Jean Villiers de l'Isle-Adam wrote the novel *L'Eve future* (1880–1886), in which Edison manufactured an artificial woman at Menlo Park.

1879. On April 29, Cleveland, Ohio, used the arc light combined with a dynamo developed by Charles F. Brush to illuminate its Public Square. The following year, New York also adopted the Brush lighting. Brush later played a part in the founding of General Electric.

1881. Marshall Field, who had begun work as a $400–per-year clerk a decade earlier, now owned what was to be one of the finest department stores of the period. His gift of $1 million to the Chicago Exposition in 1893 made possible the Columbian Museum, which became the Field Museum of Natural History.

1883. On May 24, President Chester A. Arthur and Governor Grover Cleveland opened the Brooklyn Bridge. Designed by John Roebling, who was killed in an accident during its thirteen-year construction, it was the longest suspension bridge (1595 feet) in the world; like the Eads bridge, it used Bessemer steel.

1884. Designed by William LeBaron Jenney, Chicago's ten-story Home Insurance Building had a steel skeleton. In 1892, the twenty-two-story Chicago Masonic Temple would dwarf it. By 1898, New York had six such skyscrapers, although the twenty-story Flatiron Building did not rise until 1902, nor did the sixty-story Woolworth Building until 1913.

1888. Although Cleveland had also pioneered a mile-long electric trolley in 1884, not until four years later did Frank Sprague succeed in operating a citywide electric trolley line in Richmond, Virginia. By 1895, more than 800 streetcar lines were in operation. From them evolved the interurban lines which fanned out across such states as Ohio and Indiana. As early as 1895, Cleveland and Akron were linked; Sandusky remained at the center of another web serving both Toledo and Cleveland until 1938[27]; a Wooster and Cleveland line operated until 1930. Although they granted customers a greater mobility, they also restricted passengers. As with the major railroads, a person could only go where the tracks went. Thus, for example, one could never ride directly from Wooster to Akron, Columbus, or Cincinnati. Another form of the electric railway, the subway, opened in Boston in 1897. The Interborough Rapid Transit started a tunnel in New York in 1900.

1890–1900. A colorful part of the 1890s came from the widespread craze for the bicycle. At the height of its popularity, for example, some 50,000 Clevelanders enjoyed the freedom given them by wheels.[28] Yet a bicycle cost $100 to $125, a price that undoubtedly restricted its use.

1890. John D. Rockefeller and Charles F. Brush provided some of the ingenuity and money needed to open the Cleveland Arcade on Memorial Day. Joining Euclid and Superior Avenues, it housed 112 bazaarlike shops as well as a variety of offices on its four tiers. High above—at more than 100 feet—a glass roof protected the structure.[29]

1892. Thomas Edison and the Thomas Houston Company consolidated to form General Electric, with Charles A. Coffin as president.

1893. In the same year that Westinghouse won the contract to illuminate the Chicago Exposition, his company built generators to harness Niagara Falls. In 1895, it delivered the first electricity to Buffalo.

1895. Marconi discovered wireless telegraphy, but not until 1901 did he send a message from Cornwall, England, to St. John's, Newfoundland. Soon all oceangoing ships were required to have the wireless.

1901. On January 10, Anthony F. Lucas brought in an oil strike near Beaumont, Texas; within eighteen months another strike turned a frontier town in Indian Territory into a booming Tulsa. In March, under the leadership of J. P. Morgan, United States Steel was incorporated. With a capital of nearly $1.5 billion, it controlled three-fifths of the steel-related industries in the U.S. It owned most of the Mesabi range in Minnesota, as well as other holdings in Wisconsin and Michigan. In 1905, with Judge Elbert H. Gary as its chairman, in order to have a base near Chicago, it built Gary, Indiana, out of wasteland bordering Lake Michigan. By the outbreak of World War I it produced more steel than Great Britain, France, and Germany combined.[30]

1903. On December 13, during a span of fifty-nine seconds at Kitty Hawk, North Carolina, Wilbur and Orville Wright flew their aeroplane a distance of 852 feet. Essentially, the press ignored their effort, as did the military, for at the time Count Frederick von Zeppelin commanded the public imagination. In 1900, with the support of the Kaiser and funds coming from public subscription, he had flown a rigid ship for twenty minutes.

1907. In Buffalo, New York, Ellsworth M. Statler built the first hotel to offer every guest not only a private room but a private bath.

1909. Henry Ford decided to specialize in the Model-T. In 1913 he initiated the assembly line. His aim, he repeatedly said, was to make the automobile available at a price everyone could afford. He paid his assembly-line workers a minimum of $5 for an eight-hour workday. Originally, the cost of a Model-T had been $950; by 1924, it had been reduced to $290 (without a self-starter).[31]

One has a variety of reactions to these innovations and inventions. Undoubtedly, at an ever-accelerating pace, the decades between the 1870s and World War I saw the beginning of what has been called America's infatuation with the machine. One is tempted to refer to those years as the opening of the Age of the Engineer, for his achievements—ranging from bridges and skyscrapers through dynamos and automobiles to phonographs and the wireless—have given the late nineteenth and twentieth centuries their shapes and sounds. Certainly they support Commager's contention that the 1890s proved to be an American watershed. On this side of them "lies the modern America, predominantly urban and industrial . . . experiencing profound changes in population, social institutions, economy, and technology."[32] One notices, too, that greater economic power fell into the hands of those men who controlled the great corporations. Granted the "immense" disparity between wealth and poverty during the last decades of the nineteenth century, the thrust of those inventions and innovations emphasized two crucial areas which seem to question those historians who stress the average American's lack of education and information.[33] On the one hand, many of the developments concentrated upon transportation and communication; on the other, they attempted to make more readily available a wider variety of goods and services—a tendency which led to the mass market and the ascendency of both the department and chain stores. That emphasis implies that during the period of transition a large percentage of Americans maintained or acquired a keen interest in the world around them.

By 1887 the New York *Herald* had a daily circulation of 250,000; "the mammoth newspapers gave the cities something they needed. They furnished a polyglot, swarming population with a sense of civic identity. . . . They gave mixed classes and nationalities a common daily experience of reading."[34] Nor should one forget that the magazines, from the established *The Atlantic Monthly* to the new *McClure's*, gave the audience of the 1890s factual articles not only on the American scene but also upon distant lands and all phases of scientific speculation, often by recognized authorities. In *McClure's*, for example, Simon Newcomb, Professor of Mathematics for the U.S. Navy, reported on "Some Unsolved Problems of Astronomy" (July 1899) before addressing the question, "Is the Airship Coming?" (September 1901). He did not agree with Samuel P. Langley, who had considered "The Flying Machine" (June 1897). Percival Lowell, who wrote more frequently for *The Atlantic Monthly*, described in *McClure's* "The Planet Mars" (December 1907), while a dozen years earlier, Sir Robert Ball had entertained "The Possibility of Life on Other Worlds" (July 1895). Another favorite topic in *McClure's* proved to be the polar regions: Sir Arthur Conan Doyle, "The Glamour of the Arctic" (May 1896); Cleveland Moffett, "Race to the North Pole" (August 1893); and Dr. Frederick A. Cook, "Two Thousand Miles in the Antarctic Ice" (November 1899).

In addition to John Fiske and Percival Lowell, *The Atlantic Monthly* regularly featured Louis Agassiz and Asa Gray. Through the 1870s it also ran a series of articles by Robert Dale Owen as he gave an account of his studies of spiritual phenomena; at least once, Henry James, Sr., wrote on "Spiritualism Old and New" (September 1868). *Lippincott's Magazine* featured such titles as Charles Morris's "A New Theory of the Universe" (May 1891) and Harvey B. Bashore's "The First Days of the World" (February 1896), one of the frequent attempts to establish man in the Americas at the time of the glaciers. Perhaps one final example may illustrate the degree to which new scientific materials gained access to both the newspapers and magazines. On January 21, 1912, the *New York Times* emphasized "Professor Hiram Bingham's Report of the Yale Expedition's Findings of Several Inca or Pre-Inca Ruins"; in *Harper's Monthly Magazine* for October 1912, Bingham himself gave an account of "A Search for the Last Inca Capital" in the mountain province of Vilcabamba, Peru.

In considering sources from which the public gained information regarding matters beyond their daily lives, one should not forget Chautauqua and the Lyceum circuit. In November 1871, the New York *Herald* reported how Stanley had found Livingstone in Ujiji on Lake Tanganyika. After stopping in England briefly during the summer of 1872, Stanley returned to the U.S. and went on a lecture tour. On February 17, 1873, he told a "captivated" audience in Cleveland, "How I Found Dr. Livingstone"; on February 7, 1891, he gave an account of his own four expeditions entitled "Darkest Africa"; he returned once more during the winter of 1896–1897 to reveal the full extent of his "discoveries in the dark continent."[35]

As the twentieth century opened, the continental United States was undergoing a metamorphosis, for the United States had become the industrial giant of the world. It was the largest producer of most heavy goods and the biggest consumer of all. The country, with more than 76 million inhabitants, seemed caught in a whirlpool of change. Granted the isolation of the farm and the limitations of the small town, the metropolitan areas simply magnified the problems, particularly because their slums devoured so many of the 19 million immigrants searching for a promised/imagined America. In the two years following the 1871 fire, for example, immigration swelled Chicago's population from 300,000 to 1 million. By the turn of the century, historians estimate that one out of three persons in the major cities was foreign-born. Graphic photos tell much of the story, but a single image captures the pathos: "Seldom did the overworked laborer or his child-burdened wife have the will to venture a couple of miles to the wonderland of theatres and department stores."[36] America stood at the edge of tomorrow, but its writers and its leaders could only project their individual dreams and fears onto that future, for no one could yet tell what the outcome would be. The literary naturalism of such men as Norris, Crane, and Dreiser could examine the anguished scene. In 1908, Jack London could imagine a downtrodden proletariat attempting a future rebellion against the iron heel of the Oligarchy of the Trusts. In 1908 Hudson Maxim could envision a future city "as one enormous edifice; . . . banks of streets, arcades, and corridors, parks and playgrounds will rise one above another, tier on tier, to eye-tiring heights."[37]

Whether they explored Maggie Johnson's Bowery, sought refuge in a forgotten Eden, or projected an idyllic future society, all of the writers would search for some kind of paradise.

NOTES

1. Brian Aldiss, *Billion Year Spree: The True History of Science Fiction* (Garden City, N.Y.: Doubleday & Company, Inc., 1973), p. 20.

2. Aldiss, p. 44.

3. Mary Shelley, "Preface," *The Annotated Frankenstein*, introduction and notes by Leonard Wolf (New York: Clarkson N. Potter, Inc., 1977), p. 3.

4. On the basis of recent examination, the notable exception seems to be David Lee

Clark, *Charles Brockden Brown: Pioneer Voice in America* (Durham, N.C.: Duke University Press, 1952). He devotes a chapter, "Time the Assessor" (pp. 295–309), to an appraisal of Brown's reputation since his death, citing evaluations as late as 1904 and 1920, although emphasizing the mixed reception Brown received when he was not actually ignored. Clark refuses explicitly to give any "detailed notice" of "Scott's interest," "Godwin's tribute," or "Mary Shelley's probable debt to *Carwin* in her novel *The Last Man*" (p. 295).

5. Edith Birkhead, *The Tale of Terror: A Study of the Gothic Romance* (London: Constable & Company, 1921), p. 158; "American Authors," *Blackwood's Magazine*, XVI (1824), 425.

6. For a detailed discussion of these early sources, see Thomas D. Clareson, "The Emergence of Science Fiction: The Beginnings to the 1920s," in Neil Barron, ed., *Anatomy of Wonder: A Critical Guide to Science Fiction*, 2d ed. (New York: R.R. Bowker Company, 1981), pp. 3–87. It includes an annotated bibliography of 182 items.

7. Arthur C. Clarke, *Ascent into Orbit: A Scientific Autobiography* (New York: John Wiley & Sons, 1984), p. v.

8. Henry Steele Commager, *The American Mind: An Interpretation of American Thought and Character Since the 1880's* (New Haven: Yale University Press, 1950), p. 47.

9. L. S., "Darwinism and Divinity," *The Popular Science Monthly*, I (June 1872), 188.

10. Henry Lake, "Is Electricity Life?" *The Popular Science Monthly*, II (February 1873), 477–485, reprinted from *Belgravia*; W. G. A. Bonwill, "Why I Deny Evolution," *The Atlantic Monthly*, 44 (1889), 267–272.

11. "The Natural History of Man: A Course of Lectures by A. De Quatrefages," trans. Eliza A. Youmans, *The Popular Science Monthly*, I (June 1872), 208.

12. Jacques Loeb, "The Mechanistic Conception of Life," *The Popular Science Monthly*, LXXX (January 1912), 5–21.

13. Henry Steele Commager, p. 114.

14. Charles Hodge, as cited in Nelson Manfred Blake, *A History of American Life and Thought* (New York: McGraw-Hill Book Company, 1963), p. 427; John Fiske, as cited by Henry Steele Commager, p. 85.

15. William Dean Howells, "Novel-Writing and Novel-Reading," ed. William M. Gibson (New York: The New York Public Library, 1958), p. 24. This was the first publication of the essay which was originally a lecture for a tour through the East and Midwest.

16. William Dean Howells, p. 9.

17. Dr. Carpenter, "Epidemic Delusions," *The Popular Science Monthly*, II (November 1872), 36.

18. William Ganson Rose, *Cleveland: The Making of a City* (Cleveland and New York: The World Publishing Company, 1950). See especially the sequence of chapters beginning with "The Industrial Age 1870–1879," pp. 361–426.

19. Mark Sullivan, *Our Times: The United States 1900–1925* (New York: Charles Scribner's Sons, 1927), I, *The Turn of the Century*, 28.

20. The Editors of TIME-LIFE BOOKS, *This Fabulous Century* (New York: Time-Life Books, 1970), 1, *1900–1910*, 30–31.

21. Allan B. Forbes, "The Literary Quest for Utopia, 1880–1900," *Social Forces*, 6 (December 1927), 180.

22. Bernard A. Weisenberger and the Editors of TIME–LIFE BOOKS, *The LIFE History of the United States/1890–1901* (New York: Time-Life Books, 1974), 8, *Reaching for Empire*, 94.

23. Mark Sullivan, *The Turn of the Century*, I:29.

24. Henry Steele Commager, p. 44.

25. Frederick Lewis Allen, *The Big Change: America Transforms Itself, 1900–1950* (New York: Harper & Brothers, 1952), pp. 50–51.

26. Henry Steele Commager, p. 46. He also emphasizes "the telephone exchange, and a hundred labor-saving devices" and remarks that her emancipation had been "dramatized by the vote, and guaranteed by birth control."

27. Charles E. Frohman, *Sandusky's Yesterdays* (Columbus, Ohio: The Ohio Historical Society, 1968), p. 143.

28. William Ganson Rose, p. 503.

29. William Ganson Rose, p. 519.

30. Nelson Manfred Blake, p. 327; *This Fabulous Century*, 1, *1900–1910*, 33–34.

31. Frederick Lewis Allen, pp. 112–113.

32. Henry Steele Commager, p. 41.

33. Nelson Manfred Blake, p. 386; Richard N. Farmer, *The Real World of 1984* (New York: David McKay Company, Inc., 1973), p. 15.

34. *The LIFE History of the United States/1890–1901*, 8, *Reaching for Empire*, 37.

35. William Ganson Rose, pp. 390, 526.

36. *This Fabulous Century*, 1, *1900–1910*, 80.

37. Hudson Maxim, "Man's Machine-Made Millennium," *Cosmopolitan*, XLV (November 1908), 576.

2

The Haunted Men

Whether or not one calls the Gothic a literature of subversion, as Robert Donald Spector does, because of its "reluctance to accept the traditional, the dominant, the accepted values" of the eighteenth century, it does have a significant place in the continuing debate regarding epistemology going back to John Locke.[1] The prevailing opinion coming out of the seventeenth century held that "science and philosophy paralleled each other in being concerned with manifestations of divinity in a universe which was assumed to be permanently divine, increasingly intelligible, and so designed that man could better his lot by improving his understanding of physical phenomena."[2] (Essentially "an Enlightenment world view," it has been shared—without the trappings of divinity—by such science fiction writers as John Campbell, Isaac Asimov, and Robert Heinlein, for whom rational man gathers knowledge in a rational universe; consequently, one of the main narrative patterns of the field has concerned itself with problem solving. This characteristic leads to the frequent comparison of the sf story to the detective story and explains to some degree, at least, why both Poe and Asimov have been successful in both fields.[3])

By the late eighteenth century, however, the psychological empiricists had isolated man in a picturesque but brooding nature which one could not be certain was "reality." Given that problem, man became marooned amid the flowing impressions which his mind drew from his senses, but he could not be sure that his mind functioned properly, nor could he be certain that what his reason made of those perceptions was accurate. The Romantic poet, like Wordsworth, concentrating upon the solitary figure, explored "his own mind in its absorption of the external world as it impressed itself upon his senses, memory, and intuition of God."[4] Wordsworth proved to be one of the fortunates. As Ernest J. Lovell has shown, drawing heavily upon the Gothic novel, others felt increasingly alienated from nature.[5] J. M. W. Turner's "Dolbaden Castle, North Wales" (1810), John Martin's "The Bard" (1817), and Caspar David Friedrich's "The Cliffs at Rugen" (1818–1820) give emotional impact to the visual image of diminished man against an overwhelming landscape (so often rendered in terms of mountains or ocean). Those moderns for whom the intellectual tumult of conflicting views during the nineteenth century has been encapsulated in the idea of a quarrel about Darwinian theory may be surprised to find that as early as 1817 in *Blackwood's Magazine* an anonymous writer lamented the "separation between science and religion."[6]

The crucial function of the Gothic had been to reawaken the irrational and demonic. In *The Castle of Otranto* (1765), Horace Walpole had provided most of the essential machinery, including the suggestion that he was publishing an old manuscript which he had acquired—a deception which remained a stock narrative convention into the twentieth century. For him, the supernatural, however different its trappings, worked as it had for the Elizabethan and Jacobean playwrights: as an agent of divine justice, the wraith foreshadowed and/or helped bring about the inevitable punishment of a sinner. Retribution, predicated on the concept of a moral universe governed by a just divinity, retained a vital role in the treatment of the supernatural well into the nineteenth century, achieving one of its finest expressions in the fiction of Hawthorne.

In contrast, Mrs. Ann Radcliffe provided her audience with satisfactory natural explanations in order to establish the credibility of her "impossible horrors."[7] From this line, as early as Charles Brockden Brown, came those writers who used contemporary scientific speculation to explain away the apparently supernatural. Thus, among English writers, M. G. "Monk" Lewis and Charles Maturin perhaps most fully realized the Gothic's potential for horror in their psychological probings of characters who had their origins in such medieval legendary figures as Faustus, the Wandering Jew, and the Doppelgänger. Frederick S. Frank calls Maturin's protagonist, Melmoth the Wanderer, a "grand, godless, godlike creature."[8] From the Gothic flows the tradition of horror which survives in contemporary fiction. Inadvertently—and certainly neither they nor anyone in the nineteenth century realized it—the Gothicists opened the door to that continuum which leads to the grotesque, distorted Absurdist world. Along the way occurred a high point—in the 1980s one does not choose to say culmination or climax—during the first years of the twentieth century in that dichotomy of Freud on the one hand and Watson and the Behaviorists on the other.

From the beginning, the writers made use of a number of their readers' interests to gain the distancing necessary to make their works more acceptable: the Continental setting, the Medieval past, and the Oriental tale. One consequence was that alchemy and astrology provide most of the scientific content of the Gothic romance. Even Victor Frankenstein "chanced" upon a volume of Cornelius Agrippa and then sought the works of Paracelsus and Albertus Magnus.

Skillfully and quickly, Mary Shelley guides young Frankenstein and her readers from alchemy to contemporary science. Victor's personal, reflective narrative allows her to compress the transition. He remarks that had he known that "a modern system of science [whose powers] were real and practical . . . had been introduced," he would have "thrown Agrippa aside." Despite his dreams of "raising ghosts or devils," such daily phenomena as distillation "and the wonderful effects of steam" had not escaped his attention. Two years (and two paragraphs) later, after he watched lightning destroy a great oak, his father tells him of electricity, builds a small machine, performs a few experiments, and makes a kite for the fifteen-year-old Victor. The kite, drawing lightning from the clouds, completes "the overthrow" of the alchemists. At seventeen he enters the university at Ingolstadt, where, after another denunciation of the alchemists, he becomes the devoted student of M. Waldemar, who enumerates the "miracles" which modern natural philosophers have performed. Waldemar concludes, "They have acquired new and almost unlimited powers; they can command the thunders of heaven, mimic the earthquake, and even mock the invisible world with its own shadows." Only then does Victor undertake the studies which lead to his "infus[ing] a spark of being into the lifeless thing that lay at [his] feet."[9]

Waldemar's celebration of science remains unique in the fiction of the early nineteenth century. More importantly, however, since Mary Shelley has allowed Victor to create life so soon, she becomes free to show the effects of such an act upon Victor Frankenstein, Robert Walton, and the nameless creature. Before Frankenstein reveals his success, he first protests that his narrative is not the "vision" of a madman, and he then refuses to tell the eager Walton the secret of "bestowing animation upon lifeless matter" lest it lead Walton, as it did Frankenstein, to "destruction and infallible misery." He underscores Mary Shelley's judgment of him when he laments the fate of one "who aspires to become greater than his nature will allow."[10]

The novel becomes a tale of retribution involving the sin of intellectual pride. Yet the story is not that of Victor Frankenstein alone; there are three narrators. Walton's isolation in the Arctic—a favorite setting throughout the century—provides an exotic means of obtaining a contemporary setting that still removes the action from a familiar everyday world. Walton's "ardent curiosity" reveals that he, too, is guilty of the sin of pride. He rationalizes that he will be a benefactor of mankind by discovering the Northeast Passage to Asia; his words echo Frankenstein's as he speaks of his "enthusiasm" and "favourite dream." In familiar terms—exploration—he sets the stage for Frankenstein's more bizarre, more "terrific" confession. Of Frankenstein as a Faustian/godlike figure little need be said. Once he confronts his creature on Montanvert near Mont Blanc, the monster's narrative introduces a new perspective. His account of his rejection by society takes up much of the second volume of the novel. One sees it as the thematic core. In the context of the Shelley circle, one can easily read it as a disguised plea for tolerance toward the individual.

After Frankenstein destroys the female whom he is building as a mate for his creature, because he fears that he will loose a race of devils on the world, his monster kills Victor's bride on her wedding night. Driven by guilt and remorse, as much as by hatred, Frankenstein pursues him into the Arctic. Ironically, before dying of exhaustion, Frankenstein exhorts Walton's crew not to forsake their original undertaking but to continue on to the pole, thus assuring their place as "benefactors" of mankind. But the final scene belongs to the creature. Emphasizing his abhorrence of himself and asking, "Am I to be thought the only criminal, when all human kind sinned against me?"—he flees into the night, seeking his own death. Mary Shelley gave modern science its first myth in *Frankenstein*.

Twenty years earlier, Charles Brockden Brown had adapted the Gothic to an American setting in *Wieland, or The Transformation* (1798). Despite a number of ties to Germany especially, the narrative takes place on the Schuylkill River near Philadelphia sometime between the "conclusion of the French and the beginning of the revolutionary war."[11] Even more important than this shift from anything remotely medieval, however, are two other matters which gave direction to American fantasy. First, Brown drew upon current scientific data and speculation to explain the apparently supernatural. Second, in the character of Theodore Wieland, for the first time in American fiction, however briefly, Brown dramatized a case of dementia, appealing in his "Advertisement" to "Physicians and to men conversant with the latent springs and occasional perversions of the human mind" (p. 3) in order to gain authority for his portrayal.

Brown's choice of narrator, Theodore's sister Clara Wieland, a young woman of feeling, proved unfortunate because she allows the storyline to go astray. Initially, however, she concentrates effectively upon two actions providing the cornerstones of the central mystery. The original point of departure is the religious obsession of her father. He built a stone temple somewhat removed from the house where he could worship in solitude. His own mental imbalance revealed itself when, certain that he had failed to perform some spiritual duty, he believed that some "strange and terrible" death awaited him. One night at the temple spontaneous combustion burned him, but he did not immediately die. For her account of the incident Clara must rely upon her uncle whose "belief is unalterably attached to natural causes" (p. 21), although she acknowledges that as she has grown older she has wondered whether or not the accident illustrates divine intervention into the affairs of men. Brown inserts a note referring to instances of spontaneous combustion reported in learned medical journals.

The second action does not occur until some six years after Theodore's marriage to Catherine Pleyel. Before turning to it, Clara remarks upon her brother's gravity but gives more attention to the high quality of his scholarship. He is the equal of Catherine's brother, Henry Pleyel, with whom he quibbles about scholarly details. Theodore is the first to hear a mysterious voice speak to him. One evening he leaves Henry and the two women only to return, asking if Catherine has left their company. Assured that she has not, he faces a dilemma, for near the temple her voice warned him of danger. Although Pleyel argues that "an auricular deception" took place, Clara fears that Theodore's senses have been the victim of a delusion. "The will," she asserts, "is the tool of understanding, which must fashion its conclusions on the notices of the senses" (p. 39). Only then does she explain that Theodore has always believed that "a direct and supernatural decree" caused her father's death. To prove that Theodore did hear

Catherine's voice, a second incident occurs; both he and Pleyel hear her voice announce that Pleyel's beloved Baroness de Stolberg has died in Leipzig.

The question of the accuracy of sense perceptions not only foreshadows Theodore's fate but also provides a heightening of Clara's vacillating speculations regarding supernatural and natural explanations of the voices. At this point, however, the narrative loses much of its focus. Quite simply, Brown made too much of a good thing. Clara abandons Wieland as she turns to a description of her sensibilities and the supposed threat to her virtue. A young writer expanding his first novel, Brown lost himself amid the conventions of Richardsonian sentiment and seduction. Clara introduces a stereotypical Faustian character, Carwin, whose voice fascinates her. At one point he suggests that the voices she, Theodore, and Pleyel have heard may be of human origin because "mimickry [is] so very common" (p. 85). No less than four times does she hear voices. Carwin appears at the threshold of her bedroom. Pleyel, whom Clara decides she loves, denounces her—"how art thou fallen!" (p. 117)—after hearing two voices, Clara's and Carwin's, discuss their passion. A note from Carwin sends Clara back to her bedroom where she finds Catherine dead.

When Wieland tells Clara that Catherine and their children are dead, she temporarily loses her mind; only when she recovers does her uncle, Thomas Cambridge, formerly a surgeon with the British army in Germany, give her a copy of the transcript of Wieland's confession. Those few pages (pp. 184–196) allow Wieland to describe his own religious obsession, climaxing in Clara's house when a radiant figure and a voice tell him that "in proof" of his faith, he must kill Catherine. He does. The voice then demands the sacrifice of his children; he acquiesces to the will of God. Cambridge explains to Clara that he knew of many such cases of "maniacal . . . illusions" in Germany. Brown inserts a note: "Mania Mutabilis. See Darwin's Zoonomia, vol. ii, Class III. 1, 2, where similar cases are stated" (p. 202).

When Clara encounters Carwin, he admits that he "sported with [her] terrors" (p. 222) and confesses his part in each incident (Clara's maid, Judith, with whom he had an affair, aided him), but he denies prompting Wieland to murder. Acknowledging his misuse of his power, he cannot name it; thus Brown inserts a lengthy note describing *"Biloquium,* or ventrilocution," in which he refers to the "work of Abbe de la Chappelle" (p. 223). In a final scene permitting a gamut of emotions, Theodore, still crazed, intends to kill Clara even as she converses with Carwin. When Clara explains Carwin's activities and when Wieland directly questions Carwin, he admits his "contrivance" (p. 247). Although Wieland recognizes Carwin is a "daemon" rather than God, he still attempts to kill Clara; only when Carwin's voice tells him *"to hold,"* does he come to his senses. He commits suicide. To strain for exotic interpretations seems unnecessary, for Clara declares that as he realizes his error, "Wieland was transformed at once into the *man of sorrows"* (p. 258). What is more important, through trickery, the latent morbidity which he inherited from his father—heightened by the manner of his father's death—transformed him into a madman.[12]

One regrets that Brown did not always maintain better control over his material by eliminating—or decreasing—his attention to Clara's feelings (which were themselves more than slightly morbid), but his strength lies in his portrayal of Wieland's madness and in his appeal to scientific thought to support his case study. He alone backed up his fiction with notes to accepted authorities. Not until near the end of the nineteenth century would the reader find anything like it except in Mary Shelley.

Washington Irving also achieved a kind of uniqueness. Although attracted to the Gothic, he apparently could not take it seriously, for through innumerable "adventures" he toys with its machinery, even in "Rip Van Winkle" and "The Legend of Sleepy Hollow." His humor permeates "The Devil and Tom Walker"—told to Irving and a fishing party by a Cape Cod whaler—while he intrudes a pleasant but unneeded tale into the episodic "Dolph Heyliger." Constantly, one is aware of his presence through his personal comments and references to the circumstances in which a story was told. (Not surprisingly, three of his finest works—"Rip Van Winkle," "The Legend of Sleepy Hollow," and "Dolph Heyliger"—supposedly have been taken from the manuscripts of Diedrich Knickerbocker.) Always the effect of horror is tempered by humor. One can best see the result by comparing the tone of "The Devil and Tom Walker" to that of William Austin's "Peter Rugg, The Missing Man" (1824), both of which make use of the image of a traveler riding eternally through the night. Irving's image is further diminished when the Cape Cod whaler informs his audience that one may still see the "very hole" from which Tom dug Captain Kidd's treasure. In short, his tales have little or none of the dramatic and emotional intensity of either *Wieland* or that kind of story identified with *Blackwood's Magazine*.

Thus, in the present context, Irving's most noteworthy effort remains "The Adventure of the German Student," although even there his narrator must briefly intrude, exclaiming, " . . . but I should first tell you something about this young German." Because Gottfried Wolfgang had indulged in "fanciful speculations on spiritual essences . . . his health was impaired; his mind 'diseased.' " His dreams envision a beautiful woman. Once this is established, the narrative concentrates upon a single incident. One night in revolutionary Paris he finds the young woman in the Place de Grève and persuades her to share his rooms; they pledge their love forever. In the morning after briefly leaving her asleep, he returns to find her dead. The police officer informs him that she had been guillotined the day before. Wolfgang goes mad, certain that the fiend has possessed him. The horror—with the macabre detail of her head rolling on the floor—remains traditionally Gothic. In answer to a question, the narrator insists that the event cannot be doubted: "The student told it me himself. I saw him in a madhouse in Paris." To say that Irving satirizes the Gothic with this ending or that it initially resembles Poe but really "undercuts the plausibility" of the tale detracts from the achievement of both authors.[13] Given the interlocking structure of *Tales of a Traveller*, in which "Adventure of the German Student" appeared, Irving could not avoid the linking envelope. (In his best tales dealing with psychological abnormality, Poe did not intrude in such a manner.) Irving anticipated, if he did not achieve, the ambiguity of later writers. Did the event actually take place? Can the reader believe the testament of an inmate of a madhouse? One cannot be certain, for Gottfried Wolfgang shares the diseased mind of Theodore Wieland and the other Gothic protagonists.

In England, *Blackwood's Magazine* "kept Gothicism alive from the 1820s through the 1840s,"[14] as well as shaped much of the work of Edgar Allan Poe. It contained tales of retribution, like James Hogg's "The Mysterious Bride" (1830), in which the ghost of a beautiful woman returns to haunt, marry, and destroy the descendant of the Laird of Berkendelly who dishonored and abandoned her,[15] but *Blackwood's* gained its fame (and notoriety) from the story concentrating upon the reactions of a character to a singular, bizarre situation. Its contributors moved beyond the conventional, expected examination of the heightened sensibilities of a beleaguered heroine or the anguished broodings of a Gothic villain. Using such "natural events" as premature burial, spontaneous combustion, and cataleptic trances, for example, they minutely and explicitly described the psychological reactions of a character, often making use of the first-person narrator to increase the impact of the experience. Their analyses added horror upon horror until the practice exhausted itself; indeed, as though aware of their excesses, the authors joked at their efforts, as when the narrator of "Crocodile Island" (1833) complains, "I have just got to that point in a tale I am writing for next month's Blackwood, and curse me if I know how to get naturally away from Crocodile Island."[16] The key lies in the word naturally, for the writers abandoned the supernatural in favor of supposedly mundane events, however exotic.

Poe's indebtedness to *Blackwood's* has been amply documented; the late Thomas O. Mabbott declared that the journal "provided a source for ideas made use of, one way or another, in many of Poe's stories."[17] Close examination of his work reveals that as a journalist in need of materials, Poe borrowed widely and adapted his sources to his own ends. Yet throughout the 1830s he returned again and again to *Blackwood's*; one suspects that the magazine both fascinated and repelled him. He named Blackwood Blackwood as one of the group who would tell *The Tales of the Folio Club*, and he gave the subtitle, "A Tale neither in nor out of 'Blackwood,' " to "Loss of Breath," an early effort intended for that volume. But his most successful satire of the magazine remains "The Psyche Zenobia (How to Write a Blackwood Article)," in which he first allows Mr. Blackwood to explain the methods of his authors to Zenobia and then appends "A Predicament," a parody ridiculing the sensations of Zenobia as the minute hand of a clock decapitates her. (It was published separately in 1838 as "The Scythe of Time," the name Zenobia gave to the minute hand.) In the often-cited letter of April 30, 1835, to Thomas W. White, Poe showed wide acquaintance with specific stories, while in a letter of February 11, 1836, to J. P. Kennedy, he spoke of "the extravagances of Blackwood."[18] Yet as late as 1842, in his review of Hawthorne's *Twice-Told Tales*, in referring to the need to achieve a single effect, he cited "Tales of Effect, many fine examples of which we[re] found in the earlier numbers of Blackwood." Of his most famous stories, "The Pit and the Pendulum," certainly draws from William Mudford's "The Iron Shroud" (August 1830) as one of its many sources.

An element of burlesque and satire occurs in Poe's work throughout his career, but he soon escaped the excesses of the early "Metzengerstein" and "The Assignation," so obviously imitative. In "Ligeia," regarded as one of his finest tales,[19] although the first-person narrator echoes the conventional protagonist not only as he speaks of his opium dreams but also as he implies his "incipient madness" and remarks upon the "mad disorder" of his thoughts, Poe found his direction. His concentration upon the single effect proved crucial, for he focused on terror. However much his characters dwell on female beauty, love, death, and consciousness, Poe captures them in a moment of horror which strips them of the last vestige of sanity. More effectively than his predecessors, in his best fiction Poe dramatized glimpses into the realm of madness. "The Black Cat," "The Cask of Amontillado," "The Fall of the House of Usher" (though its narrator is an observer), and "The Tell-Tale Heart" come immediately to mind, as do "The Pit and the Pendulum" (despite the arrival of the French army) and "William Wilson," whose concern with the Doppelgänger anticipates the later concern with multiple personality. Perhaps through the influence of Poe especially, the story dwelling upon madness became highly popular in America and remained in vogue in such magazines as *Cosmopolitan, The Atlantic Monthly*, and *The Black Cat* as late as the turn of the century.

Ironically, Poe's treatment of abnormal psychology did not in itself contribute to the development of science fiction,[20] although modern psychology has illuminated his stories. This seeming paradox emphasizes that his "perfection" of the *Blackwood's* story led to a kind of cul de sac. *Blackwood's* contributors had delighted in compiling the explicit reactions of a character to a bizarre situation not involving the supernatural. In doing this, they had turned their backs on the demonic universe of the Gothicists. They had reduced their world to physical and psychological sensations whose validity of experience they themselves came not to accept, as illustrated by both the satire of Poe and the breakdown of "Crocodile Island." When Poe pushed those sensations into the realm of madness, there was no place left to go. Despite the continued popularity of that kind of sensational story, it could not develop further until a new perspective was taken of the material, whether or not it involved the supernatural.

The differences between Poe's "The Oval Portrait" (1842) and Hawthorne's "The Birthmark" (1843) may suggest something about the needed shift in perspective, a shift that had begun while Poe wrote some of his finest tales.[21]

In "The Oval Portrait" (first published as "Life in Death," 1842), referring specifically to Mrs. Radcliffe and a castle in the Apennines, Poe allows his narrator, victim of "incipient delirium," to discover the portrait of a lovely young woman among many paintings. In the book describing them, he finds her story. A young bride, she hated "the art which was her rival," but she posed for her husband, "a passionate, and wild, and moody" artist. He paints her life into the picture. After exclaiming, "This is indeed *Life* itself!"—he turns to find her dead. The idea of the tie between life and an inanimate object may be implicit, but Poe ends on the shock of the beauty's death. In "The Birthmark" (1843), Hawthorne looks back to "a man of science" in the last century "when the comparatively recent discovery of electricity and other kindred mysteries of Nature seemed to open paths into the region of miracle." Aylmer insists upon removing a blemish from the cheek of his lovely bride, Georgina. Throughout the narrative, Hawthorne enumerates Aylmer's past failures—the flower, the daguerreotype, the elixir of life—before Aylmer experiments upon Georgina. His science fails him. She dies. One thinks of Victor Frankenstein, who played God. Hawthorne stresses the sin of pride when he allows the dying Georgina to console Aylmer: "Do not repent that . . . you have rejected the best the earth can offer." The emphasis rests upon the moral implications of the action, not the action itself.

Both writers dealt with mesmerism. The best—and it is good—that Poe achieved occurs in "The Facts in the Case of M. Valdemar" (1845). The mesmerist keeps Valdemar in a trance long after his physiological death; released from the trance, Valdemar "*rotted* away" beneath the hands of the narrator, the mesmerist. Again, there is the shock of action. In contrast, Hawthorne used mesmerism—or any experiment—to enhance his characters. *The Scarlet Letter, The House of the Seven Gables, The Blithedale Romance* serve as examples. His central concern remained with sin and retribution. Perhaps "The Hollow of the Three Hills" most vividly illustrates the shift in tone as it transforms all of the shopworn machinery of the Gothic. During "those strange old times" a woman and an old crone meet in a "hollow basin," a circular pit, which could lie anywhere; "such scenes as this (so gray tradition tells) were once the resort of a Power of Evil and his plighted subjects." The woman—"smitten with an untimely blight"—wishes to learn of those whom she abandoned; described as a wanderer, the lady kneels with her head on the knees of the old woman who begins her incantations ("a prayer that was not meant to be acceptable in Heaven"). Whether auditory hallucinations or the exclamations of physical beings summoned up, the sounds contrast sharply with the voices heard in *Wieland*. In speaking of one wraith who seeks an "auditor," Hawthorne characterizes all of the Gothic protagonists: " . . . each member of that frenzied company, whose own burning thoughts had become their exclusive world." In response to the lady's implied request, the death-bell sounds, "bearing tidings of mortality and woe to the cottage, to the hall, and to the solitary wayfarer, that all might weep for the doom appointed in turn to them." There comes a "measured tread" before one learns that she has died; "she lifted not her head."[22]

No other brief tale evokes more powerfully the themes which haunted Nathaniel Hawthorne; nor does any other contrast him more sharply with Poe. Those themes led him finally to the fragmentary romances involving a bloody footprint and the elixir of life. In America at midcentury, Poe and Hawthorne brought one impulse to a finish, although a few may read several of Fitz-James O'Brien's enchanting stories as studies of madness.

Thus, before the end of the Civil War, only Oliver Wendell Holmes' *Elsie Venner* (1861) indicated one direction in which the American handling of abnormal psychology would develop. *Elsie Venner* anticipates the increasing interest in multiple personality which marked the last decades of the century. Holmes sketched the scientific background only in nontechnical generalizations which are always kept in the background. The village physician who attends Elsie throughout her brief life explains something of the mystery surrounding her personality only after her death. When Elsie's mother was pregnant, she was bitten by a rattlesnake; in some inexplicable manner that incident marked Elsie, causing her to have a dual personality. In her abnormal state she partook of the habits of a snake. The doctor, however, dismisses this phenomenon as "an accidental principle" which he had hoped would disappear as she grew older. Holmes made no appeal to outside authority, nor did he cite a similar case to increase the plausibility of his basic concept.

Between the Civil War and the early twentieth century particularly, the treatment of the supernatural in fiction, like that of the interplanetary voyage, became the battleground for those who wished to maintain the old Christian values or to substitute a framework based upon such cults as the Theosophists. For example, as late as 1908, in the "Foreword" to *The Shadow World*, a fictionalized account of Hamlin Garland's experience with psychical research, Garland explained, "This book is a faithful record . . . of the most marvelous phenomena which have come under my observation during the last sixteen or seventeen years. I have used my notes (made immediately after the settings) and also my reports to the American Psychical Society (of which I was at one time a director)."[23] Such magazines as *The Atlantic Monthly* carried numerous articles dealing with psychical research. Both Henry James's brother William and his father played important roles on the American scene, as did Sir Arthur Conan Doyle somewhat later in England. The basic issue was a simple one: whether or not the individual writer could accept the findings of the new psychology which led within a generation to Carl Jung, Freud, and Watson. There was, of course, no single reaction, often even in the writings of a given author.

In terms of literary history, perhaps the most important line of development occurred among those writers who came to explain away the supernatural in terms of hallucination. In Britain, the most important single figure at midcentury was Sheridan LeFanu in such tales as "Green Tea." In America, although their fiction was very different, Henry James and Ambrose Bierce arrived at a similar goal. If one looks for a single turning point, one may find it in Henry James's unsigned discussion of the supernatural in literature in *The Nation* (November 9, 1865), in which he suggested that "a good ghost story, to be half as terrible as a good murder story, must be connected at a hundred different points with the common objects of life."[24] In that article, he compared Mrs. Radcliffe and Wilkie Collins, to her detriment, while praising *The Woman in White* (1861) for its "introduction into fiction of the mysteries at our own door." In this way did one of the major voices calling for literary realism reject Gothicism. In his later study of Hawthorne, James lamented "the want of reality and the abuse of the fanciful element" in *The Scarlet Letter*, observing, too, that "the element of the unreal is pushed too far" in *The Marble Faun*.

Yet subsequent critics have agreed that James's early contributions to the ghost story followed the manner of Hawthorne. The earliest of these, "A Romance of Certain Old Clothes" (*The Atlantic Monthly*, February 1868), focuses upon a proud and jealous woman, Rosalind Wingate. Although the supernatural is never brought onstage, divine retribution apparently punishes her for her acts against her sister. By implication, the ghost of her sister strangles her. "DeGrey: A Romance" (*The Atlantic Monthly*, July 1868) recalls Hawthorne's *The House of the Seven Gables* in that it turns upon the curse laid upon the DeGrey family by a medieval knight whose daughter married into the family; the curse kills the women whom the DeGrey men love. When the current fiancée curses the curse, she must watch young DeGrey die from no apparent cause. She goes mad. In "The Ghostly Rental" (*Galaxy*, 1876), the daughter of Captain Diamond pretends to haunt him after he has cursed her lover. He dies, only to return to haunt his daughter. Of these earliest stories, James reprinted only "A Romance of Certain Old Clothes," the last time in *Stories Revived* (1885). He did not publish another ghost story until 1891.

In the interval Ambrose Bierce published the majority of his macabre tales. Although his artistry would improve, he had found his basic storyline as early as "A Holy Terror" (*The Wasp*, December 3, 1882). It concentrates upon a single incident. Believing that he has struck a vein of gold in a graveyard, a prospector, Jefferson Doman, finds that to stake his claim he must open a fresh grave. As night approaches, he realizes that he must move the coffin; to do this he must stand in the grave as he enlarges it. Bierce reminds one of Poe and *Blackwood's* as he dwells upon the prospector's reactions, but his language differs greatly: "He was intensely observant; his senses were all alert; but he saw not the coffin. As one can gaze at the sun until it looks black and then vanishes, so his mind, having exhausted its capacities of dread, was no longer conscious of the separate existence of anything dreadful."[25] As he digs, his imagination calls up a vision of the "livid corpse of the dead woman"; when he strikes the coffin so that it bursts open, he dies of fright. The narrative shifts; months later a party visiting the graveyard declares the claim to be fool's gold.

Unfortunately, as yet the sequence of Bierce's stories has not been established because most of them appeared in Hearst's *San Francisco Examiner* between 1887 and 1891; he did collect them in two volumes, *Tales of Soldiers and Civilians* (1891)—later changed to *In the Midst of Life*—and *Can Such Things Be?* (1893). However different Bierce's stories may seem, they are united by a common theme. In "The Boarded Window," a frontiersman named Murlock prepares the body of his wife for burial. He awakens to find a panther dragging her body toward the window of the cabin. He shoots at the animal but loses consciousness. Reviving, he finds that his wife had not been dead; the panther had killed her but not before she bit off a piece of its ear in her agony. By implication Murlock dies from the shock. In "The Eyes of the Panther," Irene Marlowe tells Jenner Brading that she cannot marry him because she is insane, the child of a woman who had been driven mad by an encounter with a panther. Bierce inserts his own account of that event—a story within a story—to gain a terse objectivity. Irene disappears into the forest; Brading shouts a warning because he believes that he sees the bright eyes of a panther. A final brief scene reports that, aroused one night by the scream of a panther, he shoots the creature, only to trail it into the brush and find he has killed Irene. In "The Middle Toe of the Right Foot," the husband of a woman who has been murdered is forced to stay alone overnight in the house in which she lived. By morning he has died; in the dust are the footprints of children and a woman identified as the murder victim by her missing toe. The first-person protagonist of "The Secret of Macgarger's Gulch" dreams—or awakens to an hallucination—that a man kills a woman with an axe; an abrupt shift of scene to a later period reveals that a woman who dwelt in the cabin had long ago disappeared. In "Staley Fleming's Hallucination," the protagonist dreams of being attacked by a dog belonging to a murdered man; he is found dead with the marks of a dog's teeth on his throat. Jerome Searing, a scout during the Civil War and protagonist of "One of the Missing," regains consciousness to find that he faces his own gun. Certain that it will kill him if he moves, he nevertheless tries to discharge it; he dies of fright. Only then does the reader learn that the gun was discharged when he fell. Such a situation is base deception by Bierce, but it points to his central theme.

Often cited, "The Man and the Snake" builds upon a similar deception. Visiting the home of a well-known scientist who keeps his collection of snakes in a wing of his house, Harker Brayton reads by chance a passage from a medieval book attesting the hypnotic power of snakes. Brayton scoffs, but soon afterward in the privacy of his room, he sees a snake under the bed. He tries to leave, but something compels him to move toward the snake:

Again he took a step forward, and another. . . . The man groaned; the snake made neither sound nor motion, but its eyes were two dazzling suns. . . . He heard, somewhere, the continuous throbbing of a great drum . . . and thought he stood in the Nileside reeds. . . . The music ceased. . . . A landscape, glittering with sun and rain, stretched before him. . . . In the middle distance a vast serpent, wearing a crown, reared its head out of its voluminous convolutions and looked at him with his dead mother's eyes. . . . Something struck him a hard blow upon the face and breast. He had fallen to the floor. . . . And every movement left him a little nearer to the snake. (pp. 85, 86)

At this point Bierce breaks the narrative, shifting to the scientist and his wife in another part of the house. They hear Brayton's scream, find him dead of a convulsion, and reveal that the snake is stuffed, with shoebuttons for eyes. Deception, yes; but Bierce dramatizes the hallucination in terms so modern that one recalls Eugene O'Neill's dramatic study of fear *The Emperor Jones*. (No suggestion that Bierce influenced O'Neill is intended.) Whatever the variety of his stories, Bierce worked upon one central theme: the dramatization of fear. His basic premise may be found in *The Devil's Dictionary*: "Ghost—the outward and visible sign of an inward fear."[26]

The implications of race memory in "The Man and the Snake" lead to four stories in which Bierce allowed his protagonists to rationalize their fears. The central figure of "The Secret of Macgarger's Gulch" muses upon "that element of hereditary superstition from which none of us is altogether free" (p. 34). One of the characters of "A Watcher by the Dead" echoes this idea: "The superstitious awe with which the living regard the dead . . . is hereditary and incurable" (p. 74). The most elaborate statement occurs in the reflections of Brainerd Bysing in "A Tough Tussle," in which the sentry scares himself to death:

"I suppose it will require a thousand ages—perhaps ten thousand—for humanity to outgrow this feeling. Where and when did it originate? Away back, probably, in what is called the cradle of the human race—the plains of Central Asia. What we inherit as a superstition our barbarous ancestors must have held as a reasonable conviction. Doubtless they believed themselves justified by facts whose nature we cannot even conjecture in thinking a dead body a malign thing endowed with some strange power of mischief, with perhaps a will and a purpose to exert it. Possibly they had some awful form of religion of which that was one of the chief doctrines, sedulously taught by their priesthood, as ours teach the immortality of the soul. As the Aryans moved slowly on, to and through the Caucasus passes, and spread over Europe, new conditions of life must have resulted in the formulation of new religions. The old belief in the malevolence of the dead body was lost from the creeds and even perished from tradition, but it left its heritage of terror, which is transmitted from generation to generation—is as much a part of us as are our blood and bones." (p. 301)

Thus did Bierce make use of the scientific speculations of the 1880s and 1890s. In two tales he created a basic situation which became popular and was widely imitated, though never so fully explained. In "The Suitable Surroundings," a writer of ghost stories challenges the protagonist to read one of his manuscripts alone in a deserted house in the forest at night. Startled by the hoot of an owl, he extinguishes his candle; in the morning he is found dead. "A Watcher by the Dead" illustrates both Bierce's theme and method. In the initial scene in a room in San Francisco, an unnamed young man examines a corpse covered only with a sheet; satisfied, he blows out his candle to save it. The second scene goes back to an office on Kearney Street, where Dr. Halberson explains man's inheritance of fear to his colleagues, Dr. Harper and Dr. Mancher. Harper names Jarette as a man who will meet Halberson's conditions and stay with a corpse in a locked room all night, while Mancher offers to play the part of the corpse. The narrative returns to Jarette, musing about his growing concern, as he hears footsteps. Bierce again breaks the flow of action. In the morning Dr. Halberson and Dr. Harper find a crowd in the room surrounding a dead body. Harper declares that he had warned Halberson that Mancher would kill Jarette. Harper and Halberson flee to Europe. Seven years later, in a final scene, Dr. Mancher approaches them in Madison Square, New York, and tells them what happened that night. Jarette died of fright, and Mancher, caught in the original situation, went crazy; he curses the two for not having released him. In short, he was driven mad by his fear of something which he completely understands, a situation which he has brought into being.

Bierce enhances the impact of his material by breaking his narrative into carefully juxtaposed scenes. He varies the pattern with each story, often relying on dialogue to set up the situation and to reveal the final consequences. Increasingly, he takes the action offstage in that he prepares for the central action but shifts at the moment of the crucial encounter. He usually relies on a third-person narrative in order to downplay any emotional reactions. Often he himself intrudes. Such fragmentation frequently produces irony, as evidenced by the seemingly neglected "The Moonlit Road," in which he presents three perspectives of the same action. The first narrator reports the strange death of his mother and the later disappearance of his father. An old man recalls vague memories of killing a wife whom he thought unfaithful and being driven into amnesia—perhaps madness—when he saw her ghost. The mother then establishes her innocence, gives the details of her murder by someone whom she cannot identify, and tells of her attempts to come back in order to communicate with her husband and son to assure them of her well being and continued love. Her husband fled, and she has never been able to communicate with her son. Granted that "The Moonlit Road" deals with a ghost as an actual being rather than an hallucination, it nevertheless substitutes a fresh kind of horror for that inherited from the Gothic and Poe.

In sharp contrast to Bierce's here-and-now dramatic scenes, Henry James achieved much the same result by closely examining "what someone felt about something"[27]; yet even in those few stories in the 1890s when the ghosts are presented as physical actualities instead of as an hallucination, they fulfill Bierce's definition: "the outward and visible sign of an inward fear."

Although some question must remain as to whether or not James interpreted his earlier efforts in light of his theories at the time he wrote the prefaces to the New York edition, he did speak of "Sir Edmund Orme" (1891) as the portrayal of "a state of *unconscious* obsession or, in romantic parlance, hauntedness."[28] In her youth the heroine's mother rejected the suit of Sir Edmund; now, with her daughter still indecisive toward the narrator, the mother's emotional anxiety calls up Sir Edmund's ghost. Both she and the narrator are aware of it, but the daughter sees Sir Edmund only after she has consented to marriage. Her mother, at the height of her concern, dies of a heart attack.

"Sir Edmund Orme," however, was not the first time James had portrayed an obsession; his earliest examination of that state of mind had occurred in "The Last of the Valerii" (1874), although he did not then make use of the supernatural to point up his theme. The Italian, Conte Valerio, a natural man not unlike

Hawthorne's Donatello, warns his American wife that if she continues to dig for antiquarian statuary, he will not answer for his wits, because for him the statues are ghosts. He becomes fascinated by the figure of a Juno "so exquisite it could hardly be inanimate"; "the unholy passions of his forefathers revived."[29] Not until it has been buried again does his excited state of mind cease. Here is James's basic formula for his most thorough studies of a psychological case, for the protagonist, through his own imagination, creates the supernatural from the natural, often naming the object or disclosing the relationship which causes unrest. In this manner, though by different means and with different emphasis, James reached the same point as did Bierce: man's evocation of the supernatural through his individual fears and anxieties.

The first story in which the obsession results in an actual hallucination is "Nona Vincent" (March 1892). Allan Wayworth has created an ideal woman who gains expression through his play *Nona Vincent*. Infatuated with a Mrs. Alsagar, he believes her the basis of the character, but she protests, implying that he is in love with his character. When the play goes into production, he is dissatisfied with the way in which Violet Grey plays the role. On opening night each woman accuses him of being in love with the other; this he denies vigorously. In a highly emotional state he returns to his apartment, where he has an hallucination in which Nona Vincent comes to him, staying with him for some time. This experience releases him from the obsession. At the play's next performance he finds Violet brilliant and in the end marries her.

Both "The Altar of the Dead" (1895) and "The Beast in the Jungle" (1903) provide variations in that the obsession serves as a point of departure for moral studies, while "The Real Right Thing" (1899) stands unique in that—recalling "Sir Edmund Orme," perhaps—two people share an obsession. When Ashton Boyne dies, his wife delegates his friend George Withermore to write a biography, making use of all his personal papers and letters. From the first day, they both sense Boyne's presence but think it signifies his sanction of the work. More and more, however, Withermore feels that the "presence" disapproves. So strong does the impression become that when he next tries to write, he encounters a shadowy apparition, which Mrs. Boyne says she also sees. Evidence in the text implies that she "sees" it at his suggestion. When they abandon the project, the presence is felt no longer. One can perhaps overlook "The Great Good Place" (1900) since its denouement reveals that it is a dream experience.

Partly because of the implications regarding motivation, the most terrible of these stories remains "Maud Evelyn" (1900). A series of dialogues between the narrator and Marmaduke—the action is all offstage—indicates how Marmaduke comes to share the obsession the Dedricks have concerning their daughter who died some years ago when she was fifteen. This method of distancing the action through the screen of dialogue—together with an initial frame similar to that of "The Turn of the Screw" in that a Lady Emma tells the story—gives it a flat, reportorial tone adding to its eeriness. Initially, Marmaduke reveals that the Dedricks "live for" Maud Evelyn; she is "with them in the sense that they think of nothing else.'' In a second encounter, he speaks of her as though they were engaged; in the next, of the many gifts he has given her, even recalling ''about each one the particular thing she said.'' The climax comes when the narrator sees Marmaduke in mourning and is told that he has ''lost his wife.'' Quietly, he explains that ''the more we live in the past, the more things we find in it. . . . They so wanted it for her that we've at last seen our way clear to it. . . . Maud Evelyn had *all* her young happiness.''[30] The horror lies in the ease with which Marmaduke comes to share the Dedricks' obsession. One may debate whether he believes it as strongly as they or simply takes advantage of a good thing. He is the only one of James's protagonists who does not share that ''anxious state'' of mind to which Ford Madox Ford referred.[31]

One wonders whether or not the impact of ''Maud Evelyn'' would have been greater had Marmaduke been the narrator, as the governess is in ''The Turn of the Screw'' (1898). James's successful efforts to distance that story from the here-and-now by having Douglas produce a manuscript which places the action somewhere near midcentury may lead the reader to forget that the experience at Bly was but one incident in the career of a young woman who continued to work as a governess. That was the basis of her relationship with Douglas, who obviously remains infatuated with the memory of her. Since the way one reads the story depends upon how one interprets the behavior of the governess, the reaction of Fred Lewis Pattee as early as 1923 remains significant:

So fundamental was [James's] scientific habit, his recording only that which came within range of his material experience, that the story may be read not as a ghost story at all, but as the record of a clinic: the growth of a suggested infernal cliché in the brain of the nurse who alone sees the ghosts, or her final dementia which is pressed to a focus that overwhelms in her mind every other idea, and makes the children her innocent victims. As such it becomes a record unspeakably pathetic. The boy becomes a brave little martyr. It is a triumph of science over romance.[32]

Granted that in his assessment Pattee may be no less ambiguous than James himself, one must recall that such a reading did not provoke controversy for at least a decade until Edna Kenton and Edmund Wilson added Freudian paraphernalia branding the governess a sexual neurotic.

In his ''Preface'' to the New York edition of ''The Turn of the Screw,'' James asserted, ''Make the reader *think* the evil, make him think it for himself, and you are released from weak specifications''; in the *Notebooks* he had already declared, ''The whole of anything is never told.''[33] Certainly, James did not tie himself to ''weak specifications.'' The text leads the reader, like Pattee, to make inferences. As Douglas sets up the established convention of the old manuscript, the suggestion occurs that the young governess accepted the position because she was infatuated with the master. For a moment, perhaps, one witnesses her jealousy as Mrs. Grose tells her that her predecessor, Miss Jessel, ''was also young and pretty—almost as young and almost as pretty, Miss, even as you.''

She recollects immediately "throwing off" the remark that "he seems to like us young and pretty," but then she asks whether or not Miss Jessel was "careful—particular." Mrs. Grose demurs—"about some things, yes"—but she "won't tell tales."[34] Almost at once, then, one is led to speculate about her predecessor.

More importantly, after she learns that Quint is dead, in the only passage in which she refers to herself in the third person, the governess herself observes that "nobody in the house but the governess was in the governess's plight" (p. 467). Once her narrative has begun, the reader has only her impression and memory of what happened at Bly from which to draw evidence. When Mrs. Grose answers her question by saying that Quint was "too free with every one" (p. 468), and when she recapitulates the circumstances of Quint's death, she acknowledges:

I scarce know how to put my story into words that shall be a credible picture of my state of mind; but I was in these days literally able to find a joy in the extraordinary flight of heroism the occasion demanded of me. I now saw that I had been asked for a service admirable and difficult; and there would be a greatness in letting it be seen—oh in the right quarter!—that I could succeed where many another girl might have failed. (pp. 470–471).

Her inexperience, emphasized as early as the framing device, and her own notion of her role at Bly restrict her understanding of what she encountered and, therefore, what she recalled. Nor should one forget that she alone infers that the children know of the presence of the ghosts and that they have kept the knowledge to themselves (p. 474). Moreover, when Mrs. Grose admits that her predecessors "were both infamous," the governess insists, "I must have it now. . . . Come, there was something between them" (pp. 476–477). She later asserts that the ghosts wish to "get to" the children for "the love of all the evil that, in those dreadful days, the pair put into them" (p. 498). From the evidence of the text, one must accept that she alone saw the figure of Miss Jessel at the lake (pp. 496–497). In short, what occurred at Bly must be regarded as a tissue of the governess's judgments and imaginings.

In the text there is also the ambivalence of the manner in which Miles addresses her—"My dear. . . . dear!" (pp. 518, 520)—a manner that he could have learned as readily from Peter Quint as from either his uncle or the persons at school. The ambiguity of the text reaches a high point, of course, in the climactic scene when she and Miles are alone. When she urges him to explain what happened at school, he confesses that he did not steal but that he said things, though to whom or even how many remains unspecified. She refers to her own "sternness" and then shrieks as she realizes that a ghost has made its appearance. Miles responds by asking, "Is she *here*?" Staggering and gasping, the governess hears Miles give her back "with a sudden fury . . . 'Miss Jessel. Miss Jessel,' " as well as ask in surprise, "It's *he*?" (p. 549).

The narrative of the governess represents the essence of James's technique as he insisted that the reader "think the evil," thereby releasing him from weak specifications. The reader must share the governess's ignorance on crucial matters: the relationship between Peter Quint and Miss Jessel, why her predecessor left Bly, and why the narrator frightens little Flora, who at 8 years of age must be less knowledgeable than Miles. The recent tendency to infer that Miles and Peter Quint had a homosexual relationship seems no more strongly implied than that Miles had some exotic relationship with Miss Jessel or witnessed something between her and Peter Quint. Nor can such implications be dismissed out of hand, for among other details Mrs. Grose admits that she was "afraid" of Quint, who "had everything to say . . . even about *them*" (pp. 469–470), so that the governess gains an impression of "the sinister figure of the living man" whose ghost she saw. Perhaps Miles seeks a relationship with the youthful governess (certainly she would have seemed an older sister, as she well may have to Douglas, only ten years younger than she). Knowledge of Victorian society permits a whole range of speculations regarding governesses.

In terms of the structure of the narrative, once the governess has arrived at Bly, a repetitive pattern sets in. She discusses or thinks about the trouble at the school; she cannot decide what action to take; she encounters either Peter Quint or Miss Jessel. The one incident which makes all interpretations of the nameless young woman suspect occurs soon after her arrival when, without previous knowledge, she describes the wraith whom Mrs. Grose identifies as Peter Quint. "The Turn of the Screw" resists any simplistic reading. Not only must the reader face the ambiguities of Henry James, but almost certainly an unreliable narrator. Yet when compared with James's other ghostly tales, "The Turn of the Screw" seems James's most complex case study of a person in an anxious state of mind.

James stands unique in that he did not, like Bierce, refer explicitly to inherent fear and race memory, nor did he make use of a trained psychologist, as did William Dean Howells in *Questionable Shapes* (1903) and *Between the Dark and the Daylight* (1907). Howells permits the psychologist Wanhope to attempt a scientific explanation of each of the stories told by members of a dinner club. Among them is "The Angel of the Lord," whose protagonist suffers an intense fear of death, causing him to believe that a tramp wandering through the woods is the angel of death sent for him. He runs wildly after the tramp and is killed in a fall. The protagonist of "Though One Rose from the Dead" develops the obsession that his deceased wife will return to him, for they had been psychically close during life. Believing that he hears her voice, he rushes into the fogbound surf and is drowned. In "A Case of Metaphantasmia," the nervous traveler projects his dream to a girl in a nearby sleeping compartment of a train. When she cries for help, he goes to her, although remaining in a somnambulant state. Of this phenomenon Wanhope asserts, " . . . but of course we can't accept a single instance as establishing a scientific certainty" (p. 110).

Ironically, Howells echoes both Bierce and the psychological empiricists of a century earlier as he explains to his companions, "We cannot tell what influences reach us from our environment, or what our environment really is, or how much or little we mean by the word. The sense of danger seems inborn, and so possibly is a survival of our race life when it was wholly animal.'' This is not to suggest that the authors had come full circle. Wanhope's response suggests that the accumulating evidence of discoveries throughout the nineteenth century has sharpened the dilemma. A kind of pathos comes through his voice as he remarks, ''Men like James and Royce, among the psychologists, and Shaler, among the scientists, scarcely leave us at peace in our doubts any more, much less our denials. . . . For all psychology is in a manner dealing with the occult'' (p. 204). If anything, he emphasizes the dilemma as he differentiates between the psychologists and the scientists.

Of the three writers—Bierce, James, and Howells—several of Bierce's plots were most often imitated, although no one could match his sardonic humor nor his ironic perspective. Yet in *Montezuma's Castle* (1899), a collection of stories drawing on the local color of the American Southwest, Charles B. Cory echoed Bierce in ''The White Tanks,'' in which a half-breed Mexican Indian becomes the victim of a practical joke. Bitten by a rattlesnake whose fangs have been removed, he dies of fright. Even more obvious are two selections from Harle Owen Cummins' *Welsh Rarebit Tales* (1902). The protagonist of ''The Fool and His Joke'' wagers that he can disinter a corpse at midnight and remain with it until morning in a haunted house. The man with whom he wagers gives him a gun loaded with blanks and then plays ghost. The protagonist goes mad, as does the central figure of ''The Man Who Was Not Afraid.'' He bets that he can go into a mausoleum and take a string of pearls from the throat of a newly interred corpse. He does not know in which coffin she lies, nor has he been told that one casket contains the mutilated body of a tramp cut to pieces by a train. In the morning he is found crazed, playing with parts of the tramp's body.

Although several critics have suggested Bierce's influence on Stephen Crane's ''The Black Dog: A Night of Spectral Terror'' in *The Whilomville Stories*, not collected until 1949, such an inference too easily forgets that Crane, like many of the early literary naturalists, shared Bierce's belief that fear provided the dominant motivation of mankind. Thus, by 1907, in *The White Darkness*, Laurence Mott could abandon Bierce's central theme and tone while adapting the basic incident to his own ends. In ''The Dark Thing at Hatchet Lake,'' one night Baptiste Clement must pass the lonely lake where Jack Arnold has drowned. He is certain that he sees Jack; the narrative breaks off; the next morning searchers find him frozen to death, his face contorted by fear. As late as 1925, the anarchist in F. Britten Austin's ''The Infernal Machine,'' published in *Thirteen*, is apprehended while trying to smuggle explosives aboard the liner *Gargantuan* to destroy it. While he is interred below decks, his imagination transforms a minor collision into a major catastrophe, particularly because he has become thoroughly disoriented. He does not survive the darkness.

This matter of influence remains tricky. In the same volume, *Thirteen*, Austin's ''Under the Lens'' has been compared to Holmes's *Elsie Venner*, because it builds on the premise that inherited characteristics largely control mankind's behavior. One forgets that by 1925 genetics had begun to take its place in the popular imagination. Austin referred only to "germ plasm," but at one point he did speak of people as "machines."

Despite Edith Wharton's acquaintance with James, his influence on Wharton's *Tales of Men and Ghosts* (1910) must remain no more than conjecture, because both writers relied so heavily on psychological realism. Hardly has the protagonist of "The Bolted Door" killed his wealthy cousin before his conscience makes him confess the crime. No one believes him; an "alienist" tells him that the idea of murder is one of "the commonest forms of hallucination" (p. 44). The compulsion, like that of the Ancient Mariner, forces him to stop people on the street. Only then do his friends commit him to an asylum; only then does a newspaper reporter acknowledge that he accidentally discovered that the confession was true. The narrator of "The Eyes" has immersed himself in his study of the Gothic novel. When he repeatedly experiences visitations by the "worst eyes" he has ever seen, he diligently applies himself to "explaining them on scientific principles. They were hallucinations" (p. 255). He cannot free himself, however, until he leaves the woman whom he professes to love and isolates himself; implication suggests that the eyes represent his guilt about a homosexual encounter.

When one goes beyond such works as these, major problems of evaluation arise, partly because the field of psychology was so new that many of the writers were not well informed. Indeed, one may infer that during the years before the end of the century some of them were misinformed. Not the least of the problems resulted from the development of psychical research which, for some, made synonymous mind, soul, and spirit. For example, in laying the basis for the explanation of how a medium can help solve the murders which occur in *Zaléa: A Psychological Episode and Tale of Love* (1900), Rufus Cummins Garland suggests that psychology is not new, for "the phenomena of the soul and mind have long been investigated by many able and learned men" (p. 59). Nor should the contemporary reader of the 1980s forget that while such individuals as J. M. Charcot and William James were creating a new science, many of the writers of fiction were using materials which are now accepted as areas within parapsychology. Moreover—and here lies the chief value of much of the fiction—attitudes toward the field changed as the period progressed, not always because writers became better informed.

As late as *The Weird Adventures of Professor Delapine of the Sorbonne* (1916), George L. Johnson took Delapine through a number of séances which led him to accept spiritualism, thus providing incidental background to two love stories. Hamlin Garland's *The Shadow World* (1908), as noted, was little more than an essay recapitulating his experience with psychical research; he presented the latter portion as a series of dialogues between him and a skeptical scientist and concluded that he would "go wherever science leads," although hoping that human life was "but a link in the chain of existence." Then, too, there was Sir

Arthur Conan Doyle's *The Land of the Mist* (1926), in which a strangely passive professor George Challenger plays the role of skeptic but finally is convinced that communication with the dead can occur. There must be a universal order, insisted Doyle, heartbroken at the loss of his son during World War I.

Stanley Waterloo used a sentimental love story in *The Seekers* (1900) to cloak an attack upon Christian Science and the use of opiates in patent medicine. In contrast to his British contemporaries, however, through his protagonist he voiced a severe attack on orthodox Christianity: " . . . the miracles of the New Testament have lost their power over the modern mind as attesting divinity in the Great Healer. The best teachers of Christianity of the waning century have paid small attention to the miracles of Jesus, have said or written little even of his miraculous birth and resurrection. They have insisted more and more upon his teachings" (p. 131). Waterloo took a hard line; although as early as a prefatory note to *A Double Life; or, Starr Cross* (1884), Herbert E. Chase had expressed the confusion of the period: " . . . when the science of neurology is conceded to be the whole science of man . . . when the hitherto-hidden secrets of electricity are being exposed but not understood . . . when the secret of what constitutes the human mind is so rapidly discovered . . . [then mankind must be ready to] accept truth in whatever form it may come" (p. 3). Although he began his tale by focusing upon an inventive child prodigy, it soon became a mishmash of unexplained identities and spiritualism. As late as 1933, however, J. D. Beresford's *The Camberwell Miracle* focuses upon the successful career of the faith healer, Martin Davies, who possesses "powers that can't be accounted for by any mechanistic theory of the universe" (p. 322). It ends up by affirming "the powers of love."

At one pole of the range of stories dealing with the mind-soul-body puzzle are those stories which dealt with suspended animation, reincarnation, and transmigration. As early as 1873, calling upon science and archaeologists to believe his tale, Leonard Kip allowed his first-person narrator and Ursula, "a simple Alpine maiden of sixteen," to discover *Hannibal's Man* encased in a glacier. Revived, the Carthaginian soldier eventually fights the narrator for the hand of Ursula. Apparently because tolling Christmas bells startle him, he blunders during the fight and falls into a crevasse where the lovers leave him. A generation later, Edwin Lester Arnold's English country gentleman, Louis Allanby, excavates a Roman tomb on his land, thereby discovering a body whose epitaph reads, "Marcus Lepidus, the Centurion, is Asleep; Tread Lightly." By an act of will, Allanby revives the Roman officer. Spiritually akin, they show affection for the same woman, whom Lepidus identifies as a reincarnation of Prisca Quintilia, the girl he loved in Rome. Arnold made use of the Centurion as a means of gently satirizing the manners of English country society, particularly their hesitancy in affairs of the heart. The more ardent Lepidus, who proves attractive to Priscilla Smith, forces her to make a choice between him and Allanby. Reluctantly, perhaps, but dutifully, she chooses the English squire; Lepidus takes the draught they have prepared for the loser and returns to his crypt.

In 1890, Arnold had taken Phra the Phoenician through a series of wonderful adventures involving reincarnations at various stages of history—ranging from Roman Britain through the Elizabethan Age—which attracted the imagination of the end of the nineteenth century. Throughout those lives, Phra pursues but never wins the Celtic princess whom he had wed in early Britain. Stanley Waterloo avoided such romance in *A Son of the Ages* (1914), taking his protagonist as far back as "Scar, the Link," although the most notable episode involves the sinking of Atlantis. Waterloo's book has importance because, like such writers as Jack London, he relied upon the premise of race memory.

The emphasis upon prehistory continued in one of the few novels in which the African estates of Tarzan, Lord Greystoke, simply provided a backdrop for Edgar Rice Burroughs. After an earthquake, Tarzan's party finds and revives Nu of the Niocene from suspended animation; another quake transports Nu and the attractive, restless Virginia Custer—reincarnation of his ancient love, Nu-tal—back to a prehistoric world where *The Eternal Lover* (1925) demonstrates his prowess by killing a sabre-toothed tiger. Burroughs deliberately made the ending ambiguous. On the one hand, the entire narrative seems the dream of Virginia Custer, who remains uncomfortable in modern society; on the other, Tarzan and his companions do find a cave in which the bones of a caveman and a tiger are intermingled.

The most important American treatment of the theme of reincarnation occurred in Jack London's *The Star Rover* (1915). Imprisoned and tortured in San Quentin prison as a dangerous revolutionary, Professor Darrell Standing learns how to induce a self-hypnotic catalepsy whenever he is forced into a straitjacket. This trance liberates his soul so that he may relive past incarnations. His astral projections take him not only to sixteenth-century France and the American frontier but also to Korea and to Judea, where he serves as the commander of a legion under Pontius Pilate. London at least implied the concept of race memory when he allowed Standing to explain the mental sensitivity which permitted him to learn astral projection. Although *The Star Rover* may be judged London's slightest novel, the popularity of its subject matter led to the publication of *The Twenty-Fifth Man* (1924), supposedly written by Ed Morrell, who taught Professor Standing the secret. That latter novel, however, is no more than a grisly tale of prison life.

Edgar Fawcett's *The Ghost of Guy Thyrle* (1895) gains historical importance whether one reads it as an astral projection ("a cosmic voyage") surpassing that of Darrell Standing, or as the hallucination of an Oxford student, Raymond Severnay, fascinated by the work of the Society for Psychical Research.[35] After visiting a supposedly haunted house owned by his brother Cecil, Severnay tells of his encounter with the spirit of Thyrle and then recounts Thyrle's adventures. Having discovered a drug which releases his soul from his body, Thyrle ranges the earth, becoming a critic of society as well as an observer, and explores the ruins of a once-grand civilization on the moon. During that journey a rival arranges the cremation of Thyrle's body so that he is trapped; he can neither return to his mundane life, nor can he enter the realm of the dead. He journeys to a wide variety of worlds before again returning to earth in order to find someone who will die voluntarily so that he may share the death and thus enter the realm of the dead. The doctor whom Cecil has consulted declares Raymond mad, suffering from hallucinations. They find Raymond dead. Certainly the framework adds only an ambiguity to the novel; Fawcett seems to hide behind the device as well as behind his remarks about seeking a new, realistic mode which readers will find acceptable. This impression becomes stronger when one recalls that he had already written "Solarion" (1889), a variation on the Frankenstein theme published only in *Lippincott's Magazine*.

A part of the concern with psychical research emphasized both the "trance medium," as the individual was called, and the role of hypnotism. Richard Harding Davis attacked as fraudulent the séance and any idea of communicating with the dead in *Vera the Medium* (1908), but in the introduction to Etta DeCamp's *The Return of Frank Stockton* (1913), Stockton himself is made to declare, "[An author] can continue his work after passing out of the material body, providing he finds one yet in earth-life, as I have, through whose patience and sympathetic vibrations it is possible to write and present to the world proof of continued existence" (p. 11). DeCamp explained that the breakthrough came in 1909 during an experiment after she had read William T. Stead's account of his experience as an automatic writer.

In contrast, a medium plays a crucial role in Rufus Cummins Garland's *Zaléa: A Psychological Episode and Tale of Love* (1900). Confronted by the murder of a wealthy Frenchman, M. Paul Dumons, in Washington, Major Byrne believes that that crime is somehow related to the murder of his fiancée, Marie Chantelle, in New Orleans three years earlier. He enlists the aid of a detective, Edward Sanford, whose orthodox investigations get him nowhere. Then to his aid comes Professor Lawson, a member of "the Society for the Study and Advancement of Psychology." He is both a teacher of science and a trance medium, whose eyes burn with "the fire of longing—longing for knowledge of the Great Universe and its Creator"; Lawson refers to "the shadowy domains of the psychical world," and he asks, "If science discovers new and startling things, why should Christians refuse to believe them? These things, whatever they may be, are simply the results of the productive force of Christianity's God." Byrne and Sanford agree that "Christianity must go hand in hand with science if it would survive" (pp. 36, 40, 41). However dated such phrasing may make the story, Lawson also notes the importance of dreams, which always have about them "something of the supernatural" (p. 43).

After a séance, during which Lawson apparently solves the case, he refuses to divulge his findings until Sanford has heard Mlle. LaFontaine in Gounod's "Romeo et Juliette" the next evening. With little prompting, she readily confesses to both murders, her secret apparently having been revealed by "Paul's own words" during the séance with Lawson. Both murders had been acts of jealousy against a man who had wronged her. As Zaléa Gonzales she had borne

Dumons' son; then she studied music in Paris. She killed Marie because she had heard rumor that Dumons' parents had arranged for Marie to marry him; she killed Dumons because she heard that he was to have dinner with the French ambassador's daughter. Abruptly she dies, as though exhausted, but after a year her spirit returns to acknowledge that the crimes were committed by her baser self and to admonish both Byrne and Sanford to practice a "broad, true, humane Christianity."

Zaléa was not unique. Without benefit of Christian repentance, *Ilian: A Psychological Tale of the Civil War* (1888) by Chaplain James J. Kane, U.S.N., had also dealt with a "great crime and [its] punishment." The crime, of course, is seduction, in this case that of a beautiful Southern girl by a Boston professor. She curses him and all his descendants just before she dies in childbirth. Their illegitimate daughter, Ilian, becomes the instrument of the curse when she persuades the professor's legitimate son, Adrien, to betray the North and spy for the South. Although she loves Adrien and marries him, they never live together as man and wife, because Ilian's recurrent hallucinations warn her against him. After he dies, she learns her true identity and seems to revel in emotional horror at having come so close to the unspeakable sin of incest.

In the introduction, Chaplain Kane had assured his readers that the psychological incidents in the novel were not "uncommon" and were drawn from personal experience. He is present as a character at Adrien's death, suggests that he was under the influence of narcotics, and declares that his soul accompanied Adrien's to the borderland of death, where spirits took Adrien but rejected him because he did not wear the mark of death. He offered a special appendix to the novel in which he explained that a plant grown in Mixtecapan, Mexico, "induces sleep similar in all respects to the hypnotic state. The subject answers with closed eyes questions that are put to him, and is completely insensible. . . . That certain drugs and plants have the power of developing 'hypnotism' and psychic exaltation is a fact which every intelligent person must acknowledge" (p. 379). Granted that the explanation is sensational for its day, through it Kane implied that a narcotic condition had caused his own experience after Adrien's death and that such a hypnotic state may explain Adrien's treachery. More importantly, for the first time since Charles Brockden Brown, an author appealed to a specific outside authority to explain away the apparent supernatural.

As one reacts to the melodrama of *Zaléa* and *Ilian*, a central problem becomes clearer. Some years ago, Lionel Stevenson remarked that even "during the decades while realism was nominally in the ascendant" the tradition of fantasy flourished.[36] He spoke of the early twentieth century, but his judgment remains as applicable to the last decades of the nineteenth century. One recalls Henry James's praise of Wilkie Collins. What becomes evident is that in the most effective fantasy of the period, the authors clothed their work with the protective coloration of realistic detail. One thinks of Bierce and James as well as Robert Louis Stevenson's *The Strange Case of Dr. Jekyll and Mr. Hyde* (1886), the classic study of dual personality. In short, the writers intruded an element of fantasy into a fictional world which replicated the familiar external world as closely as possible. But the problem involved technical matters—such as point of view—as much as content. Thinking of Bierce and James, one understands that there was no single solution. The lawyer Utterson vividly presents the mystery of Jekyll and Hyde, but only the statement of Henry Jekyll gives an adequate explanation of the relationship between the doctor and his alter ego.

When, for whatever reasons, the writers did not achieve this mastery of their materials, the results seem much too melodramatic and extreme. For example, in Francis Howard Williams' *Atman: The Documents in a Strange Case* (1891), a student of psychic philosophy, Professor Perdicaris, attempts an experiment joining the "pure spirit" of Margaret Haviland and the soulless, "animal woman" Mlle. Felice into a single being. When he fails, he commits suicide. Williams attempted to bolster the feasibility of the venture by citing diaries, journals, and even an extract from the *Times*. Other writers attempted to shore up their efforts by appealing to such a figure as the psychologist Wanhope. Still others couched such psychological material in an acceptable moral—that is, Christian—framework. But even then, as though uncertain what to do with the psychological phenomena—or perhaps as though afraid of it, especially when they could not satisfactorily explain it—they relegated it to the background and placed their principal emphasis upon a love story. The practice often resulted in flawed stories in which the background and central action did not fuse successfully into an effective unity. In short, they mismanaged their materials, perhaps because they did not understand the phenomena well enough to bring the diverse elements together.

Examples of such mismanagement can be easily found throughout the period. As early as "The Queen of Sheba" (1877), Thomas Bailey Aldrich introduced that storyline which turns upon the heroine's amnesia. In this instance, the protagonist encounters a lovely young girl wandering through the New Hampshire countryside; she informs him that she is the Queen of Sheba; he learns that she is the inmate of a nearby asylum, thought to be incurably insane. Several years later in Europe, he falls in love with a charming beauty closely resembling the young woman in New Hampshire. Not until she is bedridden with a severe cold so that the doctor must enter the scene, does the protagonist learn that she is the same girl and that she has been completely cured of—and does not remember— a strange mental disorder which followed an attack of typhoid fever. The knowledge that she is not the victim of "hereditary doom" removes the last impediment to their marriage. William Dean Howells did much the same thing in "A Sleep and a Forgetting" (1907), in which the young woman becomes amnesiac after seeing her mother killed at a railroad crossing. Again a doctor effects a cure through a discussion of her recurrent dreams. She does not give a detailed account of them, however, nor does the doctor provide an analysis. The cure simply takes place so that she can marry her young man.

Mary Cruger's *Hyperaesthesia* (1886) purports to be a medical study whose historical importance arises from Dr. Frank Hilton's suggestion that physical and mental illness are somehow related, perhaps the earliest hint of the researches which have led to the study of psychosomatic medicine. The most successful sequence in the novel involves those scenes in which Hilton distracts his patient, Clare Ashton, from the physical anguish of her "morbid supersensitiveness of the nerves" by tattooing a wristlet on her arm at her suggestion. Implicit is the suggestion of a kind of hypnosis. But the main action of the novel is dominated by the mother of Hilton's former fiancée who disappeared after she heard him protest their engagement following a brief shipboard romance. Pretending to be the girl's ghost, the mother haunts the young doctor but finally announces that her daughter is alive, waiting for Dr. Hilton to fulfill his vow. Only when a medical colleague proves the girl dead is Hilton free to marry the young woman of his choice—Clare Ashton's sister-in-law.

Another doctor, the central figure in Edward Bellamy's first novel, *Dr. Hei-denhoff's Process* (1880), has discovered the way to erase guilt from a patient's memory. The narrator exclaims that through such a procedure the "figurative promises of the Gospel would become literally true" (p. 12). Dr. Gustave Hei-denhoff carefully explains his procedure in an extended passage. Since science has learned that certain "nerve corpuscles or fibers" of the brain record specific "sensations and the ideas directly connected with them," and since science has also found that the galvanic battery has the power "to destroy or dissolve morbid tissues," he has invented a device capable of removing the memory of sin from his patients' minds (pp. 95–97). "They have already repented," he hastens to explain. "My process . . . only completes physically what is already done morally" (p. 105). Unfortunately, Dr. Heidenhoff does not cure the heroine of the shame and memory of her seduction by a former suiter; the narrator awakens to learn that she has committed suicide. (Waking from a dream, like the old manuscript, became a stock convention throughout all of the motifs of fantasy; by and large it seems to have been used when the author sought release from a situation which he could not or did not want to explain. Seldom, if ever, did the dream ending in itself result in a satisfactory resolution.)

An even stronger commitment to Christianity shapes the theme of Irving Bachellor's *The Master of Silence* (1892). In America, Kendric Lane finds his uncle, a scientist specializing in the psychic and occult (his laboratory is complete with a galvanic battery). Given the opportunity to raise his motherless son, the scientist sees in young Rayel's life "a grand experiment" allowing the boy to retain the inborn ability—unknowingly shared by all humanity—to communicate telepathically. The scientist insists that his son has Christ-like powers. Although "Rayel, the wonderful," cannot speak, he can read a person's thoughts and dreams, recording his reactions to them in brilliant paintings. At the uncle's suggestion, Lane teaches Rayel to speak and takes him into society where he gains a reputation as a fine artist and an eccentric, although the deceit and selfishness of society appall him. At this point, the storyline becomes ensnared by a scheme of Lane's stepmother, now remarried, to obtain Lane's fortune. Rayel defeats her attempt but dies as a result; thus Lane is free to marry a beloved actress. Not only does Bachellor emphasize the need to be Christ-like, but he also lectures parents who may not realize that their foremost "mission—the most sacred of all trusts" is to care for their children (p. 60).

In contrast to this kind of didactic intrusion, Albert Bigelow Paine objectified the encounter between good and evil in *The Mystery of Evelin Delorme; A Hypnotic Story* (1894), derived from Stevenson's novel. In the introduction, Dr. Herbert L. Stone explains that Evelin Delorme, a student of the "Mesmeric Sciences," became the subject of a deliberate experiment after she asked him to "give her a double personality" enabling her to become, at least momentarily, a woman of the world (p. vii). After "these transformations were frequently repeated" during the next few months, she disappeared; a year later, Dr. Stone meets her *"in her assumed identity"* (p. x). The experiment has gone awry. Neither personality is aware of the other. Because both Eva Delorme and Evelin March love the same man, Paine created a love triangle which gains resolution only when Evelin March, in a jealous frenzy and thinking that she is killing someone else—a rival, commits suicide.

Paine's novel remains the most effective American study of dual personality largely because it is not so flawed as Vincent Harper's *The Mortgage on the Brain, Being the Confessions of the Late Ethelbert Croft, M.D.* (1905). In an experiment recalling that of Dr. Heidenhoff, Dr. Pablo Yznaga transforms Croft into a social lion who chases through Europe in pursuit of a young woman who needs a similar treatment because she is as shy as he was. Eventually his colleagues rescue them both. Paine kept his explanation simple, a matter of hypnotism; Harper's scientist substitutes radio-energy for Heidenhoff's galvanic battery. Paine did not moralize, but, through Dr. Yznaga, Harper launched an attack upon "meta-physician and theologian," taking the position that the universe is made up of "One Life of ALL" and that the "temporarily individualized mind may 'connect' with this reservoir of universal thought" (p. 260). In this he merely substituted a popular view of the era for an orthodox Christianity. Thus, the most interesting aspect of his argument arises from his seemingly contradictory view that reduces personality to "the sum total of the cerebral and nervous conditions and capacities found combined within a human being"; Yznaga thus disposes of "the up-start Ego," because it is not "a fixed, personal, spiritual something existing independently of the brain" but simply the "transient . . . result" of external forces on the human brain and nervous system (p. 82). One infers that Yznaga/Harper accepted this premise only if it somehow resulted in the unity of "ALL."

As a consequence of these spiritual bickerings, one of the most entertaining novels from the turn of the century remains Robert W. Chambers' delightful *Some Ladies in Haste* (1908), a parody of those novels involving changes of personality. One morning as he sits at the window of his Club, William Manners decides to use his hypnotic powers to cause "the first five ornamental young girls he chanced to observe on Fifth Avenue" to pursue and marry "five very imperfect men of his acquaintance" (p. 60). Unwittingly, both he and his fiancée are involved. The plot permitted Chambers to scoff at both the fad for hypnotism and the popular belief in love at first sight.

If Chambers achieved a lighthearted humor through the exchange of personalities, then Ignatius Donnelly used the device to give emotional impact to his denunciation of racism in *Doctor Huguet* (1891). After Doctor Anthony Huguet of C_____, South Carolina, discusses at length the black race with a number of his wealthy friends, among them the father of his beloved Mary Ruddiman, he has a vision of the figure of Christ surrounded by black hands raised in supplication; he hears Christ's voice: "THESE, TOO, ARE MY CHILDREN. FOR THEM ALSO, I DIED ON THE CROSS" (p. 86). When Huguet awakens, he finds that his consciousness has been transferred to the body of Sam Johnsing, a notorious drunken black. After he approaches Mary, clasping her hand, he is hunted by a posse for molesting a white woman. No one can doubt Donnelly's sincerity, but as his story progresses, he relies on such plot devices as having the black Huguet save the Ruddiman plantation by paying off the mortgage (after going North to Baltimore and securing a sympathetic lawyer). When he teaches the black community, the Klan whips him, and the blacks protect him. In a melodramatic finish, he returns to his own body only after his valet, Ben, is killed saving him from being shot by the false Huguet even as the Klan tries to hang him. Mary's maid, the beautiful octoroon Abigail, also must be killed by whites, though she tells him that she loved him and would have married him "despite that black skin" (p. 285). In the 1980s his advice—"To the white race I would preach mercy and charity. . . . To the black race I would preach patience and wisdom" (p. 287)—cannot be satisfactory, but in 1891 he was the only popular writer courageous enough to speak to the problem.

The turning point in the treatment of psychological phenomena came, perhaps not so surprisingly as first impression suggests, in the stories dealing with the so-called "scientific detective." One pauses momentarily over Edwin Balmer and William MacHarg's *The Achievements of Luther Trant* (1910). Once again the issue involved realism, for in their introduction the coauthors stressed that Trant, a "one time assistant in a psychological laboratory, now turned detective," makes use of "real" methods and "real" tests in his police work. Through such procedures "modern men of science are at last disclosing and defining the workings of the oldest of world-mysteries—the human mind" (p. i). Although modeled after Sherlock Holmes in that he relies heavily upon his powers of deduction, Trant also employs the newest inventions available to the criminologist, including a device anticipating the lie detector.

Even more adept both as a lab technician and an inventor was Arthur B. Reeve's fashionable Craig Kennedy, whose New York-based exploits were faithfully reported by Dr. Jameson in *Cosmopolitan* between 1911 and 1915. In retrospect, his most important case proved to be "The Dream Doctor" (August 1913); in it Kennedy gives explicit attention to Freud's theory of dreams and then proceeds to the "psychanalysis [*sic*], the soul analysis" of Madeline Maitland, whose husband had been poisoned by Dr. Arnold Masterson, to whom she had once been engaged. She dreams at least once of being attacked by a bull which turns into a serpent and has the face of Masterson. When Reeve expanded the story into the first two episodes—"The Dream Doctor" and "The Soul Analysis"—of the volume *The Dream Doctor* (1914), he added nothing new to his discussion of Freud as it had appeared in *Cosmopolitan*. The split simply gave more emphasis to his account of Freudian theory.

"The dream," Kennedy explains, "is not an absurd and senseless jumble, but a perfect mechanism and has a definite meaning in penetrating the mind. It is as though we had two streams of thought, one of which we allow to flow freely, the other of which we are constantly repressing, pushing back into the subconscious, or unconscious. . . . But the resistances, the psychic censors of our ideas, are always active except in sleep. . . . Seldom does one recognize his own repressed thoughts or unattained wishes" (p. 34). Before turning to his analysis of Mrs. Maitland's dreams, he declares, "Sex is one of the strongest of human impulses, yet the one subjected to greatest repression" (p. 35).

"The Dream Doctor" introduced Freud to readers of popular fiction. Reeve expanded that initial discussion somewhat in "The Psychanalysis," published in *The Treasure Train* (1917):

"[The psychanalysis] is a new system. In the field of abnormal psychology, the soul-analysis is of first importance. Today, this study is of the greatest help in neurology and psychiatry. . . .

I think you are already familiar with the theory of dreams that has been developed by Dr. Sigmund Freud of Vienna. But perhaps you are not aware of the fact that Freud's contribution to the study of insanity is of even greater scientific value than his dream theories taken by themselves.

Obsessions and phobias have their origin, according to Freud, in sexual life. The ibsession represents a compensation or substitution for an unbearable sexual idea and takes its place in consciousness. In normal, sexual life, no neurosis is possible, say the Freudists. Sex is the strongest impulse, yet subject to the greatest repression, and hence the weakest point of our cultural development. Hysteria arises through the conflict of the libido and sex-repression. Often sex-wishes may be consciously rejected but unconsciously accepted. So when they are understood every insane utterance has a reason. There is really method in madness." (pp. 56, 65)

In *Atavar, The Dream Dancer* (1917, reprinted 1924), Kennedy employs Freudian analysis as he solves the murder of Guy Hawtrey, one of the men attracted to the dancer Natalie Lisle. Because of her role as Astarte, Natalie has come to think of herself as a double personality. Kennedy finds that she dreams of herself as the Stone Age woman, Gel, fleeing from two men and rescued by a third. In a recurring somnambulistic state, she also performs a sensual, nude dance. After giving her the Jung word-association test, Kennedy helps her solve her personal problems. She overcomes a kind of frigidity (against which she rebels in the somnambulistic dance) and rejects two older suitors in favor of a childhood sweetheart.

Once Freudian theory entered American fantasy, it remained, although not always so clearly explicated as in the Craig Kennedy stories. One wonders, for example, how much Cleveland Moffett drew upon knowledge of Freudian theory in the novel *Possessed* (1920). Despite the implication of the title, one cannot be certain whether Moffett wanted to exorcise his central character, Penelope Wells, or to portray her as a split personality. His discussion of female sexuality remains one of the most notable of the period.[37]

Freudian theory undercut the simplistic dichotomies of absolute moral good and evil and of the body and soul, premises on which writers relied for their portrayals of dual personalities. Without them the results could be confusing, as in Waldo Frank's *Chalk Face* (1924), in part because the disjointed narrative strongly implies the madness of John Mark, the young psychologist who has undertaken self-analysis. Although the storyline centers on Mark's love for Mildred Fayne, Frank's chief interest lay with those scenes in which Mark hallucinates and encounters a man with a chalk-colored head. The figure is a creation of Mark's imagination; it provides the means by which he deceives himself. He projects his evil actions onto the man with the chalk head in order to hide from himself the fact that he has killed his parents as well as Philip LaMotte, a rival suitor, all of whom could have prevented his marriage to Mildred. After a crucial sequence in which dream and reality fuse together, Mark understands that the man with the chalk head is a part of himself. He believes that he has willed Chalk Face into being to commit the murders for him. At least one reviewer asserted that Mark "recognizes chalk face as his other self,"[38] thereby falling back upon the literary tradition of dual personalities rather than Freud. When Mark confesses the murders to Mildred, she abandons him—apparently to madness.

Whatever else, John Mark is a victim of his imagination, as is Edward Chesworth in Arthur R. Rees's *The Threshold of Fear* (1926). Although Freudian theory is essential to both novels, what Waldo Frank attempts to achieve through elaborate symbolism, Rees gains through simplicity and directness. Partly through an interest in a young woman, Haldham, the first-person narrator, takes a job as chauffeur-mechanic whose principal task is to transport Edward Chesworth, described as an invalid because he has suffered a nervous breakdown. Haldham learns that Chesworth is being cared for by a Dr. Penhryn, whose library includes a wide range "of works on the process and oddities of human thought . . . from the days of black magic to the psychotherapeutics of the modern analytical school. Some of the latter I recognized: Freud, Bleuler, and Jung. . . . " They are the books, Haldham decides, of "an alienist or specialist in nervous disease" (pp. 90, 91). Through the influence of the young woman, the sister of Chesworth and the niece of Haldham's employer, Chesworth confides in Haldham, telling him of Herbert Musard's expedition into Peru to find "the birthplace of the earliest civilization on this globe" deep in the mountains, "the last undiscovered spots" in the world (p. 133). Not only was Chesworth the sole survivor after his companions died in an avalanche, but he was told by an Indian that he had violated "the Valley of Ghosts," and that he had "sinned against Death by seeking his place'' (p.166). Chesworth believes that he drowned, lying for four days on the bottom of a lake before the Indian gods interceded on his behalf with Death. Chesworth recalls that when he regained consciousness in the Indian's hut, his mind seemed "curiously blank" as though, like Adam, he "had been created fully grown, with conscious faculties but no past" (p. 163).

His narrative could well have stood alone, for tales of such expeditions remained widely popular, but Rees gave the familiar story a new dimension by having Haldham's narrative serve as a frame. Although Chesworth got back to civilization, he suffered a nervous breakdown. When Haldham finds him, despite the care of Dr. Penhryn, he is growing worse, for certain signs, like the recurring sound of an Indian drum, have convinced Chesworth that death has come for him. There is no suggestion that he is insane; rather, he is being frightened to death.

Only Dr. Penhryn's death saves him, for Haldham and his companions find among Penhryn's papers evidence that he used Chesworth as a subject of an experiment to discover what threshold of fear man could withstand before going mad. Not unlike Frankenstein, Penhryn "sought to wrest from the darkness of the universe in which we walk those secrets of existence which we are not permitted to know" (p. 243). To gain his end, with Chesworth he had employed suggestion and, consequently, autosuggestion, for he worked on the premise that "the subconscious mind is the actual controlling force of the human entity" (p. 241). Although Haldham and his companions are not certain whether or not such theories form an actual science, they read from Penhryn's papers that " 'there exists an underworld of the mind of which we know nothing. . . . The subconscious mind is the real soul of man, where our lives and destinies are shaped without our knowledge. . . . When man discovers the secret of the subconscious, and how to use it aright, he will be master of his immortal soul and the dark universe in which he dwells' '' (pp. 244, 245).[39]

In his papers, Penhryn had explained why Chesworth reacted as he did: "Death often comes as the result of suggestion, because the fear of it works upon our subconscious and brings about swift physical decay" (p. 249). "We are all the slaves of imagination," he concluded; "Imagination and suggestion. These two qualities govern us all."

Ironically, perhaps, by relying upon Freudian theory, essentially, Rees had arrived at the same end that Bierce gained: the dramatization of fear. In doing so, he opened wide the depths of inner space and showed it as a labyrinth of terror. There was no peace in the dark world which the psyche revealed. If writers were to attain paradise, they must search elsewhere.

NOTES

1. Robert Donald Spector, "Introduction," *The English Gothic: A Bibliographic Guide to Writers from Horace Walpole to Mary Shelley* (Westport, Conn.: Greenwood Press, 1984), p. 6.

2. Charles Coulston Gillespie, *Genesis and Geology* (Cambridge: Harvard University Press, 1951), p. 6.

3. See Thomas L. Wymer, "Perception and Value in Science Fiction," and Thomas D. Clareson, "Many Worlds, Many Futures," in Thomas D. Clareson, ed., *Many Futures, Many Worlds* (Kent, Ohio: Kent State University Press, 1977), pp. 1–26.

4. Geoffrey Bullough, *Mirror of Minds: Changing Psychological Beliefs in English Poetry* (Toronto: University of Toronto Press, 1962), p. 143.

5. Ernest J. Lovell, *Byron: The Record of a Quest. Studies in a Poet's Concept and Treatment of Nature* (Austin, Tex.: The University of Texas Press, 1949), pp. 138–175. Lovell asserts that the literary background influencing Byron's attitude toward nature came primarily from the Gothic novel. He calls it the "Zeluco theme," giving it the name of the villain in John Moore's *Zeluco* (1789). Most simply, the premise states "that a villain or any other character with feelings of guilt, misanthropy, or excessive gloom can derive neither pleasure nor spiritual comfort from a contemplation of nature" (p. 139).

6. "Review of New Publications," *Blackwood's Magazine*, 1 (April 1817), 73. The anonymous reviewer made that remark as he began discussion of Thomas Chalmers' *A Series of Discourses on the Christian Revelation, viewed in Connexion with the Modern Astronomy*.

7. Anthony Trollope, as cited by Spector, p. 6.

8. Frederick S. Frank, "The Gothic Romance 1762–1820," in Marshall B. Tymn, ed., *Horror Literature: A Core Collection and Reference Guide* (New York and London: R. R. Bowker, 1981), p. 113. Frank provides one of the finest brief comprehensive evaluations of the original Gothic movement; he augments it with an annotated bibliography of 422 items. He says of Melmoth the Wanderer: "This grand, godless, godlike creature has mortgaged his soul to the devil and is condemned to wander through time in search for another sufferer or sinner in such agony that Melmoth will be able to trade destinies with him and obtain the rest of death." He cites Edmund Burke on the sublime as well as both H.P. Lovecraft and G. R. Thompson to suggest the scope of the Gothic. He asserts that Lewis "altered the course of the Gothic novel and completed the transition to the demonic-irrational begun by Beckford" (p. 24).

9. Mary Shelley, *The Annotated Frankenstein*, With an Introduction and Notes by Leonard Wolf (New York: Clarkson N. Potter, Inc., 1977), pp. 40–72 *passim*.

10. Shelley, p. 66.

11. Charles Brockden Brown, *Wieland, or The Transformation. Together with Memoirs of Carwin the Biloquist. A Fragment*, edited with an introduction by Fred Lewis Pattee (New York: Harcourt Brace and Company, 1926), p. 4. Page references in the text are to this edition. In his "Selected Reading List" Pattee refers to a London edition of 1822 subtitled "An American Tale," (p. xlviii), but he does not add that phrasing on the title page of this edition.

12. On occasion, too much has been made of Carwin's suggestion that "my only crime was curiosity" (p. 231). He speaks in specific reference to perusing Clara's books: "I opened and found new scope for my curiosity in your books."

13. Brian Attebery, *The Fantasy Tradition in American Literature from Irving to Le Guin* (Bloomington, Ind.: Indiana University Press, 1980), p. 37; Robert E. Morsberger, "The Short Fiction of Irving," in Frank N. Magill, ed., *Survey of Modern Fantasy Literature* (Englewood Cliffs, N.J.: Salem Press, 1983), 5:1557–1558.

14. Benjamin Franklin Fisher IV, "The Residual Gothic Impulse 1824–1873," in Tymn, *Horror Fiction*, p. 178.

15. James Hogg, "The Mysterious Bride," *Blackwood's Magazine*, 28 (December 1830), 943–950.

16. "Crocodile Island," *Blackwood's Magazine*, 33 (January 1833), 105–112. The story illustrates how convoluted and self-defeating the *Blackwood's* tradition became. The first-person narrator, an Oxford student, establishes the scene as the Golden Cross Inn. He listens as another student tells a traveler of an adventure which happened to him among the American Indians. Abruptly, he breaks off his first-person narrative and asks the advice of the traveler because he cannot figure out an ending. Denouncing the "lying scribler," the traveler angrily departs. The frame, especially the ending, destroys any effectiveness the tale may potentially have had. The quotation occurs on p. 112.

17. *Edgar Allan Poe: Tales and Sketches: 1831–1842*, ed. Thomas O. Mabbott (Cambridge and London: Harvard University Press, 1978), p. 357.

18. Mabbott, p. 51.

19. Mabbott, p. 305.

20. E. F. Bleiler, "Edgar Allan Poe," in E. F. Bleiler, ed., *Science Fiction Writers: Critical Studies of the Major Authors from the Early Nineteenth Century to the Present Day* (New York: Charles Scribner's Sons, 1982), pp. 11–18. Bleiler specifically dismisses such stories as "The Black Cat" and "William Wilson" from consideration because "abnormal psychology in itself, unless rendered fantastic by other elements, has never been considered science fiction" (p. 17). Others may choose to argue with him, especially since abnormal psychology and horror have provided material for sf since *Frankenstein*.

21. Mabbott, p. 661. Mabbott cites the comparison between the stories made by Arthur Hobson Quinn in *Edgar Allan Poe* (1941), p. 301. He refers to Quinn while summarizing a "succession of interpretations of the meaning" of Poe's story made since midcentury. One may well be either amused or horrified by their variety.

22. Nathaniel Hawthorne, "The Hollow Between the Hills," *Twice-Told Tales*, ed. William Charvat, Roy Harvey Pearce, and Claude M. Simpson (Columbus, Ohio: Ohio State University Press, 1974), pp. 199–204 *passim*.

23. Hamlin Garland, *The Shadow World* (New York: Harper & Brothers, 1908), p. iii.

24. Henry James, *Notes and Reviews*, preface by Pierre de Chaignon la Rose (Cambridge: Harvard University Press, 1921), p. 110.

25. Ambrose Bierce, "A Holy Terror," *The Complete Short Stories of Ambrose Bierce*, Compiled with Commentary by Ernest Jerome Hopkins (Garden City, N.Y.: Doubleday & Company, Inc., 1970), p. 251. All references to Bierce's stories are to this text.

26. *The Collected Works of Ambrose Bierce* (New York and Washington: The Neal Publishing Company, 1911), VII, *The Devil's Dictionary*, 115.

27. Henry James, *The Art of the Novel*, ed. Richard P. Blackmur (New York: Charles Scribner's Sons, 1934), p. xvii.

28. *The Novels and Tales of Henry James* (New York: Charles Scribner's Sons, The New York Edition, 1909), 17:xxiii–xxiv.

29. "The Last of the Valerii," *The Ghostly Tales of Henry James*, edited with an introduction by Leon Edel (New Brunswick: Rutgers University Press, 1948), pp. 70–102.

30. "Maud Evelyn," *The Ghostly Tales of Henry James*, pp. 608, 611, 621, 624, 625.

31. Ford Madox Ford, *Henry James: A Critical Study* (New York: A. & C. Boni, 1915), p. 225.

32. Fred L. Pattee, *The Development of the American Short Story* (New York: Harper & Brothers, 1924), pp. 206–207.

33. *The Novels and Tales of Henry James*, 12:xxi–xxii; *The Notebooks of Henry James*, ed. F. O. Matthiessen and Kenneth B. Murdock (New York: Oxford University Press, 1947), p. 18.

34. "The Turn of the Screw," *The Ghostly Tales of Henry James*, pp. 450, 451.

35. Brian Stableford, "The Ghost of Guy Thyrle," in Frank N. Magill, ed., *Survey of Science Fiction Literature*, 2 (Englewood Cliffs, N.J.: Salem Press, 1979), 869–872. Stableford reads it as a "cosmic voyage" and gives much attention to the "epistolatory proem" in which Fawcett defended the "rationalistic raiment" which he gave to the novel while saying that it should not be read as a ghost story. Fawcett exemplifies, in this case at least, those writers who had difficulty with their chosen subjects during the period.

36. Lionel Stevenson, "Purveyors of Myth and Magic," *Yesterday and After, 11, The History of the English Novel* (New York: Barnes and Noble, 1967), 111–154.

37. For a discussion of *Possessed*, see chapter 5.

38. A. Donald Douglas, "Waldo Frank—Poet," *The Saturday Review of Literature*, November 1, 1924, p. 244. Douglas is lavish and evasive in saying that Frank would prefer to "translate his intimations into symbols of pure poetry [rather] than into character, action, . . . or men and women both symbolic and actual." He concludes, "Like Arthur Machen, Mr. Waldo Frank is a very fine poet and a consummate artist (in tone poems) who chooses to write in the form of the novel."

39. Prior to Rees's *The Threshold of Fear*, the most significant use of the subconscious mind in American science fiction had occurred in Thomas A. Stoddard's *The Quest* (1909), though only in way of explanation. Early in that novel, apparently believing that he has murdered Enos Holmes, Dr. Williams disappears from New England. The rest of the narrative follows his adventures with various Indian tribes on the Orinoco River. Five years later when his wife finds him, he becomes ill. Upon recovery, he can recall nothing of his adventures in South America. A man who has studied psychology concludes "that when the doctor awoke from the effects of the blow given by the murderer he was in a subconscious condition or state of mind, and remained so until discovered by his wife" (p. 166). The novel then ends with the question of whether or not "the sub-conscious mind knows things" that the individual does not know and wonders "how . . . it come[s] to this knowledge."

3

"The War to End All Wars"

The brief flurry of the Spanish-American conflict led William Ward Crane to recall briefly certain "Fanciful Predictions of War" in *Lippincott's Magazine* (November 1898). In referring to the short story "The End of New York," the single American title which he evaluated, he sounded very like his European contemporaries when he asserted that "it helped to call general attention to our depleted and old-fashioned navy and our unprotected harbors."[1] The story succeeded as propaganda, he implied, because it had "excited" interest and thus had helped "to remedy these evils." Without specifying titles, Crane noted that the earlier American apprehension concerning "the immense dormant power of China" now seemed "absurd" after Japan's easy victory, although he warned that "at some time of European conflict or disorganization, a great Asiatic uprising, electrified by some common fanaticism, might be a fearful menace to the Aryan race." Among British titles—he named none by Continental writers—he regarded Wells's *The War of the Worlds* as "the most fanciful of all those fictions" and likened "The End of New York" to Sir George Tomkyns Chesney's *The Battle of Dorking: or Reminiscences of a Volunteer*. He urged serious consideration of all these novels, "for they may help to prevent their own fulfillment. As notes of warning they may serve a useful purpose." In his final appraisal, he again sounded very much a part of the smugness of his generation when he declared, "They are, in fact, strong evidences of that keener intelligence and wider outlook which distinguish our era from the days when magazines and newspapers were still in embryo."

There is no need to reexamine in detail *The Battle of Dorking* (1871), a task which I. F. Clarke has done so well,[2] except to emphasize that Chesney's narrative did establish a tone which was to echo through various motifs within science fiction from the 1870s on. Told in retrospect by the Volunteer who had been an eyewitness to the action and was now a grandfather, the story gains much of its effectiveness from the completeness of the disaster; as Clarke suggests, "There was no hope for a revival of national greatness."[3] In this acceptance it reminds one of Jack London's *The Scarlet Plague* (1915) in that both have a crushing finality about them.

Published in *Blackwood's Magazine* (May 1871), *The Battle of Dorking* was reprinted as a sixpenny pamphlet in June and sold 80,000 copies within the month; John Blackwood's letters attest to both "the realistic skill of the story, which had an almost startling effect," and its immediate popularity among such persons as A. W. Kinglake, Colonel George Moncrieff, and Edward Bulwer–Lytton.[4] The reaction may have been precipitated by the quick victory of Germany over the highly regarded French army, but it was sustained by the complex anxieties of a nation committed increasingly to the self-imposed responsibilities of a worldwide empire. Chesney had dispatched parts of the British army to India (an uprising), to Canada ("difficulty with America"), and to Ireland ("the talked-of Fenian invasion"), while he dispersed the Fleet to the West Indies, the China Seas, and the northern Pacific shore of America so that the British Isles lay open to German attack.

Although the concern of the navy men focused increasingly on Germany because of the growth of its fleet, England never had a single enemy; the nations crowding every border were suspect. By the end of the century, Great Britain had fought every major nation of Europe alone or in combination in a multitude of imaginary wars. For example, Sir William Laird Clowes and Alan H. Burgoyne collaborated on *The Great Naval War of 1887* (1887), in which France defeated Britain; Clowes repeated the French success in *The Captain of the "Mary Rose": A Tale of Tomorrow* (1892). In *For England's Sake* (1889), Robert Cromie guided English arms to victory over Russia, which had tried to take India from the crown. They renewed hostilities in his *The Next Crusade* (1896), when England joined with Austria to oust Turkey from the Balkans, while the Russians sided with Turkey only because they wanted Constantinople for themselves. *The Great War of 189–* (1893), by Admiral Philip Colomb and his collaborators, portrayed a continentwide struggle between an Anglo-German alliance and Franco-Russian forces. The journalist William LeQueux allowed the French to invade Sussex and besiege London in *The Great War in England in 1897* (1894) but turned the tide of battle after Britain's loyal ally, Germany, took Paris on November 16. Although the first-person narrator—and sole survivor—of Fred T. Jane's *Blake of the "Rattlesnake"* (1895) wonders why Germany has not come to the aid of the British, the flotilla of torpedo boats like the "Rattlesnake" disposes of both the French and Russian fleets. As late as Captain Cairnes' *The Coming Waterloo* (1901), with Germany and Austria as allies, a British army invades France.

Whoever the enemy, however, seapower determined the victor. In retrospect, given the nationalistic tensions rising out of an era of aggressive imperialism which reinforced—indeed, created—the armaments race, one cannot be too surprised at the accepted, widespread feeling that a major war would occur inevitably early in the new century. For example, John Byrn-Scarlett, the protagonist of Cutcliffe Hyne's *Empire of the World* (1910), declares that everyone knew that sooner or later Germany would attack one of the Western powers. Nor should one be surprised that Great Britain, an island kingdom dependent economically on its colonies and overseas trade, was concerned about maintaining naval strength. Yet one does feel that seapower and the threat of invasion blinded almost all of the writers to the realities of any impending conflict, even after the Boer War. Prior to H. G. Wells's *The War in the Air* (1908), the majority of the novelists predicated victory or defeat on control of the seas and/or the outcome of a major battle between fleets at full strength.

Victory in Cromie's *The Next Crusade* meant transforming the Mediterranean into "a British lake" (p. 202). In *The Final War* (1896), an extravaganza giving part of its attention to campaigns in Germany, France, and Russia, Louis Tracy mentions machine guns once in passing; artillery and cavalry dominate the land fighting. Although Cairnes gave little specific information, he did conclude that because of the innovations in weaponry in general, "the well-trained few will annihilate the half-trained multitude in the fighting of the future" (p. 364). Nor can one comprehend the disbelief expressed regarding Sir Arthur Conan Doyle's "Danger," published in the *Strand Magazine* (July 1914), which warned that submarine warfare could cut off Britain's food supply and force surrender. Charles Gleig had dramatized that possibility as early as *When All Men Starve* (1898), which ended with the breakdown of all civil and police authority in England. One comes away from a consideration of the British treatment of the future-war motif with the impression that the new naval hardware excited the enthusiasts—the journalistic writers in particular—but that no one appreciated the changes that the new weaponry would bring to modern warfare. One must agree with I. F. Clarke's analysis: "Save for rare exceptions, [these stories] are distinguished by a complete failure to foresee the form a modern war would take. . . . This was inevitable. It was the result of the now familiar time-lag between the rapid development of technology and the belated abandonment of ideas, mental habits, and social attitudes that the new machines and the new industries had rendered out of date."[5]

To put it another way, the writers were so caught up in the immediate problems of Europe and the empire that for the most part they did not exploit the imaginative possibilities. An exception occurred in Tom Greer's *A Modern Daedalus* (1887), when the protagonist, John O'Halloran, solves the problem of flight by strapping himself into mechanical wings; he drops dynamite bombs by hand, thereby gaining Irish Home Rule after he has trained a number of Irish youths to fly as bombers. E. Douglas Fawcett's *Hartmann the Anarchist* (1893) tries unsuccessfully to destroy London by bombing it from a zeppelinlike ship in 1920. To return to the international scene, aeroplanes remained few and far between. One of the most notable (with four propellers) provides the means by which the Englishman John Strong hopes to bring peace to the world in W. Holt-White's *The Man Who Stole the Earth* (1909). With deadly accuracy he, too, drops dynamite bombs by hand. By no means a parody of the future-war motif, the narrative nevertheless degenerates into a Balkan romance in which Strong pursues

King George II of Balkania, who flees to Paris in a balloon after kidnapping his daughter, Princess Diana, whom Strong wishes to marry. In a final sequence, three of Strong's planes defeat three of the Kaiser's; so impressed is the Kaiser that he declares undying friendship and offers to give the bride away at the forthcoming wedding. Although the Irishman, John Castellan, invents a combination submarine-aeroplane which he gives to the Kaiser in George Griffith's *The World Peril of 1910* (1907), the triumph of British arms is lessened by the threat of a comet's collision with the earth. The most advanced weapon was employed by an American writer, Roy Norton, whose *The Flame: A Story of What Might Have Been* (1916) was published only in London. A mysterious scientist develops "a queer shaft of flame. It was a flame of unearthly hue, terribly steady, incredulously bright, and having a quality and density approaching organic matter" (p. 242). He uses it against the Germans along 200 miles of the Western Front; at least half a million of the enemy are blinded. Germany surrenders, and the scientist, revealed as an American, Robert Wentworth, rules a peaceful world as a benevolent dictator for twenty years before his death.

Whether the protagonist is the American scientist, Robert Wentworth, or Blake of the "Rattlesnake," he has little importance as an individual personality. Like Beowulf, King Arthur, or Sir Galahad before him, his importance lies solely in his actions. One must agree with Clarke, as noted elsewhere, that in the future-war motif the writers sought to create a heroic "myth for an industrial civilization of ironclads and high-speed turbines, a new and violent *chanson de geste* for an age of imperialism, told in the inflammatory language of the mass Press."[6] Consequently, the most memorable British works from the period remain those which break the pattern. The earliest is P. G. Wodehouse's delightful parody *The Swoop* (1909), in which Clarence Chugwater, a boy scout, saves England. No less than eight invasions occur simultaneously; the barbarous hordes, ranging from German and Russian armies to Young Turks and Moroccan brigands, suffer from colds and coughs due to the English summer. Significantly, *The Swoop* is the one novel by Wodehouse which has not been extensively reprinted.[7] The second work is Saki's *When William Came* (1914); to achieve its satire, the narrative concentrates upon such characters as Cecily Yeovil, who endures the conquest by becoming a part of the social scene. Her acquiescence proves ultimately unimportant, for as one of the German officers remarks, to win England the Germans must capture the hearts of her youth. Ironically, perhaps, in light of Wodehouse's earlier parody, the British boy scouts do not show up for a parade where the Kaiser proudly anticipates reviewing his new subjects. At the outbreak of the war, as though looking back to previous glory, Arthur Machen provided the short story "The Bowman" to the *Evening News* (September 29, 1914), which grew into the legend of the Angels of Mons. Later, Machen produced *The Terror: A Fantasy* (1917); concerned with a number of mysterious deaths throughout England, the narrative ends with the manuscript of a letter suggesting that because of the brutality of the war, the animals have joined together against mankind.

The obvious exception to those who foresaw a simple British victory, of course, is H. G. Wells. He stood apart from the popularizers. In *The War in the Air* (1908), he discerned that air power can destroy cities but cannot occupy countries so that warfare can lead only to the downfall of modern civilization. In *The World Set Free* (1914), he predicted that science would master the atomic bomb by midcentury and that such knowledge rendered separate political nations obsolete. In these novels, he suggested the direction which the future-war motif would take after World War I, especially in postwar Europe.

One characteristic among the British novels, particularly those by the journalists, was the growing concern for Kaiser Wilhelm as an individual. It usually resulted in sympathetic portraits of him, even when he commanded the legions of the enemy. It is as though by appealing to him, the journalists felt that they could avert his hostility; they seemed to feel that somehow he must be won over to the British view. Of all the world leaders he most often became a character in the novels. One hesitates to name the first novel in which this occurred, but he made a major, though brief, appearance in Louis Tracy's *The Final War* (1896), already a crucial work in that the United States comes to the aid of Britain against a coalition of France, Russia, and Germany. In that novel, after Bismarck reminds the Kaiser of the folly of warfare against England, Wilhelm sends a letter to Queen Victoria; Dr. Jameson of South African fame kidnaps him and takes him to London, where Victoria decrees that he not be treated as a prisoner. Instead, he and the Prince of Wales enter into arbitration. Admitting from the outset that this "war is a terrible blunder" (p. 314), the Kaiser finally agrees to peace and total disarmament of Germany when the Prince of Wales reminds him that America and Britain—"the Saxon race"—are now leagued together in what will be the last war. Although the implication remains that Germany will one day be admitted to the partnership, at the close of hostilities, the U.S. and Britain jointly issue "An International Proclamation," in which they assert that "the Divine Will" has outlawed war and made Britain and America "the instruments to accomplish the task" (p. 353). The decree then enumerates the principles by which the Saxon race will rule the world; significantly, no nation, Asiatic or European, is referred to as an inferior race, although the two ruling nations will settle "permanent boundaries . . . and the adjustment of Colonial areas"[8] (p. 354).

All in all, subsequent American writers made more of the Anglo-Saxon alliance than did the British, who seemed simply to accept it once someone had thought of it. But the British showed increasing friendliness toward Kaiser Wilhelm, especially during the first decade of the new century. In George Griffith's *The Great Weather Syndicate* (1906), the young American geologist who can manipulate the world's weather, Clarence Arkwright, obtains an interview with the Kaiser and asks him to call off his scheduled army maneuvers since they pose a threat to European peace. Although Wilhelm is such "an honourable gentleman" that he reacts angrily to the kidnapping of Arkwright's fiancée and sister by a rival syndicate, he refuses to call off the military operation. Arkwright challenges him to a duel, threatening to inflict bad weather on Germany if Wilhelm does not call off his plans. The Kaiser later recalls Arkwright to a special meeting at Potsdam, where he denounces and finally arrests Baron Oscar Vanderlé, who was responsible for the kidnapping, and detains Oscar and Falkner Merindin, who lead the opposing weather syndicate. He persists in his attempt to seize Arkwright's weather station on Mount Brockden in Germany, only to find that the Baltic ports and the Kiel Canal have frozen over, that Germany has been visited by a mixture of summer and wintry weather, and that 100,000 men and 200 guns have been marooned in a dense fog as they attempted an assault on Brockden. Wilhelm asks for an armistice which is refused, admits that he planned widespread warfare, and finally surrenders. But he refers to Arkwright as a sportsman, gives his word that henceforth he will advocate peace, and with little persuasion gives Arkwright's sister Clarice in marriage at a ceremony in the chapel of the Marble Palace at Potsdam. Three years earlier, in *The Lake of Gold* (1903), after bringing about extensive social reform in the United States, Griffith simply had the Kaiser kidnapped so that Germany, Britain, and the United States could form a new Triple Alliance to assure the peace of the world. As noted, John Strong, the protagonist of W. Holt-White's *The Man Who Stole the Earth* (1909), engaged the Kaiser in an aerial duel and became his staunch friend, while the Kaiser gave Princess Diana in marriage. Even an American writer, Roy Norton, arranged for Wilhelm to be kidnapped and held in custody in the American Northwest in *The Vanishing Fleets* (1908). Although the tone remained very different because the novelists were dealing with a warrior and a gentleman, the British obsession with Wilhelm anticipates the eventual American obsession with Asia.

To some degree, at least, Clarke oversimplified when he asserted that the United States initially remained "outside the conflict of the imaginary wars" because as a nation the U.S. "lacked the strong and permanent sense of a foreign menace required to touch off tales of future wars."[9] The earliest American portrayal of an imaginary conflict appears to be the work of a professor at William and Mary College, Beverly Tucker, whose *The Partisan Leader: A Tale of the Future* (1856, 1861) climaxed when Virginia "lifted the soiled banner of her sovereignty from the dust" (p. 392) and became an independent nation.[10] The second effort, the anonymous *What May Happen in the Next 90 Days* (1877) dealt with another civil war. The dispute over the results of the 1876 election causes Grant to establish himself as a dictator, the "Protector of the Republic." Governor Rutherford B. Hayes of Ohio calls out the state militia. A retrospective letter from the narrator to his nephew indicates that the fighting which broke out in Ohio and New York spread throughout the U.S., continued for years, and devastated the country.

Although various narratives at the turn of the century made use of a number of rebellions and civil wars, only one suggested conflict between the whites and the black minority in the United States. Yet even in *The Next War* (1892), King Wallace did not resort to open warfare, for when a plot to poison their employers on a certain date fails, the American blacks flee into Southern swamps and subsequently disappear. Whoever Wallace was, one must read the novel as a fantasy of wish fulfillment using some of the conventions of the future-war motif. Only Ignatius Donnelly confronted the plight of the blacks more boldly.

America's first international enemies were Great Britain and Spain. As various writers reminded their audience, the U.S. had fought two of its wars with Britain, but one infers that this animosity came more from an Irish influence than a continuing, pervasive hatred of the British. The role of Spain resulted from the dream of a Manifest Destiny which included much of Central America, at least, and reflected the tension which ended in the Spanish-American War. After the Cuban escapade, a single novel satirized militarism and American imperialism; that occurred in Ernest Crosby's portrait of *Captain Jinks; Hero* (1902). His love of toy soldiers and uniforms determines a career that leads him from the John Wesley Boys' Brigade to East Point and the Cubapines; it ends only with the failure of his presidential candidacy. Not surprisingly, Crosby also attacks Germany (Tutonia).

In *The King's Men* (1884), Robert Grant and his collaborators pictured an England at an indefinite time in the future when the ruins of St. Paul's Cathedral could be seen to the east of London. Emigration had drained the island, while the financial bankruptcy of its aristocracy, the failure of foreign trade, and the loss of India to Russia had reduced British power. The exiled King George V held court in Boston, while the elected president, O'Donovan Rourke, had been deposed by radicals. The storyline becomes little more than court intrigue as Loyalists fail in their effort to return George to the throne. Henry Standish Coverdale's *The Fall of the Great Republic* (1885), published anonymously, provides an elaborate narrative frame, supposedly a report presented in 1895 to the Board of European Administration in the Province of New York. Britain, France, and Germany had united to conquer the United States after their embassies had been attacked during widespread civil strife. The narrative delineates the social and political ills which engulfed the U.S. following the Civil War. The nation became the haven of undesirables from Europe, including Irish exiles who plotted a number of brutal crimes, among them an attempt to assassinate Queen Victoria and her cabinet.

Donald Mackay's *The Dynamite Ship* (1888) proves to be an armed American yacht which permits the Irish League to bombard London and destroy the Houses of Parliament, thereby gaining independence for Ireland. In the same year, Samuel Barton took up the conventional cry of unpreparedness and encouraged the rebuilding of the American Merchant Marine in his prefatory note to *The Battle of the Swash, and the Capture of Canada* (1888). Canadians welcome the American invaders, and when the British fleet is defeated, both Canada and the West Indies become American territories. Barton touched on what was to become one of the central themes in the American treatment of the future-war motif; an American scientist develops a weapon—in this instance a self-destroying, electrically powered torpedo boat—which assures the American victory.

If Chesney's *The Battle of Dorking* provided the basic form and theme for the European treatment of imaginary wars, then Frank Stockton's *The Great War Syndicate* (1889), first serialized in *Collier's Weekly*, gave the fullest initial expression to at least two themes which made American treatment of the motif distinctive. At the same time, his novel remains unique in that he gave full responsibility for the war effort to twenty-three men, "all great capitalists," who promise to restore peace within a year and insist that the army and navy, though still controlled by the government rather than by the Syndicate, refrain from any but purely defensive action. Then the council puts American science to work developing new weapons. Two are little more than cautious extrapolations from the drawing boards of the period: a heavily armored vessel and a submarinelike "crab" (resembling the *Monitor* in appearance) capable of seizing a ship's propeller in a clawlike appendage, thereby rendering the ship immobile. The third, however, is the first of the "ultimate" weapons developed by American science; called an "Instantaneous Motor," it is a bomb detonated by electricity instead of gunpowder. Of it Stockton wrote:

These bombs were cylindrical in form and pointed at the outer end. They were filled with hundreds of small tubes, each radiating outward from a central line. Those in the middle third of the bomb pointed directly outward, while those in the front portion were inclined forward at a slight angle, and those in the rear portion backward at the same angle. One tube, at the end of the bomb, and pointing directly backward, furnished the motive power.

Each of these tubes could exert a force sufficient to move an ordinary train of passenger-cars one mile, and this power could be exerted instantaneously. (pp. 15–16)

In motive power, to some extent at least, the "Instantaneous Motor" anticipated the jet engine.

The Syndicate directs a small force to move against a Canadian port in order to show the world the power of its weapons. After the Canadians refuse to lower their colors, the American commander fires an experimental shot into the bay; then after permitting evacuation, he orders the fort destroyed. All spectators witness the effectiveness of the Motor:

There was no report, no smoke, no visible sign that the motor had left the cannon, but at that instant there appeared—a vast aperture in the waters of the bay, which was variously described as from 100 to 500 yards in diameter. . . . At the same instant the sky above the spot . . . was darkened by a wide-spreading cloud. . . .

Five seconds later a vast brown cloud appeared on the Ft. Pilcher promontory. This cloud was nearly spherical in form, with an apparent diameter of 1000 yards. . . . The great brown cloud quickly began to lose its spherical form, part of it descending heavily to the earth, and part floating away in vast dust-clouds, borne inland by the breeze, settling downward as they moved, and depositing on land, water, ships, houses, domes, and trees an almost impalpable powder.

When the cloud had cleared away there were no fortifications and the bluff on which they had stood had disappeared. (pp. 30, 34–35)

Despite the difference in the forces involved, one cannot escape noticing the similarity, in miniature, between the explosion and effect of the Motor and those of the A-bomb.

Only one further demonstration is necessary; a coastal fort on the English Channel is destroyed. Immediately, the businessmen of both nations form an enlarged Syndicate whose aim is to outlaw all future war and lead the civilized world to new heights. By suggesting this scheme, Stockton anticipated even more than Andrew Carnegie implied when in 1893 the latter voiced the opinion that the U.S. and Britain "should enter into a political union."[11] Perhaps more importantly, Stockton pointed out that this millennium could be achieved only because the "Instantaneous Motor" proved to be the ultimate weapon:

The ministry now perceived that the Syndicate had not waged war: it had been simply exhibiting the uselessness of war as at the present waged. Who now could deny that it would be folly to oppose the resources of ordinary warfare to those of what might be called prohibitive warfare. . . .

The desire to evolve that power which should render opposition useless had long led men from one warlike invention to another. Everyone who had constructed a new kind of gun, a new kind of armor, or a new explosive, thought that he had solved the problem, or was on his way to doing so. The inventor of the "Instantaneous Motor" had done it. (pp. 120, 123–124)

This yoking together of a highly advanced weapon with a desire for universal peace provides the thematic core of the American treatment of the future-war motif.

Unlike Stockton, James Barnes gave much attention to political background in *The Unpardonable War* (1904), the last conflict between the U.S. and Great Britain. Barnes used the opening chapters of the narrative to warn against the dangers of yellow journalism and a political victory by a third party. After denouncing strikes, the forty-four-hour week, a payment of less than 6 percent dividends, and a government-sponsored building program involving "public parks and people's playgrounds," Barnes assured his readers that the reaction of the public to such doings meant that the "people's party"—labor, socialists, and Populists—would lose the next election. To keep that party in power, a newspaper editor and a cabinet secretary incite the U.S. to war against Britain. They rationalize their action in terms of the acquisition of Canada as well as the fact that "Ireland would be free."

Although disputes in the Yukon and on the fishing banks of Newfoundland are cited as due cause for war, no fighting takes place until after the British fleet sails toward the Panama Canal. In the fog a British and an American ship approach one another. This gives the American commander an opportunity to test new weapons: the "Ewart Locator" and the "Westland Obliterator." Hopefully the former will ascertain "the size, direction, and speed of any vessel within a radius of a hundred miles—a method entirely separate from the wireless system of communication." The latter "was intended to destroy by overwhelming or burning out, an enemy's aerial plant. It was entirely new and practically untried'' (p. 74). The weapons blow out the electrical systems of both ships so that they collide in the fog. Somewhat later, disaster strikes the American navy when a ''half mile length'' of sea explodes after a submarine strikes a mine, destroying all nearby ships. Barnes asked, ''Had the inventor, over his drawing board, been warned of such possibility? There was no time to think. The fact was proved. One experiment in modern warfare needed no further trial'' (p. 174). In this manner, Barnes anticipated radar while rejecting the submarine.

At this point, the scientist Westland, ''the Wizard of Staten Island'' (undoubtedly he represented Edison), insists that he intends to end all war by means of his newly developed electrical device which explodes all known types of gunpowder. He then urges the President to become head of a league for the suppression of war and explains that he has discovered that the newspaper editor and the cabinet minister were agents of Germany and Russia, who had hoped Britain and the United States would exhaust themselves in the struggle. Despite this evidence and desire for peace, the British army advances into Maine, if only to provide Westland with the opportunity to test his new invention. It proves successful:

Science had rendered military advancement worthless, fighting had gone back to the first principles—and first principles were obsolete. Gunpowder was useless; the school of the sword and buckler had vanished; archery was dead—to revive it ridiculous; and these things belonged now to the age of romance—an age that was gone forever with the decay of the symptoms of barbarism. (p. 340)

Thus begins an era of world peace. The ''People's Party'' is soundly beaten in the election, and Theodore Roosevelt—of whom Barnes wrote, ''Too bad he ever came to the conclusion that two terms in Washington were enough'' (p. 40)—reenters public life. Britain and America sign a grand alliance.

Spain did not fare so well. Park Benjamin's ''The End of New York''—the story to which Crane referred in 1898—snatches victory from the Spanish after its fleet has leveled Manhattan's skyscrapers with heavy artillery and nitroglycerin bombs dropped from balloons. First published in *Fiction Magazine* (October 31, 1881) and reprinted in Scribner's anthology *Stories by American Authors*, V (1884), it emulates the established European pattern, even to Benjamin's anguished lament regarding an inadequate navy and unprotected ports. He emphasized the humiliation of defeat by having the Chilean fleet relieve New York and defeat the Spanish. Only in one passage does the story attain a separate identity; that occurs after ''Mr. Thomas A. Edison announced that he had invented everything which, up to that time, any one else had suggested.'' Told that his idea of using magnets to pull Spanish ironclads onto the rocks is not original with him, Edison waxed indignant: ''Somebody suggested this notion had been anticipated by one Sinbad the Sailor, whereupon Mr. Edison denounced that person as a 'patent pirate' '' (V, 102). Throughout the period before World

War I, Benjamin was the only writer of fiction to attack Edison personally, for the international press, both fiction and nonfiction, made him a popular hero epitomizing inventive genius.

In contrast, using his novel as a vehicle for a tirade against both the coinage of silver and severe unemployment—declaring that "it was time for War" (p. 59)—John H. Palmer opened *The Invasion of New York* (1897) with a moment of pageantry guaranteed to appeal to the most jingoistic American hearts. In accordance with a treaty of annexation, on July 4, 1898, the U.S.S. *Maine* and the necessary marines have come to Honolulu to take possession of the islands. Palmer referred to "the new state of Hawaii" (p. 28). After the Japanese population attacks the marines during the annexation ceremony, the U.S. has no recourse but to declare war on both Spain and Japan. Palmer then staged battles with each fleet individually. As the Spanish fleet attempts a surprise attack on New York before the U.S. Navy can intercede, it becomes the victim of the planning of the military engineers as it passes through the Narrows, for unknowingly it has entered a cleverly designed trap:

From Fort Hamilton on both shores had been arranged a line of torpedoes, each directed toward the channel. Their propelling force was compressed air, first from tubes in which they rested, then from their own reservoirs. . . . The mechanism by which they were set free consisted of magnets and levers actuated by an electric battery ashore. . . . Scientific in design, awful in anticipated results, this sinister product of civilization lurked beneath the waters, a concealed volcano. (pp. 78–79, 80)

Although each Spanish ship fires a single shot at Fort Hamilton, no gun responds until 500 torpedoes annihilate the Spanish ships, leaving little for the American navy to do. Palmer had prefaced the ambush with the declaration that this "was the moment to test in actual warfare a device so terrible in conception, so delicate in construction, that when adjusted for service the concussion from a great gun was considered sufficient to endanger its probable efficiency" (p. 78). On August 29, 1898, only four Spanish ships survive such "devilish ingenuity."

The Japanese fleet succeeds much better initially in that it bombards San Francisco, where the "single pneumatic dynamite gun, of which so much had been expected, failed at the first discharge" (p. 101). That fleet, led "by the two battleships with their eighteen inches of armor," is beaten decisively in a running battle off Hawaii, but it is defeated in a manner befitting the sailors of "Japan, that rising power of the Pacific" (p. 95). The confrontation with Asia—focused most often upon Japan—provided the final dominant theme in the American treatment of the future-war motif.

Of the European effort, Clarke declared that "the nationalistic emotions of the period found their natural outlet in a new mythology of imaginary wars which were no more than a picture of the world rearranged to suit a nation's desire."[12] Undoubtedly, that judgment applies to American contributions as well, but one senses that it fails to measure adequately the depth of the tension between a perhaps naive but nevertheless sincere idealism and a blatant jingoism which shaped the American works. The Europeans had been here before, whereas—as Louis Tracy suggested—the United States was new to the field because history had compressed the whole of the technological revolution into the generation following the Civil War. One too easily forgets that, at least in its modern form, the literary myth of the Western frontier and the cowboy was created simultaneously with the myth of the engineer/scientist as the shaper of society. In both mythologies, the American writers sound much like a young boy bragging loudly of his own accomplishments in a simple, straightforward, naive manner; before World War I the quality of cynicism had not yet intruded.

One can hear much of that tone in the way in which the writers presented not only the scientist and his work but also the use to which those inventions were put. For example, in Stanley Waterloo's *Armageddon* (1898), David Appleton's development of "a great torpedo-shaped thing with an aluminum exterior" powered by electricity (p. 26) provides the central thread of the narrative (Helen Daggart, his fiancée, names it the "Wild Goose"), but a second concern is the construction of a Nicaraguan canal. After completion of the canal, a coalition of European nations attacks, apparently believing, as Waterloo averred, that ownership of the canal meant ownership of the seas. Although Britain and Japan aid the Americans and their combined fleets pummel the "Slavs" and the "Latins," the turning point comes only when Appleton brings his dirigible-type craft into the fray. "What happened then," the narrator declares, "changed what will be the story of all wars of the future" (p. 220); by hand he drops packages of dynamite which sink the Russian flagship and several other major ships, although the "Wild Goose" crash lands into the ocean and is destroyed. Appleton declares that with aerial warfare added, international conflict will end, for there "can be no safety for anyone." To Helen's question, "Why do we make these killing machines then, if they are not to be used?"—Appleton replies:

To have a world at peace there must be massed in the controlling nations such power of destruction as may not be even questioned. So we shall build our appliances of destruction, calling to our aid every discovery and achievement of science. When there are but chances about war, when it means death to all, or the vast majority of all who engage in it, there will be peace. (pp. 258–259)

In this case that means providing weapons for the Anglo-Saxon alliance, including Holland and the Scandinavian nations, as well as Germany, though it fought on the side of the Latin-Slavic coalition. (Japan, whose naval prowess had impressed the Americans and British, becomes one of the victorious council.) At a Conference in Amsterdam the victors inform the rest of the world:

"We are the conquerors. Rightly or wrongly, we consider ourselves the approved of Providence in directing most of the affairs of the world, and we propose, for the present to direct them. We do not intend to take your territory, but we do intend to establish our authority as paramount, and centuries may pass before you again acquire the position you lately held relatively, even if you develop a different growth. We believe that we are the people most adapted for population of new lands and propose to act in accordance with this idea.'' (p. 242)

Consequently, the defeated nations are excluded from Africa, which is assigned to Britain. Undoubtedly expressing the conservative reaction to the flood of new immigrants during the 1880s and 1890s, Waterloo closed America to further immigration: ''There is room for the Hun and Latin steerage loads in South America'' (p. 244).

The fervor of this outburst surpassed even that of Benjamin Rush's *Anglo-Saxons, Onward! A Romance of the Future* (1908), which both celebrates the career of President John Morrison, whom both political parties nominated by acclamation in recognition of his military and diplomatic prowess, and recounts the idyllic romance of his daughter Helen and John Howard, a Southern gentleman and an alumnus of V. M. I., who incidentally leads a combined British-American army to victory over the Russians and Turks. The victory over Spain in 1898 had initiated the ''phenomenal'' growth of America: ''Isolation! Seclusion! Effeminating inaction! were thrust aside as unworthy of race and nation. Anglo-Saxons, Onward! became the watchword of the Americans in the closing years of the nineteenth century'' (p. 58). In addition, the new expansion ''had offered a vent or safety-valve to the restless, enterprising young men of the nation, who prior to this happy relief had begun to feel crowded and grow restless, adopting all kinds of visionary and dangerous doctrines'' (p. 59). As noted, paradoxically, the most ridiculous and yet in one sense historically important of alliances had been described ''allegorically'' two years earlier in Gregory Casparian's *An Anglo-American Alliance* (1906), in which through a deliberate operation the American girl Margaret MacDonald had undergone a sex change so that as Spencer Hamilton she could marry the English girl, Aurora Cunningham, with whom she had long had a schoolgirl infatuation when they were students at a Ladies' Seminary at Cornwall on the Hudson.

In contrast, the fullest idealization of a scientist occurred in Simon Newcomb's *His Wisdom, the Defender* (1900), an account of the career of Archibald Campbell, Professor of Molecular Physics at Harvard University. Presented by future historians after Campbell's death, the narrative portrays his rise to power as a benevolent world dictator. The nation first reacts to his activities after the disappearance of his fleet of 250 small, power-driven boats, each manned by members of his secret society, ''The Angelic Order of Seraphim,'' made up of college men. Subpoenaed by Congress, he explains the nature of his discoveries:

''I am free to say that the boats are not propelled by steam power, but by etherine through the action of therm.

''These are terms which I have applied to certain new agencies discovered by me. I mean by etherine a new form of matter having relations to the luminous ether, not possessed by any other matter formerly known to man. Therm is an agent somewhat akin to electricity, also discovered by me, and still unknown to the scientific world. By these two agencies I can exercise force and produce motion in ways never before known." (pp. 86–87)

Not until he unveils an airship capable of space travel does he reveal his political thinking. Knowing that free use of his "ultimate" energy would precipitate a second, devastating industrial revolution because of its suddenness, he insists that he retain "the power to guide the revolution. I could bring about its benefits without its attendant evils. To do this my power must be absolute" (pp. 110–111). His proposal that he rule a federated world-state meets open antagonism. Only after he and his "Seraphim" defeat the German army, the British navy, and a combination of French and Austrian forces do nations grant his demands. At once he declares himself "Defender of the Peace of the World," abolishes war, and asserts that "dependent peoples" will be ruled "in accordance with their laws and traditions" (p. 319). One must read this in terms of African and Asiatic peoples so that *His Wisdom, the Defender* expresses perhaps the most tolerant racial view among the early American novels. The nations willingly give up their sovereignty, and Campbell rules benignly. Throughout the period he best represents the scientist as a father figure instigating a world utopia.

The figure of Edestone in J. Stewart Barney's *L.P.M.; The End of the Great War* (1915) voices a far harsher doctrine. When the American Secretary of State sees in the proposal for peace a period of U.S. domination, Edestone acts on his own. He goes to the European rulers with motion pictures of his giant, fortresslike flying machine in action. To the king of England he unveils his deepest motivation:

"I am an American and I am proud of it. Not because of the great power and wealth of my country, nor its hundred and odd millions of people made up of the nations of the earth, the sweepings of Europe, the overflow of Asia, and the bag of the slave-hunter of Africa, which centuries will amalgamate into a *cafe au lait* conglomerate, but because I am proud of that small group of Anglo-Saxons who, under the influence of the free air of our great country, have developed such strength that they have up to this time put the stamp of England upon all who have come in contact with them. . . . In your presence and that of Almighty God, I dedicate my life to my people, the Anglo-Saxons." (p. 102)

During the same interview Edestone explains the secret of his flying fortress in terms that his audience can understand:

"I have invented an instrument which I call a *Deionizer*. With this, so far as regards any phenomena of which we are conscious, I am able to change the electrical condition of an object, provided that this object is insulated from contact with the earth." (pp. 106–107)

He has developed another antigravity device.

Although the British King pledges his support, the Kaiser attempts to obtain the secret and the airship through threats and violence. Edestone gains his support only after annihilating one major military installation each day for a week. Having gained his audience, he assembles the rulers and outlines his plan for an authoritarian state unlike anything seen in the American treatment of the motif:

He scoffed at the theory of majority rule, equality of man, and perpetual peace through brotherly love. . . .

He then established a very limited ruling class, which he called, for the lack of a better name, the Aristocracy of Intelligence, over which he placed a head of absolute power, backed with sufficient force to see that its wishes were carried out. . . .

He suggested that the Race problem might be entirely solved by segregating the races of the world, and giving over to them a portion of the earth sufficiently large to support them in the climate and surroundings to which they were accustomed. (pp. 414–416)

Barney unquestionably thought that the government begun by Edestone would produce an ideal state.

Although perhaps more technocratic, it reminds one of the governments ruled by an oligarchy of Trusts which both George Allan England and Jack London, for example, feared and prophesied in such novels as *The Iron Heel* (1907). In this context, then, it expresses the political tensions in the U.S. in the early years of the twentieth century. In its disregard for the individual, for deviations from the norm, and for the emotional and intellectual makeup of society, it theoretically predicts a state as intolerant as any seen in the twentieth century.

The tone of Hollis Godfrey's *The Man Who Ended War* (1908) differs sharply because it is presented as a mystery. An unknown scientist delivers an ultimatum to the nations of the world. They must disarm immediately. To show his power he causes battleships of the United States, Great Britain, and France to disappear. James Orrington, a newspaperman; Tom Haldane, his friend and a scientist; and Dorothy Haldane, Tom's lab assistant and Orrington's beloved, set out to solve the mystery and gain a story. Because the sensitive "reflectoscopes" in Haldane's laboratory register a strong electric current at the precise moment that the ships disappear, although they are thousands of miles from the lab, Haldane theorizes that the scientist makes use of "some radio-active generator, some means of wave disturbance greater than anything we have yet attained" (p. 53). He develops a device capable of tracing any electrical or radioactive "wave" to its source. Then begins a game of hide-and-seek—important because instead of being mere decoration, Dorothy provides the motivating drive—which ends in the British Channel during a great battle between the British and German fleets. One by one the fighting ships vanish (they do not sink). When the annihilation is complete, a submarine surfaces for a moment; "The Man," a scientist and writer introduced only in the opening scene of the novel, becomes visible. He dies; one may infer that he is mad. When the three have made explanations to the rulers of the principal nations, the powers call for a world disarmament conference to be held at The Hague. The Kaiser alone remains adamant until he understands more thoroughly the power of such a weapon. The world thus assured of peace, Orrington and Dorothy—who holds a master's degree from Barnard—confess their love and flee to Paris to buy a trousseau.

In the same year, Roy Norton's *The Vanishing Fleets* (1908) presents a comparable mystery. As a Japanese fleet steams toward Hawaii, it disappears without a trace. The nations of the world concur that such "total destruction" is unwarranted because no "civilized nation would have chosen deliberately to exterminate its enemies" (pp. 87–88). Britain sends its North Sea fleet to demonstrate off the eastern coast of the U.S. It, too, disappears. Simultaneously, during a fog in both London and Berlin, the King of England and the Kaiser vanish, while one of the missing British dreadnaughts reappears in the Thames estuary—undamaged but without a crew.

A flashback reveals that when an American scientist—whose daughter is his lab assistant—undertook an experiment to show naval authorities a new alloy he had developed, something unforeseen in his combination of "electricity and metallurgy" resulted in the first occurrence of true levitation. He explains:

"My friends, by the discovery of an alloy of metal and metalloids we have created a new substance, which when an electrical current of certain potentiality is passed through it becomes intensely radioactive; infinitely more so than radium. Through these machines my daughter and I have produced electrical manifestations hitherto unsuspected and unknown. The metal itself, while radioactive to a certain degree, does not become intensely so without the application of the excitant current." (p. 217)

Since levitation—that is, an antigravity force—is a major effect of this new force, the scientist immediately solves the problem of flight by inventing the "radioplane." His planes attack the Japanese fleet off Hawaii, carrying each ship aloft by means of magnetic power and taking them to a large lake somewhere near Seattle. The commanding officers of the British fleet agree to be moved after they have witnessed the levitation of one of their own ships. When the King and the Kaiser have also been taken to the lake, the President asks their aid in ending all war and establishing a necessary alliance.

At first refusing to cooperate, the Kaiser is detained in a hunting camp in the Pacific Northwest, where he befriends his American guards. At last he agrees to support a conclave of nations:

"We all change, I suppose as we advance. I have learned that one may have his ideas changed by accident. I have known for many days what it is to be free to think, to learn profound lessons in philosophy from the forests and streams, and have come nearer to men of the American nation than I had ever hoped. I have formed new friendships, and by the camp fires at night have been given other views of life, of men and humanity, by a most admirable teacher." (pp. 328–329)

In this speech, Kaiser Wilhelm gives expression to several interrelated ideas which seem a fixed part of the American imagination at the turn of the century. First, if the leaders of the major countries would sit down in open discussion, they would quickly straighten out whatever difficulties seemed to exist between nations. Second, because European diplomats and rulers had been trained in a completely different, perhaps cynical philosophy, if they had the opportunity to share with Americans the natural setting of the western continent, they would somehow be affected by the transcendental idealism which traditionally formed the core of American thought. In short, if the rulers of the world were to meet at a Walden pond, as individuals they could be inspired to cure the ills of the world. One must infer the importance of this idea in shaping American thinking: how else explain the efforts of Henry Ford and Woodrow Wilson to secure a moral peace at a conference table?

Even when the scientist was mad, as in Arthur Train and Robert William Wood's *The Man Who Rocked the Earth* (1915), first serialized in the *Saturday Evening Post* in the autumn of 1914, the same idealism prevailed. An unknown scientist broadcasts an ultimatum in July 1915 insisting that the stalemated European war be ended. When his message goes unheeded, he lengthens the sidereal day and tilts the earth's axis, as he had promised. An international conference takes place at the White House, with the President being asked to act as intermediary between the statesmen and the unknown PAX, the call letters which the scientist uses. The German representative, Count Von Koenitz, demands further evidence of PAX's power; thus, he cuts through the Atlas Mountains, allowing the Mediterranean to flood into the Sahara. A report filed by an acting U.S. consul in Algeria gives the first description of PAX's ship:

... it was a cylindrical ring like a doughnut or an anchor ring, constructed of highly polished metal, the inner aperture being about twenty-five yards in diameter. The tube of the cylinder looked to be about twenty feet thick, and had circular windows or portholes that were brilliantly lighted.

The strangest thing about it was that it carried a superstructure consisting of a number of arms meeting at a point above the centre of the opening and supporting some sort of apparatus from which the beam of light emanated. This appliance was focused down through the Ring and could apparently be moved at will over a limited radius of about fifteen degrees. (p. 65)

Not only is "The Flying Ring," as it came to be called, the most advanced in design of any of the ships dealt with in the future-war motif, but its "beam of light" is the most advanced weapon, as evidenced by its effect on the Arabs accidently caught in the ray as it cut through the mountains: "Five days later all three began to suffer excruciating torment from internal burns, the skin upon their heads and bodies began to peel off, and they died in agony within the week" (p. 68). Such was the first description of radiation sickness published in a widely circulated American magazine.

Although Count Von Koenitz agrees to an armistice (the Kaiser has abdicated and the Russians have taken Berlin), the remainder of the narrative becomes a race between a German expeditionary force and a single American scientist, Bennie Hooker, Lawton Professor of Applied Physics at Harvard, to reach PAX in his retreat hidden in the interior of Labrador. In a chapter which functions solely to establish the knowledgeability of the eccentric Hooker—who "take[s] a crack at the fourth dimension" when he needs relaxation and admits "spacial curvature's [his] hobby"—Hooker indicates the communication and borrowing of ideas among members of the international community of science. To Thornton, the senior astronomer at the Naval Observatory in Washington, he explains the source of PAX's power:

. . . All you need is the energy [to tilt the earth's axis]. And it's lying all around if you could only get at it. That's just what I'm working at now. Radium, uranium, thorium, actinium—all the radioactive elements—are, as everybody knows, continually disintegrating, discharging the enormous energy that is imprisoned in their molecules. It may take generations, epochs, centuries, for them to get rid of it and transform themselves into other substances, but they will inevitably do so eventually. They're doing with more or less of a rush what all the elements are doing at their leisure. A single ounce of uranium contains about the same amount of energy that could be produced by the combustion of ten tons of coal—but it won't let the energy go. Instead it holds onto it, and the energy leaks slowly, almost imperceptibly, away, like water from a big reservoir tapped only by a tiny pipe. "Atomic energy" Rutherford calls it. Every element, every substance, has its energy ready to be touched off and put to use. The chap who can find out how to release that energy all at once will revolutionize the civilized world. It will be like the discovery that water could be turned into steam and made to work for us—multiplied a million times.

If, instead of that energy just oozing away and the uranium disintegrating infinitesimally each year, it could be exploded at a given moment you could drive an ocean liner with a handful of it. You could make the old globe stagger round and turn upside down! Mankind could just lay off and take a holiday. (pp. 100–101)

When a German general commanding an artillery division breaks the armistice by using a great new gun to bombard Paris, the Flying Ring cruises over the Western Front and obliterates the village of Champaubert, the artillery division's position, turning it "into the smoking crater of a dying volcano" (p. 171). Enraged perhaps to madness, PAX announces that on September 10 he will drastically shift the poles of the earth, changing Europe to an Arctic tundra. His effort fails. An explosion kills him and all but one of his staff, while the German forces die in a "reeking marsh," because the explosion diverts the flow of the river up which they are advancing, thereby grounding their motor boats and barges. Hooker arrives at the site later on; with the aid of a machinist, the sole survivor, and a colleague who comes in by plane, he flies the Ring to Washington. In his absence, the nations have destroyed the last vestiges of militarism, even the uniforms, throughout the world. Each continent has united into a coalition, all of them agreeing to meet in an annual world congress to be held at The Hague. "Each state enforced local laws, but all were obedient to the higher law—the Law of Humanity—which was uniform through the earth" (p. 225). Never again did either an American or a European contributor to the future-war motif express such idealism.[13]

Perhaps not surprisingly, none of the relatively infrequent imaginary wars with Germany was published after the U.S. entry into World War I. As early as *"Bietigham"* (1886), published under the pseudonym John W. Minor, conflict with Germany, "the worst-hated nation in Europe [but] unquestionably the most powerful" (pp. 29–30), had played a significant role in bringing an end to imperialism and starting a series of revolutions which eventually produces a United States of Europe and results in world peace. Joining an allied army made up of British, French, Italian, and Spanish troops, American forces fight in a campaign aimed at such fortresses as Metz and Strasbourg. They take part in the decisive battle of Hoheneck—complete with cavalry charge.

No other American author involved the armies of the U.S. and Germany until H. Irving Hancock, a prolific writer of boys' series books, permitted the Imperial army to undertake "The Invasion of the United States" in four volumes, all issued in 1916. He readily used the young men whom he had previously guided through West Point and Annapolis.[14] Beaten back from Boston and New York, they rally in western Pennsylvania and Ohio, but despite their determined effort in *Making the Stand for Old Glory*, the Army of the Alleghenies needs the aid of an army from Brazil, which enters the conflict because the U.S. had once invoked the Monroe Doctrine to aid Brazil. While Hancock echoed convention by declaring that America's unpreparedness must be blamed for the invasion of 1920, he differed from his contemporaries in that he drove his point home by emphasizing that even victory costs "most of the United States Navy as it had existed in the spring of 1920," as well as 85 percent of the regular army (p. 253).

The increasing vehemence of American feeling against Germany in 1916 may be measured by the serialization of two novels aimed at a popular audience: Thomas Dixon's *The Fall of a Nation* in the *National Sunday Magazine* and Cleveland Moffett's *The Conquest of America* in *McClure's Magazine*. Dixon's novel was unique in that it did not give American science any chance to save or rescue the nation which had been surprised and occupied. Little more than a diatribe against Germany and the German-American population, it turns on the efforts of a secret society of American women. Each member "dates" a German officer or soldier and kills him, while the women's menfolk seize ammunition dumps and communication centers. Victory is that simple when one puts her mind to it.

Moffett created "The Committee of Twenty-One," a combination of businessmen, military leaders, and scientists who band together after the occupation of the country. He played that occupation for all of the emotion he could rouse. When the German fleet attacks New York, for example, some 5,000 youths between the ages of fifteen and eighteen, "members of the Athletic League of New York Public Schools," armed with no more than 125 rifles, stand off the invaders until they are forced to retreat, leaving seventy comrades "qualified as sharpshooters to remain and face almost certain death" (pp. 62, 64). In a chapter entitled "Thrilling Incident at Wanamaker's Store When Germans Dishonor the American Flag," a little boy of seven begins to sing "America" when someone plays it; the adult audience joins him. The Germans do not punish the Philadelphians.

Dedicated to "the Aero Club of America," the novel turns on three battles. In the first, the Americans annihilate a German army by igniting thousands of gallons of oil—donated by Standard Oil—which have been buried beneath the battlefield. In the second, a fleet of airplanes dumps tons of liquid chlorine on another German army. But the U.S. does not achieve final victory until the third when Thomas A. Edison develops a radio-controlled torpedo which permits "an insignificant airforce" to destroy "a great fleet" so that the U.S. is able to dictate the terms of peace. One infers that Moffett reflected the changing American mood when he wrote:

We may be sure that wars will continue on the earth. War may be a biological necessity in the development of the human race—God's housecleaning, as Ella Wheeler Wilcox calls it. War may be a great soul stimulant meant to purge mankind of evils greater than itself, evils of baseness and world degeneration. We know there are blighted forests that must be swept clean by fire. Let us not scoff at such a theory until we understand the immeasurable mysteries of life and death. We know that, through the ages, two terrific and devastating racial impulses have made themselves felt among men and have never been restrained, sex attraction and war. Perhaps they were not meant to be restrained. (pp. 20–21)

Perhaps the single most important characteristic of the future-war motif, as dealt with by both American and European writers before World War I, was that by and large the novels dealt with the here-and-now, projecting forward in time no more than a few years. In this the motif anticipated—or established the formula for—such later works as Eugene Burdick and Harvey Wheeler's *Fail Safe* (1962). However, whether told by the Volunteer who fought at Dorking; by John W. Minor, who gave three lectures in Denver in 1932 tracing the effects of the war in *"Bietingham"*; or by future historians who provided a biographical tribute to Professor Archibald Campbell, founder of the world society in *His Wisdom, the Defender*, the retrospective narrative—certainly not unique to the future-war motif—reveals a second characteristic significant in the evolution of the motif in that it describes not only the conflict but also the far-reaching consequences of the events of the struggle. These narratives were in the minority, for the motif grew out of an urgency, an immediacy, too myopic to go beyond jingoistic or frightened consideration of the dangers of a current situation—that is, the clash of nationalistic interests during the late nineteenth and early twentieth centuries. Thus, whether projecting a nationalistic or racial bias, the writers created seeming paradises dominated by their own countries.

As such, the novels quickly became dated. Almost a century later, after the mindless brutalities ranging from World War I to Vietnam, the greatest number of them evoke a sense of futility and, perhaps, something of wonder. As purposive literature they belie the ability of science fiction to predict accurately, for none of the authors dealing with the European scene foresaw the stalemate of trench warfare brought on by the new technology. As cautionary tales they did not teach the nations not to fight. So as a group most of them retain, at most, a historical interest, because they give some insight into a state of mind (and society) which ended abruptly with the machine guns of August 1914. In literary terms, many of the narratives told from a retrospective point of view contributed to the development of that narrative technique which created the alternative future history—most often used as a vehicle to picture either a utopian or dystopian society.[15]

What has been said of the fiction dealing with imaginary European wars can be applied, by and large, to the American confrontation with Asia, although that conflict endured for a longer time and had a more complex psychological base. The taproot of the hostility goes back to the importation of Coolie labor into California, as evidenced by Pierton W. Dooner's *Last Days of the Republic* (1880), an essaylike tome which denounces the Chinese immigrants—supposedly in the words of J. W. Marshall, Chief Justice of California—as "a race of people whom Nature has marked as inferior, and who are incapable of progress or intellectual development beyond a certain point" (pp. 186–187); however, they prove to be superior to the American blacks who "rapidly and noiselessly disappeared—perished, it seemed, by the very act of contact" (pp. 95, 127) when Chinese labor was introduced and welcomed into the southeastern states. Dooner chronicled the infiltration, the political takeover of states where Chinese labor had been introduced, the seizure of all territory below the thirty-seventh parallel, and finally open warfare. From the early stages of the conquest, Dooner suggested, the Chinese intermarried with American women (p. 127), thereby adding the fuel of miscegenation to his tirade. After resistance and a terrible famine, America is destroyed as a nation, reduced to a Chinese province. Robert Wolton essentially echoed Dooner in *A Short and Truthful History of the Taking of California and Oregon in the Year A.D. 1899*, published in 1882, the year of the Chinese Exclusion Act. Possibly of greater interest because of its tie to Edward Bellamy's *Looking Backward* (1888) is Arthur Dudley Vinton's *Looking Further Backward* (1890). Professor Won Lung Li, the successor to Professor Julian West, delivers a series of lectures at Shawmut College, in which he gives close attention to the Chinese conquest of America beginning in 2020, although his primary aim is to show the weaknesses in Bellamy's projected utopia.

Not all of the novels were so effective as Vinton's. In *A Dream of Conquest* (1889), Lloyd Bryce struck out satirically in all directions, although part of the storyline involves a war between the U.S. and China, the American navy being virtually wiped out and New York evacuated. Before the narrator awakens from his dream, the beleaguered Americans suggest that a society matron, Mrs. Percival T. McFlusterer, marry the second-class mandarin, Wang-Chi-Poo, who early declares that "Melican woman all foot and all tongue" (p. 28). Something of a similar problem seriously mars Oto Mundo's *The Recovered Continent; A Tale of the Chinese Invasion* (1898); in a two-part narrative, Mundo did not adequately develop any of the topics he introduced. The narrator, Esden, falls against an electric wire in 1874 and seems to awake in 1926, but he indicates that he is not sure that he did not simply dream of being in the future; at the end of the second part, he is uncertain whether or not he exists simultaneously in both time periods. Given this confusion, the reader finds that the first portion of the narrative pictures an America expanded to include Canada and Greenland, whose climate has been changed so that it is habitable. Another line of action involves a deliberate experiment which transforms the simpleminded Toto Topheavy into a genius. The second part of the narrative shifts to 1933 and the several years subsequent, during which time Toto Topheavy leads an army of some 400,000 Chinese which defeats European powers and America at the Battle of Constantinople. Although Toto is identified as the anti-Christ, after he survives an assassination attempt, he flees to Greenland, where with Esden's grandson, he helps to establish "A Provincial Government of the World"; he then expresses the desire to use all the explosives in the world to cut a canal across the Isthmus of Panama. This mishmash simply provides another index of the topics popular at the turn of the century; it also provides one of the best examples of the difficulty the writers had controlling their materials.

Before major concern shifted from China, M. P. Shiel, the eccentric English writer, created the myth of "The Yellow Peril" in the novel *The Yellow Danger* (1899), first serialized in 1897.[16] He turned loose an army of 150 million "yellow men" to overwhelm Europe. Not satisfied with a British naval victory, he infected the few survivors with the germs of "putrid cholera" and put them ashore on the Continent. Within weeks, Chinese-occupied Europe is laid waste, although even Americans participate in a last battle which "degenerates into a debauch of hell" (p. 386). So often violent, Shiel gave voice to an almost paranoid racism.

Equally brutal is Jack London's story "The Unparalleled Invasion" published in *McClure's Magazine* (July 1910). Presented as an excerpt from Walt Mervin's *Certain Essays in History*, the narrative reports the action by the United States and the nations of Europe in 1976 when they are no longer able to cope with China because it has been awakened by Japan—whom it defeated decisively in 1922—and because its population has approached the billion mark. Appalled, the Western powers agree to a truce among themselves; then they follow the suggestion of a scientist, Jacobus Laningdale, a professor employed by the New York City Health Office. First they blockade all of China's borders, both land and sea, and then they literally bombard it with every known infectious germs. China perishes. (The plague germs produce a hybrid which is finally isolated and studied.) Not until 1982 do the nations colonize an empty China; in 1987, at the Convention of Copenhagen, they agree never to use among themselves "the laboratory methods of warfare" they had used against China. In the essay "The Yellow Peril," published in *Revolution and Other Essays* (1912) though apparently written in Manchuria in 1904, London declared, "War is to-day the final arbiter in the affairs of men, and it is as yet the final test of the worthwhileness of peoples" (p. 269). He wrote of the Japanese dream of domination and warned of the danger to the West should Japan "undertake the management" of 400 million Chinese.

In contrast, although J. Hamilton Sedberry made use of electro guns, electro cannons, and electro bombs and projected the final war "between the Caucasian and Mongolian races" into the years 2005–2007, his *Under the Sign of the Cross* (1908) focuses upon the love between William Hastings, a Virginian who rises to the rank of commander-in-chief of the American forces, and Beatrix Clifton, daughter of the English commander. If one can imagine the language, characters, and storyline of Sir Walter Scott or one of the sentimental novels dealing with the American Civil War cast into the twenty-first century, then one has the essential quality of Sedberry's romance. The plot thickens with a kidnapping (a beautiful Southern girl by a villainous English naval captain), assorted rescues (that of Beatrix when her horse almost runs over the edge of a cliff into the Bosphorus, to say nothing of saving her and one Ann Patterson from a Turkish harem), Anglo-American rivalry for the hand of the dazzling Beatrix, swordplay (highlighted by a duel between Hastings and Sir Lambert Seville, who desires his cousin Beatrix), and General Clifton's dismissal of Hastings as an unqualified suitor because at that moment he is merely a captain. This affair of the heart is resolved happily after a tremendous battle which determines both that Christianity will not give "place to Paganism" and that "the Heathens were destined to be overcome and driven back to the Orient" (p. 448). Although the valiant enemy is referred to as Mongolian or the "yellow peril"—which persists in cavalry charges, although the West has armored cars—the only officers are labeled as Japanese.

The Japanese seized center stage, of course, following their unexpected victory over the Russians. *The Yellow War* (1905) gathered together a number of sketches, many of them first published in *Blackwood's Magazine*. Their highly pro-Japanese author, who identified himself simply as "O", declared that although the incidents were fictionalized, each represented "some living actor in the terrific drama with which [he] ha[d] been intimate during the past year" (p. vi). He concluded that "Militarism, the curse of the past, will be the curse of the future" (p. 101).

Marsden Manson's *The Yellow Peril in Action; A Possible Chapter in History* (1907), a brief pamphlet which apparently was the first fictional treatment of a war between the U.S. and Japan, projects a defeat in 1912 depriving America of the territories acquired in the war with Spain and denying it any share of the commerce in the Pacific. "Europe [stands] amazed and almost aghast" at the outcome (p. 19), while Congress enacts legislation prohibiting any immigration for ten years and denying forever the franchise to any person not born and educated in the United States. Few other authors gave attention to the commercial implications of such a conflict, and only Roy Norton in *The Vanishing Fleets* (1908), as noted, asserted that America's primary aim was to achieve world peace. In that same year, Captain Richard Pearson Hobson published a three-part article, "If War Should Come!" in *Cosmopolitan*, in which he estimated that the Japanese could land an army of 500,000 men on American soil within four months, one of his alarmist predictions. In the collection of stories *The Battle for the Pacific*, Rowan Stevens' "Sorakachi-Prometheus" focuses upon an American scientist, Adams, who invents an electrically controlled airplane as well as leashing the power of lightning into a destructive ray. Ironically, Adams had secreted himself in Japan, where, as the almost legendary scientist Sorakachi, he obtained financial support from the Japanese government. The bloodiest fighting of 1908, however, occurred in the widely popular novel *Banzai!*, first published in Leipzig under the name Parabellum, the pseudonym of Ferdinand Heinrich Grautoff, who attempted to make "Old Britain" the villain of the piece by emphasizing its financial aid to the Japanese. Germany, of course, aids the United States by recognizing the Monroe Doctrine. Helped by both the Japanese and Chinese inhabitants of the west coast states who rise in rebellion (Grautoff makes no distinction between them; he lumps them together as "the yellow peril"), the Japanese armies penetrate the American mainland. A defeat near Ft. Bridger, however, ends the invasion—perhaps somewhat arbitrarily.

Equally racist in tone is J. U. Giesy's *All for His Country* (1915). After Mexico attacks the United States, Japanese troops hidden aboard a ship coming into San Francisco Bay for repairs seize the Presidio. With the aid of Japanese inhabitants—"For years they had been waiting and preparing. In many communities they actually outnumbered the whites, and they all rose at once" (p. 102)—the invaders occupy much of California before the Americans retreat to Utah and Nevada. New York has been bombed; the fleet, destroyed. Although from the first Giesy complicated the storyline with internal political dissensions and business rivalries as well as a love story, the central action concerns Meade Stillman's development of an "aero-destroyer," an all-metallic plane shaped like a torpedo and fueled by radium. Making use of an antigravity power, it can fly at 200 mph. When Bernice Biddy Gethelds goes to Utah to search for Stillman, Harold Darling, who loves her platonically, accompanies her. He flies the aero-destroyer and annihilates the Japanese fleet before he dies, thereby assuring the U.S. of victory. Because Stillman and his ship have been called the miracle needed to save the nation, Giesy concluded the narrative with the remark that "the Supreme Miracle is Love"—after Bernice and Stillman have agreed to marry.

After World War I, in such a novel as *The Orphan of Space* (1926), the pseudonymous Captain Glossop warned against "the terrible results of the Yellow Peril combined with Bolshevism" (p. 1) when Germany, Russia, and China undertake world conquest. But most British novelists turned from the excitement of new armaments and the celebration of glorious victories. They portrayed a future world after cataclysmic war, whether civil or international, has reduced civilization to barbarism, if indeed, mankind has survived. Among the best of these were Edward Shanks' *The People of the Ruins* (1920) and John Collier's *Tom's A-Cold* (1933), published in America as *Full Circle*. In Francis H. Sibson's *Unthinkable* (1933), after the survivors of a South African Antarctic expedition struggle northward because no relief ship has reached them, they realize that modern society has destroyed itself in a war whose cause they do not know; they echo the early H. G. Wells of, for example, "The Star" (1898) and *In the Days of the Comet* (1906) when they resolve to build again *"and build better."*

The most notable exception to this pattern was S. Fowler Wright's *Prelude in Prague; A Story of the War of 1938* (1935), published in America the following year as *The War of 1938*. In perhaps his most "realistic" novel, Wright predicted with good accuracy the effect of mass bombing on an open city even before the Spanish Civil War showed Europe what awaited it in the 1940s.

In America, although the "Yellow Peril" had become a villain throughout popular adventure and mystery fiction, the obsession of the American future-war motif with an Asiatic enemy continued. For the most part, however, even when giving attention to the development of advanced weapons, the novels were thematically tired. Roy Snell's *The Seagoing Tank* (1924), aimed at a juvenile audience, asserted that wealthy Oriental yachtsmen acted as spies for their unspecified governments.

Hector Charles Bywater assured his audience that he did not intend either to foment tensions between the U.S. and Japan, despite the immigration controversy and the conflict of commercial interests in the Far East, or to suggest that conflict between the nations was "close at hand or inevitable"; nor did he choose "to sacrifice reality for the sake of dramatic effect" by bringing a Japanese fleet either to Hawaii or allowing its army to "overrun the Pacific Slope" of America (p. vi). The resultant chronicle of *The Great Pacific War; A History of the American-Japanese Campaign of 1931–1933* (1925) gives so close a month-by-month description of the engagements in the western Pacific that libraries have sometimes cataloged it as history rather than fiction. In *Pacifico* (1926), W. B. Shearer emphasized the influence of Germany upon the militarism of Japan and ended the novel's action with an aborted revolt in the Philippines, although the storyline centers on the efforts of Commander Truxton Rogers and the beautiful Rena Garrett to keep precious secrets from falling into the hands of Japanese agents. F. Britten Austin used the story "In the China Sea" to warn that Japan would attack Guam; it was published in the collection *The War God Walks Again* (1926), in which most of the stories are dominated by bombing and poison gas attacks. Francis Beeding's *The Hidden Kingdom* (1927) pursues the diabolical German chemist Professor Kreutzemark from western Europe to Outer Mongolia, where he hopes to establish himself as a religious figure and lead the Mongol hordes to world conquest.

The degree to which exhausted themes were mixed together can be illustrated by the mishmash of contradictions in W. D. Gann's *The Tunnel Thru the Air; or, Looking Back from 1940* (1927) and by the demented racism of Solomon Cruso's *The Last of the Japs and the Jews* (1933). Declaring the Bible to be a "wonderful book" containing all scientific laws and presenting the narrative as the biography of a deeply religious American leader, Robert Gordon, Gann described an attack upon the U.S. by Japan, which is soon joined by a coalition of nations including England, Germany, and Russia. Despite apparent defeat and imminent occupation by the armies of the alliance, America relies upon her scientists to produce a variety of weapons, including a vacuum through which U.S. planes can fly without being seen, as well as a sleeping gas. Now the American commander Gordon prepares himself spiritually for what must come. During a period of six days he undertakes the destruction of buildings in the enemy capitals as well as the gassing of their populations. On the seventh day he returns to New York to await their surrender (p. 393). After their capitulation, at a conference in New York in August 1932, he is introduced as "the greatest and most just man since our saviour Jesus Christ was on earth" (p. 408). Warning his audience that America has a weapon capable of destroying "every living soul on the earth," he asks them to remember that the U.S. victory "is according to God's plan and God's will" (p. 410). He then marries a childhood sweetheart, Marie Stanton, and rules the United Kingdom of the World.

Such hypocrisy is surpassed only by the indiscriminant genocide of Cruso's volume, dedicated to "the Rulers, Statesmen, Diplomats, and Militarists of the Caucasian Race, the white Aryans, who fell on the battlefields of Europe, Asia, Africa, America, and Australia in the period of 1980–1985, A.D." Presented as a future history, although one cannot be sure whom the speaker represents, the narrative opens with the assertion that by 2390 (p. 5) "a mighty army of Indian warriors stood ready to repel the expected invasion of the white enemy," and by 2490 (p. 9) "countless numbers of Redskins" roamed the Western Hemisphere. They retain "primitive weapons [and] picturesque Indian attire" (p. 6). Nothing more is made of this point of departure, for the narrative recapitulates the worldwide slaughter. After a diatribe against the Soviet five-year plan and socialism in general, the capitalistic nations band together to overrun all of Russia in 1942. Their puppet Czar, Kiril I, is as much "admired by the capitalistic world as Mussolini was for producing Fascism" (p. 44). Whether or not the Mongols oust the Kuomingtang government from Nanking before an unusually terrible Pacific storm "swallows up" the islands of Japan in 1962 remains debatable, but by the end of the 1960s the Caucasians and Mongols are locked in battle. Despite possessing airships "created by superhuman intellect" (p. 188), the whites are finally defeated after a series of battles, the greatest of which begins on July 25, 1981, during which cavalry charges prove decisive, as they did in 1942 during the Russian campaign. Sometime during the interval of four decades, 16 million Jews, "almost the entire Jewish population of the world . . . [was] completely wiped out" (pp. 23–24); again, 11 million Jews died "in their beds [murdered] by white people who killed them systematically, quietly, with knives, swords, and bayonets" (p. 216). Nevertheless, a million Jewish Americans take up arms and grimly await an Asiatic invasion (p. 286). To make certain that no Japanese survives, the Pacific coughs up the islands, before they sink once more. At the end, Jeremiah, an American Indian, weeps for the hundred million who have died in the U.S.

In contrast to such irrational mayhem, Edward Gawain—the pseudonym of Edward Penray—presented a carefully structured though formulaic invasion of the Americas by "unknown peoples out of Asia" in *The Earth-Tube* (1929). Although the "most charitable estimate of these [invaders] places them somewhere between the African native and the early American Indian" (p. 57), their society is dominated by science and technology; their strength lies in their use of a "super" metal, undulal, so heavy that they cannot build either airplanes or ships with it. To conquer Japan they had to build a bridge from the Chinese mainland; for whatever reasons, they turn their backs on Europe and tunnel through the earth to attack the Western Hemisphere. From an island off the coast of South America they build a causeway and attack Montevideo and move northward against the U.S., now a nation encompassing Central America and Canada. Their juggernaut tanks are unstoppable until the American scientist, King Henderson, discovers that liquid air destroys them. Before a final victory which sends the Asiatics scurrying to the city they have built at the mouth of the earth-tube, Henderson suggests that somehow they have created machines that are alive (p. 263). Gawain showed an ambivalence toward the science of the invaders: he was fascinated by it, but in that it provided the basis of a culture which lived by a cruelly impersonal philosophy devoid of mercy, he seemed horrified by it. Perhaps that impression results from his genuine delight in science *per se* and his need within the novel to portray the Asiatics as "fiends." His motives were plainly mixed, for after victory which destroys the enemy, Americans acquire "a new economic system which guarantees that never again shall any man be made a slave by other men" (p. 309). He provided no details, but throughout the novel Mui Salvos, a spokesman for the Asiatics, attacks the exploitation of factory workers, several times referring to them as slaves and machines.

One of the most effective American portrayals of an imaginary war occurred in Floyd Gibbons' *The Red Napoleon* (1929), because the famous journalist cast himself in the novel as first-person narrator; implicit in the narrative framework is the idea that he has spent some time with Karakhan of Kazan, the Mongol ruler of the U.S.S.R., during the dictator's exile in Bermuda after his defeat in 1936. Now in 1941 as a representative of the World Press, Gibbons sends out daily reports on the dying man who had so nearly conquered the world. He has also had the opportunity to write the biography of Karakhan who assumed power in Moscow after the assassination of Stalin on November 2, 1932. Gibbons could not have selected a better framing device. It allows him the authority of his personal experience: " . . . in 1928, I returned to America from Europe, a confirmed pacifist. I was sick of war. As a correspondent I had been in wars for the preceding fourteen years" (p. 3). He is able to slip in a few necessary details—mention of his first meeting with Karakhan in a garrison town on the Volga in 1922; Karakhan's marriage to the American woman, Lin Larkin, a member of the American Communist Party, who went to Russia in 1921; the expulsion of French and British forces from Southeast Asia following the unification of China; and the revolt of North Africa against Europe in 1931—before he bridges the years to the summer of 1932 when he covers the European flu epidemic and famine for the Chicago *Tribune* syndicate. Almost casually, he reports that he then had the opportunity to travel across the entire North African front and so had the fortune to obtain from the Allied General Staff documentary evidence of Russia's support of the native rebellion. This leads to his assignment to Moscow so that he is on the scene when his acquaintance Karakhan takes power.

Although Gibbons documented as carefully as did Bywater (he provides, for example, an appendix giving the naval strengths involved in the final battle of the Windward Passage off Jamaica), he gave his narrative a vivid immediacy through such devices as his newspaper dispatches. His friendship with Karakhan gives him a freedom of movement within the narrative that he would not otherwise have; for example, the Asiatic invaders permit him to parachute behind American lines so that he can report first hand the futile resistance of the Americans and Canadians before he is again captured by Karakhan's forces. Despite the detail of the fighting, the narrative is much more than an account of Karakhan's sweep through Europe, beginning with the invasion of Poland on January 2, 1933, followed by the invasion of Mexico and the struggle for Canada and the U.S. (Boston falls by Christmas 1934). From the beginning of the frame, Gibbons' central theme builds upon the idea of a race war, for Karakhan's instructions to his troops have been "CONQUER AND BREED" (p. 2) so that thousands of children are born to the white women of Europe and America in the wake of his conquering armies. Granted the impact of the idea of miscegenation on the readers of the period, Gibbons obviously sides with Karakhan, giving him the final statement, "The hatred between the colours and the species must be stamped out. . . . I recognize but one race—the HUMAN RACE" (p. 463). Gibbons indulged in some of the conventional fantasies of the period: the demise of the old order and the formation of a U.S. of Europe; the union of America and Canada—the result of the Canadian plebiscite of 1937—into a strong nation reaching from Mexico to the Arctic, by implication the future bastion of Western culture. Yet his central warning remains the need to solve the problem of races. One cannot readily accept John Gardner's verdict that the vision is "emphatically presented as that of a madman, a misfit."[17] From the outset, Gibbons accepted the view sympathetically, though commenting frequently upon the hatred it evoked from the West. In taking this position, Gibbons remained unique among both American and Western European writers, if only that he was more explicit in naming the problem. One may perhaps question the effectiveness of *The Red Napoleon*, but one cannot ignore its dark vision nor dismiss it as just another war story in which the author is obsessed with the details of battle.[18]

Although Sinclair Lewis depicted the rise of an American Fascism in *It Can't Happen Here* (1935) and Hendrik Van Loon pictured a Nazi attack on America—aided by a fifth column—as late as *Invasion* (1940), throughout the 1930s the emphasis in popular fiction continued to focus on the threat from Asia.

Since one cannot be certain how widely the novels circulated, the most important development of the 1930s saw the shift of the future-war motif to the pages of the mass market pulp magazines. The history of the pulp magazines deserves a more thorough study than has, with few exceptions, yet been made, but one premise remains comparatively secure. In response to a volatile market during the 1930s, they gave their audience what the readers wanted, or they did not survive. Ignoring the development of the magazines specializing in science fiction, fantasy, and horror, one observes two patterns. First, a number of titles— such as *G-8 and His Battle Aces, The Lone Eagle, Sky Fighters, Flying Aces, Wings,* and *Aces*—romanticized the activities of the World War I aviator; he emerged as the one folk, or culture, hero from the quagmire of the Western Front. Because he acted as an individual, he could easily be identified with the knightly warriors of the past, an association made both in fiction and nonfiction. Often he acted as secret agent and trouble shooter, thereby helping to set the stage for those who played the deadly game of espionage after World War II, culminating, perhaps, in James Bond, Agent 007.

More importantly in the present context, the pulps became the vehicle chronicling the adventures of such stalwarts as *Dusty Ayres and His Battle Birds* and *Operator 5*, whose harried but valiant efforts beat back untold Asiatic invaders. For a time, Richard Wentworth, *The Spider*, originally conceived as a rival of Lamont Cranston, *The Shadow*, pitted himself against the Yellow Peril. Important as were these series, the stories published in *Argosy* very probably reached a wider audience because of the success of the Munsey chain from the first decade of the century; moreover, *Argosy* remained the only weekly magazine. In the issues of February 24 and March 3, 1934—supposedly "reprinted" from the *Argosy* of February 1 and 8, 1953—Murray Leinster dealt with King Lun, dictator of New Asia, as he launched the "War of the Purple Gas" against America. Despite the derring-do of such men as Lieutenant Sid Terrill, only through the effort of American science does the U.S. overcome the advantages given the Asians by the Oriental physicist, Toyen Itso. As late as May 27, 1939, Arthur Leo Zagat published "Tomorrow," the first of three novelettes concerned with the survival in mountains near the Hudson River of a group of American teenagers, led by Dikar, in a country reduced to wilderness and occupied by a savage aggressor. Dikar remembers "the Long Ago" when he and his mother fled before the invader; a voice in his dreams insists that "the black and yellow men .·. . have come out of the East to make this world a Hell" (p. 26). On the cover, the image of a Japanese soldier straddles an America in flames; the blurb demands, "Will your children walk in chains as slaves of the Yellow Horde?" In the June 17 issue appeared the second installment, "Children of Tomorrow," in which Dikar and his bride Marilee are among those who escape from a concentration camp; the discovery that Marilee is pregnant makes Dikar resolve that he "shall lead the Bunch down from the mountain to an America retaken for freedom and liberty" (p. 36). In the issue of September 9—on the stands as Hitler invaded Poland—the reader learns that Dikar and the Bunch are children who were evacuated from New York before it was destroyed. They pledge themselves to resist the Asafrics led by Viceroy Yamamoto, but the U.S. remains enslaved.

In retrospect, given the emotional impact and racism of the popular fiction, whether novel or magazine, one realizes that by the 1930s, at the latest, there never was a question *if* America would fight the Asiatics—Japan. The only question was *when*. For there can be little doubt that from Chesney's *The Battle of Dorking* to Arthur Leo Zagat's conquered America, the future-war motif gave voice to some of the deepest anxieties and hatreds of the Western imagination. (In a sense it became a self-fulfilling prophecy.) Had it ceased with World War II, one might dismiss it as an interesting though unpleasant insight into the high period of Western imperialism, but the future war remains a part of popular literature, whether it manifests itself in the endless novels dealing with international crises and espionage or in the speculations of General Sir John Hackett and his NATO collaborators in 1978 regarding *The Third World War: August 1985*.

NOTES

1. William Ward Crane, "Fanciful Predictions of War," *Lippincott's Magazine*, 62 (November 1898), 716–717.
2. I. F. Clarke, "The Break-in Phase: The Battle of Dorking Episode," *Voices Prophesying War* (New York and London: Oxford University Press, 1966), pp. 30–63.
3. Clarke, p. 34.
4. Mrs. Gerald Porter, *Annals of a Publishing House: William Blackwood and His Sons* (Edinburgh and London: William Blackwood and Sons, 1898), 3, *John Blackwood*, 298–303.
5. Clarke, pp. 68–69.
6. Clarke, p. 127; see Thomas D. Clareson, "The Emergence of Science Fiction: The Beginnings to the 1920s," in Neil Barron, ed., *Anatomy of Wonder* (New York and London: R. R. Bowker Company, 1981), p. 15.
7. Clarke mentions this neglect, p. 154. As late as the autumn of 1981, I failed to find any reprint in London; *The Swoop* was conspicuously absent from the many Wodehouse paperbacks then available. Richard Bleiler of the Ohio State University Library called my attention to *The Swoop: and Other Stories by P. G. Wodehouse*, ed. David A. Jasen (New York: The Seabury Press, 1979). That appears to be a small edition which may have been remaindered. I know of no paperback edition in the U.S. or Canada.
8. When the President finally declares war, thereby becoming Britain's ally, Tracy intrudes a passage which remains infuriating in its rhetoric and condescension:

The whole country was inflamed with fire of martial ardour.

For it was what the American in his heart yearned for. To stand among the nations, no longer youthful, immature, undeveloped; no longer to be patronised as a land of promise; no longer the excitable irresponsible country which older civilisations indulged with a smile; but as a strong man, equal in power, in wealth, in wisdom, to the oldest of the great peoples of the earth—this was what he had so ardently desired.

And now he had stepped forth, free from boyhood's privileges, a giant into the arena, and was

standing side by side with England—the ally and defender of the greatest country that the world
had known.

At last would commence the real national history—the history of a people made one by suffering
and by activity. For America could not look back upon her first melancholy war with England, still
less on the ghastly struggle amongst her own sons, and regard these as the prouder epochs of her
life. Civil war cannot make a people great. America longed for some such splendid struggle as this
that was now before her, a struggle against all Europe, as the starting point of a new and glorious
period in her history, as something which would give her character and solidity, and establish her
place firmly amongst the nations. (p. 212)

9. Clarke, p. 44.

10. *The Partisan Leader* makes up an intriguing two volumes. The first volume indicates that it was printed in Washington by John Caxton in 1856; apparently Rudd &
Carleton reprinted it in New York in 1861. A note suggests that it was written in 1835
and 1836 "as a tale of the future" and was published in 1836 by Duff Gordon "but
afterwards suppressed." An "Explanatory Introduction" emphasizes that secessionists
infiltrated the Democratic Party and were responsible for almost everything from the
annexation of Texas to Buchanan's Cabinet. The main storyline traces the friendship of
President Van Buren with the father of the Trevor family. It makes passing reference to
the Yankees' setting the slaves free (p. 14).

11. Clarke, *The Pattern of Expectation 1644–2001* (New York: Basic Books, Inc.,
1979), p. 107.

12. Clarke, *Voices Prophesying War*, pp. 120–121.

13. More than twenty years later, Train recalled the collaboration in which Professor
Wood of Johns Hopkins provided "scientific data in great wads" after they had agreed
on the central action of the novel. In the too brief reminiscence, he suggests that they
call PAX's ship *"The Flying Doughnut"* and says that *Cosmopolitan* engaged them to
write a "follow-up" serial. He gave his greatest emphasis to their prediction of the great
German cannon, "Big Bertha," citing an article from a New York paper which "printed
verbatim my description of the first discharge of our apocryphal cannon towards Paris."
Arthur Train, "The Man Who Rocked the Earth," *My Day in Court* (New York and
London: Charles Scribner's Sons, 1939), pp. 329–333.

14. Hancock focuses upon Dick Prescott, a graduate of West Point. At the beginning
of the series he is a lieutenant; at its end, a general. Hancock makes mention of Dave
Darrin and Dan Dalzell, whom he took through Annapolis, but he keeps them offstage
during the invasion, implying early that they have been killed aboard a submarine. Unlike
his predecessors and contemporaries, Hancock gave very little attention to naval affairs
after the initial invasion near Boston.

15. Milo Hastings' *City of Endless Night* (1920), originally serialized in *True Story*
as *Children of "Kultur"* (1919), uses a conflict between the United World and the remnant
of Germany surviving in a subterranean city beneath Berlin in the year 2151 as a point
of departure. The reflective first-person narrator, later identified as the American scientist
Lyman de Forrest of Chicago, gains access to the city-fortress by accident and is able to
bring about its downfall. Because the novel centers on the efforts of the protagonist and
because it serves as a means of denouncing German "kultur," *City of Endless Night*
remains a fine example of an early dystopia and is only peripherally related to the future-
war motif. By the time John Palmer and Hilary Saunders collaborated on *The Seven
Sleepers* (1925), British agents in the here-and-now prevent the chemist, Professor

Kreutzemark, from organizing German capitalists and military men in a conspiracy to start a new war to regain the glory lost in 1918.

16. To appreciate the extravagance of Shiel, see such a discussion as Brian Stableford, "The Yellow Danger," in Magill, *Survey of Science Fiction Literature*, V:2525–2528.

17. John Gardner, "Afterword," in Floyd Gibbons, *The Red Napoleon* (Carbondale and Edwardsville, Ill.: Southern Illinois University Press, 1976), p. 484. Gardner remarks, "But his [Karakhan's] vision—the vision of Floyd Gibbons, in fact—is emphatically presented as that of a madman, a misfit, a creature who has every reason to hate not only whites but all benighted, narrow-minded humanity. All the good characters spew out without thinking a view antithetical to Karakhan's." One questions this reading of Gibbons, who repeatedly emphasizes that Karakhan's views evoke the hatred of the white race.

18. Brian Stableford, "Science Fiction Between Wars: 1918–1938," in Neil Barron, *Anatomy of Wonder*, pp. 88–124. Stableford quite correctly speaks of the pessimism resulting from World War I, but in his only notice of Gibbons, an annotation to *The Red Napoleon* (p. 108), he dismisses the journalist as one claiming "to have been motivated by a horror of war, but [who] takes the usual fascinated interest in planning the campaigns of the would-be conqueror." Gibbons follows established conventions in describing the battles; his keenest interest seems to lie with the politics.

4

"The Machine-Made Millennium"[1]

On the one hand, as shown, medical men and so-called psychologists conducted experiments which revealed them to be students of the occult, while on the other hand, certain geniuses developed weapons which assured their nations of victory over all adversaries. Everett Carter has complicated any easy account of the emergence of the scientist as hero by showing that the background of industrial expansion in the 1860s produced an "atmosphere of material expansion [in which] the inventor became the new hero. . . . The admiration for the scientist became a commonplace of realistic fiction. As the clear-eyed observer, he was portrayed as seeing through sentimentality to the truth."[2] In stressing the importance "of the empirical attitude toward truth and morality," Carter cites characters ranging from DeForest's Dr. Ravenel to Ruth Bolton in *The Gilded Age*. Early in the 1960s, John B. Hamilton focused upon the importance of medical doctors in nineteenth-century American fiction as he emphasized the point that one must distinguish between science fiction and science in fiction.[3]

Mary Shelley's *Frankenstein* should be the starting point. Stripped of his Faustian stature, however, Victor Frankenstein is nothing more than a "mad" scientist, the prototype of those demented, usually one-dimensional villains whose thirst for knowledge and lack of humanity threaten to destroy mankind. Ironically, he and his nameless monster have become the incarnation of science as a danger to civilization. The problem becomes apparent in the early fiction. In Charles Brockden Brown's *Wieland*, Thomas Cambridge tells Clara of analogous cases which he encountered while a British military surgeon in Germany, but Brown must intrude footnotes to give the scientific explanation of Theodore's psychotic state. Uniformly, recent critics have dismissed Edgar Allan Poe's stories from the field of science fiction.[4] When his protagonists are not madmen or travelers they are most often mesmerists, as is "P——" in "The Facts in the Case of M. Valdemar." Von Kempelen's discovery smacks of alchemy, for he learns how to transform brass into gold. What gives some of Poe's fiction the aura of sf is the matter-of-fact, realistic tone with which his narrators describe circumstantial detail, although on close analysis that detail is often little more than jargon even at the time it was written. One should recall, for example, that until late in the century the new psychology did not develop a terminology adequate to discuss the phenomena with which it was concerned; similarly—and let the future-war motif provide the initial examples—the inventors often dismissed the technical explanations of their "gadgets" as either unnecessary or so complicated that the readers would not understand. (One cannot resist looking ahead to note that the block exposition of the "nuts and bolts" of sf hardware became a characteristic of the fiction in the early Gernsback magazines, a quality which subsequent writers and critics have deplored.)

Mesmerism and alchemy infest the lesser stories of Poe's successor Fitz-James O'Brien, who sought to base his terror on the rational and scientific instead of the traditional supernatural. Despite its sentiment and rhetoric, his "A Terrible Night" (1856) anticipates the direction of Ambrose Bierce. When the first-person narrator and his close friend spend the night in a lonely cabin in the forest, they are terrified by their half-breed host. In their fear they resolve to take turns remaining awake. Believing that the half-breed is about to knife him, the narrator shoots him. Actually asleep and dreaming, he has shot his best friend. Medical doctors explain that he suffered from "somnolentia"—sleep drunkenness. In "The Pot of Tulips" (1855), an orthodox ghost story, O'Brien concludes with the assertion that he could, if he chose, "overwhelm" the reader with "a scientific theory . . . reconciling ghosts and natural phenomena." Of course, he refrains from doing so.

One of O'Brien's most widely known stories—especially acclaimed by Sam Moskowitz because of its apparent influence on A. Merritt[5]—"The Wondersmith" (1859) deals with the successful efforts of Herr Hippe and his gypsy colleagues to infuse wooden mannikins with the captive souls of "demon" children; sold as toys during the Christmas season, the mannikins will come alive on New Year's Eve and kill the children into whose homes they have been introduced. Violently anti-Christian, the gypsies (a euphemism in this story for Jews) hope to gain revenge against those who have stolen the world from older gods. With swords coated by a poison obtained from the Macoushu Indians of Guiana, the mannikins revive prematurely and kill Herr Hippe and his companions. As suggested elsewhere, "there is no suspense nor surprise; there is no adequate characterization."[6] In modern fantasy, the use of satanic mannikins, whatever their relationship to the medieval Golem, appears to have begun with O'Brien.

Although in "How I Overcame My Gravity" (1864) the narrator invents a globe in which he may fly, his explanation of how a whirling copper sphere overcomes its gravity comes out as jargon. Catapulted into free flight, the globe disintegrates. At that point, O'Brien undercut his entire effort by having the narrator wake from his dream. Repeatedly, one infers that the early writers relied upon the dream vision, even in so slight a story as this, either to get themselves out of some narrative corner or to avoid rational, scientific explanation.

In contrast, three of O'Brien's tales add significantly to the storylines which shaped subsequent science fiction. The narrator of "The Lost Room" (1858) returns to find that revelers have taken over his usually dark and gloomy room. They invite him to join them; when he refuses, they make him cast dice for its possession. He loses, and they eject him. Although he briefly glimpses his old room, he finds himself beating against a blank wall. His room has vanished, as though it had never existed. For once, a mid-nineteenth–century author did not imply that his narrator is mad. Thus, "The Lost Room" introduces the concept of multiple levels of space and, perhaps, time.

The same economy and unity govern "What Was It? A Mystery" (1859). This late story also exemplifies effectively that strength which Frederick Lewis Pattee found in O'Brien's work when he said that O'Brien added "a sense of actuality to Poe's unlocalized romance" by setting his fiction in a familiar New York City.[7] The narrator explains that his landlady and her boarders want to move into a house on 26th Street between Seventh and Eighth Avenues simply because they believe that it is haunted. After a "month of psychological excitement" passes uneventfully, the narrator and Dr. Hammond—who smoke opium together—speculate about the nature of "the greatest element of terror." That night—the narrator adds a touch of realism by specifying that it is July 10—in the darkness of his room, "something" falls onto the narrator while he is in bed and attempts to strangle him. Overcoming it, he finds in the light that it is invisible. His feeling that he has lost his sight provides the greatest terror. He grows angry at his companions' reactions; they laugh—until they sense the creature's physical being. He and Hammond have it chloroformed so that they can have a plaster cast made of what proves to be a misshapen dwarf with a grotesque face. A fortnight later it starves to death. The idea that the plaster cast has been placed in a museum on 10th Street adds a significant detail establishing the reality of the event. (The editors of *The Atlantic Monthly* heightened this effect by adding a note which suggested that there would be a special exhibition.) Through his handling of point of view, the realistic detail, and his restraint, O'Brien created a story which remains essentially timeless. His story leads to Maupassant's "Le Horla" and Bierce's "The Damned Thing," among those which were to deal with nonhuman, invisible species.

"The Diamond Lens" (1858) has been generally regarded as O'Brien's finest story; essentially, however, it looks backward to Poe and the Gothic, although opening a new world to modern fantasy. Very carefully, the first-person narrator reveals his obsession with the science of microscopy and his dream of obtaining a perfect lens. At a séance, the spirit of Leeuwenhoek advises him to obtain a 140–carat diamond and subject it to electromagnetic currents which will realign its atoms. To secure the diamond he kills. Through the perfect lens, in a world within a drop of water, he sees and loves a beautiful woman—Animula. Seeking to escape his enchantment with her, he flees his room to attend the performance of a famous dancer. Compared to Animula, he finds her gross. Returning to his room, he discovers that his beloved Animula is dying because the drop of water in which her world exists has evaporated. A final episode suggests that he is mad and thus, as in Irving's "Adventure of the German Student," questions the credibility of the entire episode. "The Diamond Lens" may well be the finest of these ambiguous, transitional tales. Certainly it led such a later writer as Ray Cummings to the subatomic universe of the golden atom.

The concept of a perfect lens also underlies William H. Rhodes's "Phases in the Life of John Pollexfen," collected in the posthumous volume *Caxton's Book* (1876), probably the single most important book in terms of an emerging American science fiction published by that date.[8] The photographer-chemist, Pollexfen, seeks the perfect camera lens so that he can achieve color photography. To do so, he buys the living eye of the impoverished Lucile Marmont, who readily surrenders her eye for the advancement of science. Although the first-person narrator several times refers to Pollexfen as a monster, an echo of Hawthorne sounds through the climax of the story when Lucile's betrothed, Charles Courtland, voluntarily gives up one of his eyes so that neither of the lovers will be a perfect beauty or come to regret the imperfection (mutilation) in the other.

In "The Telescopic Eye," nine-year-old Johnny Palmer has eyes which permit him to see and describe the lunar surface. Once an oculist has examined Johnny with an "opthalmoscope" and pronounced his eyes flat and elongated instead of round, Rhodes uses Johnny's vision as a point of departure to satirize literary portrayals of lunarian societies. The boy does need a telescope in order to describe Mars and its inhabitants. "The Earth's Hot Center" pretends to be the correspondence of the United States Consul at Bruges to Hamilton Fish, Secretary of State, reporting a conscious experiment by a combination of European governments to drill to the center of the earth. The story is heavy with geological data; however, the venture ends in a volcanic eruption in the North Sea bed which threatens to "devastate" Belgium, Holland, and Denmark, to say nothing of connecting the British Isles with the European mainland. The catastrophe is downplayed, however, by the formality of the report. Again, Rhodes's purpose seems primarily satirical.

In an introductory memorial tribute to Rhodes, the editor of the volume says of the California lawyer and judge who wrote only occasionally:

His fondness for weaving the problems of science with fiction, which became afterwards so marked a characteristic of his literary efforts, attracted the especial attention of his professors [at Harvard Law School, 1844–1846]; and had Mr. Rhodes devoted himself to this then novel department of letters, he would have become, no doubt, greatly distinguished as a writer; and the great master of science fiction, Jules Verne, would have found the field of his efforts already sown and reaped by the young Southern student. [Rhodes was born in North Carolina and lived in Texas before settling in California.] (pp. 6–7)

The most important story in the collection, "The Case of Summerfield"— first published in the Sacramento *Union* for May 13, 1871, and then issued separately in both 1907 and 1918—established the American prototype of those mad scientists who, most often through greed or a desire for power, threaten to destroy civilization.[9] This type of story became a significant element in the development of the catastrophe motif as a dominant, popular form of science fiction, because it freed the motif from a reliance on purely natural disasters.

In Rhodes's story, the chemist, Gregory Summerfield, has developed a "pill of [his] own composition and discovery" (p. 25) which accelerates the fiery effect of mixing potassium and water by liberating oxygen gas. He demonstrates the effectiveness of his secret by dropping the pill into a tenth of the water which the narrator had originally drawn into a washbasin: " . . . a sharp explosion took place, and in a second of time the water was blazing in a red, lurid column half way to the ceiling" (p. 27). Unless the citizens of San Francisco pay him $1 million, he threatens to ignite the oceans of the world, thereby destroying the earth. Convinced of Summerfield's power, the first-person narrator, Leonidas Parker, communicates with a group of wealthy citizens. When they cannot raise the ransom and persuade Summerfield to allow them to attempt to gain the rest of the money in New York, Parker kills the chemist. Rhodes structures the tale in such a way as to remove all mystery from it. The reader is told that these papers were found among the effects of the late Leonidas Parker; there follows a newspaper report of the disappearance of Summerfield and the discharge without trial of Parker. The body of the narrative focuses upon the dramatic scene in which Summerfield demonstrates his ability and makes his demand; Parker then summarizes the attempt to raise the money and simply refers to his deed while arguing justifiable homicide. Rhodes attempted to make the threat more feasible by referring to a variety of novas which mankind had observed, one as recent as 1866.

Early in the narrative, Summerfield echoes Victor Frankenstein, but simply to say this does not take into account the shift in narrative tone from that of the guilt-ridden voice of Dr. Frankenstein. The change in narrative tone occurs after Summerfield declares, "I feel like a God! and I recognize my fellow-men but as pygmies that I spurn beneath my feet" (p. 22). Summerfield evokes none of the pity that one feels for Faustus and Frankenstein. When one speaks of the modern treatment of the Frankenstein theme, one must recall that, unlike Mary Shelley, the authors did not want their readers to feel pity for the villains. The one exception to this generalization occurs in those few novels like *The Man Who Rocked the Earth*, in which the figure of PAX acts out of a love of humanity and a hatred of tyranny and in his madness quite probably does not realize the consequences of his actions. Yet even here the author does not tolerate the scientist's acting like God. PAX must die, killing himself in his own experiments.

Summerfield's family tree flourished, although the majority of his descendants were so wizened and stereotyped that they could be dismissed in a catalog. Among his more distinguished British cousins are Wells's Dr. Moreau and Griffin, the invisible man. Especially in the case of Moreau, however, one soon learns that the scientist is a means to an end instead of the end itself. As has been shown, *The Island of Dr. Moreau* (1896) serves as a vehicle for Wells's satire.[10] On the one hand, Edward Pendrick learns that the human effort to codify behavior ("The Law") is essentially ridiculous because it is impossible to reconcile Darwinian theory and an orthodox concept of God and morality. On the other hand, after Moreau's death, he comes to understand the inadequacies of the concept of the natural man. One infers that back in England his seeing the beast in the face of every human whom he encounters unnerves him, as it may have unnerved Wells himself. Moreau, of course, feels no guilt or remorse in his experiments; his lack of compassion makes his world much more brutal than that of Victor Frankenstein. In *The Invisible Man* (1897), the scientist Kemp, who initially sympathizes with Griffin, ends up by calling him "mad . . . inhuman," for his reign of terror appears to be Wells's statement that the miraculous developments of science can be misused by an evil genius.

In American fiction, the early novel of Garrett P. Serviss, *The Moon Metal* (1900), is notable primarily for the ambivalence which Serviss displays in his treatment of the mysterious Dr. Max Syx. The discovery near the South Pole of gold deposits so rich that gold becomes as common as iron precipitates a worldwide financial crisis. Syx appears before an international council of bankers, offering to replace gold with a new metal, artemisium, which can be obtained only from his mine in the Grand Tetons near Jackson Hole. He asks for military protection for his mine, and he demands a payment of 1 percent "on the circulating medium," as well as an agreed upon amount to be used in the arts. While this arrangement will maintain the essential status quo among financial powers, it also makes him the richest and most powerful man in the world.

Had a young engineer, Andrew Hall, not been suspicious of Syx and investigated the mine, the arrangement might have lasted indefinitely. Hall discovers that through the use of "a form of electric action more subtle in its effects" than anything yet known (pp. 130–131), Syx draws his metal in a "shaft of flying atoms" from the moon (p. 138). Once Syx's monopoly has been broken, he disappears from the United States and teaches scientists in various parts of the world the secret of his process. Thus, hundreds of rays devastate the moon, while the metallic dust almost reduces the earth to ruins. The governments of the world finally unite their efforts so that the production of artemisium is rigidly controlled.

Recalling his last encounter with Dr. Syx in the Tetons, Hall admits that without understanding why he did so, he called Syx a "black Satan" (p. 162), yet he had never "entertained any enmity" toward Syx, although he "always regarded him as a heartless person, who had purposely led thousands to their ruin for his selfish gain" (pp. 162–163). An odd touch ends the account, for Hall imagines that Syx's face somehow becomes that of the man in the moon. One must infer that Serviss wanted to tell a story that celebrated the mysteries of science and that he used Syx to present a puzzle that must be solved, for no real harm comes to anyone. His basic attitude is perhaps best expressed in the opening passage of the chapter entitled "Better Than Alchemy"; before Hall is allowed to reveal Syx's secret, the narrator explains:

I come now to a part of my narrative which would have been deemed altogether incredible in those closing years of the nineteenth century that witnessed the first steps toward the solution of the deepest mysteries of the ether. (p. 124)

Throughout his other novels, Serviss celebrated both the scientist and science, so that in this early work one can assume that a young writer simply made use of established conventions but could not portray Syx as a true villain.

Serviss's attitude toward science stands in sharp contrast to Raymond MacDonald's in *The Mad Scientist; A Tale of the Future* (1908). One could dismiss MacDonald's novel as an extravagant parody were it not for the sense of despair at the heart of its outcry against the newest discoveries of science. The narrative opens with an emotional attack upon Wall Street and contains a brief account of warfare between capital and labor which reaches a climax when the "entire [American] army of 75,000 was simply wiped out" and the President was assassinated (pp. 150–151). So stunned are the people "that no one thought of continuing the struggle" (p. 160). Such slaughter is instigated by Maxim Folk, described at one point as "this modern Satan" (p. 158). For no ideological reason, he supplies the disgruntled delegates of a national convention of the United Laborers of America with weapons (called "electro-death") when they make "treasonous utterances" against the government and march on Washington. Thus fifty groups of ten men each are able to kill the President and annihilate the army.

When MacDonald first introduced Folk early in the narrative, he made certain that no one could doubt his villainy:

Maxim Folk was first and foremost an iconoclast, a disrupter, a student of Nature, yet not to take delight in observing her wonders, her marvels, her beauties, but to turn to his own account, if possible, her conditions, her laws.

His natural leanings were not to turn his powers to the enlightenment of men; neither did he delight in the grandeur and sublimity of Nature. He sought knowledge rather to destroy than to build; he delighted in public upheavals. He wanted to fight Nature with her own forces, and to witness with his own eyes the destruction done. Pandemonium was to him a thing of pleasure, an ideal amusement. A devils' council might have taken pleasure in his suggestions. (p. 27)

As though this were not sufficient, he carefully explains that "it was advanced knowledge of the powers of radium and electricity which enabled Maxim Folk ... to perform the scientific wonders with which he alternately deluded, excited, frightened or destroyed the fellow beings with whom he came into contact" (p. 191). Somewhat earlier, Professor Kaye and Detective Egan, who pursue Folk relentlessly throughout the novel, watch as he deliberately sets a lake on fire; before simply driving away from them in his automobile, he promises that one day he will "touch off the Atlantic Ocean and light the whole damned orb! That will be a conflagration worth witnessing" (p. 72).

Although he is captured and brought to trial, he escapes and seizes the battleship *Behemoth*, levitates it, and after a year returns to attack New York City and ships of the U.S. Navy with a form of energy (extreme downward pressure) emanating from an electric gyroscope. Only when the eclipse of the moon cuts off light rays from Folk's ship, now high in the stratosphere, does the *Behemoth* plunge to earth, a flaming meteor, thus freeing the world "forever from the frightful plagues and murderous amusements of the mad scientist" (p. 242).

Such excesses should be laughed at, but from his tone throughout one recognizes at once that MacDonald takes them seriously. Abruptly, halfway through the narrative in a chapter entitled "Folk's Scientific Magic," MacDonald stops the action to comment upon Madame Curie's discovery of radium; one senses the depth of his feeling as he laments that the "discovery of radium has wholly upset previously existing theories as to matter originating in some seventy elements" (p. 189). He refers to alchemy as he writes of transmutation of elements and the interchangeability of heat, light, and electricity. But the intensity of his reaction does not become wholly apparent until at the trial of Folk the prosecuting attorney lashes out not at Folk but at science itself:

" . . . science has wrested from Nature a new manifestation of remarkable power—a power mischievous in its very inception and diabolic in its effects. In consequence, man to-day is burying his hopes, his ambitions, his love of home and country. He sees naught but an existence of utter chaos and desolation, a desolation maddening in its conception, as his fellows are daily slaughtered without reason, and apparently without cause. It is by the irony of fate that we with our puerile laws are to-day trying this prisoner on the mere charge of murder. The prisoner, though guilty, is but an accomplice, and Science is the principal. Were it possible, I would ask that Science be indicted, for hers is the sin. . . .

" . . . Already man has delved far into the mystic realms until Nature, jealous of her secrets, has disclosed an agency that may assist evil intentions to bring an end to all things human. It is now for us to take a determined stand, and forbid forever this too deep prying into Nature's laws. Too much knowledge is proven to be a dangerous thing. Let us do our part as wise citizens to force into oblivion the spread of such murderous science as that put forth by Maxim Folk." (pp. 211, 217)

What one could otherwise discount as a poorly executed mishmash of sensational action and stereotyped characters must be recognized as one of the earliest voices, perhaps the first, condemning the discoveries which have subsequently led to the threat of nuclear holocaust; what MacDonald's prosecutor says may now read like shopworn clichés, but it anticipates many of the charges heard in America since World War II. Various critics and authors have spoken of science fiction as a literature of ideas, as though that were the only criterion which counted; here, then, however absurdly framed in the narrative itself, appears one of the ideas which has been increasingly verbalized for the past generation.

A familiarity with these new theories and the control of all forms of energy provides the point of departure for the storyline of Stewart Edward White's *The Sign at Six* (1912). Its protagonist, Percy Darrow, had figured in the earlier novel, *The Mystery* (1907), but in this sequel he is given center stage, for he must track down the madman who threatens to destroy New York. The unknown genius makes himself known through a series of notes to the capitalist McCarthy, who "quite simply, at that time owned New York" (p. 4); he demands that McCarthy surrender himself for judgment and punishment. As proof that he has the power to destroy McCarthy, he promises to send a sign at six o'clock. The first sign is the complete blacking out of the Atlas building, where McCarthy has his offices. Even the flashlights brought into the building by repairmen fail, although they work again as soon as they are taken outside. The second sign, occurring the next day, is a complete silence, centering again around the Atlas building but spreading throughout the city. The third sign is the failure of light throughout the city.

When the first phenomenon occurs, one of the newspaper editors instructs his reporter:

"And if the scientific men haven't any other notions, ask 'em if it's anything to do with the earth passing through the tail of [Halley's] comet." (p. 26)

After the second phenomenon occurs, Darrow decides to aid the police; it is he who first sees the common property of the phenomena:

The logical mind would therefore examine these things to see what they have in common. The answer simply jumps at you: *Vibration*. Electricity and light are vibrations in ether; sound is vibration in air or some solid. Therefore, whatever could absolutely stop vibration could necessarily stop electricity, light, and sound. (p. 121)

As the warnings continue they take on a definite religiosity, naming the sender variously as "the Lord's anointed" and the "right hand of God" and threatening total destruction. Darrow worries that the unknown scientist has powers which he has not yet revealed:

"Suppose he can go one step further and, even for the barest fraction of time, should be able to stop the vibrations of heat."

"That is annihilation."

"On a wholesale scale. It means the death of every living thing from the smallest insect to the largest animal, from the microbe to the very lichens on the stones of Trinity." (pp. 154–155)

All of this information Darrow conveys to a rival scientist who has been called in by the authorities. Because the two men hate each other as a result of the rival's theft of some of a colleague's secrets, a kind of contest develops between them—a deadly contest, for the last warning threatens total destruction. While his rival searches for a wireless station outside the city, Darrow finds the crazed scientist in the office next to McCarthy's. (He has deduced this location from two facts: the weakness of the signals and the immediate knowledge that the sender has of McCarthy's actions.) As they struggle at the controls of the apparatus, the madman dies, lapsing into an imbecility as something in his brain snaps. Finding his manuscript, Darrow says of his secret:

"It's the biggest thing—and the simplest—the world has ever known in physics . . . but it's got to go. . . . The man has perfected a combined system of special tuning and definite electrical energy . . . by which through an ordinary wireless sender he can send forth into the ether what might be called deadening or nullifying waves." (pp. 243–244)

In his hands he holds four pages that contain the formulas which would give their possessor untold power. Without hesitation Darrow burns the manuscript; he explains his action:

"This is probably the greatest achievement of the scientific intellect; but it must go. It would give to men an unchecked power that belongs only to the gods." (pp. 245–246)

White's *The Sign at Six* remains noteworthy for a number of reasons. First, except for the final encounter, it keeps the mad scientist offstage so that the narrative emphasis can remain focused upon Percy Darrow. Through this technique it emphasizes the solution of a puzzle. (On both counts it brings to mind Hollis Godfrey's *The Man Who Ended War*.) Equally important, however, is its final theme: there are areas of knowledge into which man should not trespass.

Perhaps these variations in the treatment of the "mad" scientist are sufficient to indicate the American treatment of the theme. After World War I, the activities of the evil geniuses proliferated in the works of such a writer as Austin J. Small. In *The Death Maker* (1926), Jann Vorst breeds bacteria and develops hybrids whose poison he intends to insert into the food supplies of the world, thereby destroying mankind. In *The Avenging Ray* (1930), Carlo Damian invents a "Degravitisor" by which he can disrupt the cohesion of molecules; he believes that he has been chosen by God to punish a wicked world. One of the most memorable is Edmund Snell's *Kontrol* (1928), in which the genius, Dr. Guriev, attempts to transplant first-class brains into first-class bodies. Although his creatures are described as being dead, they begin to build a great technological center on an isolated island which is destroyed by a volcano. The number of "mad" scientists is legion, even playing a dominant part in such pulp magazines as *G–8 and His Battle Aces*, where Herr Doktor Kreuger presented monthly terrors which threatened the Allied forces on the Western Front. Such figures survived in the fiction because they provided a mixture of horror and science in a puzzle to be solved by a heroic protagonist.

Among the many critics and enthusiasts who have praised Jules Verne, none has been more eloquent than E. F. Bleiler:

Historically there can be no question that Verne is by far the most important personality in the science fiction form before Wells. Indeed, although Wells was a superior artist . . . Verne's overall influence has been greater. . . .

Entire chains of development are based on Verne's work. The invention story of the American dime novel was a lurid, low-grade exploitation of what Verne worked out with great thought.[11]

This is a superlative assessment of Verne's position, particularly since it comes from the editor of the two-volume anthology *The Frank Reade Library* (1979); in his introduction to that collection of thirty-five titles from the Frank Reade, Jr., series—which he refers to as "the utmost in science-fiction adventure" during the 1880s and 1890s, Bleiler emphasizes that "the ultimate genesis of the Frank Reade stories was Jules Verne."[12] Such a verdict creates two problems.

Usually writing under the pseudonym "Noname," Luis P. Senarens chronicled the adventures of the teenager whose "speculative inventions" provide an intriguing index to the accomplishments and imaginings of American technology during the last decades of the nineteenth century. Undoubtedly, his stories provided formulaic patterns for other writers, as well as establishing patterns of expectations among their readers. (Amusingly, what seems to be a virtually complete run of Frank's exploits sits on the shelves beside the novels of Charles Reade in the Bodelian Library.) It is general knowledge, however, that the idea did not originate with Senarens. At least the first three or four numbers were written by Harry Enton. The potential of such a series came from the publisher Frank Tousey when he saw a reprint of Edward S. Ellis's *The Huge Hunter; or The Steam Man of the Prairies*, which Bleiler calls "the first of all science-fiction dime novels."[13] So far as Jules Verne is concerned, this is the crux of the first problem, for Bleiler suggests that he saw Ellis's novel "reissued as *Beadle's Pocket Novel #40*, January 14, 1876," a date some years after the translation and publication of Verne's works in America.

Although Sam Moskowitz salutes Verne for making "science fiction a popular form of entertainment in most of the Western nations of the world," he points out that Ellis's *The Steam Man of the Prairies* first appeared as #45 in Irwin Beadle's *American Novels* in August 1868, a year before any of Verne's works were published in the U.S. In an outburst of enthusiasm, he declares that the "invention story" had been developed by Ellis, Enton, and Senarens "before the translations of Jules Verne. They did not need Jules Verne."[14] The problem is further complicated by the fact that *The House of Beadle and Adams* lists the first publication of Ellis's prototypical work as #45 of *Irwin's American Novels* in August 1868; subsequent printings occurred in the *Half Dime* series on October 3, 1882, and in the *Dime* series on January 27, 1885.[15] No mention is made of an 1876 imprint. The question becomes whether Ellis shaped his tale from essentially American materials and whether Verne subsequently influenced Senarens.

The more serious problem arises when one examines the storylines of Verne's novels, as Mark Hillegas did in the 1960s.[16] One comes away with the impression that he was far more interested in science (especially geography and geology) and inventions (forms of transportation) than he was in the scientist. In the sixty-five volumes of the Verne canon, the great majority of protagonists must be described as explorers or travelers. When a scientist does intrude himself, he usually serves as Verne's textbook (Bleiler's "father figure"). The members of the Baltimore Gun Club can hardly be classified as scientists, while both Captain Nemo and Robur, according to Bleiler, "have been ancestors of literally scores of dynamic outlaws with superior technology, who prey on the rest of the world" (p. 581). One can argue that the "purest" scientists appear in *The Five Hundred Millions of the Begum* (1879). Yet there can be no doubt of Verne's worldwide influence. In writing of Cleveland, William Ganson Rose reports that "Jules Verne's fantastic best seller, *Twenty Thousand Leagues Under the Sea*, appeared in 1870, and moved quickly from stores to many family bookcases at $3.50 a copy. The Alger stories reached the height of their popularity" (p. 367).

Nor can one doubt the popularity of Lu Senarens' Frank Reade, Jr., stories. Like Verne's work, Senarens' tales reflected actual speculations and experiments already in progress, as well as the fascination with geography. When one examines the thirty-five titles collected in *The Frank Reade Library*, a number of characteristics become obvious. As though they provide a variant on the dime novel concerned with the Western frontier, some ten of the first twenty stories have their settings in the West. Increasingly, they move to the international scene, and increasingly they concern themselves with submarines and, especially, airships. Similarly, the source of power shifts from steam to electricity. Except for the descriptions of the machines—especially in the opening chapters and during encounters with admiring country folk—there is little or no scientific data in the narratives. The storylines are dominated by miscellaneous adventures during a variety of journeys. In that the inventions are used for moral good—which, for Senarens, included personal gain—one can say they read like a blending of Verne and Alger. In "Frank Reade, Jr.'s Great Electric Tricycle, And What He Did for Charity" (dated October 5, 1892), Frank wagers $2,000 against the bicyclists, Spreckels and Harrison, that he can beat them by at least forty-eight hours in a race from Chicago to New Orleans. After various incidents on the road, most of which involve robbers or persons attempting to keep him from winning, he triumphs and gives his winnings to an orphanage in Chicago. One may say that various means of transportation set apart his stories, just as athletics set apart the exploits of Frank Merriwell.

But Frank Reade, Jr.—actually his father, when one considers Harry Enton's earlier contributions—became the prototype of a legion of boy inventors and boy explorers. Weldon Cobb made use of Frank Edison (Can there be a more obvious double indebtedness to history and fiction?), whom he described in *A Trip to Mars* (1901) as "the nephew of a noted scientific savant" (p. 8). Within a decade, Tom Swift made his initial appearance.

Symbolically, the name of Tom Swift has come to represent all of those teenage geniuses whose activities shaped so many boys' adventure series books at the turn of the century. Yet neither the relatively late date of publication (the first five titles in 1910) nor the literary quality of the novels turned out under the house name Victor Appleton adequately explains why Tom Swift remains the best remembered of the youthful inventors. The survival of Grosset & Dunlap into the 1940s as a publisher of adventure stories aimed at a juvenile audience seems the decisive factor. Consequently, one is tempted to bypass the young savant from Shopton to examine a less well known series in order to discover the patterns recurring in such fiction.

In *The Boy Inventors' Flying Ship* (1913), Richard Bonner records the further activities of Tom Jessop and Jack Chadwick, who live on the estate of Jack's father, himself an inventor, near the small town of Nestorville somewhere in the vicinity of Boston. Bonner reminds his readers that in their first outing, *The Boy Inventors' Wireless Triumph* (1912), Tom and Jack had "many stirring adventures" in Yucatan and helped to find Tom's long-missing father, "an explorer and naturalist." The two boys then contributed to the development of *The Boy Inventors' Vanishing Gun* (1912) "in spite of the machinations of a gang of rascals."[17] Sometime during this interval the boys had designed the *Flying Road Racer*, which navigated both the road and the sky. In *The Boy Inventors and the Diving Torpedo Boat* (1912), they had converted the *Racer* into a submarine, *Peacemaker*, which "proved of material aid to some Americans beleaguered by blood-thirsty negro revolutionists in Cuba." In addition, "in this book both the boys increased their mechanical ability and learned self-reliance and manliness in many a hard test of those sterling qualities" (p. 16). Now, for some weeks during time "exclusive of their studies in the Technical College that both attended in Boston," they had transformed the *Racer* into the *Wondership* by adding pontoons to the cylindrical body, introducing more powerful engines, and building metal doors which could be closed to prevent high seas from capsizing the ship by making it a water-tight cylinder. They had already tested it in flight, its green and red lights needed during the night flight creating a journalistic sensation, leading one observer to declare that it must have been a comet. As they awaited a final test which would prove whether it was also seaworthy, Dick Donovan, the youngest reporter for the *Boston Evening Eagle*, tracked them down and spied on them in order to get a scoop.[18]

After "going over every nut and bolt" (p. 5) of the *Wondership* in the opening chapter, Jack and Tom use it to reach Professor Dinkelspeil's yacht, *Valkyrie-of-Bremen*, which briefly flies a distress signal off the New England coast. They are captured by mutineers, ride out a hurricane, and are forced to remain in the engine room for two weeks (p. 99) to maintain the faulty engines. By the time they are at the mouth of the Amazon, the mutineers abandon them on a supposedly sinking ship, but they escape, because despite the original threats of the mutineers, the *Wondership* has been "lashed firmly to the boat deck" (p. 77). Although facing such "dire peril[s]" as swordfish and a whale with her calf, the boys, their fathers, and Dick Donovan join Professor Dinkelspeil in his expedition to the headwaters of the Amazon, where, he is certain, the giant sloth Mega-therium has survived since prehistory. They use the *Wondership* to reach the highlands, where they face an anaconda, "marching ants," and a hostile Indian Tribe led by the villainous Chekla before they find both the Megatherium and a treasure of diamonds. Dick Donovan contributes to the success of the expedition by photographing Jack, Tom, and the professor standing beside the body of the sloth which the boys have just shot; that photo "has since been reproduced in countless periodicals throughout the world" (p. 298). The diamonds fetch "a surprising price in the States," and Tom Jesson and Jack Chadwick—"the ingenious lads"—undertake construction of a new invention.

Undoubtedly, some critics will laugh or sneer at such a tale, dismissing it as unworthy of any attention. To do so overlooks a number of significant matters which characterize any popular, formulaic fiction. First, Bonner mixed several of the important motifs of the period in order to appeal as widely as possible to his audience. Secondly, in the 1980s with its concept of the global village, one must not forget the lack of mobility of Bonner's audience. (Certainly at least until after World War II, the journey from the country/town to the city remained a central literary theme in American fiction as well as a major personal experience in many American lives.) Bonner took his readers to the unexplored corners of the world, and the *Wondership* stood by conveniently to afford the means of transportation, quickly moving across thousands of miles. (The way in which it is "lashed firmly" to the boat deck reminds one of a horse at the hitching post.) Third, the ships throughout his stories—and thus invention in general—gained some of the romantic aura of the distant, exotic places which they allowed the travelers to visit. At a time of technological innovation and expansion surely the romantic aura not only helped create an appropriate, needed climate aiding that expansion but very probably introduced a number of the youthful readers to areas which provided their future careers. As suggested in regard to Verne, the inventions may well have been more important than the fictional inventors, or perhaps it would be more accurate to say that the readers could imagine them-selves as the inventors of such splendid machines.

Nor should one assume that the audience for such adventures was made up entirely of teenage boys. Katherine Stokes created the "Motor Maid Series"; a publicity blurb on an unnumbered page of *The Boy Inventors' Flying Ship* de-scribes the first of these "Wholesome Stories of Adventure," *The Motor Maids' School Days*: "Billie Campbell was just the type of a straightforward, athletic girl to be successful as a practical Motor Maid. She took her car, as she did her class-mates, to her heart, and many a grand good time did they have all together. The road over which she ran her red machine had many an unexpected turning,—now it led her into peculiar danger; now into contact with strange travelers; and again into experiences by fire and water. But best of all, 'The Comet' never failed its brave girl owner." Margaret Burnham wrote the "Girl Aviators' Se-ries"—"Clean Aviation Stories." Of the initial title, *The Girl Aviators and the Phantom Airship*, the blurb remarks, "Peggy won well deserved fame for her skill and good sense as an aviator. There were many stumbling-blocks in their [Peggy's and her brother Roy's] terrestrial path, but they soared above them all to ultimate success."[19]

Although Robert C. Givin's *A Thousand Miles an Hour* (1913) does include Leonora Loveday, "an exceedingly pretty girl [who] had considerable experience as an aeronaut" (p. 10), in a flight that allows the earth to turn beneath an almost stationary ship and includes an extended tourist excursion through Japan, most of the novels, whether intended for a juvenile or adult audience, did not give primary attention to a young woman for her own sake. Yet the stories of inventions intended for a juvenile audience should not be consigned to the dime novels or series books and be abandoned. In *Through the Earth* (1898), Clement Fezandie spent much of the narrative describing how a renowned engineer builds a tunnel from Australia to New York, but sixteen-year-old William Swindon volunteers to take the first journey in order to help his widowed mother financially as well as to secure enough money to become a mechanical engineer. Writing as Tom Graham, Sinclair Lewis concentrated in *Hike and the Aeroplane* (1912) on the efforts of Hike Griffin, a student at Santa Benicia Military Academy in California, to help Martin Priest convince the war department to take an option on Priest's plane, but that is only the continuing thread in a narrative which includes various wrecks and an encounter with Mexican bandits. By the 1920s, A. Hyatt Verrill documented the achievements of the youthful "Radio Detectives," Tom Pauling and Frank Putney, although one senses that his greatest interest lay with his accounts of the adventures of boy explorers in various lands.

A number of novels focusing upon inventors did aim at the adult market. They developed in two directions. On the one hand, they produced a number of delightful eccentrics—Hayden Carruth's *The Adventures of Jones* (1895), S. E. Chapman's *Doctor Jones' Picnic* (1898), and Edgar Franklin's *Mr. Hawkins' Humorous Adventures* (1904)—intended as comic though sympathetic portrayals of the inventive genius. Perhaps because it is a novel rather than a series of anecdotal short stories, the most successful of these is William Wallace Cook's *The Eighth Wonder* (1906–1907), in which a scientist who has been cheated out of his inventions by the oil trusts attempts to gain revenge. He seeks "to corner the electrical supply of the country" (p. 45). He intends to accomplish this by attracting every particle of electricity in North America to the giant electromagnets that he has set up in the Black Hills of South Dakota. He believes he can do this because of the nature and origin of electricity:

Who is there on the face of the globe that knows exactly what electricity is?—There is so much electricity in the world—just so much in the United States, just so much in Europe, just so much in Asia. But it is used over and over again. . . .

. . . electricity is ether, simply ether, charged with a peculiar property native to virgin iron. This property was given off while our planet was in a molten, formative state. With the cooling of the mass, the door was shut and the electrical essence forever imprisoned.

The ether that absorbed this essence became the common electricity of commerce and the arts.

It is not possible that any more of the mysterious property can be released. The world has what it has, and it can never have any more or less. (pp. 46, 135–136)

Instead of interrupting the flow of electricity, however, his experiments with the electromagnets cause the axis of the earth to shift, "deflecting the north pole—dragging it down toward the ecliptic."[20] As a result he is branded a "world-wrecker" and troops are sent against him. In the end, the government rights the wrongs done to him by retiring him on a pension, while his companion, the youthful narrator, goes to work for the government and is permitted to marry the "girl of his choice."

More frequently, as noted earlier, the scientist as hero became the scientific detective, of whom Arthur B. Reeve's Craig Kennedy remains the principal example. He invented a new device—the telelectrograph to transmit photographs by telephone, the telegraphone to tape phone conversations, and the sacchari-meter to detect the amount of sugar held in a solution, among others—virtually every month in *Cosmopolitan* from 1910 to 1915. Often the scientist joined forces with a journalist, as in Albert Dorrington's *The Radium Terrors* (1912).

As a result, the number of novels in which a scientist's activities provide the point of departure or in which he solves a mystery are innumerable. But the number of times when the author attempts a sympathetic study of character are few. Frank Stockton focused upon Roland Clewe in *The Great Stone of Sardis* (1898), but whatever his intentions, the bulk of the narrative dwells upon two interlocked adventures. The first is the successful journey to the North Pole by means of a special submarine. The second results both from Clewe's discovery of a kind of super x-ray that permits him to see through the strata of the earth and from his invention of a gun that sinks a projectile fourteen miles into the earth. Stockton describes the ray as

. . . a photic force somewhat similar to the cathode ray, but of infinitely greater significance and importance to the searcher after physical truth. Simply described, his discovery was a powerful ray produced by a new combination of electric lights which would penetrate down into the earth, passing through all substances which it met on its way, and illu-minating and disclosing everything through which it passed. (p. 21)

By means of this ray, Clewe learns that the surface shell of the earth is only fourteen miles thick and that it ends in something akin to glass. Since his new gun will, conveniently, bury a projectile that deep into the earth, he rigs a car so that he may descend through the shell. By so doing, he learns that the core of the earth is in reality a giant diamond, apparently produced by the pressure of the crust. One infers that Thomas Edison provided the model for Roland Clewe, but less clear is Stockton's reason for emphasizing the romance between Clewe and Mrs. Margaret Raleigh. She is entirely sympathetic to his investi-gations, for she has been his partner and actually majority owner of the laboratories they operate at Sardis. At the end they marry and are, of course, extremely wealthy. Stockton, unfortunately, included a villain taken from the dime novels, Ivan Rovinski, a Slav whose chief effort is the attempted sabotage of the submarine. One suspects that in this case, at least, as opposed to *The Great War Syndicate*, Stockton attempted to create a narrative of novel length by incorporating many of the conventions readily available to him. The result is not entirely effective.

In many ways, the most effective portrait of a scientist occurs in Edith Wharton's short story "The Debt," which appeared in her volume *Tales of Men and Ghosts* (1910). In it she concentrates upon the study of Galen Dredge, whom she would represent as one of the great scientists of the period:

Dredge's *Arrival of the Fittest* [is] the most important contribution yet made to the development of Darwinian theory, or rather to the solution of the awkward problem about which that theory has had to make such a circuit. Dredge's theory will be contested, may one day be disproved; but at least it has swept out of the way all previous conjectures, including of course Lanfear's great attempt, and for our generation of scientific investigators it will serve as the first safe bridge across a murderous black whirlpool. (p. 127)

In this passage, Edith Wharton comes as close to referring to concrete scientific data as she does anywhere in the story, for her primary intention is to give a biographical sketch of Dredge, showing his development from an awkward country youth to an accomplished theorist. As a young student in college he early becomes the protégé of the distinguished Lanfear, whose *Utility and Variation* has been regarded as the final word concerning Darwinian theory:

If [Lanfear] did not describe the young man as his pre-destined Huxley, it was because such comparison between himself and his great predecessor would have been distasteful to him; but he evidently felt that it would be Dredge's part to reveal him to posterity. (p. 134)

Here is the basis for the central conflict of the story. Dredge's ability is great and he soon establishes himself as a notable scientist, but even then he follows Lanfear much like a faithful puppy. Lanfear names Dredge to be his successor to the endowed chair of Experimental Evolution at Columbia, which position was endowed specifically for Lanfear and his chosen successors. No sooner does Dredge assume the chair after Lanfear's death than he begins a series of lectures attacking the hypotheses of *Utility and Variation*. The public is shocked; his personal friends, the narrator, and Lanfear's son remind him that his duty is to make public Lanfear's great work. Then he reminds them that Lanfear once said "a scientific hypothesis lasts till there's something else to put in its place" (p. 136).

With this he silences them and wins their approval by asking what they think Lanfear would have done if he himself had arrived at a theory which replaced his presently accepted theories. There can be only one answer, for when Lanfear

published his own volume, he replaced and destroyed the works of his predecessors. In this manner, Dredge reveals that his fundamental duty is to the search
for final truth, a duty to which Lanfear had also devoted himself.

Much of the quality of "The Debt" arises from its narrative technique, for
by means of a series of dialogues and quickly sketched scenes Edith Wharton
concentrated solely upon a study of character, omitting completely any violent
onstage physical action. In this way she shows that the same devices and themes
which so many writers treated with romantic extravagance could be used as the
basis of a realistic study of character.

For much the same reason, *The Mystery* (1907), a collaboration between
Stewart Edward White and Samuel Hopkins Adams, remains perhaps the most
effective novel of the period. Its basic storyline provides still another example
of the quest for the ultimate energy, but White and Adams achieve an effect
which recalls the best of Wilkie Collins, Ambrose Bierce, and Jack London
through their control of perspective. They divide the narrative into three sections,
each of which is presented from a different point of view. Quite literally they
present a mystery, but in presenting its solution they do not move toward melodrama; rather they slowly reveal the consequences of a central action upon
various characters.

Part One presents a situation analogous to that of the famed *Marie Celeste*.
In the south Pacific, the U.S. cruiser *Wolverine* discovers a deserted yacht.
Twice, prize crews are put aboard her and twice during the night they disappear.
During the second night, after the ships become separated, the men aboard the
cruiser observe elaborate volcanic and electrical disturbances toward the southwest. In the morning they find only one of the yacht's lifeboats; in it, in an
exhausted condition, lies a well-known journalist, Ralph Slade.

Part Two, the major portion of the novel, is devoted to a flashback in which
Slade tells the story of the yacht's voyage into the Pacific. He smuggled himself
aboard because he learned that the ship had been hired by a famous scientist,
Karl Augustus Schermirhorn, noted for his "telepathy and wireless waves theory" (p. 57). Schermirhorn has theorized that by combining rare volcanic gases
with such radioactive substances as uranium and radium, he can produce the
ultimate energy. To do this, however, he must perform certain dangerous experiments at the scene of an active volcano. For this reason he chooses an isolated
island in the Pacific.

The majority of Part Two deals not with Schermirhorn's experiments but rather
with the effect of the voyage on the "motley" crew. Because the professor has
a brass-bound chest which he guards closely (it contains pure radioactives, it is
later revealed), and because certain members of the crew are acquainted with a
rare book on the transmutation of metals, they believe him to be an alchemist
and the chest to be filled with gold. They become sullen and rebellious. The
narrative becomes a study of their deterioration during their inactivity while the
experiments are performed. One of the most vivid scenes occurs when the crew,
including Slade, is driven to blood-lust while hunting seals in a great cave and

slaughters the seals by the hundreds. The climax comes when the experiments are ended; as the volcano begins an eruption, the crew—seized by both fear and desire—kills Schermirhorn and steals the ship. At sea, one crew member opens the chest. A chemical reaction takes place. The ship begins to burn and the crew is lost in an attempt to escape.

When Slade suggests that Schermirhorn's assistant, Percy Darrow, might yet be alive on the island, the cruiser returns to search for him. Thus, Part Three becomes Darrow's personal narrative, in which he explains the nature of the experiment; he does this primarily by means of his characterization of Schermirhorn:

"Along how many lines of activity that mind played. One of them was the secret of energy! Concentrated, resistless energy. Man's contrivances were too puny for him. The most powerful engines he regarded as toys. . . .

"It was natural that he should turn to the most prominent radio-active elements, uranium, thorium, and radium. But though his knowledge surpassed that of the much-exploited authorities, he was never satisfied with any of his results." (pp. 263–264)

Although neither technical details nor a generalized description of the experiment is ever given, Darrow does reveal that it was successful, that Schermirhorn produced the ultimate energy, celestium. Of the professor during the period of the crucial final experiments, Darrow states:

"The doctor ceased to be a companion. He ceased to be a human, almost. A machine, that's what he was. . . . His whole force of being was centered on his discovery. It would make him the foremost scientist of the world; the foremost individual entity of his time—of all time, possibly. Light, heat, motive force in incredible degrees and under such control as has never been known. The push of a button, the turn of a screw—Oh, he was to be the master of such power as no monarch wielded! . . . Power unlimited, absolute power was his goal. With his end achieved, he could establish an autocracy, a dynasty of science; whatever he chose.—Oh, it was a rich-hued, golden, glowing dream; a dream such as men's souls don't formulate in these stale days—not our kinds of men. . . . The Teutonic mysticism—you understand. And it was all true. Oh, quite." (p. 262)

The extent of celestium's power proved that it was the ultimate energy:

"Yes, he was to cure mankind. Or kill, kill as no man had ever killed, did he choose. The armies and navies of the powers would be at his mercy. Magnetism was to be his slave. Aerial navigation, transmutation of metals, the screening of gravity." (p.276)

Instead, he was killed by ignorant men who thought him an alchemist possessing a chest of gold. His secret, of course, died with him.

Although *The Mystery* shares with the other novels in its period a lack of technical information and an emphasis upon suspenseful action, it differs radically from the others in that it makes the conventions secondary to the study of the characters' reactions to the two basic situations, the appearance of the derelict vessel and Schermirhorn's experiments. Whereas many of the other novels present a group of stereotyped characters scrambling through a series of episodes, often ill-connected, *The Mystery* gains a unity and depth by presenting all of its action in terms of what it means to the characters, individually and collectively. Thus, the reader is shown first the reactions of the cruiser's officers and men to the mystery of the yacht, then the reactions of the uneducated, superstitious crew to Schermirhorn's experiment, and finally the reactions of a scientist to those experiments. Because the characters are emphasized, the readers more easily identify with them, thereby increasing acceptance of the one scientific premise that they are asked to accept; namely, that an ultimate energy can be produced by the interaction of rare volcanic gases with radioactive substances. In short, White and Adams made a decision unlike that of many of their contemporaries; essentially they kept the melodramatic action offstage. As a result, they achieved a study of the "effect" of a premise upon their characters, a criterion which recent critics and authors alike declare lies at the heart of the most effective science fiction.

For the most extravagant portrait of the scientist as hero, one must turn to Hugo Gernsback's *Ralph 124C41 + : Thrilling Adventures in the Year 2660* (1925), first serialized from April 1911 to March 1912 in Gernsback's magazine *Modern Electrics*. Gernsback divided his attention three ways. First, he sketched quickly a federated world government based upon socialistic principles, but politics takes the background to his catalog of technological "gadgets" which make that future state an earthly paradise. Second, a major portion of the narrative is surrendered to descriptions of those devices, although—surprisingly, in terms of Gernsback's own activities and knowledge of science—Gernsback gave only the vaguest general explanations of how and why any one gadget worked as it did. At the opening of the novel, for example, Ralph is experimenting with Radium-K in an attempt to perfect a method of suspended animation. Gernsback's first description of the radium shows that he presented a speculation as dated as anything written by the most untrained writer of the period:

In 2009, Anatole M610 B9, the great French physicist, found that Radium obtained all its energy from the ether of space and proved that Radium was one of the few substances having a very strong affinity for the ether. Radium, he found, attracted the ether violently and the latter surging back and forward through the Radium became charged electrically, presenting all the other well known phenomena. (p. 53)

Noteworthy are the reliance upon electricity and the total disregard of atomic theory, which was known at the time.

Not only does the inclusion of innumerable mechanical devices reflect Gernsback's own fascination and optimism, but they provide an essential backdrop for the portrait of Ralph himself. Against this background—and its jargon—Gernsback relied as did so many of his contemporaries upon the love of Ralph for the lovely Alice 212B 423 as his main storyline, the third element he gave his attention to. The novel is innovative, however, for he pictures "the other man" as a villainous Martian, Llysanorh', who kidnaps Alice and takes her into space. Pursued into space, rather than give her up, he kills her with a dagger. Thus the supreme test of Ralph 124C41 + as a man, a lover, and a scientist comes when he must operate on the corpse of his beloved Alice in order to restore her to life (pp. 195–206). He succeeds, though the "agony" and "heart-breaking foreboding of the past weeks" (he has kept her in a state of suspended animation) cause him to fall, unconscious, at the moment of his triumph.

One sequence perhaps best indicates Gernsback's attitude toward his protagonist. It occurs after Ralph sees Alice for the first time:

. . . It was not for him to think of these things, he told himself. He was but a tool, a tool to advance science, to benefit humanity. He belonged, not to himself, but to the Government—the Government, who fed and clothed him, and whose doctors guarded his health with every precaution. He had to pay the penalty of his + . To be sure, he had everything. He had but to ask and his wish was law—if it did not interfere with his work.

To the World Governor, Ralph complains:

"I am nothing but a prisoner." . . .

"You are a great inventor," smiled the Governor, "and a tremendous factor in the world's advancement. You are invaluable to humanity, and—you are irreplaceable. You belong to the world—not to yourself." (pp. 41, 42)

Both in terms of Ralph's action and the description of him, the novel expresses an adulation of scientific genius unequaled among its contemporaries. Within the context provided by Gernsback, it seems appropriate that the scientist resurrects his beloved amid the technological paradise he and his predecessors have created.

NOTES

1. Maxim Hudson, "The Machine-Made Millennium," *Cosmopolitan*, 45 (November 1908), 568–576. Both I. F. Clarke and I, at least, have made frequent reference to Hudson's article. Its title symbolizes the potential of which America, especially, dreamed at the start of the new century.

2. Everett Carter, *Howells and the Age of Realism* (Philadelphia: J. B. Lippincott Co., 1954), pp. 91, 92.

3. John B. Hamilton, "Notes Toward a Definition of Science Fiction," *Extrapolation*, 4 (December 1962), 2–13.

4. See, for example, Brian Aldiss, *Billion Year Spree*, p. 54; E. F. Bleiler, "Edgar Allan Poe," *Science Fiction Writers* (New York: Charles Scribner's Sons, 1982), pp. 11–18; Peter Nicholls, ed., *The Science Fiction Encyclopedia*, pp. 464–465.

5. Sam Moskowitz, "The Fabulous Fantasist—Fitz-James O'Brien," *Explorers of*

the Infinite (Cleveland and New York: The World Publishing Company, 1963), pp. 62–72.

6. Thomas D. Clareson, "Fitz-James O'Brien," in E. F. Bleiler, ed., *Supernatural and Horror Writers*, (New York: Charles Scribner's Sons, 1985), II:717-722.

7. Frederick Lewis Pattee, *The Development of the American Short Story* (New York and London: Harper and Brothers, 1923), pp. 155–159.

8. In *Science Fiction in America*, for example, I have acknowledged the importance of Sam Moskowitz's two collections: *The Crystal Man* (1973), the stories of Edward Page Mitchell, and *Into the Sun* (1980), the stories of Robert Duncan Milne. Both men contributed significantly to science fiction, but their stories were not collected during their lifetimes. Debate about the importance of individual magazine stories can become heated and prolonged.

9. W. H. Rhodes, *Caxton's Book,* Introduction by Sam Moskowitz (Westport, Conn.: Hyperion Press, 1974), p. iii.

10. See, for example, Robert M. Philmus, *"The Island of Dr. Moreau,"* in Frank N. Magill, ed., *Science Fiction Literature*, 3:1079–1081.

11. E. F. Bleiler, "Jules Verne," in E. F. Bleiler, ed., *Science Fiction Writers*, pp. 573–582.

12. E. F. Bleiler, ed., *The Frank Reade Library* (New York and London: Garland Publishing Company, Inc., 1979), 1:7.

13. E. F. Bleiler, *The Frank Reade Library*, 1:8.

14. Sam Moskowitz, *The Crystal Man* (Garden City, N.Y.: Doubleday & Company, Inc., 1973), pp. xx-xxi.

15. Albert Johannsen, *The House of Beadle and Adams* (Norman, Okla.: The University of Oklahoma Press, 1950), I:108, 150, 268; II:93–97.

16. Mark Hillegas, "An Annotated Bibliography of Jules Verne's *Voyages Extraordinaires*," *Extrapolation*, 3 (May 1962), 32–47.

17. William Ganson Rose, *Cleveland: The Making of a City*, p. 367.

18. Dick Donovan provides a unique kind of humor differing from the reliance of most authors on Irish and black American dialects. He indulges in what must be called nonsense alliteration: "By the long-legged Lhama of Thibet" (p. 19); "By the Horntoads of Herrington" (p. 23); "By the skyscraping sultans of Syria" (p. 51). These examples may suffice here; a minor character, Dick and his humor give way in the heat of action.

19. Neither series is included in Robert Reginald's fine *Science Fiction and Fantasy Literature* (1979), vol. 1, to which anyone working in the field must be indebted. Since all of the boys' series seem to be included (Reginald lists two variant titles in Bonner's Young Inventors series in that they differ from Bonner's references to the same stories in *The Boy Inventors' Flying Ship*), two reasons for the omissions suggest themselves. First, they may have been judged as realism instead of extrapolative fantasy; second, they were girls' series books. Exceptional heroines, like Wonder Woman, had not yet made their appearance. I have not yet had either of the girls' series in my possession.

20. William Wallace Cook, *The Eighth Wonder; or, Working for Marvels* (New York: Street & Smith, 1906–1907), p. 142.

5

Shadows of the Future: Utopia or Catastrophe?

Initiated by Edward Bellamy's *Looking Backward, A.D. 2000–1887* (1888), American utopian fiction reached a floodtide during the generation before World War I. Despite the importance of such an individual title as Theodor Hertzka's *Freeland* (1891) or the work of such a writer as H. G. Wells, quantitatively neither Britain nor Continental Europe shared the experience, probably because many British authors had already rejected the machine age. Even before Bellamy portrayed his socialist utopia, both Richard Jeffries in *After London* (1885) and W. H. Hudson in *A Crystal Age* (1887) had destroyed urbanized, industrialized England (by flood and fire, respectively). Having celebrated the fourteenth-century Peasants' Revolt in *The Dream of John Ball* (1886–1887), William Morris had his protagonist in *News from Nowhere* (1890) awaken in a future Kensington which was a socialist arcadia. In the sense of presenting an idealized medievalism, Morris anticipated G. K. Chesterton's *The Napoleon of Notting Hill* (1904). As Morris intended *News from Nowhere* to be a direct response to Bellamy, so Chesterton directly attacked the ideas of H. G. Wells.

Although I. F. Clarke declares that Bellamy succeeded because "he had invented the working model of an alternative industrial society; he had faced all the great social issues," Clarke calls Wells's *A Modern Utopia* (1905) "the most important utopia of the twentieth century, because it made the most complete act of faith in the name of progress, and because by a cruel irony of fiction it became the model from which the dominant dystopias of the last fifty years have taken their mark."[1] Mark Hillegas explicates that irony when he asserts that the "hero of the first two decades of the century became the symbol of everything most intellectuals hated, and [Wells's] vision of utopia the object of scorn," and he points to a second reason for the criticism of Wells when he suggests that *A Modern Utopia* provided an "archetypal blueprint for the scientifically planned welfare state."[2] Yet Hillegas also emphasizes that "its greatest contribution to the literature of utopian thought, is its concept of utopia as planet-wide." He enumerates three other "distinctive features": "the voluntary nobility, the *samurai*; the important role of science and technology; and Utopia seen as kinetic, not static.''[3]

The benevolent, administrative *samurai*, Wells's ''men of good intent,'' whom he equated with the Guardians of Plato's *Republic*, easily became identified with authoritarian bureaucracy, at best, as the twentieth century progressed, especially since Wells's utopia ''demands more powerful and efficient method of control than electoral methods can give.''[4] Perhaps, as Hillegas asserts, Wells's greatest insight came when he realized that modern technology would transform the world into a global village so that utopia could no longer remain isolated, as it had since the time of Sir Thomas More. Nor could it be small and self-sufficient, as so many of the actual experiments in nineteenth-century America had attempted to be. Equally important, however—and it belies J. O. Bailey's conclusion that utopia shifted from a geographical place to a condition to be achieved in the future[5]—is the concept that utopia itself will continually change as innovations are introduced into it and modify it. This insight makes Wells's vision unique, for other utopias and especially the major dystopias—Zamiatin's *We* (1924), Aldous Huxley's *Brave New World* (1932), and George Orwell's *Nineteen Eighty-Four* (1949)—all freeze their societies and maintain the status quo through totalitarian authority, always doing so in the name of Huxley's ''Stability.'' Finally, in the choice of *samurai* as the name of the ''voluntary nobility'' is another factor setting Wells apart from his contemporaries: unlike the seemingly neglected William Delisle Hay, to single him out from the legion of writers who espoused the cause of the Aryans or Anglo-Saxons, Wells was not a racist.

If his tone of voice became more strident, more anxious, as time passed, Wells reacted to the failure of society and events to fulfill his vision. Whatever the novel—*The Food of the Gods* (1904), *The War in the Air* (1908), *The World Set Free* (1914)—the thematic tension rises from the resistance of society to change and the inability of society to handle new scientific developments, whatever they may be. As early as *When the Sleeper Wakes* (1899), Wells indicated his opposition to the idea that a privileged oligarchy could gain absolute financial control of society, thereby gaining the power to regiment the workers. In that novel one sees the beginning of the split between the classes which led to the Eloi and the Morlocks of *The Time Machine* (1895). Arthur O. Lewis has recently pointed out that *When the Sleeper Wakes* ''anticipated'' the works of subsequent ''anti-utopian'' writers; he underscores the basic thesis of Mark Hillegas's *The Future As Nightmare: H. G. Wells and the Anti-Utopians* (1967).[6]

One must not forget that after the turn of the century the basic issue at the core of Wells's work insisted that science and technology would provide the means to a utopian end only if mankind reformed society and individual behavior. Although Hillegas, among others, has noticed ''the Huxleyan cosmic pessimism''[7] permeating the romances of the 1890s in which Wells warned of the precariousness of human existence *as a species*, one must emphasize that he voiced this pessimism before he embraced science, technology, and social reform as means of ensuring the survival of the human race. One may infer that that advocacy—for which he has been so frequently damned—may well have been in itself an act of desperation on the part of an individual who believed that he saw only too clearly the fate of mankind if left to the workings of nature.

Looking Backward sparked controversy in the United States especially, but Bellamy himself never became a focal point of attack as did Wells, although they both raised a number of the same issues, centralization and socialism among them. One infers that the reaction to *Looking Backward* and the variety within American utopian literature resulted, in part at least, both from the size and diversity of America and from the relative newness of American industrialization. Neither the Populist movement nor the American labor movement, as exemplified by the Knights of Labor, resembled the Fabian Socialists or the Labour Party. One says this fully aware that a consideration either of contemporary newspapers and journals or of subsequent historians indicates, as previously noted, that the period was one of tumult and transition. Jean Pfaelzer has said that the "1880s and 1890s were among the most active periods of class, race, and sex struggles in American history."[8] Kenneth Roemer has summarized the era as one when "millions of Americans were confused and distressed by the panic of 1873, the ups and downs of the 1880s, and the crash of 1893. The numerous strikes and confrontations at Haymarket Square, Pullman, and Homestead terrified workers and employers. The unequal distribution of wealth . . . heightened tensions. . . . White native Americans feared the influx of blacks from the South and the shiploads of immigrants from southeastern Europe."[9]

Although the majority of migrants came to the cities from the farms, writers from Upton Sinclair and Theodore Dreiser to Frederick Lewis Allen and his contemporaries at mid-twentieth century have seized upon the plight of the immigrant as somehow symbolic of the "poverty, filth, and wretchedness" characteristic of the urban, industrial explosion of the late nineteenth century. Their physical presence was not the only problem. As early as Henry Standish Coverdale's *The Fall of the Great Republic* (1888), novelists complained that immigrants "from the most dangerous classes of Europe" swarmed to America, bringing with them "socialism, nihilism, and their kindred poisons" (p. 12).

Removed from the scene by nearly a century, one finds no simple reason explaining why the 1880s and 1890s did not erupt into even greater violence. The novelists were often inconsistent within their own work. Ignatius Donnelly predicted a civil war taking place in 1988 between the capitalists and the so-called Brothers of Destruction in *Caesar's Column* (1891), but within a year a figure identifying itself as "THE PITY OF GOD" appears to Ephraim Benezet and gives him *The Golden Bottle* (1892) so that Benezet can create gold from nothing; he becomes instrumental in bringing about "The Universal Republic" temporarily after the outworn political creeds—"the kingships"—of Europe, led by England, have been defeated in warfare. The theme of revolution echoes through the work of Jack London and, less ardently, George Allan England, whose physicist in *The Golden Blight* (1916) develops a "radiojector" capable of turning gold into dust. A number of "peaceful revolutions" occur in such novels as Frederick U. Adams' *President John Smith* (1897), who promotes a new constitution but does not oppose industrialization *per se*.

What remains important is that for whatever reasons no revolution took place. In the opening passages of *The Big Change*, Frederick Lewis Allen contrasts the figures of J. Pierpont Morgan, "head of the mightiest banking house in the world and the most powerful man in all American business," and Eugene V. Debs, who had led the Pullman strike of 1894, had served a prison term, had "consumed Marxist literature in his cell, and had become an ardent Socialist." Advocating public ownership, eventually, of all public services, transportation, means of production, and distribution, Debs received some 96,000 votes as the Social Democratic candidate in 1900; in 1912, described—as usual—as a year of "ferment," he gained 901,602 votes, some 6 percent of the votes cast in the year Woodrow Wilson was elected. Of these two men Frederick Lewis Allen writes:

> Both Morgan and Debs would have been bewildered had they been able to foresee what the next half century would bring to the nation: how a combination of varied and often warring forces would produce an America which would not only be utterly unlike the America of 1900, but also would be utterly unlike the picture in either man's mind; yet an America in which an astonishing productive capacity would be combined with the widest distribution of prosperity ever witnessed in the world. (p. 6)

A number of factors, most importantly the problem of minorities, must qualify Allen's assertion. He does not mention the Great Depression of the 1930s and ignores the possibility that the prosperity of which he speaks may not have come about on a truly wide scale until after World War II. Given these serious modifications, his statement does have validity as of the 1920s after the initial urbanization and industrialization of the United States had been completed. Certainly, no comparable change took place in Europe after World War I.

What makes Allen relevant in the immediate context is that the "widest distribution of prosperity" took place completely outside of (one is tempted to say despite) the tumult of American utopian literature in the decades before World War I. Because a number of books have closely examined American utopias, there seems no need to repeat detailed analysis of that body of literature in a study of science fiction as a whole.[10] More than ten years ago, Samuel R. Delany admonished academic critics for wasting "a great deal of time trying to approach modern SF works in utopian/dystopian terms."[11] He asserted that the template of Victorian utopian fiction (he included American utopian fiction under that label) had always been a restrictive one in that it forced writers to "exhaust themselves by taking sides" in a "terribly limiting argument"—namely, personal reaction to a "new" society—which he translated as an argument concerning "the environment I prefer."[12] Delany suggested that in terms of the organization of society, Western man had come up with four mythic patterns: Arcadia, the Land of Flies, New Jerusalem, and Brave New World.

Someone may wish to take issue with Delany. The judgment that close ex-amination of such literary works gives insight into a culture during a specific period cannot be denied. Certainly, as noted, English fiction from the 1870s onward provided a battleground for the acceptance or rejection of modern in-dustrial society. However, when one turns to American utopian fiction before World War I, one does not find such clear-cut battlelines. Despite the commotion about the conflict between capital and labor, the impression remains that what one sees is innumerable individual dreams projected onto a linear future which is no more than an extension of their time period. Kenneth Roemer seems to reinforce this interpretation when he remarks, "The ambivalence towards change, however, was the most persistent characteristic. Almost everything about the present had to be changed, but the ultimate goal of all change was a world without change."[13] (One notes immediately that as a group the writers denied what may have been Wells's keenest insight.) Granted, some concerns recur: diet, eugenics, the single tax, sexual purity, cooperatives, the coinage of gold and silver, the disparity in wealth. But many of those interests quickly became outdated so that they give the fiction only historical value, while the general diversity of answers to the questions underlying the fiction implies that many of the writers did not understand the nature or the completeness of the transition then taking place in the United States. (This implication—or inference, if one prefers—may help to explain why the myth of the Western frontier and the myth of utopia simultaneously gained widespread popularity in the U.S.) One may debate whether the most controversial issue in this fiction involved the acceptance or rejection of some form of socialism or the preservation of Christianity.

As alchemy and mesmerism were the most prevalent sciences in the Gothic novel, so the use of electricity and aluminum and the presence of advanced forms of transportation provided staple elements in the background of the utopian novels. Unlike those societies reached by exotic journeys, for the most part patiently observant protagonists reached the future utopias through dream visions or experiments/accidents involving suspended animation. Again, for the most part these narratives involved little dramatic action; they took the form of the classic dialogues in which the appointed guide to the society did most of the talking. Consequently, when the disquisition focuses upon politics, economics, or morality—perhaps the three chief topics once the society has been described—the books read like essays.

At the one extreme, in Chauncey Tinker's well-known *The Crystal Button* (1891), the protagonist, Paul Prognosis, is transported to the forty-ninth century to the City of Tone, where study of the physical sciences has brought a tech-nological paradise; he learns, however, that the new height of civilization resulted from the teachings of John Costor, a twentieth-century prophet, a "Disciple of Truth," whose Order of the Crystal Button brought about a moral reawakening in mankind. Lying in a coma for some ten years, Prognosis enters the future world and is returned to his sick bed, without immediate recollection of the passage of time, only after a comet passes near earth in the forty-ninth century.

In a sense, Tinker has adapted the familiar convention of the dream. The reader never knows what effect the comet had on the future world. At the other extreme, in S. M. Landis's *The Social War of the Year 1900* (1872), the Second Coming of Christ establishes a new Eden in "obedience to His fixed Laws" (p. 397). In contrast, William Wonder's *Reciprocity* (1909) denounces Christianity in favor of "a practical heaven here on earth . . . where love and justice rule" (p. 165). In 2907, its protagonist finds an idyllic pastoral society made up of small farms near White River Junction, Vermont, although over the horizon New York City has swelled to a megalopolis of 20 million persons. Herman Hines Brinsmade in *Utopia Achieved* (1912) also presents a countryside dominated by well-managed farms, although New York has a population of 20 million because the United Aero Company has made possible a suburban civilization which did away with the slums of the nineteenth century. Such novels as Byron Brooks's *Earth Revisited* (1893), however, abandoned Manhattan to warehouses, offices, and wholesale businesses.

The majority of the novels did not prefer the metropolis. In *Solaris Farm* (1900), Milan C. Edson, for whom agriculture was the most important profession, argues that the best conditions for a good life occur "in the rural districts, far from the turmoil and strife, the smoke and poisonous gases of the great city" (p. 79); he also blames the "competitive system . . . for a majority of the evils which had so retarded the world's progress" (p. 133). In *Altruria* (1895), Titus Smith prefers a small Iowa town of some 3,000 inhabitants to the large city, although he wants a worldwide republic with free trade. Again, in contrast, the protagonist of Ignatius Donnelly's *The Golden Bottle* (1892), Ephraim Benezet of Kansas, builds a great city maintained by hydroelectric power at the mouth of Great Egg Harbor River in New Jersey. During the subsequent war with Europe, Canada enthusiastically joins the U.S. within a month (p. 209), while Ireland expresses "joy . . . unbounded" when its citizens see the arrival of "the long-prayed-for [American] deliverers" (p. 213). Yet in a vision Benezet is told that he should not have expected a perfect world. "Don't you know," the spirit tells him, "the universe is nothing but *work*, and we all of us . . . have no place in it but as *workers*" (pp. 310–311).

A number of authors locate their societies in the heart of Africa, as does Albert Chavannes in the novel *In Brighter Climes* (1895); the few survivors of the great rebellion of 1988 in Ignatius Donnelly's *Caesar's Column* (1891) also flee to Africa. While all of these novels emphasize the working man, the protagonists of George Gordon Hastings' *The First American King* (1908) awaken in 1975 to find themselves in an American Empire which literally encloses the Pacific Ocean and is ruled by William I. Its teachers deny the importance of the popular vote and the power of the people, for their society originated in the wave of Anglomania which swept the country in the late nineteenth century and their aristocracy gained its first recognition in Ward McAllister's 400, although one protagonist assures them that the concept of "the 400" originated as a joke (p. 78). Whatever their means, however, all of the authors shared the aim voiced by Hyland C. Kirk in *When the World Grows Young* (1888): "the perfectionment of man, mentally, morally, and physically" (pp. 188–189).

Perhaps these examples will suffice to indicate the degree to which this body of fiction presented only an extension of nineteenth-century society. The use of the future became an expedient convention allowing the writers a freedom to illustrate the fulfillment of their ideas. Yet as those novels which locate their utopias in some corner of the world (or another world) indicate, the future was no more than a convenience, while the science and technology provided no more than colorful background. One may suggest that although these novels emphasize a future U.S., they do not belong to the body of science fiction any more than do such Theosophic tracts as Thomas Blot's *The Man from Mars* (1891) and Sara Weiss's *Decimon Huydas: A Romance of Mars* (1906), in both of which Martians come to earth by means of "transmigration of the soul" and expound in essaylike monologues the wonders of Madame Blavatsky's universe.[14]

Admittedly, such a judgment may seem to be something of an overreaction. So one must underscore that the study of utopian fiction has importance *per se*, but American utopian fiction during the generation before World War I did not *originate* any convention of which subsequent science fiction made extensive use. It did reinforce the extrapolation of action and scene into the future, although as such critics as Hillegas, in speaking of Wells, have emphasized, it also "domesticated" its projections by opening the narrative in the here-and-now: thus the emphasis upon the dream or suspended animation. Because the utopian fiction concerned itself so much with the exposition of ideas and often only sketched the future world, it also reinforced the physical portrayal of that future world (though one may argue that the nonfiction magazine articles, with their illustrations, had as much influence). Some years ago, Clifford D. Simak emphasized that the physical presentation of the future world proved the most important and arduous task that the sf writer had to face.[15] Perhaps the best resolution of this seeming paradox may be found in the suggestion that as the nineteenth century progressed, the acceptance of the idea of change, with the corollary belief in unending progress, produced both a utopian fiction and a science fiction, each of which made use in its own way of similar materials so that at quick glance they appear to be one and the same.

What has not been widely emphasized is that by the end of the 1880s American writers were satirizing the concept of progress and, somewhat later, the idea of utopia. In *The Golden Age of Patents: A Parody on Yankee Inventiveness* (1888), for example, Wallace Peck declares that "with our American patents in operation, the present may be fitly termed the Century of Conveniences; for Man now journeys through life with a host of new appliances surrounding him" (p. 5). He does not focus on the achievement of a single scientist, as does Hayden Carruth in *The Adventures of Jones* (1895), but he merrily discusses such innovations as a variety of cars, the "Elite Elopement Company (Unltd.)," "The Metropolitan Lasso Company"—for rescuing hats which have blown off in the wind or obtaining waiters in public dining rooms—and the "Submarine Farming

Company," since "seaweed may become . . . a valuable food product" (p. 23). He cannot resist romance, including the episode of "The Modern Mermaid; or, the Diving Belle and Her Submarine Suitor," in which the charming Babette is confronted in her submarine garden by Nathaniel, who, because of their diving suits, can tell "the maid his Passion" only "with the expressive signs of the United States deaf-and-dumb language" (p. 49).

In Franklin N. North's *The Awakening of Noahville* (1898), two Yankees descend upon "a lost city, in a lost kingdom beyond the seas" (p. 35) and corrupt the Medieval culture—complete with a beautiful princess and a group of nobles who strike for higher wages, carrying such signs as "Eight hours a day's work" and "Down with the fake civilization of the nineteenth century" (pp. 131–132). North does not achieve the complex bitterness of Mark Twain in *A Connecticut Yankee in King Arthur's Court* (1889) nor the humor of George Randolph Chester's *The Jingo* (1912), a parody of the lost-race motif. In *Cosmopolitan*, as early as 1893, Julian Hawthorne's "June 1993" sketches a future in which "flying-machines" had made possible the abandonment of cities to "shops and manufacturies," while the "bulk of the population slept some hundreds of miles away."[16] Quite casually he mentions that the flying-machine had brought war to an end after bombs were dropped on cities: "no doubt there was a general feeling of helplessness and insecurity." When he and his guide quarrel about the lack of novelty in twentieth-century life, Hawthorne dismisses the guide as a figment of his dream, thereby relegating him "to the nothingness out of which [he had] been evoked."

Although the storyline of William Wallace Cook's *A Round Trip to the Year 2000, or A Flight Through Time* (1903) centers on the efforts of Everson Lumley to escape arrest by Detective Jasper Kinch, Lumley flees into the "Unknown" future in a "time coupé" invented by Professor Alonzo Kelpie. In the year 2000, Lumley finds that he is famous because his book, "The Possibilities of the Subconscious Ego," led to the development of the "muglugs"—metallic robots—controlled by the minds of designated men. (Cook's novel provides one of the earliest, if not the first, appearance of metallic robots in sufficient numbers to make up a distinct working class.) Plot complications include the infatuation of Miss Tibijul for Lumley and a revolt of the muglugs; Cook's theme suggests that the people of the future "are victims of their own ingenuity, and have invented themselves into a vast community of dummies" (p. 53).

Perhaps the most significant element of the novel is Cook's open satire of the utopists. Lumley becomes acquainted with "The Nineteen Hundred Colony" made up of writers who have been stranded in the future. At one point, Miss Tibijul tells him, "So many novelists have been coming from nineteen hundred to write us up that it is a positive pleasure to meet one who has no aims in that direction" (p. 94). One of the authors informs him, "We're the great and growing order of the Nineteen-Hundreders, Rainbow Chasers, Knights of the Double-X Dope, and so on" (p. 42). He learns that the marooned writers have sworn an oath: "He must swear to keep away from the facts. . . . These times are a cultivated taste. . . . It has taken a hundred years to educate the people up to them, so how can we expect readers of our day and age to have any sympathy with such institutions? We must suppress the hard facts, gentlemen, and tint our theories with the rosy hues of imagination'' (p. 55).

(In a sequel, *Castaways in the Year 2000*, published in *Argosy* between October 1912 and February 1913, Cook unfortunately abandoned satire for a convoluted plot. Led by Tod Plunkett, fifteen of the men from 1900 become dictators, but their misrule causes revolt. They are not deposed until their army of muglugs has been soundly defeated by another army. Once they have been brought back to 1900 and have no way of returning to the future, Dr. Kelpie concludes, ''A man of 1900 in the year 2000 is a calamity. We're born exactly where we belong, and to get out of our proper times can result in nothing less than wide-spread disaster.''[17])

If the aim of the utopists was to show what reforms should be made and how they should be implemented, then one may argue that the most effective portrayal of the achievement of utopia occurred in Charles E. Bolton's neglected novel *The Harris-Ingram Experiment* (1905), published some four years after the author's death. Instead of extrapolating into the future, the narrative gives one of the widest ranging pictures of the American steel industry and the life of wealthy American society to be found in the fiction of the period. No summary can do justice to the texture of the novel. It is not noteworthy for its study of character, and when all of the strands of the plot are brought together, the result is melodramatic. Yet *The Harris-Ingram Experiment* provides a panorama of life in the U.S. equaled by few of the realists. The point of departure is the partnership entered into by Reuben Harris, a blacksmith, and James Ingram, an Englishman who had the ''good fortune to be a foreman where the first experiments were made by Henry Bessemer himself'' (pp. 141). Primarily through the development and sale of high-grade rails, their venture grew into the Harrisville Iron & Steel Company, for Ingram sold his interests to Harris. Now a wealthy man, Colonel Harris makes young George Ingram his protégé even though he wishes to sell to a British company. Those plans change, however, because outside agitators precipitate a strike and actually blow up the mill. In short, the crucial action of the novel turns on the foremost issue at the turn of the century: the confrontation between capital and labor.

To this central action Bolton adds a diverse background encompassing the travels of Colonel Harris and his family in New York City and abroad (including a voyage on the S.S. *Majestic*), an account of his daughter Gertrude's life at Vassar, sketches of the careers of Sir Henry Bessemer and Frederick Krupp, and the efforts of the Colonel's only son, Alfonso, to become an artist. In proper melodramatic fashion, Alfonso is spurned by a young Englishwoman who rejects him because he would be an artist instead of a businessman; he fakes his death and disappears into the American West, his quest for gold taking him to both Yellowstone and Yosemite. As one might guess, he appears at a crucial moment when bankruptcy threatens the project.

The strike does not reach its crisis until young George and Gertrude have married in Paris. With the plant destroyed, George, formerly a student at the Polytechnic Institute in Troy, New York, and his father-in-law undertake the construction of the finest steel plant in the world, to be powered entirely by electricity. The supervision of that task and the management of the new mill fall primarily to George, but in order to prevent future unrest, Colonel Harris not only arranges that half of the stock in the new corporation will be owned by "capital" and "half by the employees of the company" (p. 398), but he also endows a model, utopian town to be shared by management and labor. From education to freedom from poverty, all of the aims of the utopian writers of the period are fulfilled in the community of Harris-Ingram. What though Alfonso, rich with gold that he had found, must rescue the experiment at the moment of a final financial crisis? Utopia had been achieved.

From Mary Shelley's *The Last Man* through such novels as M. P. Shiel's sadomasochistic *The Purple Cloud* (1901)—to say nothing of the narratives by Jeffries and Hudson already cited—the literary vision of the future had a dark side to it. Some vast catastrophe engulfed the earth. The images of the last man alive or of Adam and Eve replenishing a ravaged earth seemed fixed in the Western imagination.

Alvarado M. Fuller's *A.D. 2000* (1890) exemplifies the manner in which the catastrophe motif insinuated itself even into utopian fiction. All of the established conventions make themselves apparent. With the aid of friends, Junius Cobb enters a state of suspended animation, awakening to find an America which encompasses the entire northern continent and is governed by a single political party. It is technologically advanced. Niagara Falls has been harnessed to provide cheap electric power, while the Gulf Stream has been dammed to provide a better climate. Much, if not all, of this advancement has resulted after a disaster taking place near Pittsburgh on August 21, 1916. On that date "a huge melting of aluminum bronze" flowed into an abandoned natural gas well; the intense heat started a chain reaction in the natural gas deep within the earth. The surface buckled so that a great Central Sea filled the Mississippi-Missouri-Ohio basin. Far from reducing the U.S. to barbarism, however, the transformation turned American attention from gas to electricity; experiments led to the development of an ultimate form of energy, "lipthalite vapor," which powers airplanes, submarines, and surface vessels (pp. 72–75).

One discovers that increasingly in the period from the 1870s until at least World War II, the catastrophe motif became one of the dominant themes shaping science fiction. It provided a basic point of departure: a problem to be solved. But that premise remained highly flexible so that a number of storylines could be built from it; moreover, the author had the choice of presenting the problem as a mystery which had to be solved before a resolution could be achieved, or the narrative could simply begin with an awareness of the threat. Granted that when sf is described in this fashion, it becomes a formulaic fiction, especially when action is emphasized. That fact still does not remove the variety. On the one hand, as in the case of H. G. Wells's "The Star" (1898), the threat may express itself in terms of such natural phenomena as the impending collision between earth and some celestial body (comets seem to have been favored at the turn of the century) or as a new and deadly plague in Jack London's *The Scarlet Plague* (1915). Wells, again, varied the pattern by introducing a threat from nature itself in "The Sea Raiders" (1896). As has been shown, the menace could also reveal itself in the workings of a mad scientist, as in William H. Rhodes's *The Case of Summerfield* (1876, 1918) or Stewart Edward White's *The Sign at Six* (1912). In still another form, the catastrophe could involve invading aliens, as in Wells's *The War of the Worlds* (1898), or it could reach the level of interstellar warfare, as in the conflict between humans and Sirians in Robert William Cole's *The Struggle for Empire* (1900). What remains important is that each of these storylines can be traced down to the contemporary scene. Cole's narrative, for example, concerns itself with the first notable example—in book form, at least—of those innumerable galactic wars between embattled humanity and rapacious alien hordes which grew into the so-called space opera commanding so large a portion of the popular and specialist magazines especially between the World Wars. From them are descended the *Star Wars* films as well as such a novel as Joe Haldeman's *The Forever War* (1975), the Nebula Award winner. Not only do the films and novel illustrate the persistence and variation within a storyline, but the great differences between them suggest something of the change taking place in sf since World War II.

Fuller's *A.D. 2000* shows how utopian fiction differed from the stories giving primary emphasis to the catastrophe motif. By and large, utopian fiction remains static; the observer, most often an individual from the society familiar to the reader, simply sees the wonders of the future world and is told how (why) they came into being. With a minimum of narrative, the novel emphasizes description and exposition: thus the frequency of the guided tour and the essentially Socratic dialogue. In like manner, although the emphasis of the future-war motif did rely more on narrative, most often the novelists were so interested in weaponry that personal experience was sacrificed to an account of a few major battles, usually between rival fleets, because the majority of writers felt assured that the next war would be decided at sea. Only on occasion, as in Erskine Childers' *The Riddle of the Sands* (1903) or Roy Norton's *The Vanishing Fleets* (1908), did the author bother to cast the narrative as a mystery. Similarly, the imaginary voyage, whether to some unexplored area of earth or to another world, so often had other interests that the dramatic conflict inherent in the threat of catastrophe was played down. All of these factors help to explain why the entire range of science fiction has been criticized for its lack of effective characterization. Certainly in many instances only stereotypical characters were needed to carry out the required action. Then, too, to some extent at least, these patterns may explain why so many of the narratives included the love story of a valiant hero and a dazzling heroine.

When all of this has been said, it still ignores the fact that even before the end of World War I at least three major thematic variations were possible within the catastrophe motif. First, civilization could be so completely destroyed that mankind, if it survived, could not climb again from barbarism. Second, antipodal to this warning was the determined resolution that society must somehow build again, and build better. Third, the narrative could celebrate the scientist or technician as the one individual—the leader—who could save civilization from ruin. A fourth theme did not gain popularity until after World War I; the author portrayed a future so radically changed that Europe and America—the Caucasian race, if one prefers—had not survived. One final observation need be made about the nature of catastrophe itself. Originally, it had been some natural phenomenon, but again by World War I—though certainly not widely in American fiction until after World War II—the catastrophe which brought about the fall of civilization was man-made.

Outside of the future-war motif, the first novel concentrating upon the fall of the United States is J. A. Mitchell's *The Last American* (1889), although Mitchell used his narrative primarily as a vehicle to attack American materialism. In the year 2951, a Persian expedition discovers the legendary continent of the "Mehrikans," landing first in the harbor of "Nhu Yok" and then Washington. The narrative takes the form of the journal of Khan-Li, a prince and admiral of the fleet, who is sufficiently knowledgeable of ancient history that he can explain what happened and voice Mitchell's criticisms. U.S. attempts to dominate world trade had led to its defeat by a coalition of European powers, while in 1927 the persecution of Protestants by Catholics—the "Murfey" regime—had brought about its internal decline. These problems the U.S. might have survived, but between 1945 and 1960 "climatic changes, the like of which no other land ever experienced . . . finished in less than ten years a work made easy by nervous natures and rapid lives" (p. 46). The storyline is fragile. In the ruins of Washington, the Persians find two American men and a woman; both men are killed in a fight after one of the Persians kisses the young woman. As the expedition leaves on July 4, 2951, a statue of George Washington topples.

Mitchell, who wrote at least one deeply religious novel, *Dr. Thorne's Idea* (1901), expresses the essence of his attack against his contemporary society early in the narrative; as the Persian ship enters the harbor of Nhu Yok, Khan-Li observes the ruins of the city and reflects:

For eleven centuries the cities of this sleeping hemisphere have decayed in solitude, their very existence has been forgotten. The people who built them have long passed away, and their civilization is but a shadowy tradition. Historians are astounded that a nation of an hundred million beings should vanish from the earth like a mist, and leave so little behind. But to those familiar with their life and character surprise is impossible. There was nothing to leave. The Mehrikans possessed neither literature, art, nor music of their own. Everything was borrowed. The very clothes they wore were copied with ludicrous precision from the model of other nations. They were a sharp, restless, quick-witted, greedy race, given body and soul to the gathering of riches. Their chiefest passion was to buy and sell.

. . . Prosperity was their god, with cunning and invention for his prophets. (pp. 28, 31)

Considering both the early date of *The Last American* and the fact that Mitchell's other contribution to the sf field, *Drowsy* (1917), focuses upon a highly romanticized journey to the moon as well as a love story, one wonders whether or not he fully realized how effective a narrative vehicle he had employed in the Persian voyage to a ruined America. Unlike most of his contemporaries he did not make a simple linear projection. By using a non-European as his narrator and by placing the action a thousand years into the future, he gained an aesthetic distancing, while—perhaps more important—the discontinuity jolts his readers to attention. Both devices came into wider use after the turn of the century, especially after World War I. Their effectiveness can best be measured by contrasting the result with such a book as Ellis Meredith's *The Master-Knot of Human Fate* (1901).

One infers that, unlike Mitchell, Meredith deliberately remains vague in terms of specific time and place. In the opening sequence an unnamed man (Adam) and woman (Robin) have climbed high into an isolated area of the Rockies: "Isn't it fine to be a mile or so above the rest of humanity and the deadly conventions?" (p. 10). She wishes that they might "pass through this gateway into paradise without descending to earth again." Meredith supplies the information that their only possible companion has descended into the valley to gain information about the "terrific disturbances . . . threatening the entire Eastern coast with annihilation." As they watch the lights of the town in the valley in the bright moonlight, a great "silver blue wave" from the north engulfs the plain and town; immediately, earthquakes and volcanic action rend the crust of the earth. Amid the noise of terrified animals, they witness the devastation, but nothing happens to them. They realize at once that God has chosen them to renew the world. The narrative becomes a kind of religious meditation whose keynote asks that mankind leave destiny to a "higher law that comes from the source of all law, whatever that source may be" (p. 217). Although Adam is critical of the twentieth century, he believes that the drowned world "was infinitely better than the lost Atlantis, better than the deluged planet of Noah, nobler and finer than the best civilization of which . . . any trace" was left (p. 217). In the American treatment of the catastrophe motif, *The Master-Knot of Human Fate* retains an importance by revealing the persistence of an increasingly uncertain religious orthodoxy. (It seems difficult to decide which literary form did more harm to orthodox religion: literary naturalism or science fiction/fantasy.)

On the other hand, an extreme romanticism also exploited the motif, as in Van Tassel Sutphen's *The Doomsman* (1906), whose society, a *New York Times* critic suggested, resembles "that of England in the early days of the Saxon settlement."[18] That same critic also berated Sutphen for explaining too "vaguely" how the "cataclysmic" change had ended modern society. The omniscient author explicitly refers the reader to the "final authority" of the historian, Vigilas, author of *The Later Cosmos*; writing in 2015—and one cannot be sure how long ago that was—Vigilas explains that the "Great Change" occurred some ninety years earlier. By implication a worldwide plague, the "Terror," quickly brought modern civilization to a standstill, partly because the authorities burned most of the cities in an effort to stop the scourge. Mankind was nearly wiped out; for some sixty years, only small groups, like the family, survived in the burgeoning wilderness. Now small communities have come into being, but the horizons of Vigilas's world have been reduced to the environs of New York City. Three groups exist: the Painted Men, or Wood Folk, a hybrid of the Indians and blacks, who have reverted to savagery; the House People, divided into two classes, the townspeople and the stockade dwellers; and the Doomsmen, descendants of the criminals who were released at the time of the Terror and immediately gathered together in New York City, which their descendants and the Stockaders have since named "Doom the Forbidden."

Once Sutphen sketched this background, however, for the most part he abandoned its potential for a plot that reads like something from a writer of historical romances like G.P.R. James. Although the protagonist is the youthful Constans of Greenwood Keep, from the opening sequence in which his sister, Issa, willingly leaves with Master Quinton Edge, the villainy of that Doomsman determines much of the course of the story. Several times he is referred to as a cavalier, and the dress of the Doomsmen and the Stockaders alike resembles that of an earlier period: in addition to Edge's ruffled cuffs, some of his men are described as "sturdy varlets . . . clad in green jerkins and armed with ashen lances pointed with steel" (p. 76). Thus despite the future setting, the narrative, both in language and action, calls up the past—complete with swordplay and crossbows.

Although Issa elopes with Quinton Edge, raiding Doomsmen sack the Stockade and kill most of the defenders. The action then centers upon Constans' attempt to revenge himself on Edge. Sutphen did not completely forget his point of departure. When Constans first ventures into Doom, Sutphen carefully—and one is tempted to say lovingly—describes the ruined city. Constans makes his way to a great library building (apparently the New York Public Library), where he finds two volumes of "an encyclopaedia of the applied arts and sciences" (p. 71). Although he is tricked by a young woman, Esmay, and captured by a youth, they soon help him escape; he takes the two books with him. Three years lapse in a single sentence, and Constans reflects upon the knowledge—"The Keys of Power"—which he has gained from the books:

. . . the lost civilization of the ancient world; how men had tamed lightning and bade it speak their will and work their pleasure; how the same vapor issuing from the pot bubbling on Matha's fire could be harnessed and made to draw a hundred wagons at once upon the old-time, steel-railed highways; how a child's hand upon the crank of a machine gun might hurl invisible death among a regiment of men and put even an army to flight.

Steam and gunpowder and electricity, what wonderful ideas were connoted in the words! The very names thrilled him with a sense of infinite power. (pp. 83–84)

Once again he ventures into Doom, wintering in the Flatiron Building, from which he may spy into the Citadel of the Doomsmen. He finds guns, which he recognizes from his reading, and understands that they will aid him in his effort to gain vengeance. Then occurs the most original episode of the book. Constans discovers a giant dynamo, still operative, powering an ancient electric chair. The priest, Prosper, regards it as a god and shows Constans the visage of the "Shining One"—the outline of a face appearing when electricity is supplied to certain circuits. Willingly, Constans becomes an acolyte. At this point Sutphen intrudes to declare:

Even among the ancient scientists the nature of electricity was but imperfectly understood, and as the night of ignorance settled down upon the world it was inevitable that the various phenomena of electrical energy should come to be regarded with ever-increasing awe. (pp. 137–138)

But the narrative must return to romance and swordplay. Constans discovers that he loves the now grown Esmay, and when the Blockaders storm the city, he and Esmay leave Edge and the enfeebled Issa to their fate. Prosper, angered by the disbelief in the Shining One on the part of the Doomsmen, sets the city on fire. Ecstatic in the fulfillment of his purpose, he mounts the throne of his god and is electrocuted (p. 270).

Sutphen tacked on a cryptic scene which promises that a renaissance is at hand. A year later, after Constans and Esmay have married, the commander of the electric cruiser *Erebus*, flying the colors of the Antarctic Republican Navy, moves steadily "towards the unknown shore" where Constans and his cohorts live in a rebuilt Greenwood Keep (pp. 294–295). One can possibly jest at the efforts of Sutphen as he tried to join together the ideas and conventions coming from the new scientific romance with the older devices of the historical romance. In many ways, *The Doomsman* may be regarded as a failure, neither fish nor fowl. Yet that a popular writer—famous for his stories about golf—attempted to make use of the fresh materials indicates something of their impact on the literary imagination at the turn of the century. Perhaps one can argue that without such transitional works, such failures, the field of science fiction could not have emerged and, more important, would not have had an audience.

The romanticism of Sutphen is no more absurd than the incidental use of the catastrophe motif in a novel like H. Percy Blanchard's *After the Cataclysm* (1901), which is essentially just another guided tour through a pastoral America. In June 1914, when "blind anarchy" reigns as a result of conflict between capital and labor as well as international strife, "an enormous star, mellow like a twin moon . . . an immensity of matter . . . " avoids collision with the earth "by the narrow margin of a hundred thousand miles" (pp. 44, 45). A thousand-foot tidal wave submerges the eastern United States, and its counterparts change the contours of all the continents. They are the first of various natural phenomena which destroy modern civilization so that mankind (and Christianity) may redeem the world. The process is completed by January 1934, the date when Blanchard's visitor from the turn of the century awakens in the new society. At one point, his guide apologetically explains that the "Public Services were not re-organized for fully five years after the Cataclysm" (p. 68). The populace forgot the need for "National establishments," although aircraft were developed.

Several short stories from the pen of Robert Barr provide examples of effective catastrophes relying heavily on science. One must also commend them for their realistic tone. In "The Doom of London" (1895) the narrator escapes from a killing fog which becomes "one vast smothering mattress" over the London area because it contains so much coal smoke. Almost the entire population dies; they suffocate during a period when there is no wind, for the continuing coal fires use up all of the oxygen under the cloud blanket. Before the narrator flees by train, he stays alive by using an American-made machine which produces oxygen gas. (One recalls the accounts of "black fog" that besieged London as late as the 1930s and required legislation by the London Council.) The title of his "Within an Ace of the End of the World" (*McClure's,* April 1900) speaks for itself. Presented as a future history recalling the disaster of 1904, it reports the circumstances of the "scientific miscalculation" which followed the efforts of Herbert Bonsel, who had served an apprenticeship at Edison's workshops, to change the free nitrogen of the air into a fixed nitrogen to be used as a basic ingredient of all foodstuffs. A small British syndicate, The Great Food Corporation (Limited), finances his venture. They succeed; competitors in other nations flourish. Although the death rate increases sharply and the Prime Minister and some of his colleagues go on an oxygen jag at a banquet, no warning comes until John Rule of Balliol College, Oxford, warns that man is burning himself up because the ratio of gases in the atmosphere has been reversed, oxygen now exceeding the amount of nitrogen. Spontaneous combustion finally kills all the inhabitants of the world except for eight young men at Oxford and, conveniently, eight young women at Vassar College on the Hudson. Once the danger has passed, the Oxford men voyage to America, where all ends happily, although Barr could not resist a glance at a devastated New York. John Rule was, of course, the great-grandfather of the present historian, who points out that the "race which now inhabits the earth is one that includes no savages and no war lords" (p. 554).

The resolution dates the work, but otherwise both it and "The Doom of London" represent one of the classic restrictions imposed on science fiction by many writers and editors as recently as the last several decades. Barr stayed within the bounds of scientific knowledge of his day; he did not resort to the unknown metals or unknown sources of energy so common to the work of his contemporaries.

The stories of Robert Barr anticipate later work, for one of the most obvious distinctions separating the older sf from that of the period after the appearance of the specialist magazines is that the early writers often simply used some scientific data as a point of departure. (As a result perhaps one should distinguish between the scientific romance and science fiction.) A case in point is another novel dealing with catastrophe, Louis P. Gratacap's *The Evacuation of England; The Twist in the Gulf Stream* (1908), which draws upon geological data. An early chapter, entitled "The Lecture," refers to both the San Francisco Earthquake and the eruption of Mt. Pelee on the island of Martinique. He explains that San Francisco lies on one of the two great volcanic rings of the world, while the Caribbean area is unstable. This data remains accurate. One infers that Gratacap may have opposed the idea of any Central American canal, for the construction of the Panama Canal triggers a series of reactions which submerge an area larger than the Isthmus of Panama itself, causes the islands of the West Indies to begin to rise (perhaps to converge into one land mass), and, consequently, diverts the waters of the Gulf Stream into the Pacific. One of his characters acknowledges that "our minds recoil before the awful powers of the natural world," declares that "man is subordinate to and the victim of circumstances," and asks, "What wonders may not the hand of God work in this marvellous reconstruction of land and water?" (pp. 99–100).

Given these conditions, Gratacap abandons science. He explores the effects of this disaster on the civilized world. Great Britain is transformed into a "part of the frozen north" (p. 130), akin to Labrador, so that the House of Commons orders the evacuation of England in February 1910, resolving to move to Australia. Significantly, although Gratacap names Wells as a "brilliant author and prophet of the New Republicanism" (p. 202), he explicitly calls Wells "half-deluded . . . with the sudden dream of starting the English nation on new grounds." Apparently because of his views suggesting "a radical rearrangement of the relations of the sexes," Wells is rejected by the British authorities in favor of "a more dignified and august group of men" including Churchill, Chamberlain, and Balfour, among others. Amusingly, in his concentration upon Great Britain, Gratacap says nothing of changes occurring to the eastern coast of the U.S. or to South America. However, "in Australia the English strength revived and broadened" (p. 314), by implication patterning itself to some degree on American society, for despite the "stupid rich Americans" and the "hateful middle-class Americans," Gratacap's protagonist—Alexander Leacraft, an Englishman serving in Washington—asserts that "the substance and spirit of the American life . . . is palpably the best life now shown in the world" (p. 305). Gratacap, however, proves to be as racist as most of his contemporaries. Here again is the classic pattern: give the narrative a scientific point of departure and then concentrate upon the particular social, economic, or political interests of the individual author.

When one turns to Jack London, one finds that thematically and technically, in his best work, he towers over his American contemporaries even though he, too, uses a specific event as a point of departure. Much recent criticism has focused upon *The Iron Heel* (1907); in presenting the fragmentary Everhard Manuscript, London created a highly effective method for his documentation of the excesses of the oligarchic Trusts which transformed the United States into an authoritarian, Fascistic state. Although its basic conflict is obviously dated, it should be considered among the finest early dystopian novels, quite probably the best by an American author in the first half of the twentieth century. Yet one can emphasize *The Iron Heel* too much, thus doing London a disservice by freezing him at a certain point in his evolving career. To do so ignores that the short novel *The Scarlet Plague* (1915) and the short story "The Red One" (1918) must rank as his finest works.

First published in *London Magazine* (June 1912), *The Scarlet Plague* thus gains an added significance because it was written and issued before World War I and the consequent disillusionment of the 1920s. Then, too, for once, London has control of both his material and the tone of the narrative. He employs a deceptively simple narrative frame in that the action takes place 160 years in the future, along an apparently linear projection of the early twentieth century, but the reader soon learns that he has entered a world unique to London's fiction. The opening statement itself implies that something has gone drastically wrong, for an old man and a young boy walk along what was once a railroad embankment. They join another twelve-year-old boy armed with a bow and arrow; the three retreat from a confrontation with a grizzly bear. In several ways the incident acts as a cornerstone for all that is to come. The old man gives the action a specific location: the approaches to the familiar Cliff House, one of San Francisco's most popular seaside playgrounds. Second, in admitting his own fear, like the literary naturalists, he voices the dominant motivation which guides everyone in the story.

He is Granser, the only human alive who remembers how the Scarlet Death destroyed civilization in 2013. Then he was James Howard Smith, the third in his family to be a professor of English at the University of California at Berkeley; now, sixty years later, he is an increasingly senile old man plagued by memories which have no meaning for these, his grandchildren. London succinctly captures the difference between them when the boy Edwin produces a tarnished silver dollar dated 2012. Granser, "cackling grotesquely," recalls that as the year when "Morgan the Fifth was appointed President of the United States by the Board of Magnates." Edwin "delightedly" exclaims, "You're a great Granser . . . always making believe them little marks mean something." Throughout the opening sequence, London builds on the tensions between a man, for whom everything recalls a lost world, and the children, like Edwin, who regard him "with the tolerant curiousness one accords to the prattlings of the feeble-minded" (pp. 18–19). Only after the three join several other boys acting as goatherds do the youngsters insist that he entertain them with his story of the Great Plague. He tries to explain to them that in 2010 the population of the world had reached 8 billion, and he loses himself in his recollections of how "bacteriologists" had conquered various diseases, although as early as 1929 they had been warned that new germs from the "invisible micro-organic world" might emerge to decimate mankind. One boy, Hare-Lip, grows angry with his "gabble," but Edwin tries to soften the derision and cruelty aimed at the old man.

Only then, after careful preparation does his tortured memory dramatize the events which haunt him. He describes the symptoms: the sudden onslaught, the scarlet rash covering the body, the cold and numbness beginning in the feet. At one point, he speaks of the period of incubation before the plague showed itself (p. 112). At another, he speaks of the bacteriologists dying in their laboratories as they attempted to analyze the germ: "They were heroes. As fast as they perished, others stepped forth and took their places. It was in London that they first isolated it" (p. 76). Too late, a German scientist developed a serum (p. 87). This attention to scientific detail throughout the narrative separated London from virtually all of his contemporaries, especially in America.

Once he establishes this panoramic background, Granser gives a vivid account of his personal experiences as panic overwhelms the citizens of the Bay area. His graphic detail—especially in terms of place—reminds one of Wells's *The War of the Worlds*. For a time, he joins members of the university and their families who quarantine themselves in the Chemistry Building of the Berkeley campus, but the epidemic forces them out of the city. As with Wells's London, one can trace their trek through the small towns surrounding Oakland and San Francisco. The sole survivor of the group, Granser spends three years alone in Yosemite before he encounters Bill the Chauffeur and Vesta Van Warden, former wife of one of the wealthiest of the Industrial Magnates and one of the seven men who had ruled the world. If *The Scarlet Plague* has a flaw, it may lie in London's description of Vesta as "the one woman" and his portrait of the founder of the Chauffeur tribe as a "wretched, primitive man" (p. 153).

This characterization of Chauffeur underscores the fact that interpreting *The Scarlet Plague* as "an almost pathological longing for a catastrophe that would sweep away civilization and restore the pre-Adamite ceremony of innocence" is a serious misreading of the text.[19] Unlike his contemporaries, London does not simply project his own period into the future. Instead, the world devastated by the plague appears to be that of *The Iron Heel*, but in *The Scarlet Plague* London's attitude differs from that of the earlier novel. (In like manner, although he portrays a revolutionary as his protagonist in *The Star Rover*, London's primary concern is no longer with Darrell Standing's role as a socialist agitator; it centers on his cosmic voyages.)

To say that *The Scarlet Plague* once more explores "the revenge of the people of the abyss against their masters" takes out of context Granser's remark: "In the midst of our civilization, down in our slums and labor-ghettos, we had bred a race of barbarians, of savages; and now in the time of our calamity, they turned upon us like the wild beasts they were and destroyed us" (pp. 105–106). The passage continues:

And they destroyed themselves as well. They inflamed themselves with strong drink and committed a thousand atrocities, quarreling and killing one another in the general madness.

One group of workingmen I saw, of the better sort, who had banded together, and, with their women and children in their midst . . . were fighting their way out of the city. They made a fine spectacle. (p. 106)

What the partial reading overlooks is that in *The Scarlet Plague* London portrays a society in which crazed fear of the plague dominates everyone. "All law and order had ceased . . . mobs of the hungry poor were pillaging the stores and warehouses. . . . The people remaining in the city . . . had gone mad with fear and drink" (pp. 85, 86). This is certainly no pre-Adamite innocence, nor is there a defense of the proletariat against the capitalist oligarchy.

To suggest that The Chauffeur speaks for London ignores the initial tension set up between Granser and the youngsters. The full statement of London's theme does not occur until the enveloping framework is closed. As Hare-Lip praises Chauffeur, Edwin, the only one of the boys who has been gentle toward Granser, expresses the desire to learn the secret of gunpowder. His grandfather, who has hidden books in a cave so that civilization may someday revive itself, reflects:

"The gunpowder will come. Nothing can stop it—the same old story over and over. Man will increase, and men will fight. The gunpowder will enable men to kill millions of men, and in this way only, by fire and blood, will a new civilization, in some remote day, be evolved. And of what profit will it be? Just as the old civilization passed, so will the new. It may take fifty thousand years to build, but it will pass. All things pass. Only remains cosmic force and matter, ever in flux, ever acting and reacting and realizing the eternal types—the priest, the soldier, and the king. . . . Some will fight, some will rule, some will pray; and all the rest will toil and suffer sore while on their bleeding carcasses is reared again, and yet again, without end, the amazing beauty and surpassing wonder of the civilized state!" (pp. 178–179)

The plague decimating California had swept throughout the world. Granser speaks as he does about the cycle of history knowing that no more than 350 or 400 humans survived along the Pacific shore; he has no reason to believe that anyone is alive anywhere else. The final image of the narrative focuses upon a small herd of horses driven to the beach by encroaching mountain lions as Granser and the boy Edwin, "skin-clad and barbaric," enter the forest. An irrevocable pessimism—the feeling that errant mankind will forever kill the dream of paradise—permeates London's vision.[20] One senses in it something of that same despair which haunted H. G. Wells during the last decades of his life.

Because the intensity of the anguish voiced by Granser also separated London from his contemporaries, a certain irony arises from the fact that *The Scarlet Plague* first appeared in the same year that two Americans, Garrett P. Serviss and George Allan England, dramatized the rebirth of civilization after worldwide upheavals. Granser's remark that the bacteriologists who sought to isolate the plague germs were heroes links the novels, for both Serviss and England celebrate the scientist as the savior of society.

In *The Second Deluge* (1912), Garrett P. Serviss gives center stage to the eccentric genius, Cosmo Versál. He tells Joseph Smith, an assistant, that no one will listen to him when he warns that soon an invisible, watery nebula will engulf the earth; yet from the moment he discovers the impending danger, he understands his mission:

" . . . That Lick photograph of the Lord Rosse Nebula is its very image, except that there's no electric fire in it. The same great whirl of outer spirals, and then comes the awful central mass—and we're going to plunge straight into it. Then quintillions of tons of water will condense on the earth and cover it like a universal cloudburst. And then good-by to the human race—unless—unless—I, Cosmo Versál, inspired by science, can save a remnant to repeople the planet after the catastrophe. . . . The fate of the whole race is at stake. If we can save a handful of the best blood and brain of mankind, the world will have a new chance, and a better and higher race will be the result. Since I can't save them all, I must pick and choose." (pp. 5–6, 11)

Only because he has developed a new spectroscope which can analyze "extra-visual rays" does he manage to glimpse the nebula, although it is so close that the earth will strike its core in less than a year. Seeing himself as another Noah, he realizes not only that he must build an ark but also that he "must devise a new form of vessel" capable of withstanding such a flood. Fortunately, he can use the "new metal, levium, half as heavy as aluminum and twice as strong as steel" (p. 12). Even so, he can save only a thousand people, for the ark must carry adequate provisions as well as the species of birds, animals, and insects indispensable to the life cycle of the earth.

Cosmo Versál shares a characteristic typical of the fictional scientists of the period (one wonders if its origin came from the public's impression of Edison): he seems to have unlimited wealth. Even before he employs 500 workmen to begin the ark—"the spectacle of this immense expenditure, the evidence that Cosmo was backing his words with his money, furnished a silent argument" (p. 30)[21]—he saturates New York by painting his warnings on every surface available to him, from "the bare flanks of towering sky-scrapers" to "adver-tising-boards along suburban roads" and strings of kites (p. 15). He had predicted correctly. New York laughs at this famous eccentric, and in the theatre a comic introduces a satirical song. But heavy rain, swollen rivers, and terrible electrical storms, whose lightning damages such landmarks as the Leaning Tower of Pisa, spark a wave of terror which sweeps across the world. As further climatic disruptions—"Signs"—occur, Versál undertakes the task of choosing those whom he must save. Momentarily overcome by the responsibility thrust upon him, he declares that such decisions "are the function of deity, not of man"; but Joseph reassures him, " . . . you *are* ordained; you must *do the work*" (pp. 73, 74).

As Serviss's spokesman, Versál echoes the widely held view that the world had grown increasingly corrupt, morally and physically, over the centuries, and he reemphasizes the similarity of himself and Noah. When he asserts that as many women as men must be saved because "the strongest moral element is in the women, although they don't weigh heavily for science" (p. 78), he again voices a popular opinion, but he rises to individuality during the period when he rejects the idea that his final choice be made on the basis of race: "No race has ever shown itself permanently the best" (p. 76). Only then does he reveal that not unexpected bias which set him and a number of others apart and very probably contributed to the antiscientific, anti-Wellsian reaction which became increasingly noticeable after the war: "I shall begin with the men of science. They are the true leaders" (p. 76).

Of the thousand places available, Versál assigns 225 to scientists, 270 to agriculture and mechanics, and 90 to medical doctors. To avoid future litigation, he includes only "Chief Justice Good." Explaining that a number of Russians will be aboard the ark, he rejects the Czar, for he "will carry none of the Romanoff seeds to my new world," but he does include the German Emperor, who "has at last got the war microbe out of the family blood" (p. 82). His most interesting selections are the President-Emperor of China ("a true Confucian") and the President of Liberia. He also chooses ten statesmen "with total disregard to racial and national lines" (p. 83). Despite his earlier remark, however, he does not select any renowned woman.

So closely do the early chapters concentrate on the speculations and plans of Versál that not until after the actual deluge begins does the reader become fully aware of Serviss's inability to create graphic scenes or sustain action. One suspects that his career as a newspaper columnist and a popularizer of astronomy account for these weaknesses. When the narrative is not made up of expository dialogue, Serviss generalizes about what occurs, as becomes particularly noticeable in the chapter entitled "The Last Day of New York." His inability to dramatize an incident shows itself, for example, when the ark runs aground "on the loftiest part of the Palisades" (pp. 143–145). Abruptly, intruding the editorial we, he shifts to Europe and to France, where Yves De Beauxchamps and unnamed companions build a "submersible"—named *Jules Verne*—and thus escape the flood. The break in the narrative is unneeded, for Beauxchamps soon sails to the ark and joins Versál. Together aboard the submarine they visit both submerged Paris and the Great Pyramid. Although *Jules Verne* must be abandoned, the mystery of the Sphinx is solved. Part of it collapses and reveals a strange face and an inscription which Versál interprets as a prophecy of the second deluge. (The intrusion of Egyptian material here, as well as in Serviss's earlier novel *Edison's Conquest of Mars* (1898), provides further evidence of the popular fascination with Egypt.)

The Beauxchamps sequence is not the only structural flaw in the novel, for Serviss prematurely reveals much of the outcome of the narrative when he switches his attention to Professor Abiel Pludder, Versál's severest critic, who refuses an invitation to join the party aboard the ark. By converting a downed aeroplane into a boat, he sails with his close friend, President Samson, from the Alleghenies to Colorado, where they find that many Americans have survived in the high Rockies. Pludder deduces that as much as a quarter of western America has escaped submersion (p. 279). Although the rains resume, much land remains above water. Pludder exclaims, *"Batholite,"* before he is abandoned in favor of Versál who gains a final glimpse of "New York in Her Ocean Tomb" viewed from a diving-bell invented by Beauxchamps.

Through much of the narrative, Versál insists that the area of the Himalayas will be the first land to emerge from the depths; what, other than Serviss's jingoism, should cause him to be wrong, one can but guess. Although he speaks of the "tectonic features of the globe" (pp. 270–271), he acknowledges that he erred in his original deduction, and he is surprised to find that the Rockies have provided a haven for mankind. Pludder explains that batholite refers to the concept of pressure upon the plastic rock within the earth "lifting up the superincumbent crust" (p. 394); Versál acknowledges that he based his deduction upon that idea. Thus he suffers no more than "the natural embarrassment of a man of science upon discovering that he has been in error" (p. 395). The manner in which Serviss handles the last half of the novel remains confusing, especially because he tacks on a last passage which suddenly makes the narrative the work of future historians who honor Cosmo Versál:

He taught his principles of eugenics and implanted deep the germs of science, in which he was greatly aided by Professor Pludder, and, as all readers of this narrative know, we have every reason to believe that our new world, although its population has not yet grown to ten millions, is far superior, in every respect, to the old world that was drowned. (p. 397)

By implication, a paradise based upon science has been founded. But the importance of *The Second Deluge* rests in the fact that, more than any other American novel, it explicitly identifies the scientist as the savior of mankind.

In contrast, George Allan England's trilogy *Darkness and Dawn* (1914) strips away such explicit thematic material in favor of plot action, especially a love story. In a subsequent article (1923), England asserts that "romance must always, if possible, be interwoven with science. The scientific warp must be shot through with the woof of human interest and love."[22] Granting that premise, the trilogy can also be identified with the neoprimitivism which characterized much of American popular fiction early in this century. Although no explanation of the cause of the basic catastrophe is given, it resembles that in Fuller's *A.D. 2000*:

The great explosion that liberated the poisonous gases [within the earth] and killed practically everybody in the world must have gouged this new planet out of the flank of Mother Earth in the latter part of 1920. The rejected portions, millions and millions of tons, hundreds and thousands of miles of solid rock—and with them the ruins of Chicago, Milwaukee, St. Louis, Omaha, and hundreds of smaller towns—are now all revolving in a fixed, regular orbit, some few thousand miles or so from the surface! (p. 393)

England never bothers with a fuller explanation of the cataclysm, for it simply provides a backdrop for adventure. In an office on the forty-eighth floor of the

Metropolitan Tower, one of the few skyscrapers left intact after an unspecified number of centuries, Beatrice Kendrick, a typist-secretary, awakens as though from a brief sleep. Conveniently for her, the man with whom she has been infatuated, Allan Stern, a consulting engineer, revives in the next office. During their first conversation, as Stern keeps her from looking out upon the ruins and encroaching forests of Manhattan, he offers her his tattered coat to cover her nudity; with "quiet, modest dignity," Beatrice assures him that her hair "protects" her very well, and that if they are indeed the only humans left alive, "this is no time for trifles" (pp. 11–12). He assures her that they should not "mourn or fear! Rather [they must] read this mystery, to meet it and to conquer" (p. 24). Even earlier, however, they have realized that they are "alone in [the] whole world . . . and everything belongs to [them]. . . . Even the future—the future of the human race" (p. 18).

They search Manhattan for the means to survive. The entire first volume, *The Vacant World*, combines the elements of a Robinsonade with an account of their fight with hideous, blue-mottled subhumans—they are compared unfavorably with Neanderthal Man and *Pithecanthropus*—who lurk in the forest.[23] (Allan and Beatrice triumph because they have guns and grenades.) Whenever Allan Stern is hard pressed, England says the same thing about him until even in its minor variations, it becomes a thematic chorus: "But still he kept on. Something drove him inexorably forward. For he was an engineer—and an American" (p. 80). At the end of the first volume, they confess their love and dream of the rebirth of civilization:

"You and I, Beatrice. . . . Just you—and I!"

"And love," she whispered.

"And hope, and life! And the earth reborn. The arts and sciences, language and letters, truth, 'all the glories of the world' handed down through us! . . .

"A kinder and a saner world this time. No misery, no war, no poverty, woe, strife, creeds, oppression, tears—for we are wiser than those other folk, and there shall be no error.

" . . . The aristocracy of idleness shall reign no more! A world without a slave. Man shall at last be free! . . . "

"And love?" she smiled again. . . .

"And love!" he answered. (pp. 164–165)

They seal the vision with "a kiss of passion and of joy."

England surrenders the second and third volumes of the trilogy to repetitive plot action, most of it centering on Allan's and Beatrice's escapes from various hazards, usually caused by the terrible convulsions of the earth long ago. In *Beyond the Great Oblivion*, Stern conveniently finds a biplane which is still operable, as well as a seemingly endless supply of the alcohol which serves as fuel. They fly westward toward Chicago, where they are forced down into the great abyss from which the new moon was torn. For a time they are prisoners of the albino descendants of the survivors of the disaster. Calling themselves

"Merucaans," these people hold vaguely to the memory of the former world. Stern must fight physically to become the chief of what he calls the Folk, but at the end he begins to transport the Folk from the Abyss to New Hope colony, which he and Beatrice had founded, an action continuing into *The Afterglow*. Before he can complete that task, the plane is damaged, and he and the few Merucaans with him must fight off the attacks of the subhuman Horde. Victory is achieved only after Stern burns the forests in which the Horde lives.

Victorious but exhausted, their numbers depleted, Stern and his companions discover that the Merucaans left in the Abyss have found their way to the surface and have come to him, to rescue him if need be. Thus the final chapters picture a flourishing society living in an idyllic landscape. Conveniently, he found a library of books in New York to speed the process, for in not more than a generation they have the service of airplanes and monorail trains. Allan remarks to Beatrice, "We must be content to have built foundations. On them those who shall come in the future shall raise a fairer and mightier world than any we ever dreamed" (pp. 668–669). Despite the love and strength of Beatrice, however, England implies that none of this recovery would have been possible had Allan Stern not had the scientific training of an engineer.

In a far less spectacular fashion, Sir Arthur Conan Doyle also gave mankind a second chance in *The Poison Belt* (1913). Professor Challenger and his party emerge from a hermetically sealed room to tour a seemingly desolated London. But everywhere people awaken as from a nightmare. The heightened moral insight which people gain as a result of the experience seems to make certain the growth of a better society. Although British writers in particular occasionally continued to give mankind a second chance, as in John Wyndham's *The Day of the Triffids* (1951), never again did American or British writers speak so assuredly of the moral reform and enlightened transformation and progress of Western society. The vision of an untroubled earthly paradise growing out of the old order, be it capitalist or socialist, vanished with the coming of World War I.

Apparently I. F. Clarke overlooked the earlier American novels when he named *Nordenholt's Million* (1923) by J. J. Connington, the pseudonym of Alfred Walter Stewart, as the "stereotype" of "the salvation myth" marking the "appearance of the scientist as saviour and superman."[24] When *Bacterium diazotans* destroys the nitrogenous content of the soil and causes a worldwide famine, Nordenholt establishes a colony of 5 million persons in the Clyde Valley; primarily through his individual strength, the "Nitrogen Area," as it is called, survives, although he does delegate increasing authority to Jack Flint, the first-person narrator. Yet Clarke is correct when he asserts that Nordenholt acts and speaks like an autocrat: "There's no idle class in the Nitrogen Area. . . . There's no Parliament, no gabble about Democracy, no laws that a man can't understand. I've made a clean sweep of most of the old system, and the rest will go down before we're done" (p. 183). Using this specific example, Clarke points out that utopia has changed: "The old faith in humanity has given place to a belief in the powers of an exceptional individual, a saviour far above the rest of the community in determination and intelligence."[25] His further observation that "this loss of faith led to the ultimate, despairing vision of that last day when the great cities are empty and all the works of men are in ruins" applies to British science fiction of the period in general, but not to *Nordenholt's Million* in particular. Nordenholt dies; Flint becomes the colony's leader. When the colony develops atomic power, it flourishes in a way that Nordenholt did not imagine—a way that makes it unique among British fiction of the period. In the last passage of the novel, Flint explains that he found himself facing a dilemma because the atomic engine had "made the employment of human labour super-erogatory" although the majority of citizens were manual laborers; consequently, his society became the builders of great cities named after the "ancient glories of myth and tradition: Asgard and Lyonnesse, Tara." As he gazes at the city of Asgard, he concludes, "For once, at least, in this world, hope has been far outrun by achievement. Splendours of which I never dreamed have come into being." Yet he undercuts this glory when he acknowledges," . . . our population is small. Asgard is only for the few who can enjoy its beauties: the many have other cities more suited to their tastes; and they have no wish to come hither."[26] Indeed, something new has come to the utopian dream; by implication, the dream of the brotherhood of man has vanished. Certainly, there is an ambivalence in the ending of this novel, probably the most optimistic vision to emerge among British writers of the postwar period.

Something of that same ambivalence occurred earlier in the major novel of Victor Rousseau (the pseudonym of Victor Rousseau Emanuel), a prolific writer for the Munsey pulps. His only novel apparently never published in a magazine, *The Messiah of the Cylinder* (1917), which Richard D. Mullen has called a "sexual fantasy" instead of an attack upon socialism,[27] deserves more attention than it has received. The point of departure of its storyline is deceptively simple: Both Herman Lazaroff and Arnold Pennell work at a Biological Laboratory outside of London. When Lazaroff discovers that the girl they both love, Esther, prefers Arnold, he tricks them both into cylinders which will keep them in suspended animation for a century; he enters a third, certain that in the new, "free" future he will stand a better chance of winning Esther. He awakens prematurely after sixty-five years; by 1980, as Dr. Sanson, he becomes one of the rulers, the scientific adviser to Boss Lambken.

He finds the world transformed by a series of revolutions between 1945 and 1978. It may well be an economic utopia, as Mullen emphasizes, but it is also a totalitarian world-state. Toward the end of the period of chaos, "the writings of the great Wells, since called the Prophet, were discovered and proved to be an inspiration of the new order" (p. 91). In a hall of fame, his statue stands among those of such men as Marx, Darwin, and Mendel. Lazaroff-Sanson explains: "We know now that Science has given Nature's complete and final revelation to mankind. We tolerate no heresies, no independent judgements" (p. 94). However much Wells was responsible for the new order, he had nothing to do with that characteristic giving this world state its individuality. Its emphasis upon eugenics has structured society into four groups, ranging from the non-defectives who have complete sexual freedom, though they must reproduce within their own group, to the morons who cannot reproduce and, even more than the two classes of "defectives," have been subjected to vivisection. Granted the obvious distinctions between the imaginary worlds, one wonders whether Huxley knew Rousseau's novel, for more than any novel prior to *Brave New World* its organization grows out of a control of genetics and, to some extent, intelligence.

This issue, particularly the vivisection, led to the outlawing of Christianity. In secret, however, the Christians have enshrined Esther and await the coming of the Messiah, Arnold Pennell. When he does awaken, he and Esther lead a revolt which overthrows the Lambken-Sanson power base and replaces it with a Christian community. Although *The Messiah of the Cylinder* explicitly denies the scientific materialism—the "Futurism"—which had dominated the twenty-first century, it retains the structure of the socialist world-state. Only its morality has changed; that is all a reader can be certain of, for the new government proclaims, "We shall have no representative government, no popular elections, no tyranny of the unthinking majority" (p. 353). As Mullen pointed out, there are only two things which the new regime "will not countenance: divorce and eugenics."[28] The reader can only hope that it will not be totalitarian. For these reasons it deserves particular attention as one of the first of the twentieth-century dystopian fictions which led to Zamiatin, Huxley, and Orwell. Even though its central concern is with eugenics, it must be regarded as one of the opening guns in the anti-Wellsian reaction, although Hillegas makes no reference to it in *The Future as Nightmare*.

Another Rousseau novel, *The Sea Demons*, first published in *All-Story* (1916) and then issued in London under the pseudonym H. M. Egbert (1924), strips away thematic material in favor of adventure and action. Except for those novels dealing with an imaginary presidency, it anticipates the American use of the catastrophe motif after World War I. At the center of the narrative lies the plot of the scientist, Ira MacBeard, to use a race of humanoid undersea creatures to conquer the world. Described as being like bees, they swarm and attack England and other countries when their new queen wishes to mate with the protagonist, Lieutenant Donald Paget, commander of a submarine. Within the catastrophe motif, at least, one may conclude that she is the first evil queen to desire the protagonist sexually. When he refuses and she dies (her life span is three weeks), her swarm of drones kill themselves and MacBeard in Skjold Fjord. An interesting sideline to this threat to mankind occurs when the warring nations of Europe end the Great War because they comprehend that mankind must be united to repel such attacks.

The emphasis upon action leads to Eric Temple Bell, who wrote as John Taine; his *Green Fire* (1928), one of his lesser achievements, concentrates upon the rivalry between two scientists attempting to develop atomic power in 1990. The successful efforts of the profit-seeking Jevis start a chain reaction throughout the universe so that matter is destroyed. Fortunately, James Ferguson, who sees himself from the outset as a benefactor of humanity, also learns the secret of controlling atomic power and thus stops the all-consuming threat to the universe as it reaches the Andromeda galaxy.

In the same year, 1990, Ray Cummings' *The Sea Girl* (1930) reworks the threat posed by Rousseau's *The Sea Demons*. As numerous Pacific volcanoes become active and the level of the sea begins to recede, Jeff Grant, Dr. Plantet, and the latter's son and daughter learn that a race which lives in a subterranean world beneath the Pacific—the Gians—plan to conquer the world. Another race, the Mdj (''Middge''), represented by the beautiful mermaid Nereid, whom young Arturo Plantet loves, also faces genocide. Jeff and his party reach the subterranean world, where they find the Amazon warriors of the Gian led by Queen Rhana, ''a woman six feet tall; full-breasted, slim of hip'' (p. 153)—and sadistic. She confesses her love for Jeff, but he prefers pretty Polly Plantet. In a struggle, Rhana breaks her own neck just before the Mdj destroy the Gian caverns. Polly and Jeff and Nereid and Arturo are left with the choice of whether to search for the Mdj, who have disappeared after their victory.

Fred MacIsaac resorts to the established convention of suspended animation in *The Hothouse World* (1931) to send his protagonist, George Putnam, into the middle of the twenty-first century, where he finds himself enshrined in the glass-domed Putnam community on Lake Champlain. He learns that the people regard him as a kind of Messiah who will help them, for they believe themselves to be the only community which has survived the new ice age that came after a comet polluted the earth's atmosphere in 1987. They are wrong; a group of supposed barbarians attacks the dome but is beaten off. When Putnam flies south after finding a plane, accompanied by Helen Ames, who has promised to choose him at the next marriage lottery, he discovers that the land south of the Carolinas now has a climate like that of earlier New England. When they return to the Lake Champlain community, they find that the citizens have revolted against the excesses of the aristocracy; an appended note explains that Putnam led a thousand people southward so that civilization was reborn in the Carolinas.

Despite the grim warnings of so many European writers, British fiction did not entirely escape such narratives of survival and rebirth. Francis H. Sibson allowed a continent, ''New Canada,'' to rise in the Atlantic basin in *The Survivors* (1932). The main storyline brings together an American girl, Joan Archdale, and Lt. Commander L. A. Fennlake of H.M.S. *Maple Leaf*. He goes to her, for she is trapped and alone aboard another ship. They fall in love, of course, and as they set sail aboard the *Maple Leaf* for England, she asks if he would have minded had they been the last man and woman.

A single passage, prompted by specific reference to an unnamed book about saving a submarine by Commander Edward Ellsburg, U.S.N., prepares for Sibson's sequel, *The Stolen Continent* (1934). After lumping together ''gangsters and politicians and corrupted policemen,'' Sibson cites various Americans, mostly military men, who represent the "real solid Nordic stuff . . . underneath" (p. 268). The plot of *The Stolen Continent* centers on the attempt of gangsters and corrupt politicians to take over both the U.S. and New Canada. Joan Archdale's kidnapping brings the lovers into the action. After the criminal attempt is defeated, a combined fleet of U.S. and British ships flies "the twin flags of Anglo-Saxondom" (p. 288). For whatever reasons, the novel did not find an American publisher as had its predecessor. It may well represent the swan song of Anglo-Saxon invincibility.

When considered in a context which includes an awareness of Rousseau's *The Messiah of the Cylinder*, Zamiatin's *We* (1924), and Huxley's *Brave New World* (1932), these latter novels seem at best superficial and shopworn. Stylistic matters aside, although only some of them saw initial publication in popular magazines, they represent that kind of action-oriented story contemptuously dismissed as "pulp" fiction—often simply another way of saying popular fiction. They must be counted, too, among those works which Robert Silverberg indignantly classified as "hollow and pointless adventure fiction."[29] Yet such a judgment must be tempered by the realization that while no storyline ever completely loses an audience or completely disappears, it obviously can grow dated and threadbare from retelling without substantive change or from failing to respond to a change in intellectual temper. Despite any such qualification, however, when one examines the American handling of the catastrophe motif during the 1920s and 1930s, no more than four works impress one as retaining any degree of timeless vitality. Perhaps surprisingly, none of them is conspicuously original.

Pierrepont B. Noyes, identified as American Rhineland Commissioner, combines the concepts of a fall from a Golden Age and history as an endless cycle in *The Pallid Giant; A Tale of Yesterday and Tomorrow* (1927). His first-person narrator seems a thin disguise of himself as he reacts to the premise "that evolution has, in past ages, developed a human type more than once, and that those human races destroyed themselves with their own inventions" (p. 28). Possessing the seemingly incidental knowledge that a British spy has learned that Germany has developed some deadly new ray, the narrator and his friend Rudge search the area of the ancient caves of France (he specifically names the Grotte de Gargas and the caves of the Haute Garrone) for evidence supporting the premise. Noyes introduces the idea of race memory in that while in a trance the woman Mraaya chants songs supposedly coming down through a line of women from prehistory. They find a book; when translated as "The Death-Ray," it gives an account of the destruction of a highly advanced civilization, suggesting that a few survivors consciously bred with the mindless brutes of the island Mrac (pp. 288–291), thereby producing a race of half-breeds, the "Gla-ni," from whom modern mankind is descended. Through a group of nine chosen priestesses, by a process of deep hypnosis, the survivors attempted to pass down their knowledge. Mraaya, of course, is of that lineage. The narrator of this story within a story concludes, "I, Rao, son of Ramil, last of my kind to look on this unspeakably lonesome, man-made desert called 'the world,'—am ready to die" (p. 296). He exemplifies another image of

Clarke's last man. Noyes's narrator closes with the obvious question whether or not history will repeat itself, but throughout he has voiced as a central theme: "Fear [the "pallid giant"] will destroy the world" (p. 35).

In contrast, Edwin Balmer and Philip Wylie played down thematic content in favor of plot action when they updated Garrett P. Serviss's *The Second Deluge*. In *When Worlds Collide* (1933), Cole Hendron leads a group which builds a spaceship to escape the threat of Bronson Beta. Not only do they observe the physical destruction of the earth, but they land on Bronson Beta, an arcadian planet which conveniently has begun to orbit the sun. (Like so many sequels, their *After Worlds Collide* (1934) falls short, largely because the dramatic conflict centers on their fight with Asiatic communists for control of the new world.)

Although one should not dismiss Robert Herrick's *Sometime* (1933) as merely a satire of modern society, as J. O. Bailey seemed to do,[30] Herrick did condemn the West for a series of wars beginning with "the Crusade of 1914–1918" and ending with a great struggle between the Caucasians and the "yellow peoples"; mankind destroyed civilization when it stood at the brink of gaining "control of the human environment" so that it could have "abolished want, famine, [and could have] practically controlled all disease" (p. 7). For reasons Herrick never adequately explains, a terrible ice age drove the remnant of humanity from America and Europe. Now a thousand years after "the geologic convulsions following the recent Ice Age," with the center of civilization at Omdurman near Khartoum, on the eve of the departure of the first expedition to search "the forgotten western hemisphere" (pp. 4, 6), one of the patriarchal leaders sums up what is remembered of Christian culture in its latter days. He is most critical of the prurient sexuality of the earlier period. One cannot be certain what racial hybrid survives in Herrick's novel.

Perhaps the finest American work of the period remains Stephen Vincent Benét's "By the Waters of Babylon" (1937), which echoes London's *The Scarlet Plague* in that it pictures a future America fallen to barbarism. Artistically, it is a major triumph, for quickly Benét "sets up a tension between familiar details associated with the American Indian and foreboding implications of a future catastrophe. . . . he exploits [this tension] through structuring the entire story as an account of an Indian Medicine–dream quest, embodying in it three themes . . . the initiation of a boy into adult society, the collapse of present-day civilization, and the conflict between the individual and his mythos."[31] John, son of John, who will one day be spiritual leader of his people, journeys to ruined New York, where amid the desolated towers of Manhattan, he realizes that the ancients were humans like himself. In his vision he sees the destructive bombing which wastes the city. Reflecting that perhaps "in the old days, they ate knowledge too fast," he resolves, "We must rebuild." Although anticipating the spread of the horror which he witnessed in the bombing of the Spanish Civil War, Benét nevertheless voices the affirmation which is more characteristic of American science fiction than that of any other nation.

A small group of peculiarly American novels vividly illustrates the shift away from the dream of a utopian future to a sense of imminent disaster. By and large they retain a historical value, but they are hopelessly dated, for they make use of imaginary presidencies to voice the anxieties of their individual authors. The title story of Herbert D. Ward's *A Republic Without a President* (1891) focuses upon an incident in which the president and his wife are kidnapped by a patriotic zealot who wishes to prove that the U.S. "can never afford to be careless of its defenses and of the treasures which they protect" (p. 55). American women rise "*en masse*" to help secure the stipulated ransom. Frederick U. Adams' *President John Smith* (1897) introduces a new constitution which does away with the Senate and ensures everyone the right to work, while Frank Barkley Copley's *The Impeachment of President Israels* (1912) results from the anger of Congress because he will not declare war against Germany. In the same year, the protagonist of Edward M. House's *Philip Dru: Administrator* (1912) becomes the leader of those opposed to a dominant eastern political machine and successfully leads a civil war in which all of the states west of the Mississippi combine their strength. For seven years after victory, Dru serves as "Administrator of the Republic" during a period in which the U.S. engulfs the North American continent from the Arctic to the Isthmus of Panama. Except for a brief scuffle with Mexico, this end is achieved peacefully. Women are given the franchise.

Women also prove a decisive factor in the election of 1940 in William H. McMasters's *Revolt: An American Novel* (1919). McMasters was undoubtedly sincere in his denunciation of the power which "big money" had in American politics, but the final resolution of the storyline largely negates his attack. When Roger Morton learns that his father, John Paine Morton, Chairman of United Trust Company, has named the presidential candidates of both political parties during the last three elections (p. 40), he resigns from United Trust to help form the Revolutionist political party. After a bitter campaign in which his father attempts to stifle the new party and even arranges the kidnapping of his son's fiancée, Marta Falmouth, the Revolutionist party wins; it makes use of the one newspaper chain that his father cannot control, emphasizing particularly the Gilmore Movie News Service to bring its message to the people. After Roger and Marta have been married following the victory, John Paine Morton comes to their hotel suite to tell his son, "You are the cleanest, hardest and squarest fighter this country ever produced . . . and I'm glad you won" (p. 279). He then learns that the man whose campaign his son has managed, Dan Holman, has appointed him Secretary of the Treasury because the senior Morton is one of the world's foremost financiers.

In the novel *1943*, written in 1922 by a "Mr. X," whose identity has not been discovered, the protagonist, Walter Gordon, awakens after twenty years of suspended animation to find America dominated by the iron will of the reformers who make up the American Puritan Church. Through their pressure, amendments to the Constitution have been passed enforcing prohibition of alcohol and tobacco as well as strictly governing women's dress. One of its leaders,

Knowles, informs Gordon, "that when a number of people live together in a community, the good of the community is greater than that of any one member of it. . . . We seek to make the American people perfect, or as near perfect as possible for human beings to be" (p. 167). But Gordon finds corruption still prevalent: ships described as "Floating Hells" are anchored off the three-mile limit, subterranean nightclubs where anything goes exist in Washington itself, the use of drugs is widespread, and, of course, the real political powers behind the American Puritan Church are ruthless men given to quality alcohol and imported cigars, while their police minions are trigger-happy. Only after Gordon has become fully aware of the scene does he become the presidential candidate of the American Liberty Party. After a campaign, during which an assassination attempt on Gordon is foiled by a young woman who is herself killed, he emerges the president-elect.

As one might expect, the popularity of these novels peaked during the Great Depression. Although they give insight into the national anxieties of that period, as did Sinclair Lewis's *It Can't Happen Here* and Hendrik Van Loon's *Invasion*, they do not find a single solution. In sharp contrast to the decades before World War I, the central issue is not that of socialism. Brian Barry, the imaginary president in Shaemas O'Sheel's *It Never Could Happen; or, The Second American Revolution* (1932) speaks for all of the protagonists who wish to rid the U.S. of corrupt government and poor economic conditions when he asserts, "We will not overturn the American social system. We will purge it drastically to restore its health. . . . Not revolution, but restoration, re-birth—that will be our purpose—the Renascence of traditional America!" (pp. 61–62). The core of O'Sheel's novel, presented as a future history, is the first-person narrative of General Elmer Hicks, whom Barry asked to act as commander in chief of what had once been called the Bonus Army. Supposedly edited and published in 1982, Hicks's narrative is entitled *The Veterans Revolution of 1932*. It is his task to seize Washington from conservatives who attempt a coup, while Federal troops disperse a force of "Reds" converging on the city. The major battle takes place against "a force of gunmen, gangsters, and private detectives . . . mustered in Chicago," the hirelings of "a clique of bankers and reactionary capitalists" (p. 159).

Something of the same concern for organized crime exists in George F. Worts's *The Phantom President* (1932). When the so-called "Big Four," the capitalists who run American politics, decide that Theodore K. Blair, "the cleverest practical economist in America, if not the world" (p. 24), does not have the charisma to win an election, they find a criminal and murderer, Peter Varney, who can pass as Blair's double. Varney is easily elected; he attempts to seize complete control of the presidency, for Blair had acquiesced to his use in the campaign. A touch of spice is added to the plot when the communist, Zarinov, reveals that he knows there are two presidents; he threatens a "bloodless revolution" by revealing the truth to the American people. Varney is assassinated, and Blair willingly surrenders his position for exile and anonymity, giving up "the malignant spell of power" (p. 362).

Perhaps something of the angry despair of the 1930s and the degree to which these novels expressed the fantasies of the period is most fully illustrated in Thomas F. Tweed's *Gabriel Over the White House* (1933). Tweed thought it necessary to use an automobile accident to change President Hammond's personality and political outlook. Hammond abandons an inept conservatism to side with the unemployed. Instead of political reform, however, he denounces "the American political system . . . reactionary State Legislatures . . . [and] the mismanagement of the funds Congress had voted for public works in the States" (pp. 83–84). He adjourns Congress and rules as a benevolent dictator. Through Peale Lindsay, who has grown wealthy because his firm had the exclusive rights to television and who becomes the Secretary of the Department of Education, Hammond maintains control of the public through his "television talks" (this seems to be the first extensive use in fiction of government-owned television). Although hoodlums in Chicago have gunned down a number of marchers in a parade of the Unemployed Citizens' League, not until the government undertakes the manufacture of alcohol does civil conflict break out. Primarily through the use of a federal police force, the "Green Jackets," the struggle ends in the "crushing of the most active elements among the gangsters and gunmen in New York and Chicago" (p. 195). In addition, Hammond builds a concentration camp on Ellis Island, where anyone using a gun in a crime is imprisoned, the majority of them executed.

Although he repudiates the League of Nations, with the cooperation of Britain and France, Hammond does intervene in Asiatic affairs. Air power destroys the Japanese navy. In chairing the conference at London leading to the formation of a World Council, which will have the only military forces allowed to exist, Hammond emphasizes not only the effect of air power on naval forces but suggests that any future land fighting will be done by "small professional armies, equipped with every mechanical and chemical device that science and malevolent genius could achieve" (p. 228). A new world capital, "International City," is built in the north of Ireland, and Hammond's last proposal is that the U.S. transfer almost all of its gold reserve to a new International Central Bank to bring economic stability to the world. Significantly—for dramatic effect in all probability—Tweed chose to have President Hammond again injure his head in escaping assassination by a criminal. Learning what he has done during the three years of his term, he plans to repudiate everything on national television. Before members of the administration can take action, he dies of a heart attack.

In *The President Vanishes* (1934), originally published anonymously, Rex Stout permitted President Stanley to be kidnapped, although he had attempted to seclude himself so that he would not have to ask Congress to get the U.S. involved in another European war. Much of the action of the narrative is concerned either with looking for the president or with the schemes of Lincoln Lee to lead the Gray Shirts to power in the U.S. The novel ends with a long passage—the president's speech—declaring that America must never be part of another European war.

John F. Goldsmith's *President Randolph As I Knew Him* (1935), presented as the biography of a president holding office in the 1950s and 1960s, insists that there is "no material difference between a system of large collectivistic monopolies and trusts and a system of communism. The net result of either is slavery for the common man" (p. 161). His major accomplishment, however, is the creation of a new United Nations, although one article states that "Asiatic and African populations shall not be entitled to representation in the international legislature, excepting those of the Union of South Africa and Algeria, and similar peoples of an advanced Western civilization" (p. 209). In contrast, Samuel Hopkins Adams gave no thought to international agreement in *The World Goes Smash* (1938); in 1940, the struggle of Hugh Farragut, the New York District Attorney, against organized crime leads to a civil war ended only after the development of the Azrael bomb, which brings Chicago and New York to the edge of ruin and causes widespread blindness wherever it is dropped. In a sense, Adams ignored the rest of the world, for Communism and Fascism have destroyed Europe. Perhaps the importance of these novels lies in the suggestion that they express the despair of an America which had foreseen the possibility of an earthly paradise but found instead the nightmare of depression from which there seemed no escape.

Of the nineteenth-century novels which portray a future society dominated by women, Walter Besant's *The Revolt of Man*, first published anonymously by Blackwood in 1882, understandably draws criticism, especially from the feminist critics of the 1980s. Two centuries after the "Great Transition," during which women gained complete political, social, and economic control of Britain, Dorothy Ingleby, Professor of Ancient and Modern History at Cambridge, both acknowledges that she obeys and reverences her husband and helps the youthful Lord Chester foment a revolution returning all power to men. At one point, she tells the youth, " . . . now compose that sermon which will show that Man is the Lord and Master of all created things, including—Woman" (p. 134). Besant's position obscures the skill with which he effects a complete reversal of sex roles in the early half of his narrative, a skill not equaled until Victoria Cross's *Martha Brown, M.P., A Girl of Tomorrow* (1935).

Besant's satire may be read at another level. In his projected society only "elderly ladies were rich enough to take a husband and face the possibilities of marriage. . . . Nothing, ladies complained among each other, was more difficult than to win and retain a young man's love" (p. 48). The Duchess of Dunstanburgh's proposal of marriage to Lord Chester, who loves his second cousin, Constance, Lady Carlyon, precipitates the revolution. Besant seems to use the reversal to underscore his satire of his own society in which wealthy old men married young women. This must be read as a device to heighten his ridicule, for otherwise his basic premise—that only older women can afford to marry—would hasten the extinction of humanity. He thus comes out on the side of romantic love, a fact that will not appease his feminist critics.

Perhaps Besant's taking power from women who had it intensifies the reaction against him. *The Revolt of Man* does not make the most outrageous statement at the turn of the century about the place of women in society. At one end of the spectrum, in *Zoraida; A Romance of the Harem and the Great Sahara* (1895), William LeQueux's protagonist brings his bewitching Arab wife, Zoraida, back to London, where, of course, she creates a sensation in the social world. At the other end, in *The Incubated Girl* (1896), Fred T. Jane perverted current interest in Egyptology by allowing Blackburne Zadara and Professor Wilson—who closely follow the instructions of an ancient papyrus—to hatch an egg which they had found in a temple dedicated to Isis. When it produces a girl child, whom they name Stella, Wilson is relieved that they have not produced "a Frankenstein monster" (p. 13). Zadara denounces the "new woman" who would permit young girls to know "everything of all vices and diseases . . . everything of their anatomy and the causes of sensations" (p. 18). He intends to train Stella in the paths of virtue and chastity, but at eighteen she more nearly resembles the femme fatale than perhaps any other young woman in the science fiction of the period. At one moment she makes advances to Wilson's son Meredyth, an artist, while at the next she caresses the model Susie Montmorency. Yet through Meredyth, Jane continues to prate about innate modesty and natural goodness.

After sketching Natasha, *The Angel of the Revolution* (1894), George Griffith created "a beauty to enslave and command [having] the fatal loveliness of a Cleopatra, a Lucrezia, or a Messalina . . . such a woman as would drive men mad for the love of her" (p. 15); she is *Olga Romanoff; or, the Syren of the Skies* (1894), who schemes to restore the Russian empire. Her efforts are foiled less by the Aerians than by a comet which brings catastrophe to much of the world. In *The Great Weather Syndicate* (1906), Griffith gave as much attention to romantic love as to science or the efforts of Arthur Arkwright to prevent Kaiser Wilhelm from starting a worldwide conflict. Not only does a rival syndicate intend to divert the Gulf Stream and tilt the axis of the earth so that Britain and much of Europe will be transformed into Arctic tundra, but its leaders encourage Baron Osbert de Vanderlé to kidnap Arkwright's sister, Clarice, and his fiancée, Eirene Hockley. The ensuing automobile chase (perhaps one of the earliest in popular fiction) lasts from the Savoy Hotel in London to Brussels, where the damsels are rescued and the Baron and his wife meet horrid deaths. During the chase, Arkwright inadvertently becomes a British diplomatic courier; through this circumstance, Arkwright learns of the Kaiser's desire to open conflict in 1907, and, acting independently, he confronts Wilhelm. They fight their battle, as noted earlier; always a gentleman despite his militant ways, the Kaiser gives Clarice in marriage to a socialist, Ralf Forman, who is in reality the son of an unnamed earl. The Kaiser also "bestowed the hand" of Arkwright's Aunt Martha upon his father-in-law, Eustace P. Hockley, for Arthur Arkwright and Eirene

Hockley are also united in marriage. The three couples have bungalows—"winter pleasure-houses"—in a once harsh area of the Sahara, which the Great Weather Syndicate has turned into a green and fertile paradise.

Such romance continued on both sides of the Atlantic, although in post-war Britain it often took on a more satirical, if not bitter, tone. Leslie Beresford provides one of the more notable examples in *The Venus Girl* (1925). When Milton Hastings puts on an armlet which he thinks is from Peru, a beautiful young woman appears magically in his bachelor apartment. She reveals that by donning the Bracelet of Bhor, Queen of Venus, he has summoned her and that her mission is to "win the love of an Earth-man and take him with [her] back to Venus" (p. 174). When he resists, she causes various women to flirt openly with him; the girl, Una, becomes an observer and critic of British society. At one point she declares, "Love here isn't a bit like Love in Venus, where each girl seeks out her man. Here it is all the business of the man, and there is not much Love in it. Here, it is like buying and selling. . . . There is much sorrow: there is much which is stupid; and there is little which is real Love" (p. 173). Hers is one of many voices to denounce marriage: "That is what makes all your men look so miserable, and your women have such pinched faces" (p. 174). Hastings continues to resist her offer of love and finally awakens from an attack of brain fever to find that both Una and the bracelet have vanished. He is free to marry his fiancée, Barbara Wainwright, who had inspired him to write an opera.

In sharp contrast to Leslie Beresford's narrative are the exaggerated emotion and melodramatic storyline of Juanita Savage's *Passion Island* (1928). A variant of that type of Robinsonade in which an unmarried man and woman are marooned on a Pacific Island—apparently originating with *Foul Play* (1868) by Charles Reade and Dion Boucicault—*Passion Island* concentrates on the beautiful Joan Tregenn, "a born coquette," who is responsible for the suicide of a married man. She flees from his widow; in San Francisco she is saved from the vengeful woman by Hilary J. Merrifield. He condemns Joan, however, telling her that her "chief amusement in life was breaking men's hearts and destroying their souls" (p. 27) and insists that she accompany him to the island of Muava, where he will teach her "the meaning of love and suffering" (p. 60). Even earlier, "between kisses," he declared, "I am your master" (p. 40). After she has been possessed physically—"Joan's brain was reeling and her whole body seemed aflame" (p. 115)—she confesses her love for him. After capture by natives and suitable rescues, they are finally married.

At first glance, *Passion Island* does not seem related to Victoria Cross's *Martha Brown, M.P., A Girl of Tomorrow* (1935), a utopian view of thirtieth-century Britain in which women dominate society. It achieves, as noted, the most complete reversal of sex roles of any novel of the period. Martha explains to her husband ("Manie") that she "can't have [him] always with [her]":

"I told you that before I married you, didn't I? A woman has her own life to lead, her own aspirations to fulfill, her own work to do. The man has the household and the children. I sacrificed four years of my life practically to give you our three children, not for myself. I did not want them, but I thought they would make an interest and pleasure for you." (p. 10)

Once the reader becomes familiar with this shift, the narrative catalogs the accomplishments of the society. They reflect many of the topical interests of the period; there is no unemployment, no dole, no vivisection, no air pollution, no butchers, because laws prohibit the slaughter of animals for food. A parish rector toasts the twentieth century, for it was then "that woman first stirred and felt her power. It was then she first gained her vote at twenty-one. The Flapper Vote it was called" (p. 29). What made the essential difference, however, "was the passing away of prostitution. . . . Women, haunted and worried by the presence of the disease which overclouded and spoiled the most delightful pleasure given to the world" (pp. 36, 37), seized control of sexual matters. They adopted a policy of free love, taking their one law from the disease-free animal kingdom, where "the female will never mate except from her own wish and will" (p. 37). Once this principle is established, the storyline becomes a chronicle of Martha's affairs with her various lovers.

But from early in the narrative a blemish appears in this utopia. Apologizing because he has had a child with a beautiful but unintelligent fisher girl who served as a model for his painting, one of Martha's lovers, Carlo, explains that the "key to the highest passion is that sense a man has, that while conquering a woman's body . . . the woman is giving him, for the moment at least, her whole soul—that she is responding to him, calling to him, to hold and clasp and possess her spirit as well" (p. 90). Another lover, Gerald, like all men, fails to realize "that a woman can enjoy suffering, be happy in misery under certain conditions" (p. 151), especially in pregnancy and child birth and in waiting for an absent lover.

She meets an American, Bruce Campbell Campbell [sic], who encourages her to come away with him "for pleasure, for joy, for life!" (p. 222). Referring by implication to America, he remarks that many "of the other men out there . . . are still like the twentieth century people" (p. 206); he then launches into an elaborate image describing how they break a horse ("terrify it, injure it and hurt it. . . . Then they mount it, and, of course, the creature tries to throw them. . . . Sometimes the horse is killed, sometimes the man is killed"); in contrast, by implication, because Bruce seems to care and is gentle, "a sleek, beautiful creature, whinnying with pleasure, comes up to [him] of its own accord, and [they] are off and away" (pp. 206, 207). Martha agrees to go away with him, though carefully making financial provisions for her husband and children, her lovers, and her charities. When another lover threatens her with a gun, Bruce overcomes him and insists that she leave with him at once: "The magnetic current of his will passed into her through his touch, drowning all resistance to him in her, leaving only the desire to please him" (p. 255). Although the language differs,

Martha Brown echoes the response of Joan Tregenn. Both indulge in the submission which was a requisite to the romantic love of the period.

By consensus, critics agree that the most sympathetic treatment of equality for women occurred in J. D. Beresford's *The Goslings* (1913), published in America as *A World of Women* in the same year. Essentially, the narrative concerns itself with the aftermath of a world catastrophe, for a plague sweeps out of the Orient and Russia to kill virtually all of the men of Europe and Britain. Women flee London, which, as a symbol of the old culture, dies by the ensuing autumn. Then as the women establish small communities throughout the home counties in particular, a single law becomes apparent throughout the new society: " . . . every woman had a right to her share in the bounty of Nature, and the corollary was that she earned her right by labour" (p. 217, *A World of Women*). What has been overlooked to a large extent is that in addition to the new role assigned to women, Beresford used the catastrophe to bring about a dissolution of the class structure and a universal triumph of socialism.

Jasper Thrale, the protagonist who brings warning of the plague, is initially highly critical of the women of the period, in part because "women had no fascination for him" (p. 23, *Goslings*). He asserts that "Mrs. Gosling hadn't the power to conceive an abstract idea; she had to make some application of it to her own particular experience before she could understand the simplest concept" (p. 24, *A World of Women*); he continues his tirade by denouncing the fact that there are so many shops in London devoted to women's clothes, chiding them because they spend so much on "little frivolous, stupid odds and ends . . . frippery . . . [in response to] the sex instinct." Because they do so, Thrale exclaims, " . . . what terribly unintelligent fools women must be" (pp. 25, 26), asserting that they are imitators of immodest Frenchwomen and the victims of fashion designers. He is much more eager for the arrival of socialism and much more concerned because as each society seems almost ready to achieve an ideal state, some outside force breaks it down.

Only when Thrale becomes the chief mechanic in the village of Marlow does he begin to modify his opinions; he works with and falls in love with the young woman Eileen. Their relationship gains a platonic maturity when they go together downstream in order to open all of the weirs on the river to prevent flooding. Yet their relationship is not so well accepted by the community as is the male prostitution of Sam Evans. Although Evans was something "outside the experiences of these women," they accepted him "as an outcome of the new conditions." Beresford intrudes the authorial voice to declare that the "mass of women were quite unable to think out a new morality for themselves" (p. 300, *Goslings*). Although no suggestion is made that the old order will return, the chance to explore the potential for societal change is cut short by the arrival of a shipload of 1200 men from America, where the plague attacked both sexes and did not mean death for the men. Eileen reiterates the established British theme: "We've got such a chance to begin all over again, and do it better." At least twice, she and Beresford assert that there will no longer be "class distinctions and sex distinctions," while Eileen declares that there will be no more marriage, for it "was a man's prerogative; he wanted to keep his woman to himself, and keep his property for his children" (pp. 323, 324, *Goslings*).

Always granting Beresford's sincerity and hope for the equality of women, one must nevertheless suggest that the most successful British novel dealing with the topic remains Ronald A. Knox's *Memories of the Future* (1923), supposedly the memoirs of Opal, Lady Porstock, covering the years 1915 to 1972, although written in 1988. After a nasty remark about "all the H. G. Wells–tedium that manhood endured" (p. ix), Knox establishes himself as editor of the memoirs. The novel succeeds because, told as a reflective first-person narrative by Lady Porstock, it accepts the fact of women's equality instead of delivering a sermon or an ultimatum. As a result the narrative gains a rich texture because Lady Porstock can give attention to small details as well as topical concerns. For example, she explains that she was the first woman to be president of the Oxford Union, and she slips in the fact that Indian Home Rule was granted in 1938. She traveled on business to America in 1944, at the height of the Anglo-American Entente, and she married Wilson J. Harkness of Connecticut, who had purchased one of the titles sold by Britain as a means of paying off the war debt. He became Lord Porstock, but he disappeared during a helicopter flight to France in 1963, so that Lady Opal lived as a widow. She brings the narrative to an end on the eve of a war which Britain has survived, though she gives no specific detail. In many respects this is one of the most effective future histories, although one is perhaps most impressed by the sense of continuity the narrative produces rather than the violence of revolution. Things continue, though change takes place.

In America Mary Griffith had published "Three Hundred Years Hence" as part of *Camperdown; or, News from Our Neighbourhood* (1836) in which Edgar Hawkins falls asleep and awakens in an America whose quality of life has been enhanced by the moral influence of emancipated women. The shift of power had begun when an unnamed millionaire died and bequeathed his property and fortune to the erection and support of a college for orphan girls modeled on that founded by Stephen Girard. One woman had developed a new form of power which superseded the use of steam and compressed air, but the narrative is so brief that it can only suggest the changes which have taken place. One is perhaps most surprised to find that an author who suggested social and economic reform solved the problem of race by transplanting the whole of the black population to Liberia and reimbursing the former slave owners. Yet the utopia, so often discussed, has historical importance because of its date.

The promise of Agnes Bond Yourell's *A Manless World* (1890) is not realized. Visiting his bachelor uncle, Arthur Fielding learns that the old man believes that sometime in prehistory mankind disappeared from the world; the species could no longer procreate because of the gases the earth had encountered in space (p. 16). To illustrate his theory, Uncle Matthew suggests that once again such a plague has struck; the entire narrative expands this supposition and becomes a vehicle for violent anti-Semitism—the extermination of all Jews in North America—because a Jewish doctor has found a cure but will not share his secret. Anarchists take over the world as nations despair. Few survive. Abruptly, Fielding is released from his uncle's fantasy by the sight of a photograph of his bethrothed, Estelle Whitmore: "Her features seemed to have grown beatified. They now breathed truth, devotion, unselfish love, and a divine purity" (p. 167). Dismissing his uncle as one who experienced "a love disappointment in early life," Arthur goes out of the house to "commune" with the night.

In the same year William Hosea Ballou celebrated ballooning in *The Bachelor Girl; A Novel of the 1400*. During a storm, while riding a frightened horse in a park, a fashionable young New York woman, Lily Carolyn Douvre, becomes entangled in the guy ropes of a balloon flown by the wealthy Englishman Captain Pegassus [*sic*]. Amid an encyclopedic history of the free balloon, they fall in love as the storm takes the *Americus* out to sea. To preserve the secret of their flight they sink the balloon before returning to New York. Four years later, writing as G.H.P., George Haven Putnam published *The Artificial Mother: A Marital Fantasy* (1894), whose first-person narrator builds a robot to tend the new twins, his sixth and seventh children. As his wife Polly rescues the babies and demands to know what "frightful experiments" he is subjecting her boys to (p. 31), she accidentally destroys the robot, and her husband wakens from his dream.

Because these works are so slight (*The Artificial Mother* is no more than a pamphlet), the first American science fiction novel outside the imaginary-voyage motif to make an extended statement regarding woman's place in society was Harriet Stark's *The Bacillus of Beauty* (1900), in which a deliberate experiment transforms Helen Winship into the most beautiful woman in the world. The brief initial narrative of John Burke, to whom Helen became engaged just before going to New York for postgraduate study, establishes two important points. First, within a few months she has become so lovely that momentarily John fails to recognize her (pp. 18–19); second, Professor Darmstetter, the physiologist with whom she studies, tells John that beauty and goodness are synonymous (p. 31). Helen then becomes the first-person narrator, protesting at the outset that what she writes is the truth. She quickly recapitulates her youth; she consciously tried to maintain her appearance and manner because she was extremely plain—"My face was hopeless." The central theme is reinforced when a teacher, Miss Coleman, tells her that it is a woman's "duty to be beautiful" and that the means of attaining that beauty are good health and intelligence. Miss Coleman also admonishes her never to wear a corset (pp. 60–61).

In New York Helen soon becomes the favorite student of Professor Darmstetter, who reveals that he has discovered a bacillus which speeds up the process of evolution, thereby changing the very nature of a person and also producing a greatly increased beauty. He offers her the gift; she agrees to be the first to undergo the experiment. (Implicit in the idea, of course, is another expression of the turn-of-the-century certainty that evolution/progress is working its way toward perfection.) Her mirror soon tells her that she is beautiful; Darmstetter is, indeed, "the gray and withered Pygmalion of [her] Galatea" (p. 97).

With the change Helen gives up her study of science; increasingly proud and selfish, she involves herself in the workings of fashionable society. Although she falls in love with the fiancé of a friend, she schemes to capture the heart of young Lord Strathay and through marriage to him to gain a place high in the hierarchy of British aristocracy. In many ways, the central scene of the novel occurs when she angrily confronts Professor Darmstetter, accusing him of wanting to give the bacillus to other women. He acknowledges his desire to conduct further experiments before making public his secret for the good of the world (the flaw of the novel is the professor's English): "I must try the Bacillus vit' a blonde voman, vit' a brunette voman, vit' a negro voman—it vill be fine to share t'e secrets of Gott and see v'at He meant to make of t'e negro. . . . I must try it vit' a cripple . . . vit' an idiot, vit' a deaf and dumb voman. I must set it difficult tasks, learn its limitations" (p. 227).

She forbids him to do so; he calls her his Frankenstein (p. 229). In the ensuing quarrel he dies of a heart attack. Ever more selfish, Helen falls deeply into debt and scorns both John and her father, although they both help her financially. She finds beauty a barren gift, for she learns from a friend, Cadge, that no office in town will hire her: "Men won't subject their clerks to the white light of beauty; wives won't stand for it. . . . This is the other side of all that rot about Woman's Century and Woman's Widening Sphere. Never go into an office, Miss Winship; my wife won't, when we're married" (pp. 266, 267). Even a theatrical agent warns her that "many beautiful women think beauty as an asset is worth more than it is; it makes them careless about studying while they're young, and it won't last—" (p. 280). Increasingly paranoid, she thinks that any accident might harm her beauty, and detesting anything that is ugly, she claims that she was lured into society and then abandoned.

John Burke becomes the final narrator. He discovers a last letter in which Helen acknowledges that the "Bacillus has defeated every wish it has aroused" (p. 338). Moreover, she suggests that Darmstetter gave her death as well as beauty, for in some manner the effect of the Bacillus has begun to wear off. Confessing that she did not love John and planned to marry him only so that he could pay her debts, by implication she kills herself by drinking poison. Again by implication, John destroys the professor's secret and plans to marry the crippled Emily, though at the moment he can think only of Helen. Variations of this theme in which women were given youth and beauty recurred through a number of novels; for example, Marie Corelli's *The Young Diana* (1918), Gertrude Atherton's *Black Oxen* (1923), and Amy Roberta Ruck's *The Immortal Girl* (1924). In none of them does the protagonist gain happiness from these gifts. Marie Corelli's *The Young Diana* repeats the deliberate experiment of *The Bacillus of Beauty*; the reader last sees Diana May as the "reigning beauty" in Paris, although she has become coldly inhuman in her isolation.

The essentially somber tone of these indictments of physical beauty contrasts markedly with the lighthearted humor of Robert W. Chambers. If his voice seems at times to join those who question the aspirations of the younger women of the period before World War I, that tendency is compensated for by the fact that his satire is aimed primarily at science. A writer for the popular magazines, Chambers had first gained critical attention for his fantasies, chief among them *The King in Yellow* (1895) and *The Maker of Moons* (1896), but by the turn of the century he had already written portions of the episodic novel *In Search of the Unknown* (1904), publishing a large segment of it as a two-part serial in *Cosmopolitan* (July-August 1897).[32]

In contrast to his contemporaries, he established his irreverent tone in his prefatory note to *In Search of the Unknown*: "It appears to the writer that there is urgent need of more 'nature books'—books that are scraped clear of fiction and display only the carefully articulated skeleton of fact. Hence this little volume, presented with some hesitation and more modesty. . . . the writer trusts that it may inspire enthusiasm for natural and scientific research, and inculcate a passion for observation among the young." (One should not overlook the distinct possibility that Chambers also scoffed at the realists and naturalists publishing at the turn of the century, many of whose works were colored by a neo-primitivism.)

Throughout *In Search of the Unknown* Chambers exploited the nineteenth century's growing fascination with prehistory and exotic fauna. His first-person narrator, Harold Kensett, resigns a government position to assume his "congenial duties as general superintendent of the water-fowl department connected with the zoological gardens then in the course of erection at Bronx Park, New York" (p. 2). Despite his own skepticism in the project, he first undertakes an arduous three-day journey by rail and ship southward to Black Harbor on the Atlantic Coast to obtain living specimens of the great auk from Burton Halyard. He loses the auks and their chicks overboard when he struggles in a small boat with the so-called "harbor-master," a creature whom Halyard believes to be one "of the last race of amphibious human beings" who live in the deepest part of the Atlantic Ocean (p. 27). The encounter provides the climactic action of the episode, but although Chambers built toward it, much of its potential is lost because of the pervasive humor characterizing Kensett. He next goes to Graham's Glacier in the Hudson Mountains of Canada in quest of mammoths (even Jack London wrote a story in 1901, "A Relic of the Pliocene," whose narrator hunts a mammoth, though his narrative has the flavor of a tall tale). Kensett and the youthful Professor Dorothy Van Twiller pursue the mammoth to a great sheet of water; there out of the mist emerges "a woman's splendid form, upright from the sky to the earth, knee-deep in the sea," certainly an apparition which calls up memories of Poe's Arthur Gordon Pym. Indeed, Kensett recognizes its "strange cry" as "the hail of the Spirit of the North warning us back to life again" (p. 73). For days he carries Professor Van Twiller "pickaback" before Elbon Indians rescue them.

At the International Scientific Congress during the Paris Exposition in 1900, he becomes involved in a scandal when he helps the Countess Suzanne d'Alzette hatch four eggs of the giant ux. The curtain opens revealing to the distinguished audience "four enormous chicks, bearing on their backs the most respected and exclusive aristocracy of Europe" (p. 107). After spending several years in disgrace in Java, he is summoned to go to Florida near Cape Canaveral in search of a thermosaurus, the episode published separately in *Cosmopolitan*. His final adventure takes him to Antwerp, where he searches for his great-aunt's "Crimson Diamond"; the tale becomes a parody of psychical societies and transmigration, for his great-aunt has become a white cat which accidentally swallows the diamond.

Were these scientific misadventures not enough, Harold Kensett instantly falls in love with every pretty girl he meets, and each rejects him. He becomes infatuated with Burton Halyard's nurse; she marries Halyard. He adores Dorothy Van Twiller. Although she had not suffered physically because he had carried her, "the awful experience had produced a shock which resulted in a nervous condition that lasted so long after she returned to New York that the wealthy and eminent specialist who attended her insisted upon taking her to the Riviera and marrying her" (p. 74). The Countess d'Alzette is already married. As part of his instructions before he departs for Florida, he hires Miss Helen Barrison as stenographer. He is attracted to her. In Florida he meets Daisy Holroyd, daughter of the professor who claims the thermosaurus exists. Although he and Daisy become constant companions and survive an encounter with the thermosaurus and some prehistoric birds, she chooses to marry Professor Bruce Stoddard, while Helen Barrison—in reality a graduate of Barnard and a Doctor of Entomology—prefers a young man who has accepted the chair of Psychical Phenomena at Cambridge. In Antwerp, although Wilhelmina Wyeth, who tries to explain the concept of transmigration to him, becomes his fiancée and can accept the fact that his grand-aunt is a cat, she cannot accept the complications. His grand-aunt has kittens (p. 283).

A decade later Chambers tried to repeat the pattern in *Police!* (1915); his protagonist, Percy Smith, Curator of the Department of Anthropology at Bronx Park, is the reincarnation of Harold Kensett. The misadventures and the pretty girls are also present, but the narrative never attains the light touch of *In Search of the Unknown*. Apparently it was his last attempt at satire; thereafter he turned to the melodrama of such works as *The Slayer of Souls* (1920). During the years before America's entry into World War I, however, he did produce three other satires. The parody of transmigration anticipated *Some Ladies in Haste* (1908), in which William T. Manners performs an experiment involving psychic influence. It serves as a point of departure for some playful jesting with fashionable society and love at first sight. Manners, for example, retires from New York to a farm and falls in love with his landlady, Ethra Millicent Barris, the young aristocrat whom he compelled to get rid of her servants and lead a bucolic life.

Chambers' most effective work during this period was *The Green Mouse* (1910), another spoof of psychic influence. Once again in the prefatory note, Chambers voices his intent: " . . . it is a comfort to believe that, in the near future, only literary and scientific works suitable for man, woman, child, and suffragette, are to adorn the lingerie-laden counters of our great department stores. . . . the author politely offers to a regenerated nation this modern, literary, and highly scientific work, thinly but ineffectively disguised as fiction.''

After four years at Harvard, two in postgraduate study and another two in Europe to ''perfect himself in electrical engineering,'' William Augustus Destyn must support himself as a professional magician, because no one will finance his attempt ''to invent a wireless apparatus for intercepting and transmitting psychical waves'' (p. 2). He himself has somehow become impoverished, being able only to rent a suite of two rooms on Central Park West. Although he rescues a young woman whose horse has run away and they are attracted to one another, nothing happens until she comes to his door, asking if she actually saw a pea-green mouse, one of his stage props. Destyn and Ethelinda Carr fall in love at once. Despite his unwillingness to seek financial aid from anyone in his former sphere of society, Ethelinda takes William home to her wealthy, crotchety father, Bushwyck Carr. After she threatens to follow Destyn around the country exhibiting green mice, her father agrees to help the young inventor. The couple marries immediately.

In a meeting chaired by Sacharissa, Ethelinda's sister, William proposes formation of The Green Mouse, Limited. He explains that he has discovered and can control those invisible psychic currents which identify persons predestined to fall in love and marry, even though they have failed to do so in previous incarnations. First, he collects all ''psychic emanations'' from an individual:

"Then I saunter up to some man, place the instrument on a table—like that—touch a lever. Do you see that hair wire of Rosium uncoil like a tentacle? It is searching, groping for the invisible, negative, psychical current which will carry its message.''

"To whom?'' asked Sacharissa.

"To the subconscious personality of the only woman on earth whose psychic personality is properly attuned to intercept that wireless greeting and respond to it.'' (pp. 52–53)

Sacharissa remains skeptical although William assures her that a month earlier he had tried the instrument on the Carr footman, who promptly married ''a perfectly strange parlor maid.''

Sacharissa contends that with such a machine there ''would be no fun in it,'' but she agrees to a further experiment. Blindfolded, she will pick a name from the Social Register. The first time she selects her own name; over Ethelinda's objections, she chooses again. When Killian Van K. Vanderdynk comes to the Carr residence, he is trapped between floors in an elevator. Sacharissa feeds him chocolates through the grill; then she marries him. Sybilla, one of the beautiful Carr triplets, inadvertently exposes herself to the gadget. She protests:

"What a perfectly unpleasant way to fall in love—by machinery! . . . I had rather not know who I am some day to—to like—very much. . . . It is far more interesting to meet a man by accident, and never suspect you may ever come to care for him, than to buy a ticket, walk over to a machine full of psychic waves and ring up some strange man somewhere on earth.'' (pp. 191–192)

In an extended sequence she encounters a man whom she believes to be a paper hanger working in her home; at one point he identifies himself as Prince George of Rumtifoo (p. 212), and she succumbs to the psychic waves and agrees to marry George Gray, III, even before he meets her father.

In the face of such success, the Carr girls, their father, and their husbands erect a giant building facing Madison Avenue between Eighty-second and Eighty-third Streets. It has a thousand private operating rooms, a marriage license bureau, and an emergency chapel equipped with "first aid clergymen." They plan to inundate the U.S. with circulars:

ARE YOU IN LOVE? IF NOT, WHY NOT?
Wedlock by Wireless. Marriage by Machinery.
A Wondrous Wooer Without Words!

No more doubt; no more hesitation; no more uncertainty. The Destyn-Carr Wireless Apparatus does it all for you. Happy marriage Guaranteed or money eagerly refunded! . . . Why waste time with costly courtship? Why frivol? Why fuss?

There is only ONE mate created for YOU. You pay us; We find that ONE, thereby preventing mistakes, lawsuits, elopements, regrets, grouches, alimony. . . .

THE WORLD IS YOURS
for $25.

(pp. 219–220)

Flavilla, another of the Carr triplets, is one of the few "unregenerate reactionists" who refuses to follow the lead of her sisters. In a rather precipitous ending, as she rehearses near Oyster Bay in the costume of a mermaid, she meets Henry Kingsbury, a yachtsman, and falls in love with him at first sight, as Ethelinda did with William. In short, after having a great deal of heavy-handed fun, Robert W. Chambers comes down on the side of romantic love.

He repeats that decision in a slighter satire, *The Gay Rebellion* (1913). Originally published in part in *Hampden Magazine* (1911), this episodic narrative provided Chambers with the chance, as his prefatory notice announces, to have fun with the craze for "The Science of Eugenics" which swept America at the turn of the century. When four highly eligible bachelors disappear in the Adirondacks, Curtis Langdon and William Sayre are sent out to get a newspaper story. Sayre encounters a young woman whom he calls Amourette—the title of a poem he wrote—and falls in love. Despite initial protestations, she remains passive as he literally carries her away to marry her. Langdon is caught in a net by Ethra Leslie, who takes him to the New Race University and Masculine Beauty Preserve, where he learns that a group of beautiful young women— whose ideal is the cult of the cavewoman—intend to capture only the most perfect male specimens to court and start a super race. Like Sayre, of course,

Langdon does not qualify, but he and Ethra are ruled by their hearts instead of science.

When Chambers expanded the narrative to novel length, he emphasized a nationwide strike of women which brings to mind *Lysistrata*, for "thousands of militant women" have decided that "non-intercourse with men was to be the punishment for any longer withholding the franchise" (p. 78). In England riots occur. The so called Eugenic Revolution ends when the physically unfit and unattractive rebel against the Beauty Trust (pp. 256–257). Chambers' stories are slight and dated, while his humor may at times seem forced, but he should not be condemned out of historical context. At one point in *The Gay Rebellion*, Sayre accuses Langdon of talking like William Dean Howells: "Haven't you *any* romance in you?" he asks. In *The Green Mouse*, Sybilla Carr performs an act of penance by at least intending to read Henry James.[33] Chambers wrote to entertain a select audience. That is the fault of which he is guilty. And one should not forget that at a time when both literature and science took themselves very seriously, he satirized the fads and fashions of that society, although his characters always sealed their newfound love with a first kiss.

One contemporary critic called him the "highest-priced author of the most popular magazine fiction," while another asserted that he was "the most popular writer of American fiction [of the] day."[34] In the latter article Chambers concluded by suggesting that on the eve of World War I "the splendid man is the one who is in Europe changing the map of the world, the man who is building great bridges, putting through enormous engineering feats, the man with vast courage and splendid heroism, the man who is freshening up the spirit of the universe."[35]

If in this adulation of the technician he is a man of his period, then in his assessment of contemporary women he perhaps shows a greater insight than most:

She is not half such a pretender as man, and she is much more inclined to speak the truth on vital issues than he is. The camouflage of a woman's relations to men is not in the lies she tells, but because of the lies he tells. . . . I believe every woman should be self-supporting, I believe that it is most vital that girls should be absolutely independent financially of men. . . . As to suffrage for women, I think that we men are rather pledged to give them an equal opportunity with us. . . . There is a grace, a penetration, a truth, in the instinct for honesty in the woman's mind which, when applied to art or to science, far surpasses men. In science, especially, women are better specialists.[36]

He also praised the fiction of Edith Wharton.

The ornamental young women of Robert W. Chambers' novels gave way after World War I to such figures as the protagonist of Martha Bensley Bruère's *Mildred Carver, U.S.A.* (1919), in which the young daughter of a wealthy family serves her required year in the Universal Service doing agricultural work in the Mississippi Valley. The narrative gives a close description of how she works on a large farm, learning to drive a tractor and participating in the great wheat harvest. Through her work, Mildred has removed herself from the role of the essentially passive woman; at one point, her aunt underscores that irreversible separation when she asks, "What has happened to Mildred's hands? Look at those broken nails and calluses on her fingers" (p. 187). An earlier description pinpoints the basic problem faced by women of her social status and generation:

[John Barton] saw Mildred as a singularly lovely and intelligent young American girl of the sort that New England produces so in excess of the demand that they wither in the parental gardens everywhere, or get shunted into genteel employments which are not much better than this wistful withering; but who in fortunate exceptions, are carried away into some more emotionally succulent field, where life gives them experience and love, and where they bloom into the best that this country or any other can produce. (p. 86)

Mildred is not satisfied with the idea that despite her work and increased useful knowledge, she can never "be anything but the natural 'second' in the game of some man's career" (p. 257).

Although she and John Barton, a working man, love one another, they do not marry because Mildred must take an active part in society; she declares, "[the] world is going to be better fed because I have lived" (p. 281). In addition to this novel, Martha Bruère collaborated with her husband on *Home Efficiency* (1919), in which they proposed "that for the vocation of housewife there should be as careful technical education as for the physician, the lawyer, the editor or the politician. . . . The book is a direct answer to the statement so often made that housework is mere drudgery, for it shows that the proper management of the home is one of the most complex, intellectual and difficult of professions."

However much the reader may agree with the Bruères, for the most part women writers emphasized the need for changes which would allow women more freedom as individuals. Many of the men voiced serious concern for women's morality—indeed, their sexuality. In *Possessed* (1920), for example, Cleveland Moffett concentrates upon the psychological treatment given Penelope Wells, a widow who has been decorated for valor while serving under fire in France as a nurse. After her husband's death, she faces that problem "that confronts thousands of high principled young women, widows, divorcees. . . . How could [she] adjust [her]self to life without the intimate companionship of a man?" (p. 84). The views expressed by Roberta Vallis, an outspoken feminist, regarding the equality of women in such matters seem abhorrent to Moffett; indeed, he kills her off (p. 148). Penelope becomes little more than a voice enunciating Moffett's conservative views. Although she suggests that women are liars "because centuries of oppression have made [them] afraid to tell the truth," she also asserts that "women love pursuit and are easily reconciled to capture" (p. 20). Again, while she declares "that emotional desire deliberately aroused in 'harmless flirtation' and then deliberately repressed is an offence against womanhood, a menace to the health, and a degradation of the soul," she declares that one character exasperates her with "talk about the compelling claims of oversexed individuals. Let them learn to behave themselves and control themselves" (pp. 23, 101). Through her Moffett complains of the double standard, but he includes the story of the English mother who has made arrangements "with two beautiful young matrons in her set" for her son until he is married (p. 249). Moffett's confusion—or hypocrisy—reaches its climax when Penelope acknowledges that "a woman cannot be virtuous if she longs for sensuality, or dallies with it, or dwells upon it in her thoughts, even though she refrain from sinful act. Nor can a married woman be a truly virtuous wife if she yields to perverse revellings of the imagination which defile body and soul—*even with her husband*" (p. 254). She ends up by praying, "From all defilements of love, *Dear Lord, deliver me*." The storyline is lost amidst such a diatribe. Angry as one may be at Moffett, one must nevertheless pity him, for it seems obvious that he, very probably like many men of his generation, was terrified of woman's sexuality to the extent that he could not see her as a human being. How else explain such rantings as well as the essentially European cult of the femme fatale?

In contrast, Rene Oldfield Pettersen's *Venus* (1924) seems almost naive as it presents two young women, Ve and De, who come to Earth from Venus and become a part of the Carter family at Tide End in New York. They mouth the usual indictments of marriage particularly, but they admonish their hosts, " . . . you all make too much of sex" (p. 182). Although the Venusians also speak against the stigma of illegitimacy (pp. 189–190), the Carters are the ones who denounce modern young women as represented by such "sub-debs" as their daughter Mary: "No respect for anything or anybody—no restraint in either manners or clothes" (p. 125).[37] When the visitors suggest that the young should neither mingle nor breed indiscriminately, Mrs. Carter seems somewhat upset as she asks whether they believe in birth control (p. 191). While De and Jack Carter honeymoon in space without bothering about a marriage ceremony, Ve helps Mary to see her past incarnations. She eventually brings about the marriage of Mary and Jack Dale and two other couples. Love and life itself are, of course, eternal.

The pattern of such lectures was broken by Joseph Lamarre's *The Passion of the Beast* (1928). Its narrator, William St. Clair, learns that the family of Hippolyte Dumesnil has retreated to its country estate where it lives in terror of the gorilla, Melek, which once saved the life of the elder Dumesnil in Africa. Although both father and son are killed by the gorilla, Melek loves the daughter Yvonne. As he dies of gunshot wounds after being hunted down, Melek licks Yvonne's hand. The novel is thus a scientific updating of Beauty and the Beast. It appears to be unique in the immediate postwar period, for more often the satire of society demanded that the woman be portrayed as an animal. David Garnett's *Lady into Fox* (1923) and John Collier's *His Monkey Wife* (1930) provide memorable examples. Less well known is the American title, Charles Gilson's *The Cat and the Curate* (1934), although it, too, attacks British society.

Mr. Theodore Whitten, curate of Upper Birchenthorpe-on-Sea, has problems when his black cat Susan is transformed into a beautiful woman. Whitten is shocked because she has no nightie (p. 126), and he insists that Susan sleep outside the sheets (p. 163). After several months, Susan returns to her feline form, bringing with her a single black kitten: by implication, at least, Whitten fathered the kitten (p. 313), for he kept "the good Tum" until it died. Then a respected man with a family, Theodore Whitten "went in for canaries" instead of cats. Throughout these novels there is an ambivalence toward the fact of sexuality itself.

Despite the promise of its title, Columbus Bradford's *Terrania; or, The Feminization of the World* (1930) fails to portray vividly a future world state brought about by women. Presented as a future history, it concentrates upon the love story of Amy Mortimer and Major John Goff, a minor official in the War Department. In response to his proposal of marriage, Amy, his stenographer who lost a brother in World War I, leads a universal strike against matrimony in order to bring about disarmament. In a prefatory note, Bradford cites Mrs. Carrie Chapman Catt, who said sometime earlier at a women's convention in Atlantic City "that it is 'the task of women to demilitarize the minds of the world' " (p. viii). The novel carefully documents the formation of the National Women's Party, the attainment of equal rights, and the formation of a world state. It is, as suggested elsewhere, a platonic, cerebralized *Lysistrata*, which is more verbose than dramatic or truly effective. However much Bradford may preach in favor of equal rights, one jest in particular undercuts the entire effort by revealing the temper of the period. Relative to Goff's growing love of Amy, Bradford asserts, "He may or may not have heard that saying of some wag or wit,—that stenographer girls make the best of wives because they have become accustomed beforehand to being dictated to" (p. 6–7).

Owen Johnson's *The Coming of the Amazons* (1931), an avowed "Satiristic Speculation," makes perhaps the most effective use of *Lysistrata*. Making use of the Frigidome, which induces catalepsy and slows glandular action, John Bogardus survives into the twenty-second century. Awakening in 2181, he finds a highly technological society whose dominant class of women has adopted a Grecian lifestyle. He listens attentively to his guides, Acquilla and Dianne— most of the conventions are present, including the destruction of New York City in 1984 during a European war (p. 16) and the knowledge of countless inhabited worlds, many of whose civilizations are not humanoid (pp. 202–205)—but no love story develops.

Bogardus learns that men between the ages of twenty and thirty-five are used for breeding. The most effective sequence in the novel occurs when Bogardus witnesses the parade of young men from whom the women will choose new, fresh sexual partners. He notices that their tunics reveal "the flowing lines of the graceful young bodies beneath." He decides that some of the blonds exceed "the bounds of good taste in the arrogant display of their soft shoulders and backs, with a curious fluttering divided skirt which too boldly revealed the length of their shapely legs'' (p. 212). Angrily he protests "seeing [his] fellow men reduced to this artificial slavery and parading like prospective concubines in the humiliation of a slave Mart" (p. 213). When asked if he would object if the "painted and powdered . . . debutants" were women, he replies, "Of course not." Acquilla explains to him:

"You make the mistake that men made for centuries, in believing that woman's nature was different from man's. All that you have observed in this curious display is only acquired characteristics and the acquired characteristics of the sex whose primary function is to attract the stronger. Once it was woman, now it is man." (p. 213)

Bogardus wishes to start a rebellion which will gain equal rights for men. To men imprisoned in their cells he recites the story of *Lysistrata* (pp. 232–235). He is placed on trial; by implication, his masculinity has won a number of hearts, for three women, among them Dianne, demand the right to follow him if he is cast out of the State (p. 246). The narrative breaks off; appended is a note suggesting that Bogardus wrote the narrative during eight months when he was confined in a twentieth-century madhouse. The note suggests that Bogardus feared woman and wanted to warn against "feminist progress."

Such an ending does not come as a complete surprise; a number of clues pointed to it. At one point he is asked whether he was aware in the 1920s that "economically, and in a measure morally, the women [he] rated as the weaker sex were really the despots of [his] existence" (p. 144). When one first encounters him, one also meets his wife, Ernesta, who is a feminist leader (pp. xii-xiii). Yet the ending is unquestionably disappointing, especially after the debutant scene in which Johnson so successfully voiced a now-accepted insight.

In a sense, however, Johnson's *The Coming of the Amazons* marked a final high tide in American science fiction during the post–World War I period in terms of the portrayal of women in a present or future society. George Weston's *His First Million Women* (1934) played with the idea that its protagonist, David Glendenning, was the only man in the world not left sterile by the passing of Comet Z. In Sam Fuller's *Test Tube Baby* (1936), Eleanor Garrison, a school teacher, wants her son to be "a model man—a child prodigy—a genius" (p. 10). Jimmy Garrison becomes a scientific genius, experimenting with the concept of developing embryos *ex utero* (p. 75). The stress of such work drives him to a "Jekyll-Hyde existence" (p. 200), which ends only when he is brought to trial for the murder of Augie Wallace—a criminal with whom he has planned robberies—within an hour after raping Augie's prostitute-sweetheart, Peggy Argyle. This farce ends in a courtroom scene in which Jimmy declares that the real killer is his mother because she turned him into an experiment (p. 290). She accepts the blame, begs the jury not to "send him to the chair," and declares to the courtroom that she is guilty of his crimes (p. 219). Of course, he is exonerated.

One must conclude that in science fiction which dealt with the everyday world of the present or near future or with an imaginary world of the distant future, the woman was incidental. Except in the highly stylized manner of such a writer as Robert W. Chambers, her image was, at best, indistinct. The fullest, most complex portrayal of woman during the period of the 1870s to the 1930s occurred in the imaginary-voyage motif.

NOTES

1. Clarke, *The Pattern of Expectation*, pp. 164, 213.

2. Mark Hillegas, *The Future as Nightmare: H. G. Wells and the Anti-Utopians* (New York: Oxford University Press, 1967), pp. 57, 66.

3. Hillegas, p. 70.

4. H. G. Wells, *A Modern Utopia* (Lincoln, Nebr.: University of Nebraska Press, 1967), p. 258.

5. J. O. Bailey, *Pilgrims Through Space and Time* (New York: Argus Books, Inc., 1947), p. 95.

6. Arthur O. Lewis, *Utopian Literature in the Pennsylvania State University Libraries: A Selected Bibliography* (University Park, Pa.: The Pennsylvania State University Libraries, 1984), p. 202.

7. Hillegas, p. 21.

8. Jean Pfaelzer, "The Impact of Political Theory On Narrative Structure," in Kenneth M. Roemer, ed., *America as Utopia* (New York: Burt Franklin & Company, 1981), p. 117.

9. Kenneth M. Roemer, *The Obsolete Necessity: America in Utopian Writings, 1888–1900* (Kent, Ohio: Kent State University Press, 1976), pp. 4–5.

10. In addition to the two books by Roemer and the new bibliography by Lewis, one must cite at least the following titles: Glenn Negley and J. Max Patrick, *The Quest for Utopia* (1952); Vernon Lewis Parrington, Jr., *American Dreams: A Study of American Utopias* (1947); Lyman Tower Sargent, *British and American Utopian Literature 1516–1975* (1979). This does not include the numerous dissertations and articles in various periodicals. For a complete bibliography, I suggest the Roemer volumes.

11. Samuel R. Delany, "Critical Methods: Speculative Fiction," in Thomas D. Clareson, ed., *Many Futures, Many Worlds* (Kent, Ohio: Kent State University Press, 1977), p. 290. Delany's essay was first published in *quark #1* (1970), pp. 182–195.

12. Delany, p. 288.

13. Roemer, *The Obsolete Necessity*, p. 152.

14. Other titles that should be excluded from science fiction because they serve merely as a vehicle for such monologues include the following: James B. Alexander, *The Lunarian Professor* (1909); Thomas Blot, *The Man from Mars* (1891), reissued in 1900 under the author's real name, William Simpson; Henry Wallace Dowding, *The Man from Mars* (1910); Francis W. Doughty, *A Woman from Mars* (1892); Norman R. Grisewood, *Zarlah the Martian* (1909); W. S. Harris, *Life in a Thousand Worlds* (1905); M. D. Leggett, *A Dream of a Modest Proposal* (1890); Henry Olerich, *A Cityless and Countryless World* (1893); Pruning Knife (pseud. of H. F. Allen), *A Strange Voyage* (1891); William Winsor, *Loma, A Citizen of Venus* (1897).

15. Clifford D. Simak, "Face of Science Fiction," *Minnesota Libraries*, 17 (September 1953), 197–201.

16. Julian Hawthorne, "June 1993," *Cosmopolitan*, 14 (February 1893), 450–458.

17. William Wallace Cook, "Castaways of the Year 2000," *Argosy*, 71 (February 1913), 688. One wonders when Cook wrote this novel not only because of the long interval between it and *A Round Trip to the Year 2000* but also because, unlike the rest of his science fiction, it seems to be completely lacking in satire.

18. "Nightmare Prophecy," *New York Times*, June 30, 1906, p. 419.

19. Richard Gid Powers, "Introduction," *The Science Fiction of Jack London: An Anthology* (Boston: Gregg Press, 1975), p. xvii.

20. When Granser's speech is read to undergraduate audiences without identifying the author, title, or date, they guess that it was written sometime after World War II, most often suggesting the 1950s. In contrast, they easily date (and often laugh at) passages from the most optimistic novels of the turn-of-the-century period.

21. At least twice more Serviss speaks directly to the matter of Cosmo Versál's wealth. "For mere raw material Cosmo must have expended an enormous sum, and his expenses were quadrupled by the fact that he was compelled, in order to save time, practically to lease several of the largest steel plants in the country" (p. 33). Of even more importance, when he is selecting those who will be invited to join the group on the Ark, he asserts, "I will exclude no man simply because he is a billionaire. I consider the way he made his money. . . . How could I have built the ark if I had been poor" (p. 83).

22. George Allan England, "The Fantastic in Fiction," *Darkness and Dawn* (Westport, Conn.: Hyperion Press, 1974), [p. v]. This is a photocopy of the Small, Maynard edition of 1914; England's introduction was originally published as "Facts About Fantasy" in *The Story World* for June 1923. Unfortunately, in the Hyperion edition, at least, the introduction is not paginated: thus the number I have assigned to it.

23. See A. J. Liebling, "That Was New York: To Him She Clung," *The New Yorker*, October 12, 1963, pp. 143–168. Liebling recalls that he read the first volume of the trilogy when it was serialized as "The Last New Yorkers" in the New York *Evening Mail* during March 1912. Certainly, he satirizes England's excesses, but the fact that he would write about this experience of his youth when he learned that the Metropolitan Life Insurance Company had decided not to tear down the tower indicates, as he himself says, that he never completely forgot the story. More importantly, he provides another footnote to the fact that this type of fiction reached a large audience.

24. Clarke, *The Pattern of Expectation*, pp. 229, 230.

25. Clarke, *The Pattern of Expectation*, p. 230.

26. J. J. Connington, *Nordenholt's Million* (New York and London: Penguin Books, 1946), pp. 283, 284–285, 286.

27. Richard D. Mullen, "H. G. Wells and Victor Rousseau Emanuel: *When the Sleeper Wakes* and *The Messiah of the Cylinder*," *Extrapolation*, 8 (May 1967), 31–63. Mullen states that "Emanuel's nightmare is a sexual fantasy" (p. 42), but he is so concerned with the novel's relationship to Wells that he does not explicate the statement except to refer to the temptation of the flesh, which Pennell overcomes in Lambken's "pleasure palace 'full of flowers and beautiful girls' " (pp. 44–45).

28. Mullen, p. 46.

29. Robert Silverberg, "Introduction," *The Mirror of Infinity* (New York: Harper & Row, 1970), p. viii.

30. J. O. Bailey, *Pilgrims Through Space and Time*, pp. 152–153.

31. Thomas D. Clareson, "Notes," *A Spectrum of Worlds*, pp. 120–122. The quotes are from pp. 120, 121. In view of the manner in which science fiction can become dated, the artistry of Benét is emphasized by the impact that this story always has upon under-

graduates. Unless its date is called to their attention, however, they invariably believe that the destruction of New York results from atomic bombing.

32. Robert W. Chambers, "A Matter of Interest," *Cosmopolitan*, 23 (July 1897), 315–330; (August 1897), 421–432. Sam Moskowitz refers to this separate publication in his introduction to the 1974 Hyperion Press edition of *In Search of the Unknown*. A close examination of the texts suggests there was a sharp difference in tone instead of the simple deletion of a few paragraphs.

33. Robert W. Chambers, *The Gay Rebellion* (New York: D. Appleton, 1913), p. 326; *The Green Mouse* (New York: D. Appleton, 1910), pp. 193, 194.

34. Pendennis, "My Women Types—Robert W. Chambers," *The Forum*, 9 (May 1918), 564; "The 'Play-Girl' in Fiction: Discussed by Robert W. Chambers," *Craftsman*, 31 (December 1916), 218.

35. "The 'Play-Girl' in Fiction," p. 223.

36. "My Women Types," pp. 566, 567, 568.

37. The manner in which Mary's parents and older daughter continue the passage gives an amusing insight into the period:

" . . . No respect for anything or anybody—no restraint in either manner or clothes. Look at the way they dress—only six articles of clothing and four of those are shoes and stockings."

"Really, Frances, you go too far," her mother spoke with more firmness than she usually displayed. "I am quite sure Mary dresses the same as you do."

"No, Moms," with a knowing smile, "Mary has not yet reached the brassiere-bloomer stage."

"What is that?" Mr. Carter interrupted. "I have heard of bloomers, but what is a brassiere?"

"Oh, Dad, you old simple," Frances laughed right heartily. "A brassiere is something to wrap around the ankle to keep one warm on chilly evenings." (p. 125)

Earlier Petterson had written, "Art Stanton, at this time Mary's own particular 'sheik'" (p. 54). Only such passages can make vivid the various changes which have taken place in little more than a half century.

6

Journeys to Unknown Lands

From the beginnings of history, both in oral tradition and in books like *The Odyssey*, from the Carthaginians and Phoenicians onward, the storytellers and travelers of Europe and the Mediterranean have peopled the unknown areas of the world with kingdoms and creatures unlike anything in their daily lives. The Hesperides, the Kingdom of Prester John, St. Brendan's Isles, the western continent, Brasil, "Continent Hyperboreen," *terra australis incognita*, Atlantis, and Lemuria have given form to the dream of an elusive, sought-after land in which life attained a perfection never achieved in the known world. At times, discoveries seemed momentarily to fulfill the dream: Alexander's Persia, Leif Ericson's Vinland, Marco Polo's Cathay, Cortes's Mexico, Cook's Tahiti. But always, however fabulous the Courts of Kubla Khan or the Halls of Montezuma, the idealized kingdom vanished, withdrew beyond the horizon to lure the next explorer. As time went on, Herodotus's recital of the wonders of Pompeii and Herculaneum, the Valley of the Nile, the legends of El Dorado and the Seven Cities of Cibola, and the silent monoliths of Easter Island teased the imagination. In *The Imaginary Voyage in Prose Fiction* (1940), certainly a pioneer study ranking with those of Marjorie Nicolson and J. O. Bailey, Philip Babcock Gove shows that from the Renaissance, during the great age of exploration, the account of such journeys became one of the favorite genres of fiction. He lists and describes 215 titles published between 1700 and 1800, ranging from Daniel Defoe's *Robinson Crusoe* (1719) and *Captain Singleton* (1720) to Voltaire's *Candide* (1759) and Charles Dibdin's *Hannah Hewit; or The Female Crusoe* (1796).[1]

In the nineteenth century, no single title had greater influence than did *Symzonia: A Voyage of Discovery* (1820), attributed to Captain Adam Seaborn, probably a pseudonym for Captain John Cleves Symmes of Ohio.[2] In a circular dated 1818, Symmes proposed that the earth was hollow. He revived and refurbished the theory originating with Pierre Louis Moreau de Maupertis (1698–1759), who, like Buffon, speculated about *terra australis incognita*, believing such a continent necessary to keep the earth from turning over because of the unbalanced weight of its northern land masses. Collaborating with James McBride, Symmes issued *Symmes' Theory of Concentric Spheres* (1826). Although a large portion of the public laughingly dismissed the concept as "Symmes' Hole," during the winter of 1826–1827 he lectured at Union College.

The essence of his theory states that the earth is open at both poles and that within the earth five concentric spheres are habitable on both their concave and convex sides. Beyond the hoop of ice in each polar region, the seas are open and the climate temperate, because the interior worlds receive light and heat from the refraction of the sun's rays due to the inclination of the earth's axis. (The discovery of the Ross Ice Barrier in the Antarctic in 1840 gave supposed authority to such theorizing.)

In *Symzonia*, after referring in a prefatory note to "the sublime theory" of Symmes as well as to "the application of steam to the navigation of vessels, for which the world is indebted to *Fulton*" (p. vi), Captain Adam Seaborn goes on to agree with "the opinion published by Capt. Symmes, that seals, whales, and mackerel, come from the internal world" (p. 29). Despite earlier failures to adapt steam vessels to the ocean, he realizes that he must do so if his ship is to surmount "the impetuous tides" and resist "the violent winds to be expected in the polar seas":

... Moreover, she must be of such strength as to sustain the shock of floating ice, or of taking the ground; and of such capacity as to contain fuel and provision for at least fifty men for three years, with apartments from which the external air could be excluded, and which might be artificially warmed during the rigours of a polar winter. (p. 15)

Undismayed by the problems facing him, the first-person narrator "caused a steam vessel of 400 tons to be constructed with double frames; the timbers being inclined from a perpendicular about 45 degrees; so that the outer set crossed the others at right angles" (p. 15). After giving a careful report of the ship's structure and provisioning, Seaborn announces that he set sail on August 1, 1817. Once a close account of the voyage south has been given, *Symzonia* becomes an essentially conventional description of a utopian state in which democracy has attained perfection. Yet despite "the matter-of-fact realism" of the tale, heightened by its early attention to technical detail, the chief importance of *Symzonia* lies in the choice of the Antarctic as its destination.[3] From Coleridge throughout the nineteenth century, the southern polar seas attracted such writers as Edgar Allan Poe.

Although Symmes died in 1829, at Union College he had found a disciple in Jeremiah N. Reynolds. Not only did Reynolds himself lecture on Symmes' theory, but in 1834 he presented a bill to Congress asking for monies to explore the South Polar regions. J. O. Bailey has pointed out that Poe reviewed that address in *The Southern Literary Review* and was aware of Reynolds' activities, if he did not personally know the man.[4] By the end of the 1830s, both British and American naval officers commanding ships in the area had received orders to look out for Symmes' Hole. A generation later, P. Clark argued the feasibility of "The Symmes Theory of the Earth" in *The Atlantic Monthly* (April 1873), while as late as 1909 John Weld Peck speculated about "Symmes' Theory" in *Ohio Archaeological and Historical Society Publications*.[5]

In "MS. Found in a Bottle" (1833) Poe relies on the *Blackwood's* format in that his narrator, adrift aboard a derelict vessel which is run down by an ancient ship, finds himself amid a ghostly crew acting out ritualistic duties divorced from reality. The scene echoes both "The Rime of the Ancient Mariner" and the legend of the Flying Dutchman, and it anticipates a scene in *The Narrative of Arthur Gordon Pym of Nantucket. Comprising The Details of a Mutiny and Atrocious Butchery on Board of the American Brig Grampus, on Her Way to the South Seas—with an Account of the Recapture of the Vessel by the Survivors; Their Shipwreck, and Subsequent Horrible Sufferings, from Famine; Their Deliverance by Means of the British Schooner Jane Guy; The Brief Cruise of this Latter Vessel in the Antarctic Ocean; Her Capture, and of the Massacre of Her Crew, among a Group of Islands in the 84th Parallel of the Southern Latitude, together with the Incredible Adventures and Discoveries still further South, to which that Distressing Calamity gave Rise* (1838),[6] Poe's only venture into the novel, which has been subjected to a wide variety of interpretations. A number of critics seem bewildered by the ending, while almost all overlook Pym's reference to "Nine long years, crowded with events of the most startling and, in many cases, of the most unconceived and unconceivable character" (p. 88). In many ways, the interpretation having the greatest integrity is that of Edward H. Davidson, who suggests that *Pym*'s central "theme might be called the cheating deceptiveness of reality, a subject on which [Poe] would expend his major energies in *Eureka* toward the end of his life."[7] Such a reading gains strength, for example, from Pym's prefatory note in which he laments "having kept no journal during a greater portion of the time in which [he] was absent" and thus fears that he will be unable to produce "a statement so minute and connected as to have the *appearance* of that truth it would really possess" (p. 1). Again, as a ghostly vessel whose crew appears to be "Hollanders" approaches his ship, Pym remarks, "I relate these things and circumstances minutely, and I relate them, it must be understood, precisely as they *appeared* to us" (p. 89). In short, one can argue that in *The Narrative of Arthur Gordon Pym*, Poe undertook to dramatize the dilemma which the nineteenth century inherited from the psychological empiricists: one cannot be certain that the brain perceives correctly (indeed, that it functions properly), nor can one be sure that the world as one senses it represents reality. As Davidson suggests, "Poe is asking an old question germane to philosophy and to the very bases of knowledge and being: Is what the human mind thinks is real 'really real' after all?"[8] After the initial episode in which Pym and Augustus are run down by the Nantucket whaler and before the voyage of the *Grampus* begins, Pym himself asserts, "In no affairs of mere prejudice, pro or con, do we deduce inferences with entire certainty even from the most simple data'' (p. 15). In the resultant quandary, one sees an early, generally unrecognized step toward the concept of an incomprehensible universe, a roadmark on the way to the Absurd.

At first glance, the complex subtitle of *Pym* seems merely to string together a wide variety of incidents which Poe could have taken from the accounts of actual voyages, to say nothing of fiction, in order to gain a novel-length manuscript. But closer examination implies that they may contribute to the basic questioning of reality in that they intrude unspeakable horrors into the dull, expected routine of sea voyages (for now one ignores the possibility of any satire of the romantic sensibility when Poe speaks through Pym of visions of ''shipwreck and famine; of death or captivity''). From the beginning, Arthur Gordon Pym is a properly neurasthenic young man who feels ''confused in mind'' (pp. 22, 80); whose vision, speech, and legs ''totally'' fail him (pp. 24, 37, 83); who believes himself ''feeble in the extreme'' (p. 26); who thinks that his intellect is ''bordering on idiocy'' (p. 32); and who falls into ''utter exhaustion'' (p. 54) or ''a state of partial insensibility'' (p. 82) as he goes from one ''frightful situation'' to another. He also experiences fear, seasickness, horror, and despair.

This ends abruptly when he and Dirk Peters are rescued by the *Jane Guy*, of Liverpool, Captain Guy commanding. Once they round the Cape of Good Hope and enter the southern Indian Ocean, Arthur Gordon Pym becomes a most astute, unemotional observer; the following chapters, including at least one specific reference to ''Mr. Reynolds'' (p. 137), recapitulate a history of the discoveries of recent explorers. Increasingly, the last part of the novel becomes ''a geographical fantasy, related on the one hand to the imaginary voyages of the eighteenth century and on the other to factual accounts of voyages of exploration or whaling voyages to the Antarctic.''[9] In terms of his central theme, Poe has reversed himself. Throughout the events surrounding the voyage of the *Grampus*, Pym was so physically and emotionally overwhelmed that he could not be certain that he was sane. A medley of horrors pressed in upon him. As the *Jane Guy* sails southward, Pym grows more exact and objective. Particularly on the island of Tsalal, the same potential for horror and emotion occurs; one has only to compare the prose style and the reactions of Pym to see how differently Pym handles ''frightful'' situations. For one thing, the journal entries, used only spasmodically in the early portion of the narrative, become the principal structuring device. Pym grows steady; the external world goes awry.

The change becomes noticeable only after January 14 when the *Jane Guy* passes the western edge of an ''apparently limitless floe'' (p. 141) and sails into an open sea. On January 18, they pick up a bush with red berries as well as the body of a ''singular-looking land animal'' having scarlet claws and silky white hair. They proceed to the island of Tsalal, where the only natural phenomenon Pym emphasizes is the thick, ''veined'' water (pp. 150–151). Eventually, the ''jet-black'' natives not only kill all the crew except Pym and Dirk Peters but also react strangely to the carcass of the white animal.[10] Momentarily, Pym reacts as he did earlier (p. 165) and, momentarily, Poe provides the chasms as a puzzle, but the two men escape from the island with a native prisoner in a canoe and are swept toward the south; the water assumes "a milky consistency and hue" (p. 193) and becomes so hot that it is unendurable to the touch. Again the narrative takes the form of a terse journal. At one point (March 2), Pym declares that he has learned much about the Tsalal and its inhabitants from the native Nu-Nu, but dismisses them, asking, " . . . with these how can I *now* detain the reader?" (p. 192). More importantly, a matter that seems to be overlooked, the entry, when he speaks of the "limitless cataract [which] ranged along the whole extent of the southern horizon," is dated March 9; the last two entries, when the great figure emerges as they "rushed into the embraces of the cataract" (p. 195), are dated March 21 and 22. The narrative breaks off. The entire encounter on Tsalal and the final journey make up no more than a quarter of Pym's narrative. One is at something of a loss to explain both this compression and abrupt ending except to suggest that Poe tired of the project. Yet, however rushed or fragmentary the final actions, two matters seem apparent. First, Poe's central theme does question the nature of reality, and second, despite a lack of specific reference, he did know and make use of the paraphernalia growing out of Symmes' theory.

Although the interior world remained a conventional setting well into the twentieth century, those writers who sought to complete *The Narrative of Arthur Gordon Pym* ignored Symmes. In Jules Verne's *An Antarctic Mystery* (1897, 1899), surely one of his weaker narratives, the travelers, including Dirk Peters, find Pym's frozen body at the foot of a gigantic lodestone supposedly shaped like the Sphinx. Charles Romyn Dake's *A Strange Discovery* (1899), highly imitative of Rider Haggard, allows Pym to love the incomparable Lilama, native of the city of Hili-li, founded by Roman citizens who fled the invasions of barbarians during the fourth century. Dake's basic method negates much of the sense of wonder found in both Poe and Haggard, however, for his narrator finds Dirk Peters dying in Bellevue, Illinois, with the result that discussions of such topical matters as medical practice, American politics, and even the Romantic movement in literature upstage the storyline.

By midcentury two other American imaginary voyages anticipated something of the transformation the motif was to undergo during the latter part of the nineteenth century. In the first of these, W. S. Mayo presents himself as the editor of *Kaloolah; or, Journeyings to the Djébel Kumri; An Autobiography of Jonathan Romer* (1849). More a sprawling, episodic travelogue than a dramatic story, it ranges from Nantucket and the American West—complete with Indian fights—to a voyage across the Atlantic in the *Lively Anne* and a cruise from Sierre Leone to the Congo aboard the slave ship *El Bonito*. When Jonathan falls ill of malaria, he is nursed by Princess Kaloolah, a light-skinned young woman from a kingdom in the North. He purchases the freedom of Kaloolah and her brother, Prince Enphadde, and accompanies them to their home; thus he comes to the city of Killoam in the kingdom of Framazugda, hidden on the shores of a great lake in a valley beyond the "Soudan" somewhere in the northern desert.

"Few capitals in Europe," Romer asserts, "compare with it, either in extent or the architectural elegance of its public and private edifices, the beauty of its parks, or the number of its population" (p. 458). Yet it is completely isolated from the western world, its citizens descendants of a people who came from the East, perhaps from Yemen (pp. 467–468). Romer and Kaloolah acknowledge their devotion for one another early. Their wedding provides the climax of the narrative so that Romer becomes the first American to marry a pagan princess, although the story of their love always remains secondary to the scenery. He remains with her in Killoam, sending out his manuscript with a Moor who wishes to return to his home near Fez. In a brief introduction, Mayo finds no resemblance "in matter or manner" between *Kaloolah* and Melville's *Typee*, with which it had been compared. Different as they are, the two narratives nevertheless emphasize the enchantment with idyllic settings (isolated lost cities in particular) and exotic non-European women (one thinks of Melville's obvious fascination with Fayaway) which increasingly characterized the motif as it evolved into the so-called "lost-race" novel in the last decades of the nineteenth century.

In the first such novel to employ a North American setting, Cantell A. Bigly's *Aurifodina; or, Adventures in the Gold Region* (1849), the first-person narrator stays behind when Lieutenant Wilkes' expedition leaves the northwest coast in 1837–1838. For a time he is satisfied to be a hunter along the Pacific Coast, but he decides to try to find a pass over the Sierra Mountains to Santa Fe. He encounters a party of men who have "golden hair, like [his] Saxon ancestors" (p. 18); he makes no further attempt to identify them, although he does emphasize that their "laws, manners and customs . . . do not differ radically from [his] own" (p. 45). They take him to a village high in the mountains amid scenery fit "for a royal park" (p. 23). Gold is so plentiful that it is a utilitarian metal used not only for the great gate to the village but for bathing tubs (p. 27). Although he is surprised that the women "acquiesce" so easily to having all power in the hands of "the other sex" (p. 62), he soon marries the Princess Mideeré (pp. 90–91), thereby becoming the heir presumptive to the throne. Unlike Jonathan Romer, however, he is not content to remain in Aurifodina; he undertakes a balloon voyage, landing in Kentucky and ending up in New York. Although he loves Mideeré, whom he has compared to the Madonna (p. 83), for various reasons he makes no attempt to return to her, fearing, for example, that he could never find the village.

The British published a translation of Gustave Aimard's *The Indian Scout: A Story of the Aztec City* (1861), essentially a straight western story focusing upon the adventures of a Canadian marksman—called "Flying Eagle," who evokes images of Natty Bumppo—and his affection for a Comanche maiden, Eglantine, who is "very beautiful for an Indian girl" (p. 15). Praise for Mexico City (p. 48) leads one to believe that that is the Aztec City, but incidentally at the end of the novel an unknown city, Quiepaa Tani, is discovered, and one of the Mexican leaders wishes that he could take some of the young women of the city with him "to stimulate the ardour of his allies" (p. 339). Aimard's second novel,

The Last of the Incas, A Romance (1862), has also been identified as a lost-race novel.[11]

Among the French writers, of course, Jules Verne attracted the most popular and critical attention from the mid-1860s onward. As noted earlier, Verne's most obvious influence was on the fiction aimed at a juvenile audience, yet even there his youthful companions to knowledgeable older scientists were transformed into boy inventors by American writers. Important as was his emphasis upon technology, he transformed the imaginary voyage at a time when geology and geography—the physical world itself—appealed to the popular imagination more keenly than ever before. As Peter Costello points out, Verne planned *A Journey to the Center of the Earth* (1864, 1871) to be "a geological epic," which he updated in a revised edition in 1867.[12] The descent of Professor Lidenbrock and his nephew Axel into the earth through the extinct Icelandic volcano "has probably influenced almost every subsequent tale of earlier geologic times."[13] *Twenty Thousand Leagues Under the Sea* (1870, 1872) provides a veritable encyclopedia of oceanography, ranging from coral reefs and icebergs to octopuses and lost Atlantis. *The Mysterious Island* (1874–1875), Verne's tribute to nineteenth-century progress, remains one of the finest examples of the Robinsonade, for the engineer Cyrus Harding directs his companions as they turn the primitive island into a showplace of current technology.

In his appraisal of another of Verne's most popular works, *Around the World in Eighty Days* (1873), Peter Costello pinpoints one of the major problems involved in any appraisal of Verne's place in the development of science fiction:

In 1872 the idea of a swift trip around the world was still a novelty. . . . Verne's novel dramatised the speed with which [his readers] could now travel. But he was not as yet interested in why people, as opposed to explorers, travelled to remote lands. The thing itself fascinated him, not the reasons behind it. (pp. 122, 123)

Verne's handling of the storyline of *Around the World in Eighty Days* exemplifies this characteristic. In India, Phileas Fogg saves the beautiful Aouda from cremation after the death of her husband; she joins Passepartout and Fogg, but only when the three of them arrive in London does Fogg confess his love and plan their wedding for the next day (a convenient way of discovering that he has gained a day in circling the world from East to West so that he can win his wager). This platonic relationship is the major romantic interlude in Verne's fiction. Sam Moskowitz speaks to the issue when he declares that "the love story motif is almost entirely absent from Verne's scientific romances. Until recently this was true of ninety percent of all science fiction. Readers were more interested in the theme than in the love life of the characters."[14]

Surely an examination of the novels dealt with thus far contradicts such an assertion unless one limits science fiction with some highly restrictive definition. And therein lies the basic difficulty, for Frank Magill does not include either *Around the World in Eighty Days* or *Five Weeks in a Balloon* in his surveys of science fiction and fantasy, while E. F. Bleiler excludes both titles from the second edition of his *Checklist*. Magill also relegates Rider Haggard to the realm of fantasy, listing only *She* as sf, though it is also included in a discussion of fantasy.[15] What this means is that despite the significance of the imaginary voyage as a narrative framework throughout science fiction, many twentieth-century devotees of the field arbitrarily omit certain titles from sf. To some extent this process involves the distinction between fantasy and science fiction. One cannot satisfactorily rationalize these exclusions in terms of the element of science within a particular work becoming dated. Most obviously, many individuals dismiss the lost-race motif from science fiction.

To do so is extremely parochial, showing little or no historical perspective. As suggested elsewhere, in both Great Britain and the United States between the 1870s and 1930s, the most popular form of the imaginary voyage took the form of the lost-race novel. "Most simply, that type of story reflected the impact of three interrelated areas upon the literary and public imaginations of the period": first, the renewed vigor of the explorations which sought to map the interiors of Africa, Asia, and South America, as well as both polar regions; second, the cumulative impact of geological discoveries and theories which expanded the past almost immeasurably and populated it with such creatures as Tyrannosaurus Rex, Pithecanthropus Erectus, and Neanderthal Man; and finally, the impact of archaeological discoveries and theories which—from the valley of the Indus to the depths of Africa and South America—found civilizations in the past more spectacular and mysterious than legendary El Dorado or the Kingdom of Prester John.[16]

During these decades the concept of lost Atlantis flourished as never before, because it was used to solve old mysteries and bring seeming reconciliation to new ideological quarrels. Undoubtedly, the emergence of modern journalism in search of a mass market molded much of this public reaction (one recalls Stanley's expedition to Zanzibar and Ujiji to find Livingstone). As Morton Cohen remarks, "The telegraph and war correspondents were bringing to the English at home vivid descriptions of their far-flung colonies, and these readers grew eager to participate in the adventure of Empire."[17] Peter Costello observes that even while Verne was completing *Five Weeks in a Balloon*, "Speke and Grant were still out of reach in Africa trying to settle the source of the Nile."[18] Such activities demanded a literary response; headlines frequently shaped popular fiction (one recalls the response of the literary naturalists to the "yellow journalism" in the United States soon after the turn of the century). And to dismiss geology, archaeology, and paleontology from the sciences on which the literary imagination can build is simply absurd. The refusal to include the motif in science fiction also ignores the way in which many of the themes recurrent throughout sf infuse the lost-race motif.

Sir H. Rider Haggard gave the motif its essential literary form. The anecdote relating how he wrote *King Solomon's Mines* (1885) as the result of a wager involving Robert Louis Stevenson's *Treasure Island* is too well known to repeat in detail. As in the case of Stevenson, Haggard wrote a book for boys which gained favor with the adult audience. As in the case of Verne, in *King Solomon's Mines* the "adventure was the thing, and there was plenty of it."[19] Yet in a sense he outdid Verne. In writing of *Around the World in Eighty Days*, Costello declares that "Verne was exact enough about such details as names and places, which are easy enough to look up in a gazeteer [sic], but he easily missed the substance of foreign life" (p. 122). In contrast, Haggard drew on his intimate knowledge of South Africa and the Transvaal. From his acquaintance with the warlike Zulu, he created a fierce, unbroken tribe which still ruled the unexplored interior. Although the central thrust of the narrative focuses on the search for the legendary mines, based on a map which Allan Quatermain and his companions acquired, Haggard gives most of his attention to a highly realistic yet romantic panorama of African life. *King Solomon's Mines* met with immediate success among the reviewers; ironically, the writer for *The Spectator* found it "decidedly superior to the best of Jules Verne's, and surpassing even Herman Melville's 'Kaloolah' [which] we should previously have placed at the head of this department of literary art."[20]

Once Haggard found his pattern, he repeated it in *Allan Quatermain* (1887) and *She: A History of Adventure* (1887). Both give accounts of expeditions into the unknown interior. *She* gains its distinction from Haggard's portrayal of the beautiful, apparently immortal Ayesha, "She-Who-Must-Be-Obeyed," who rules the Amahaggar tribe in the hidden valley of Kor. Two thousand years ago she had killed Kallikrates, a priest of Isis who had fled from Egypt with Amanartes, daughter of Pharaoh. Ayesha had killed him impulsively in a fit of jealousy when he rejected her love and her promise of immortality for Amanartes, already pregnant with his child. Now Ayesha believes that he has been reincarnated in his descendant, Leo Vincey, who was guided to her by an ancient manuscript left by Amanartes. Vincey returns her love, but Ayesha withers and dies when she bathes in the Pillar of Flame, the source of her immortality. Disconsolate, Leo returns to England with Ludwig Horace Holly, his guardian and the narrator. An element of mysticism enters Haggard's treatment of Ayesha, particularly when he suggests that such a love as hers and Leo's must be eternal. Ayesha fascinated Haggard, as witnessed by the existence of three additional novels devoted to her: *Ayesha, The Return of She* (1905), *She and Allan* (1920), and *Wisdom's Daughter* (1923).

"*She* took London [and America] by storm."[21] Within the year, six parodies of Haggard had been published in London and New York: *He*, attributed to Andrew Lang and W. H. Pollock; *King Solomon's Wives* by H. C. Biron; *King Solomon's Treasures*, *Bess*, and *It*, attributed to the American, John DeMorgan.[22] The title page to Munro's American edition of *He*, dated November 5, 1887, lists two additional titles as items in Munro's Twenty-five Cent Edition: #733 *Pa* and #734 *Ma*. S. J. Marshall published a serious sequel, *The King of Kor* (1903), in which he strongly implied that Leo and Ayesha would be reunited after Leo's death. The vivid background, the love story, and the enigmatic figure of Ayesha—Margaret Atwood has called her "a combination of the Ideal and the Dark Sorceress . . . re-creating . . . within the conventions of nineteenth century fiction . . . the split heroine, the tension between domestic and exotic"[23]— combined to make *She* one of the most influential books of the 1880s.

Nor should one neglect to emphasize her physical beauty. Holly is summoned to her apartment; as he waits he begins to speculate: "At length the curtain began to stir. Who could be behind it—some naked savage queen, a languishing Oriental beauty, or a nineteenth-century young woman, drinking her afternoon tea? I had not the slightest idea."[24] One infers that Holly reveals something of himself— and quite probably of all European and American men during the nineteenth century—when he imagines first that a savage queen or an Oriental beauty awaits him. Soon, from behind the folds of the curtain, appears "a white hand, white as snow, and with long tapering fingers, ending in the pinkest nails. This hand grasped the curtain, drawing it aside" (p. 107). Ayesha's first entrance is theatrical. She "unveils" herself to Holly:

. . . She lifted her white and rounded arms—never had I seen such arms before—and slowly, very slowly, she withdrew some fastening behind her hair. Then of a sudden the long, corpse-like wrappings fell from her to the ground, and my eyes travelled up her form, now robed only in a garb of clinging white that did but serve to show its rich and imperial shape, instinct with a life that was more than life, and with a certain serpent-like grace which was more than human. On her little feet were sandals fastened with studs of gold. Then came ankle more perfect than ever sculptor dreamed of. About the waist her white kirtle was fastened by a double-headed snake of pure gold, above which her generous form swelled up in lines as pure as they were lovely, till the kirtle ended at the snowy argent of her breast, whereon her arms were folded. I gazed above them at her face, and—I do not romance—shrank back blinded and amazed. I have heard of the beauty of celestial beings, now I saw it; only this beauty, with all its awful loveliness and purity was evil—or rather, at the time, it impressed me as evil. . . . The man does not live whose pen can convey a sense of what I saw. I might talk of the great changing eyes of deepest, softest black, of the tinted face, of the broad and noble brow, on which the hair grew low, and delicate, straight features. But beautiful, surpassingly beautiful as were all these, her loveliness did not lie in them. It lay rather . . . in a visible majesty, in an imperial grace, in a godlike stamp of softened power, which shone upon that living countenance like a living halo. Never before had I guessed what beauty made sublime could be—and yet, the sublimity was a dark one—the glory was not all of heaven—but nonetheless it was glorious. (pp.117–118)

Despite the ambivalence in Holly's reaction which suggests something of the Wilde days ahead awaiting British society, the description draws upon an eroticism which was to echo through the lost-race motif. The depth of Ayesha's impact on the literary imagination may be measured by the final sequence of James Hilton's *Lost Horizon* (1933). After the beautiful Lo-Tsen leaves the haven of Shangri-la, she becomes the "most old . . . most old of any one" the Chinese medical doctor at Chung-Kiang had ever seen.[25]

In view of the emphasis given *King Solomon's Mines* and *She* by Morton

Cohen and Peter Berresford Ellis, there is an irony in neither biographer's bothering with more than passing mention of *Allan Quatermain*. *King Solomon's Mines* provided Haggard with his most important setting; *She* became the most complex archetype of the lost-race heroine, but *Allan Quatermain* established the basic storyline for the motif. Quatermain himself is the first-person narrator as he leads Sir Henry Curtis and Commander John Good, R.N., past "Mt. Kenia" in quest of a mysterious white race. On a high tableland they find the warlike, sun-worshipping Zu-Vendris, who have dwelt on the shores of the great lake Milosis for a thousand years. Although Quatermain has noticed "certain ladies whose skin was of a most dazzling whiteness; and the darkest shade of colour which [he] saw was that of a rather swarthy Spaniard,"[26] nothing has prepared him for the beauty of the two reigning queens:

I have seen beautiful women in my day, and am no longer thrown into transports at the sight of a pretty face; but language fails me when I try to give some idea of the blaze of loveliness that broke upon us in the persons of these sister Queens. Both were young— perhaps five-and-twenty years of age—both were tall and exquisitely formed; but there the likeness stopped. One, Nyleptha, was a woman of dazzling fairness; her right arm and breast, bare after the custom of her people, showed like snow even against the white and gold-embroidered "kaf," or toga. And as for her sweet face, all I can say is, that it was one that few men could look on and forget. Her hair, a veritable crown of gold, clustered in short ringlets over her shapely head, half hiding the ivory brow, beneath which eyes of deep and glorious grey flashed out in tender majesty. I cannot attempt to describe her other features, only the mouth was most sweet, and curved like Cupid's bow, and over the whole countenance there shone an indescribable look of loving kindness, lit up by a shadow of delicate humour that lay upon her face like a touch of silver on a rosy cloud. (pp. 525–526)

Her sister, Sorais, is as brunette as Nyleptha is fair (once again the split between Ideal and Dark Sorceress which Atwood noted). "Royal they were in every way," continues Quatermain, "in form, in grace, and queenly dignity, and in the barbaric splendour of their attendant pomp" (p. 526). Yet when Nyleptha meets Sir Henry's gaze, Quatermain sees "the swift blood run up beneath Nyleptha's skin as the pink lights run up the morning sky. Red grew her fair bosom and shapely arm, red the swanlike neck; the rounded cheek blushed red as the petals of a rose" (p. 527). Thus does love come to the African Queen, who becomes the bride of Sir Henry and bears him a son and heir. Sir Henry Curtis was among the fortunates; most authors did not allow their protagonists to remain in an idyllic land with a barbaric maid, especially if by any remote chance she was not of European bloodstock.

Morton Cohen remarks that an unidentified publisher who had rejected *King Solomon's Mines* did not "appreciate how many readers were weary of the problem novel and how the demand for adventure and romance was again growing."[27] Such a remark becomes an understatement when placed next to the denunciation of realism and naturalism which shaped Julian Hawthorne's introduction to an American novel, William Bradshaw's *The Goddess of Atvatabar* (1892). Hawthorne's declaration helps one to understand why some critics and authors thought that a blending of science, utopian idealism, and neoprimitivism could produce a dynamic form which would give Romanticism a new heart:

Literature may be roughly classified under two heads—the creative and the critical. The former is characteristic of the imaginative temperament, while the latter is analytical in its nature. Rightly pursued, these two ways of searching out truth should supplement each other. The poet finds in God the source of matter; the man of science traces matter up to God. Science is poetry inverted; the latter sees in the former confirmation of its airiest flight; it is synthetic and creative, whereas science dissects and analyzes. Obviously, the most spiritual conceptions should always maintain a basis in the world of fact, and the greatest works of literary art, while taking their stand upon the solid earth, have not feared to lift their heads to heaven. The highest art is the union of both methods, but in recent times realism in an extreme form, led by Zola and Tolstoi, and followed with willing though infirm footsteps by certain American writers, has attained a marked prominence in literature, while romantic writers have suffered a corresponding obscuration. It must be admitted that the influence of the realists is not entirely detrimental; on the contrary, they have imported into literature a nicety of observation, a heedfulness of workmanship, a mastery of technique, which have been greatly to its advantage. Nevertheless, the novel of hard facts has failed to prove its claim to infallibility. Facts in themselves are impotent to account for life. Every material fact is but the representative on the plane of sense of a corresponding truth on the spiritual plane. Spirit is the substance; fact the shadow only, and its only claim to existence lies in its relation to spirit. Bulwer declares in one of his early productions that the Ideal is the only true Real.

In the nature of things a reaction from the depression of the realistic school must take place. Indeed, it has already set in, even at the moment of the realists' apogée. A dozen years ago the author of "John Inglesant" in a work of the finest art and the most delicate spirituality, showed that the spell of the ideal had not lost its efficacy, and the books that he has written since then have confirmed the impression produced by it. Meanwhile, Robert Louis Stevenson and Rider Haggard have cultivated with striking success the romantic vein of fiction, and the former, at least, has acquired a mastery of technical detail which the realists themselves may envy. It is little more than a year, too, since Rudyard Kipling startled the reading public with a series of tales of wonderful force and vividness; and whatever criticism may be applied to his work, it incontestably shows the dominance of spiritual and romantic motive. The realists, on the other hand, have added no notable recruits to their standard, and the leaders of the movement are losing rather than gaining in popularity. The spirit of the new age seems to be with the other party, and we may expect to see them enjoy a constantly widening vogue and influence.

The first practical problem which confronts the historian of an ideal, social, or political community is to determine the locality in which it shall be placed. It may have no geographical limitations, like Plato's "Republic," or Sir Philip Sidney's "Arcadia." Swift, in his "Gulliver's Travels," appropriated the islands of the then unknown seas, and the late Mr. Percy Greg steered into space and located a brilliant romance on the planet Mars. Mr. Haggard has placed the scene of his romance, "She," in the unexplored interior of Africa. After all, if imagination be our fellow traveller, we might well discover El Dorado within easy reach of our own townships.

Other writers, like Ignatius Donnelly and Edward Bellamy, have solved the problem by anticipating the future. Anything will do, so that it be well done. The real question is as to the writer's ability to interest his readers with supposed experiences that may develop mind and heart almost as well as if real.

"The Goddess of Atvatabar," like the works already mentioned, is a production of imagination and sentiment. (pp. 9–10)

Although Rider Haggard gave the lost-race motif its enduring form when he placed primary emphasis on the love story, American writers had anticipated him to some degree, as evidenced by Mayo's *Kaloolah*. In the last decades of the century, however, the voyage and love story often provided simply a narrative shell as the Americans attempted to inject utopian and religious materials into the motif with varying results. For example, as early as R. Elton Smile's *The Manatitlans* (1877), a German scientific expedition finds near the headwaters of the Paraguay the city of Heracles by the Falls inhabited by descendants of noble Roman families whose ship was driven by storms across the Atlantic. Their story serves only as a preliminary to the discovery by means of the "tympano-microscope" of a diminutive people infesting the petals and pistils of a flower; the 11,000-year history of the Manatitlans serves as a means of satirizing European society.[28]

As might be expected, some of the finest American works grew out of the Symmes-Poe tradition relying on Antarctica. Undoubtedly the most effective nineteenth-century satire remains Frank Cowan's *Revi-Lona: A Romance of Love in a Marvelous Land* (188?). In the "Advertisement" to the book, Cowan outlines his intentions:

This book has been written in a plain, straightforward and truthful manner, to tell how a big and brawny man with many of the vices of his sex and years and a few of the virtues, went from the backwoods of Pennsylvania to the South Pole of the Earth and found, in a volcanic or hot-water wilderness, an isolated oasis of tropic warmth and rare fertility, containing strange survivals from a bygone geologic age, and inhabited by a remnant of a former continental people, enlightened, white-skinned and of surpassing beauty, but voiceless—a perfect but petticoated paradise, where big and beautiful women ruled and little and learned men obeyed in a marvelous communistic government; where love had been suppressed for ages and kinship was unknown; and where the most stupendous and elaborate buildings were constructed without the use of metal tools; and how, by reason of his superior proportions as a man, and the novelties which he introduced in the way of ideas, microbes, seeds, and the like, he first willy-nilly and afterward, in despite of all his efforts to the contrary, disorganized the perfect commonwealth, destroyed the pure and happy people and annihilated the lovely land, with all its natural and artificial wonders. (p. iii)

Through his first-person narrator, Anson Oliver, Cowan delivers. One realizes from the initial incident, the elopement and consequent suicide of the narrator's bride-to-be, that Cowan will have none of romance. No summary can do justice to the skill with which Cowan gets his narrator, disenchanted and using an assumed name, to the town of Leota, Chile, where he is robbed of his gold and shanghaied aboard a whaler bound for the Antarctic. Accidents, murders, and the loss of all whaling boats in a fog leave him alone aboard a derelict vessel which finds its way to a mountainous land marked by volcanoes and geysers and, finally, to the harbor of a crescent-shaped city. At first, Anson is threatened with death if he does not depart. Finally, by order of the Twenty-Five Governing Women, Tobo-lulu and 200 of the harbor guard officially welcome him to the commonwealth of Revi-Lona. Being mute, Tobo-lulu must communicate by drumming, a process that Anson understands at once. He subsequently signals "by means of Morse alphabet" when he greets Nada-nana, one of the governing women (p. 35). Although she cannot understand, they exchange winks. In "a delirium of ecstacy" when fifteen beautiful young women board the ship, he impulsively kisses them all (p. 37). He learns accidentally that the women were to provide distraction while his ship was towed from the harbor, but with the discovery that the anchor is of iron, the same material as that of a great meteor whose fall was witnessed, Anson is regarded as a visitor from heaven.

The polar paradise of Revi-Lona becomes momentarily a sexual heaven. A man given to drink and promiscuity, Anson makes love to each of the Twenty-Five Governing Women. The resultant jealousy and rivalry for his affection lead first to suicide and then civil war. Beginning with the fleas aboard the ship, he brings with him some of the blessings of civilization—small pox, measles, and syphilis, all of which destroy much of the population. Although he remains faithful in his fashion to Nada-nana, his presence destroys the ideal commonwealth; that destruction is completed by famine, earthquake, volcano, and a flood that inundates the city and sends his ship outward past the ring of ice. What makes *Revi-Lona* so devastating a satire is the manner in which Cowan's handling of all romantic (utopian) conventions is undercut by the straightforward, often ribald, tone of his narrative.

Cowan treats only one convention in the same manner as do his contemporaries. He refers a number of times to "gigantic" birds, the Morgas, like the moa of New Zealand, which have been domesticated as a means of transportation. This is as close as he comes to the menagerie of prehistoric animals which some of the writers included. The convention reached its most absurd in Frank Saville's *Beyond the Great South Wall* (1901), in which a single "*Brontosaurus excelsus*" (p. 216) dominates a glacier-filled valley containing an ice-encased Mayan temple. The beast is supposedly the Mayan god Cay, described in a sixteenth-century manuscript telling of the Indians' exodus before oncoming Spaniards and their discovery in a land of ice of the physical manifestation of Cay. Throughout the remainder of the novel it pursues various members of the expedition. Trapped in a cave, because Gwen Delahay has paused to save her "puppy dog" from the oncoming monster, Captain Jack Dorinecourt prepares to shoot Gwen and himself rather than be devoured by the dinosaur whose head, thrust into the cave, has pinned them to the rear wall. In such circumstances Gwen informs

Jack that she loves him, not Lord Denvarre, from whose sinking ship Jack rescued her. A convenient earthquake kills the brontosaurus and permits the lovers to return to England to be wed.

Far more effective is James DeMille's *A Strange Manuscript Found in a Copper Cylinder* (1888), one of the more distinctly American treatments of the motif. Reputedly the manuscript of an English sailor, Thomas More, shipwrecked in the Antarctic in 1843, it echoes something of Poe's *The Narrative of Arthur Gordon Pym*. More discovers uncharted islands, is captured and escapes from cannibals, and then is swept along an underground river. Recalling that "as a boy [he] had read wild works of fiction about lands in the interior of the earth" (p. 48), he decides that he is being carried into a great cavern, but he emerges into a tropical land, a fact which he immediately explains in terms of the flattening of the earth at its poles and geothermal energy (pp. 56–57). The rest of the novel combines the love story of More and the maid, Almah, against a background cluttered with dinosaurs and an attack upon the supposedly utopian Kosekin society.

What makes *A Strange Manuscript Found in a Copper Cylinder* both significant and unique is the nature of its envelope structure. A group of Englishmen aboard a becalmed yacht rescues More's manuscript from the South Atlantic. At several points they interrupt his story to speculate about the feasibility of his report, introducing a variety of scientific and technical data to explain matters More has described. First, some of the group insist that it is a hoax of a sensational novelist, but they reconsider when they realize that its parchment is similar to Egyptian papyrus (pp. 65–68). Once they have accepted the possibility of its authenticity, they begin an argument regarding polar geography, citing the discoveries of Captains Wilkes and Ross in 1838–1840 and agree that a zone having temperate climate, at least, might exist (pp. 69–76). The next intrusion concerns fossil animals, identifying the saurians More has described as Plesiosaurus, Megalasaurus, and Ichthyosaurus (pp. 156–162). The most amusing discussion occurs when one of them concludes that the Kosekin are Hebrews: "Shem landed there from Noah's ark, and left some of his children to colonize the country" (p. 166); he prefers that to the concept of the Ten Tribes, often identified in the eighteenth and nineteenth centuries as the forefathers of the American Indian. DeMille's technique emphasizes the extent to which writers sought to provide their fantasies with realistic frames, but it also incorporates effectively and intrinsically the appeal to outside authority which began as early as Charles Brockden Brown.

In contrast, William Bradshaw's *The Goddess of Atvatabar* (1892), which turns to the Arctic to create a Symmesian world, remains the most extravagant of the American fictions portraying a lost race. Although Julian Hawthorne praises the theosophical and occult elements in the religion of Atvatabar, he proceeds to undercut his evaluation by stating that "a loftier and sublimer experience" awaits the Goddess Lyone (p. 12). Once Commander Lexington White reaches the inner world and is attracted to Lyone, she explains the underlying principle of the religion, whose center is appropriately located in the capital city named "Egyplosis":

"Life and love are synonymous. By love I mean the spiritual, ideal, romantic passion that is hopeless.
    "The pleasure that we aspire to is superior to any physical delight, and is an end in itself. It is romantic love, that blooms like a single flower in the crevices of a volcano. It is the quintessence of existence, the rarest wine of life, the expressed sweetness of difficulty and repression and long-suffering, the choicest holiday of the soul. We are willing to pay the price of hopelessness to taste such nectar." (p. 164)

White argues with her but attempts among his colleagues to praise "their oasis of love . . . and [the] purity of twin souls," but the medical doctor of the expedition denounces "this institution [as] a perversion of human nature":

"This nervous temperament, with its hysterical raptures and tears, its painful sensibility, its exalted spiritualism and irresistible sympathy, departs so far from the steady temperate sphere of action that alone can sustain alike the pleasures and disappointments of life as to become the object of pity. These are the marks of a mental disease. Ultra-romantic ideas and whimsical and unaccountable tastes are attributes of this temperament. It is a kind of insanity, not the insanity proceeding from hopeless mental aberration, but founded on a systematic train of ideas born in a heated enthusiasm. It may lead, however, to hopeless insanity." (p. 174)

A man of action who is in love, White arranges a rendezvous where he and Lyone discuss all of the merits of spiritual love (pp. 176–183); then White embraces her. "Her kiss was a blinding whirlwind of flame and tears! . . . It dissolved all other interests like fire melted stubborn steel. It was a declaration of war upon Atvatabar" (p. 183). Such apostasy leads to civil war, which the "new and formidable twin soul" wins with the aid of British and American warships sent to search for Commander White once news of his discovery has reached the outer world. Crowned king, White promises to make commercial treaties with the Anglo-American powers, although he will preserve Atvatabarese institutions and customs. Such a triumph of sexual love—the "loftier and sublimer experience" to which Hawthorne refers—illustrates vividly the essentially erotic core of the lost-race motif.
    Yet *The Goddess of Atvatabar* remains a hodgepodge of contradictions. Despite the presence of a number of conventional devices—control of the weather, "magnicity," air machines, and mechanical ostriches used not only for transportation but also for war—one of the priest-magicians ("a sorcerer") creates both the necessities for a banquet and also "the magical island of Arjeels" to the specifications of Lyone; the "abnegation of hopeless love" provides the power from which "[they] create matter such as this" (pp. 190, 192). When Lyone dies of an electric shock, she is restored to life when 10,000 worshippers

exert their soul power (in conjunction with a kind of electrical circuit making use of the super-metal, terrilium) (pp. 288–292).

As one might guess, the central target of Bradshaw's attack is Darwinian theory; he presents the "Garden of Tanje," where grow marvelous creatures "illustrative of the gradual evolution of animals from plants, a scientific faith that held sway in Atvatabar" (p. 120). Among those creatures grew the following:

There was also a flock of strange green-feathered creatures, resembling buzzards, called green gazzles, on whose heads grew sunflowers. On either side, beneath their wings, were plant roots by means of which they still sucked nourishment from the soil, as their bills had not yet been perfectly developed. . . .
. . . the yarp-happy, which seemed a combination of ape and flower. Its peculiarly weird, ape-like face was covered with a hood, and from the open mouth of each animal protruded the tongue. From the neck of the animal three long leaves radiated, the two lower leaves in each case terminating in claw-like appendages, which gave a weird expression to the zoophyte. (pp. 120, 122–123)

However paradoxical the mishmash of Atvatabar (the magic of the creation of matter and the realistic triumph of the imperialistic powers), one characteristic remained constant in terms of the motif—the beauty of Lyone:

. . . she was arrayed in a single garment of quivering pale green silk, that caressed every curve of her matchless figure. . . . She was so youthful that she could have not been more than twenty years old. . . . Her eyes were large and blue. . . . She was arrayed in a dress of soft purple silk, that, apparently, had no other garment beneath, so perfect was the revelation of her figure. (pp. 110, 113, 117)

Her hair, incidentally, is "a heavy glossy mass, of a pale sapphire-blue color, that fell in a waving cloud around her shoulders" (p. 96).

Returning to an Antarctic setting, Edward T. Bouve used the narrative frame to achieve a very different effect in *Centuries Apart* (1894). Although Bouve tried to insert a deceased "compiler" between himself and the story, it is the reconstruction of the diary of Captain Arthur Percy which was destroyed in the great Boston fire of November 1872. In a prefatory note, Bouve regrets that the diary could not have been established as the work of "a sane man, uncrazed by the fearful experience of disaster and suffering" (p. iv), for it chronicles a discovery akin to that of Columbus. Part of a Union expeditionary force sent sometime after the Battle of Gettysburg to keep Napoleon III and Maximilian from securing Mexico and aiding the Confederates (pp. 2–5), Carter and his comrades were swept by a storm deep into the southern polar sea, where they found the kingdoms of South England and La Nouvelle France. After the accession of Henry Tudor at the end of the War of the Roses, disaffected families—primarily Yorkists—had fled to France; after some years, the English exiles, together with Frenchmen led by Count de Plessis, ventured forth to obtain lands south of those held by Spain in the new world (pp. 41–45). Once Captain Percy arrives in South England, the narrative plots "The Course of True Love," as one chapter is entitled, for he loves and is loved by Lady Kate Percy, conveniently a cousin since both are descendants of the Percy family of Northumbria. When the old earl worries whether or not Kate would be happy if she were to live in the United States, Arthur replies, "The position of women is very happy in America, and your daughter would find herself, exquisitely lovely as she is, a favorite everywhere among my friends" (p. 182). His is a view not easily reconciled with those of many of Bouve's contemporaries.

Captain Percy is not the first American to reach South England. Sometime after the Battle of Gettysburg an unnamed Confederate "high officer" landed on the island but soon died, leaving Kate's father innumerable books, of which "next to Shakespeare, loved we the poesy of a certain Sir Walter Scott" (p. 88). *Centuries Apart* reads like a Scott romance, complete with a battle between the English and the French as well as a "poor mountain maiden, the daughter of a proscribed name and clan" (p. 286), who dares to love Captain Percy though she knows that he is the beloved of "peerless Katherine Percy." Yet Bouve will not permit his lovers to remain together. The ships repaired, Arthur Percy must return to the United States. After a terrible storm he is picked up as the sole survivor of the expedition (p. 332), and on the eve of Appomattox he is killed by a sniper. Yet he reveals to Tom—the supposed compiler—that as in certain novels by Scott (p. 339), he has had a premonition of his death and has seen Kate. Earlier before returning to duty, he had insisted that Tom marry his sister Catherine. Tom ends the novel wondering whether Kate waited for Arthur's return or, thinking him false, married another. In the prefatory note, Bouve established the tone for this ending when he trusted sincerely "that no enthusiastic extracts from the diary descriptive of South Polar feminine loveliness may tempt any young American viking to turn the prow of his yacht in an Antarctic direction. Probably there's little likelihood of that, however, for beauty is not sought in these later days" (pp. v-vi).

A somewhat surprising yet predictable detail occurs when the old Duke Percy describes the discovery of the southern land: they found "a pale people . . . descended from both Greek and Asiatic stock, and whose ancestors had migrated to South Africa and thence to these shores" (pp. 45–46). The lost-race motif became a highly formulaic fiction which provides an amazing index to current exploration. One can tell which areas of the world remained unexplored and so captured the popular imagination simply by glancing at trends in the novels, although subsequent authors never abandoned a setting once it had been established.

Because of the concerted effort to reach the pole at the turn of the century, as well as the series of disasters ranging from Sir John Franklin and the *Jeannette* to Andrée, the Arctic even more than the Antarctic remained perhaps the favorite American setting. In Henry Clay Fairman's *The Third World* (1904), an unnamed survivor of the Franklin expedition finds an antediluvian people of "Adamic blood" in a polar kingdom and falls in love with the Lady Noona. He remains with her, and his manuscript is found in a cave in Greenland in 1859. The convoluted plot of Harris Burland's *The Princess Thora* (1904) involves a colony of Norman French who fled from Henry I in 1105, but the storyline builds upon an impersonation which permits the supposed princess to return to England with Edward Silex, an eccentric millionaire who financed an expedition to restore the young woman to the throne. In Robert Ames Bennet's *Thyra; A Romance of the Polar Pit* (1901), the narrator saves a "Polar Valkyrie"—Princess Thyra—whose people are descended from the lost Jarl Biorn expedition of 925, while Richard Hatfield's *Geyserland; Empiricisms in Social Reform* (1908) builds on the concept of a prehistoric land bridge between Europe and America as well as the theories of such persons as Joseph Alphonse Adhemar (pp. 46–47). Supposedly the manuscript of Adam Mann, a sailor shipwrecked during a quest for the Northwest Passage in the seventeenth century, its storyline focuses upon the love of Adam and Evrona, whose "antediluvian cultured" ancestors were marooned in the new Arctic when the earth last shifted its axis. When Evrona finally openly confesses her love and urges him to stay, he replies:

"Another awaits me at home. I have asked her [twenty years ago] to let me love her. Those whom we decide to love we love forever. I met you too late, gentle Evrona." (p. 422)

Thus he returns to Holland, where recently his manuscript has been found in a Bible.

Perhaps the narrator of Albert Bigelow Paine's *The Great White Way* (1901) voices most openly the theme which implicitly shapes these storylines. In the Antarctic, an American expedition finds an agrarian communal society in an area covered "to the farthest horizon limits [by] a thick, yielding carpet of wonderful Purple Violets" (p. 224). The people are united telepathically. Long ago, legend says, a princess came from the sun to govern them, as the Inca came to the Peruvians. The narrator contemplates their life:

... Ambition and achievement—of such kind as we know and prize—seemed foreign to their lives. It was truly a "Land of Heart's Desire." ... Here, shut away from the greed and struggle of the life we know ... the lives of the people have linked themselves with the sun and the stars, with the woods and fields, with the winds and waters, and with each other, in one rare, universal chord.... They regard with sorrowful distrust our various mechanical contrivances. (pp. 236, 243, 258)

The most sensitive American, the youthful Ferratoni, who is both a scientist and a mystic, possesses a psychic power enabling him to communicate with the people telepathically. When the reigning princess chooses him to be her husband, he agrees and remains behind when his companions return to America. His action remains perhaps the most explicit renunciation of the modern technological world in any of the American lost-race novels. More than a decade later, in *The New Northland* (1915), Louis P. Gratacap remembered "The Land of Heart's Desire" as "that romantic and sufficing paradise" (pp. 93–94).

As early as William Wallace Cook's *Cast Away at the Pole* (1904), the search for the pole itself—to say nothing of the quest for an idyllic land—drew a satirical response. When Captain Salis, U.S.N., and Professor Preeble discover the tropical land of Nyll twenty-three miles from the pole, Preeble insists that the "friction of the earth in its rotation around the pole generates the heat" and resists the idea that the pole is "figurative" (p. 90). After they penetrate the veil of fog enveloping the area, in his role as "polar explorer," Captain Salis describes their discovery: " . . . the great spindle was disclosed, a mighty bulwark of celestial law and order. . . . Entranced, we stood and watched the wonderful whirligig perform its mighty revolution" (p. 226).

In 1909, William Lyon Phelps, dedicating his work to the New Haven Choral Union, made *A Dash at the Pole*, heavily laden with atrocious puns. News of Sir William Parry's achievement reached the United States not much sooner than Wallace Irwin's discovery of a "manuscript found in a ketchup bottle" reported "A New Angle on the Old Pole" in *Cosmopolitan*.[29] The most extensive and effective parody of polar adventures took shape in George Randolph Chester's *The Jingo* (1912), supposedly the recovered manuscript of one Jimmy Smith, a representative of the Eureka Manufacturing Company. From the outset, Chester dresses romantic conventions in a vernacular style. To appreciate what Chester attempts, one should contrast the entrance of Rider Haggard's Ayesha with the first view of the youthful Princess Bezzanna at play with her brother, her father, and a suitor: " . . . her cheeks and eyes flaming with the joy of the romp, and the hem of her white robe cracking behind her like a whip, revealing every lithe curve of her, [she] giggled" (p. 3). Although she refuses to marry her royal suitor, Onalyon, she does go to the shore during a storm, hoping that it will bring her "something very wonderful" (p. 10). The sea deposits Jimmy Smith at her feet, and when he regains consciousness, he first demands a cable office and then asks for his pants (p. 21). Three days later, he informs "Betsy Ann" that he has "decided not to learn [her] language. . . . So [she has] to learn American" (p. 24). Later he explains that as his ship, the *Kaisertania*, sank, he deliberately took Jones's *Handbook of Modern Shop Practise and Revised-to-the-Minute Formulas*, "thirteenth annual edition," from his trunk and then jumped overboard.

So begins the confrontation between American culture and an ancient Greek society which has somehow survived, apparently in Isola, a mountain-surrounded "niche" on the coast of the Antarctic continent (p. 93). Of course Jimmy and Betsy Ann fall in love immediately, but Jimmy tries to put her out of mind when her father reveals that a royal princess was imprisoned in a tower until she died after she had eloped with a commoner (p. 97). To no avail, however, for Princess Bezzanna responds to him, giggling, particularly after he introduces her to American fashions by fitting a gown to her.[30] The main storyline focuses upon their infatuation and the difficulties caused by Onalyon, but the thrust of Chester's satire—through Jimmy—aims at the growing materialism of America. The romance is light and the scolding delightful because as Jimmy modernizes Isola—

from interior plumbing and window glass to telephones—everything that he says undercuts his values. Yet unlike so many of his contemporaries, whether realists or fantasists, Chester is playful rather than angry. When a German aviator, losing an international race, lands and demands both gasoline and beer, Jimmy recalls the danger of European imperialism and persuades the king to declare Isola both a republic and a territory of the United States. For their wedding music Betsy Ann, ever enthusiastic, selects "The Star-Spangled Banner"; Chester is not yet finished, however, for he gives a last twist to his satire in an "Addendum" to what has been presented as a straightforward here-and-now story:

This book has been written by the editor of the *Daily Isolan* and cast into the sea, in hope that the United States of America will equip an expedition to discover Isola. The second and present territorial governor, Jimmy Smith, desires to assure the United States of the devotion and loyalty of one hundred and seventy-five thousand progressive Americans. Also, he wishes to assure the Eureka Manufacturing Company of his safety. His infant son bears the name of that great concern—Eureka Smith. (p. 394)

Surprisingly, before World War I none of the other lost-race settings evoked satire. As early as 1890, making reference to John Lloyd Stephens and Augustus Le Plongeon, Thomas A. Janvier created a protagonist in *The Aztec Treasure-House* who not only held the chair of Topical Linguistics at the University of Michigan but also wrote a book on pre-Columbian America. With the aid of a hitherto lost manuscript, Professor Thomas Palgrave braves the dangers of the jungle before finding the lost valley of Aztlan, where a fireball destroyed all the pagan idols, because Friar Antonio had been killed in the arena after preaching unsuccessfully to the Aztecs. Other explorers, including a professor, find *The Lost Canyon of the Toltecs* (1893) in the interior of the Isthmus of Panama. An incidental love story involves Mary Taylor, who disappears and must be rescued after she just happens to accompany her British father. A Christian socialist society, founded a century earlier by an eccentric Scotsman and 400 converts, flourishes somewhere in the South American wilds in Henry S. Drayton's *In Oudemon* (1900). Although its technology has far outstripped that of the outside world, its inhabitants are more proud of their accomplishments in telepathy (pp. 230–231). Moreover, they "believe with the philosopher, Emerson, that 'the virtues are natural to [them] and not a painful acquisition' " (p. 99). For example, as the narrator walks alone in the jungle, he comes upon an attractive young woman drawing on a stocking; she has pulled her skirt to her waist, but instead of being frightened at this approach, she smiles. He understands that she has withdrawn "to put herself to rights" and thinks of him as a father (pp. 104–105). In their efforts "to follow the teaching of the *Bible*" and to obey "the will of [their] Father, Infinite and Gracious," they have, of course, rejected the "evolutionary sophists [and] any materialistic notions that one may have imbibed" (pp. 174, 177). Although *In Oudemon* stands unique during the period, it does not attack science so savagely as does John Uri Lloyd's *Etidorhpa* (1895,

1914), whose narrator laments that "one by one the cherished treasures of
Christianity have been stolen from the faithful" (p. 310) and admonishes his
readers, "Beware the science of man. . . . Beware of the science of human biology" (p. 149).

Increasingly, the storyline of the novels dealing with South America grew out
of some variation of a quest for the ancient city, often identified as Manoa or
El Dorado, which remained a dominant legend from before Sir Walter Raleigh's
The Discoveries of . . . Guiana (1596) until after the disappearance of Colonel
P. H. Fawcett in 1925. The youthful protagonist of Frank H. Converse's *In
Search of an Unknown Race* (1901)—first published a decade earlier—finds such
a city near the volcanic peak Escomada inhabited by a people blending the Incas
with an even older race which at its height equaled any nation of the classical
world. The British explorers of Robert Cromie's *El Dorado* (1904) cross the
mountains of Guiana along "the great caravan route of the first civilization" the
world had known (p. 186) to begin excavations at what one of them called "The
Eden of the West" (p. 197). Although the Indians of Venezuela who threaten
the protagonists of Lloyd Osbourne's *The Adventurer* (1907) might be either
Sioux or Apache because of their ponies and manner of attack, Osbourne captures
the awe felt by the narrator and his companions as they stand amid the ruins of
Cassaquiari:

. . . the treasure was the least of it! But the crumbling buildings, acres big, all covered
with figures and hieroglyphs—the courts—the triumphal arches, lopsided and toppling—
the mystery and gloom and vastness of it beggars all description. Imagine the grave of
a vanished civilization—a London of forty centuries ago—a forgotten Rome. (p. 326)

So concerned were many of these narratives with the trek through the jungle
and the discovery of the city that any love story remained peripheral. Yet true
love often had to face the insoluble problem of miscegenation. As early as Joseph
Hatton's *The White King of Manoa* (1890), which traces Raleigh's journey to
the Orinoco, the youthful David Yarborough finds Manoa, where he marries the
Inca's daughter, Zarana Peluca, and remains to become king. But the Spanish
intrude, burning Zarana at the stake as a heretic. Angered, David destroys the
city, but he immediately returns to England, where he weds fair Lucy Withy-
combe, a childhood sweetheart. Frank Balch's *A Submarine Tour* (1905), an
obvious imitation of Verne, ranges from the Arctic and Atlantis to Port Said and
Manila, where Captain Hakke and Professor Baker witness Dewey's triumph.
On the west coast of South America they sail into a great cavern and help a city
of Incas destroy the Aztecs on a neighboring isle. Baker is "enraptured" with
the fair Actlea, who loves him but insists that they "can only *like* each other,"
for the priests will kill her if she cares too deeply for a stranger (pp. 150–151).
Although "overcome," Baker retains sufficient poise to insist that they always
"remember" one another and resumes the cruise of the *Victor*. He is swept from
the deck of the submarine near Cape Hatteras, but Captain Hakke may still be

roaming the seven seas. In Laurence D. Young's *The Climbing Doom* (1909), Waric Vagan remains in an Andean city long enough to marry Queen Zarra and have a daughter by her. Although Zarra declares that she is descended from Pizarro, Vagan takes their daughter back to America. Zarra kills herself. Clifford Smyth's *The Gilded Man* (1918) allows David Meudon to find a remnant of the Chibcha tribe in a cavern lighted by a radium sun, but the lovely Sajipona must throw herself into the radium sun because David will return to America to wed Una Leighton.

This ambivalence toward non-Caucasian women continues whatever the setting, the outcome remaining an individual decision of the writer. In *Missing, A Romance* (1896) Julius Chambers places his protagonist, Clark, among "a nation of outcasts" (p. 5) made up of black women and Spanish and Portuguese men in the Sargasso Sea. He is bewitched by Fidelle, a Creole French girl, "a creature so startingly beautiful that [he] felt [his] senses leaving [him] at the apparition . . . small in stature, but perfect in figure" (p. 50). They escape and marry, though her mother was a Creole. In contrast, Thomas Larnard, the narrator of Charles L. McKesson's *Under Pike's Peak* (1898), encounters Mahalma, daughter of an ancient race as old as any in Europe, though by implication at least partly Oriental. Although he and Oliver Esteller may compete fiercely for her affection, she dies; they bury her and return to Colorado Springs (pp. 300–301). Frank Aubrey's *A Queen of Atlantis* (1900) vividly exemplifies the dilemma. Three young Americans are abandoned in the Sargasso. The natives of the island Atlantis worship Vanina, while the king of Dilantis lusts after her and finally kidnaps her. On another island, her brother George saves the maid Myrla from a dangerous snake, but her people forbid him to remain with her (pp. 313–314), although they give him the means to defeat the Dilantians. Thus Vanina weds Owen Wydale when they return to America, while George studies chemistry. Marriott Crittenden solves the difficulty in *The Isle of Dead Ships* (1909) by marooning an American girl, Dorothy Fairfax, with Frank Howard in the Sargasso. They endure various dangers and escape, being able to marry after Howard is cleared of the charge of murdering a Puerto Rican girl, Delores Montaro, whom another naval officer married and killed, using Howard's name.

The vacillation continued. Shipwrecked in the Pacific, John Fairfax and four companions come to Matthew J. Royal's *The Isle of Virgins* (1899), peopled by a race descended from ancient Romans and seventeenth-century French but governed by women. A number of unmarried girls, among them the Princess Numeni—"a coquette of the first water" (p. 143)—are attracted to Fairfax, although he prefers Sione, the commander in chief of the royal forces: " . . . tall and of most magnificent figure . . . her golden hair. . . . her beautiful eyes. . . . she was simply a bewitching, intoxicating, ravishing dream of splendor" (pp. 108, 115–116). By conniving, they are able to choose one another at the semiannual festival when maidens select husbands. But the five survivors, Sione, Numeni, and twenty virgins secure a ship to Valparaiso so that they may return to England. In Duffield Osborne's *The Secret of the Crater* (1900), after finding a Carthaginian civilization near Easter Island, Second Lieutenant Vance simply jumps ship to marry Princess Zelkah. Although in *Toll of the Sea* (1909) Roy Norton is most concerned with a series of catastrophes transforming the Pacific basin and with the occupation of newly risen land by an Aryan race which settled both South America and the Mediterranean, he does find time for Captain James Tipton, U.S.N., to woo Princess Ayara, daughter of the ruler. The Americans in James Francis Dwyer's *The Spotted Panther* (1913) are guided through Borneo by the native woman, Nao, the Golden One, as they seek the legendary sword of Buddha.

The protagonist of Patrick and Terence Casey's *The Strange Case of William Hyde* (1916) penetrates a Pacific island to find Jallan Batoe, "another Lhassa" (p. 21), once settled by Genghis Khan's Tartars. The Sea Dyaks have wiped out the men so that only beautiful women inhabit the island. Hyde becomes involved in a triangle. He is enchanted by the queen, a golden woman, as soon as he sees her "in a marvelously wrought gown. . . . Like a gauze of mosquito netting, it showed the supple splendid form of her with each sensuous movement of her body" (p. 45). But the bewitching brunette priestess Lip-Plak-Tengga desires him: "The imperiously beautiful woman sidled against me once more, rubbing like a cat so close to me that I could feel, through the transparency of her feathery gown, the glowing warmth of her gold-limbed body" (p. 79). Purple passage by purple passage, *The Strange Case of William Hyde* remains the most openly erotic lost-race novel of its period. He flees the island after a giant orangutang kills the golden woman, his wife, as Lip-Plak laughs; now a beachcomber, he wishes that he could somehow return to Jallan Batoe.

The first-person narrator of Mabel Fuller Blodgett's *At the Queen's Mercy* (1897), an obvious imitation of Rider Haggard, remains with the capricious Lah, who is killed by the high priest. A carefully crafted tale, Arthur A. Nelson's *Wings of Danger* (1915) makes use of an Old Norse Saga, a manuscript from the British Museum, to help its explorers find a city of Vikings in the interior of Africa near so-called Skull Mountain. Although a number of references are made to Kipling and Rhodes, at one point the narrator exclaims, "What a scene for Jules Verne to describe" (p. 255). Civil strife, abetted by rival imperialistic powers, destroys the city. Ingulf, a son of the Vikings and black women, remains in the burning city with Phaïma, "a barbarically beautiful girl . . . a splendid creature, almost white (p. 278), but Sir Alan Severn returns to civilization with Norma Roylescroft, whom he has saved from the Metabeles. One other novel, Robert Ames Bennet's *The Bowl of Baal*, serialized in 1916–1917 but not published in book form until 1975, deserves mention because of the twist it gives the established convention.[31] During the war, Larry O'Brien flies deep into the Arabian peninsula, where he finds the "Lost Garden of Irem." He, too, becomes involved in a triangle involving a golden blond and an Oriental-looking brunette. At first he prefers Istara and resists the advances of Tigra, who performs a ritual dance for him which makes her his wife, if in name only: " . . . that most ancient of all Oriental dances, the Dance of the Seven Veils. . . . The creamy whiteness of the sultana's form began to gleam through the lessened thicknesses of gauze. The dancer loosened her hair so that it fell about her in a black maze'' (p. 235). Too late, O'Brien comes to realize that he loves the enchanting Tigra, ''beautiful beyond all other women—more alluring than the houri of paradise'' (p. 238). She is wounded as they fight barbaric cavemen; they flee by plane toward civilization, but in the desert she dies in his arms.

Undoubtedly, the lost-race novel gave voice to an established erotic code which titillated several generations, at least, of western men. During that same period, only four made use of innovative thematic material; as might be expected, all four concerned themselves either with the role of women in society or with race. The earliest of them and the best known, Mary E. Bradley Lane's *Mizora; A Prophecy* (1890), takes Vera Zarovitch from Siberia to a Symmesian inner world, where she finds a feminist utopia whose women have been reproducing parthenogenetically for 3,000 years.[32] The society of Mizora, obviously, is advanced technologically; interestingly, genetic engineering has turned all of the women into uniformly handsome, though thick-waisted, blonds (the waist can be understood, but why this addiction to blondness should make its way into an early feminist utopia remains uncertain). Lane vents her anger primarily against the nineteenth century's misuse of women and children as cheap labor; she advocates universal education. After fifteen years, when Wauna, one of her closest friends, returns to the outer world with Vera and dies, Vera can only write her story (found among her papers) and ''lament what man has done to woman.''[33]

Charlotte Perkins Gilman's *Herland*, originally published in 1915 but not issued in book form until 1979, has also deservedly drawn the attention of feminist critics. Three American men discover an arcadian society somewhere in the east of Canada, where the women have also reproduced parthenogenetically for 2,000 years. But the three men are permitted to marry, and therein lies the source of Gilman's most effective satire, a point that many critics appear to have overlooked or simply touched on in passing. Gilman uses the three men and their marriages to dramatize the dominant male attitudes of her society toward women and marriage. At one pole, Terry Nicholson represents the macho type which reduces women to an object to be mastered. He is a physical brute incapable of caring for anyone but himself. At the other pole, Jeff Margrave gives voice to Southern gallantry and romantic love. Yet one infers that his manners cover a selfishness as great as Nicholson's. Gilman underscores her theme through the first-person narrator, Vandyck Jennings, who acknowledges that men have invented and imposed on women the so-called feminine charms simply because they please the men. His wife reinforces and broadens his view by emphasizing that the women of Herland are mothers and people, not housewives and servants. The three men are asked to leave the society because of Nicholson's treatment of his wife.

Perhaps Inez Haynes Gillmore's *Angel Island* (1914) remains even more effective because it does not rely on an isolated feminist utopia but dramatizes its statement through the familiar conventions of the lost-race motif. Its opening recalls *The Isle of Virgins*, but the tone is immediately different. The sea has "spewed" five men onto the beach of an out-of-the-way island. Hardly have they awakened before a chance remark provokes Ralph Addington to declare, "I guess I could give up the ship's cat in exchange for a girl or two" (p. 9). When he learns that they may be on the island for some time, he reinforces his initial response: "Think of being in a place like this six months or a year without a woman around!" (p. 12). Gillmore at once labels him "an offensive type of libertine" (p. 15). For leadership the survivors look to Frank Merrill, "a sociologist traveling in the Orient to study conditions [and] a typical reformer" (p. 22). He has already admitted that "women keep up the standards of life" (p. 13), thereby eliciting Addington's response that had but one or two women survived, "the fat would be in the fire."

Almost at once they observe what they believe to be giant birds. Merrill explains that they represent "some lost species—something left over from a prehistoric era" (p. 55) and suggests that they trap a specimen or two because they have "made a discovery that will shake the whole scientific world" (p. 56). When they learn that the creatures are "flying-girls" (p. 60), Merrill wonders whether the five have "the right to capture them as ornithological specimens" or whether they must "respect their liberty as independent human beings." His speculation draws different responses from each of his companions:

"They're neither birds nor women," Pete Murphy burst out impetuously. "They're angels. Our duty is to fall down and worship them."

"They're women," said Billy Fairfax earnestly. "Our duty is to cherish and protect them."

"They're girls," Honey insisted jovially, "our duty is to josh and jolly them, to buy them taxicabs, theater-tickets, late suppers, candy, and flowers."

"They're females," said Ralph Addington contemptuously. "Our duty is to tame, subjugate, infatuate, and control them." (p. 88)

In the responses of the four men, Gillmore reveals the spectrum of roles into which men have forced women. In Merrill's question she poses her theme as she dramatizes a fable exploring the complete gamut of male-female relationships, for the men do lure the women into captivity, and each takes possession of his specimen—from the dark Chiquita to the serious Julia. Romantic love dissipates into routine; fatherhood rekindles an interest momentarily, but the men build a camp where they can be together unbothered by women and children. The men clip the wings of the women so that they must be carried because their legs are not strong enough to allow them to walk. In short, through a complex metaphor first mentioned in the title itself, a metaphor which calls to mind even Coventry Patmore's "An Angel in the House," Gillmore gives strength to her fable. The men deprive the women of their freedom and reduce them to complete dependence, although much of the time they are abandoned by those who profess to love them. In this context, the trimming of the wings becomes an excellent symbol of the manner in which the women are maimed physically and spiritually. At one point Billy exclaims, "Women don't know what's best for them. We do" (p. 149). The baby girl Angela has wings but is forbidden to fly. The final crisis comes when her wings are to be clipped. In a lengthy speech in which Julia recapitulates all that has happened on Angel Island, she declares, "There is a chain binding them to each other even as there is a chain binding them to us. And the Bond of Work is stronger than the Bond of Sex because Work is a living, growing thing" (p. 304). In order to prevent Angela from becoming as helpless as the five women, she would clip the child's wings so that she had to develop the strength to walk, but she would prefer that Angela could both fly and walk. The end offers hope, though there is no reconciliation of the basic problem.

What Gilman and Gillmore do with masculine attitudes toward women, William C. Morrow attempts to do regarding race in *Lentala of the South Seas* (1908). The narrative opens conventionally in that Joseph Tudor, the first-person narrator, and several hundred would-be colonists are shipwrecked somewhere in the South Pacific, but once again the tone differs sharply. For example, the only detail establishing a time period mentions that Tudor was trained at West Point (p. 61). Other than that timelessness, all of the conventions are there: the threat that the white intruders may be sacrificed to a heathen god, the attempt of the whites to seize the island, the native revolt which must be defeated before Lentala can be queen. But all of these are pushed into the background; the central issue remains whether or not Joseph Tudor can love Lentala, an island maid. At times the narrative is verbose for Joseph is put through a series of tests. From the beginning, Morrow seems to give himself an escape route, for Lentala has an element of "the sun's gold" in her hair as well as "blue eyes" (p. 9). Tudor infers that she and a brother Beelo had a European father and are protected by the king and his childless queen, although there exists a "deeply planted native hatred for the white blood" (p. 65). For a moment, the problem of gender arises as the boy Beelo explains that he comes to Joseph because "girls have to wear skirts . . . and girls are not as active as boys" (p. 25) so that Lentala does not have the freedom of movement. Constantly, Beelo questions Joseph about his attitude toward Lentala: "Her skin is brown. You would not trust her" (p. 36). In one exchange, knowing that Lentala is fascinated by the one white woman in the party, Joseph remarks, "She is as sweet and beautiful as Annabel, and—and—what shall I say?—more fascinating . . . souls have neither race nor color" (p. 64). In this way Morrow faces the problem which haunted the West at least throughout the age of imperialism: western man's sexual attraction for non-western women. Joseph infers that Beelo and Lentala are of mixed blood as soon as he discovers that under Beelo's clothes his skin is not as dark as the natives' (p. 121). At one point Lentala dresses like Annabel; it does "not improve her appearance," but she insists that Joseph prefers the style of the white woman (pp. 171–172). Joseph is genuinely surprised when Beelo proves to be a young woman. The disguise discovered, the youth tries to pass as Beela, Lentala's sister; she is, of course, Lentala herself who has tested Joseph from the outset.

When Joseph offers to help the king against the whites who would seize the island, the king insists, "It takes white blood to fight white blood" (p. 200). At the same time he acknowledges that Lentala is of mixed blood and asks Joseph "to manage" the whites on the island so that the natives will not be harmed. Yet he goes on to declare, "The white blood . . . is the most terrible thing in the world. . . . It never gives up; it pursues and fights relentlessly to the ends of the earth; without mercy or pity it hunts down, plunders, overwhelms, exterminates" (p. 203). Finally, Joseph and Lentala declare their love, and he remains as her consort because her duty is to her adopted people. Wordy and dated as portions of the narrative may be, *Lentala of the South Seas* faces the issue of race as no other novel in the motif did, but with imperialism at its height and the transformation of the modern world to be completed in the birth pangs of World War I, no one paid particular attention to Morrow, just as they overlooked Gilman and Gillmore.

The increasing concern for prehistory in the late nineteenth century also produced a spate of pseudohistorical novels set within the parameters of Biblical tradition. The narrator of Mrs. J. Gregory Smith's *Seola* (1878) discovers a journal supposedly giving the history of the period of the Noachian deluge. Egyptology flourished in such novels as *Pharaoh's Treasure* (1891), which reconstructs life about 1345 B.C. and ends with a Hebrew prophet lamenting the Captivity. As late as 1925, Garrett Chatfield Pier wrote a pseudohistorical novel of Moses in Egypt, *The Hidden Valley*. Innumerable archaeologists, like those in C. Bryson Taylor's *In the Dwellings of the Wilderness* (1904), opened the bewitched tombs of Egyptian princesses who drive men mad with their beauty. Rider Haggard's interest in reincarnation found imitators as late as William Henry Warner's *The Bridge of Time* (1919). Mark Twain's interest in the diaries of Adam and Eve is well known, but in Robert and Jane Speller's *Adam's First Wife* (1929) the satirical narrative is presented as the memoirs of Lilith written in the twentieth century after she had gained some degree of immortality by eating the sacred mushrooms reserved for the men of 5,000 B.C.

Those writers who could not be satisfied with Biblical antiquity created prehistoric empires at will. Essential within their work lay the myths of an Edenic continent and an Aryan (white) race, as evidenced by those themes within the lost-race motif. The desire to find traces of ancient man in the Americas fused the Aztec, Mayan, and Incan ruins, producing extravagant romances annually. Cyrus Newcomb's *The Book of Algoonah* (1884) records the migrations of Assyrian-Egyptian peoples to Asia and finally to America, where they become the Mound Builders. Frona Eunice Wait Colburn, C. C. Dail, J. G. Hilzinger, J. A. Knowlton, and Waldo Hilary Dunn contributed such romances. One of the finest, John Beatty's *The Alcohuans* (1902), records the adventures of a tenth-century Viking, Ivarr Bertholdsson, as he saves the Mound Builders from northern invaders before he visits the Toltec empire and eventually returns to Normandy. Certainly one of the most extravagant was Joseph M. Brown's *Astayanax* (1907), in which he permits both Trojans and survivors of sunken Atlantis to escape to "Amaraca." Randall Parrish's *Prisoners of Chance* (1908) pictures the Natchez Indians of the nineteenth century as descendants of the Mound Builders.

The key to the new prehistory suddenly became the lost continent of Atlantis. Ignatius Donnelly's *Atlantis: The Antediluvian World* (1882) undoubtedly triggered the concept—his book is frequently referred to well into the first quarter of the twentieth century at least—but his argument perhaps simply gave form to a widespread idea.[34] Mrs. J. Gregory Smith's *Alta* (1886) describes the sinking of Atlantis, "this Eden of the West," located in the area of the Sargasso Sea. The British author, C. J. Cutcliffe Hyne, who was obviously indebted to Rider Haggard, gave lasting form to that primeval continent in *The Lost Continent* (1900). The protagonist of David Parry's *The Scarlet Empire* (1906) finds a sunken Atlantis protected by a glass dome off the coast of America. He uses the discovery as a vehicle to attack socialism, for despite its technological expertise, Atlantis is a decadent kingdom captured by mediocrity and anonymity. Its citizens are restricted by law as to the numbers of words they may speak; marriages are arranged genetically so that physical beauty will be bred out of the race. Everyone is a number, and the population is kept content by state-approved addiction to the narcotic "Lethe weed." Certainly, Parry produced one of the early dystopian nightmares. While there is as yet no solid evidence, enough of his devices anticipate Zamiatin, Huxley, and Orwell to make one speculate as to whether or not his novel—apparently published only once—was known by the later writers. Interestingly enough, Parry remained a creature of his period in that his Atlantis, however fallen, was "the birthplace of invention and scientific discovery" (pp. 44–45) as well as the mother-continent in which the Garden of Eden flourished; its sinking caused the Noachian deluge (pp. 47–48). He also reflects the biases of his period in that he denounces labor unions as the origin of the movement which leads inevitably to socialism (pp. 62–64, 221–222).

Although Sir Arthur Conan Doyle also used the idea of a surviving sunken Atlantis as late as *The Maracot Deep* (1929), most often survivors from Atlantis—always including a beautiful princess—awakened in the contemporary world, as in Olof W. Anderson's *The Treasure Vault of Atlantis* (1925) and Erle Cox's *Out of the Silence* (1928). Increasingly, however, as in J. Leslie Mitchell's *Three Go Back* (1932), Atlantis is pictured as a primitive land which evolves into part of Robert E. Howard's Hyborian World.

The second explicit literary reaction to the new prehistory resulted in the dramatization of the life of a caveman. Because so little was known of prehistoric man until well into the twentieth century after the research of such individuals as the Leakeys, this type of story remained perhaps the most simple formulaic fiction of all. Austin Bierbower's *From Monkey to Man* (1894) suggested that oncoming glaciers had forced the "Missing Link" from an Edenic northern homeland; he also sought to explain how the snake had become a natural symbol of evil (p. 40). Prophecy foretold that the northern area would remain desolate until Adam would reclaim the land "as a Paradise Regained" (p. 230). Although Bierbower seems to have been most concerned with some reconciliation between science and traditional beliefs, he shaped the basic storyline of the caveman stories in that he introduced incidents, ranging from the discovery of fire to the use of clothing and weapons, supposedly indicative of the initial steps taken by apemen in their evolution into true men. These usually occurred within the lifetime of an individual.

To this basic pattern Stanley Waterloo added two enduring episodes in *The Story of Ab; A Tale of the Time of the Caveman* (1897), in which he first emphasizes the idea of friendship between two men before they fight to the death to possess a woman. So closely did Jack London's *Before Adam* (1906) follow this episodic plot that Waterloo sued him unsuccessfully for plagiarism. Although the concept of race memory had appeared as early as Ambrose Bierce's "The Man and the Snake," London allowed his modern man to dream of a previous existence as "Big-Tooth," who mated with "The Swift One." The narrator wonders uncertainly whether or not his descendants became true man (p. 241), but he confuses the issue by introducing a second species, the Fire People (p. 161). The popular acceptance of the motif may be measured by the publication in 1907 of William MacLeod Raines' short story, "The Cave Boy" in *Cosmopolitan*, in which the youth fights for his mate.[35] In 1914–1915, *Cosmopolitan* serialized Charles G. D. Roberts' *In the Morning of Time*, not published in book form until 1919.

Waterloo retaliated, so to speak, by combining the concepts of race memory and reincarnation in *A Son of the Ages* (1914) so that his protagonist recalls previous existences from that of "Scar, the Link" to those of Phoenician, Germanic, and Viking ancestors. One incident, "The Deluge," recalls the sinking of Atlantis. From Waterloo's contemporaries onward many writers wished to establish prehistoric man on the American continent. One of the first attempts was that of Louis P. Gratacap, who gave his attention to Lhatto, *A Woman of the Ice Age* (1906), calling her "Ageless woman! . . . the origin of human life, the vast procreative source of all civilization and all progress" (p. 40). Beyond the celebration of "Primal Woman," the novel—more essay than story—deals with the love of Lhatto for the man Ogga, who saves her when Lagk kidnaps her. It is, obviously, the same old story, although Gratacap locates the action in the Sierras (p. 43), for 30,000 years ago the climate in western America was much like that of the Great Rift Valley of Africa. Suggesting at least once that they are of an "Indian type" (p. 85), Gratacap insists that they were not "some emergence from simian ugliness, turpitude and filth. In their minds the lamp of intelligence, in their hearts the fire of love had both been lit" (p. 201). Nevertheless, they die in the desert, even as they kiss, thus beginning "the endless Poem of Life, endlessly beautiful, endlessly sad" (pp. 229, 230). As late as *The Day of the Brown Horde* (1929), Richard Tooker mixes together plesiosaurs, bison, and cavemen in the valley that now forms the Gulf of California; Kaa mates with Chee, and she is drowned when the sea engulfs the land after an earthquake. Yet even before her death Kaa realizes that "the female kind was built of undying fire that drove man on when man was weary and his mind was dead" (p. 304).

Of the early works, Gouverneur Morris's *The Pagan's Progress* (1904) subordinates all of the expected actions to the youthful Sunrise's unwillingness to accept the fact of the death of the woman Dawn, though her body lies at his feet (p. 253). He has glimpsed and pursues her spirit; as early as the prefatory note, Morris announces his theme: "Read then, how Sunrise, the pagan, was born in the dark, and having suffered at the hands of death, came to see the light glimmering beyond, and the life" (p. xv). The most original of the early novels, Ashton Hilliers' *The Master-Girl: A Romance* (1910), reverses the sex roles. Sixteen-year-old Dêh-Yān rescues Pul Yun, who has broken his leg, and takes him as her mate. Although at one point she grovels before him, exclaiming, "I want but thee" (p. 133), she develops the bow and arrow and wins a shooting contest against spearsmen (pp. 212–213) so that she becomes the leader of the tribe. She forms a special force of women archers (p. 225), but when Pul Yun dies, she immolates herself (pp. 238–241). Once again, despite the fact that, nude, she kills a bear threatening Pul Yun (pp. 79–80), there is an ambivalence in the relationship between man and woman, for she recognizes his "sex-superiority too secure in itself to need assertion" (p. 64). One senses again, as in so many of the lost-race novels, that the male audience wanted its women exotic—even Amazonian at times—but subservient.

The prehistoric spilled over into the present day, most notably in Sir Arthur Conan Doyle's *The Lost World* (1912), which established the prototype of all such survival novels. Not only did it introduce Professor George Challenger, surely one of the notable scientific eccentrics in all of science fiction, but it established the plateau of Roraima in Venezuela as a kind of shrine to the imagination, where innumerable explorers, particularly among the various boy adventurers, found their El Dorado, whatever form it might take. Interestingly, Doyle was not the first to make use of the area; it had been the site of Manoa in Frank Aubrey's *The Devil Tree of El Dorado* (1897). As late as 1927 in Alan Sullivan's *In the Beginning*, the explorers find a prehistoric valley deep in the Andes. Through atavism—the same device used by Jack London—the character Burden reverts to a creature as primitive as the cavemen they find and mates with the beautiful Mam-lo. Together with the prehistoric animals and the cavemen, Burden and Mam-lo die in a fire which destroys the valley. His comrades, however, escape. They receive a letter written by Burden before his death in which he acknowledges (enjoys) his atavism and expresses the hope that he may remain with Mam-lo forever. The same theme gains a variant expression in Edison Marshall's *Ogden's Strange Story* (1934). When Ogden's plane crashes in the Yukon Rockies, he reverts to Og, the Dawn Man, and falls in love with the Indian girl, She-Who-Laughs (surely an echo of Rider Haggard). When he is rescued, the Indian maid commits suicide, though they have declared love for one another. Returned to the United States and married to his proper fiancée, Ogden is haunted by the dark beauty of She-Who-Laughs. Unquestionably, the rejection of modern civilization, the sexual enchantment with non-European women, and a desire to prove one's masculinity all shaped these stories. But there was both an emotional and intellectual fascination with prehistory itself, as evidenced by the popularity of John Taine's *Before the Dawn* (1934), a celebration of the prehistoric world for itself—without the presence of mankind. Three modern men—archaeologist, inventor, and president of a television corporation—discover a means of looking into the remote past. Through much of the narrative their attention focuses upon Belshazzar—Tyrannosaurus Rex—from his birth to his death in the brutal world of the dinosaurs.

Although *Under the Moon of Mars*, concerned with the adventures of John Carter after the transmigration of his warrior's soul to Mars, was Edgar Rice Burroughs' first published story, Burroughs gained his lasting fame from *Tarzan of the Apes*, published first in *All-Story* (October 1912) and then in book form (1914). However much Burroughs has been reviled by critics,[36] Tarzan has recently been compared favorably with such figures as Odysseus,[37] while somewhat earlier he was described as "the only great legendary figure produced by the literature" of the twentieth century.[38] Yet to some degree, he may have overstayed his welcome, for within the last year at least one class of American undergraduates no longer responded to him.[39]

If one ignores momentarily the books, the translations, and the films, one sees that the Munsey magazines and then *Blue Book* sustained his reputation through at least two generations. For more than thirty years something about him and his adventures appealed to a wide, popular audience. Supposedly that audience was predominantly adolescent males. (Such a judgment ignores a basic fact, one which pairs him with that indomitable hero of the 1930s, Doc Savage. In the 1960s Ballantine Books reissued both Tarzan and Doc Savage titles, never letting either go out of print.) Moreover, if one includes all of Burroughs' work, not limiting one's attention to the Tarzan titles, one hears both editors and active writers alike agreeing that after Burroughs wrote, American science fiction was never the same. A number still imitate him.

Finally, however, it must be in the context of the lost-race motif that one judges Tarzan, as well as the other Burroughs protagonists who echoed him. One must emphasize that in a sense Tarzan has had two literary lives. For more than a decade, at least, Burroughs made a crucial reversal, one which ultimately proved more successful in the John Carter stories. Yet Burroughs accomplished at least three things which could only increase the popularity of Tarzan in the early decades of this century. First, Tarzan is the savage; Jane Porter, the girl from Baltimore and a farm in Wisconsin. That immediately erases the problem of miscegenation which so often shaped the ultimate outcome of lost-race fictions. Second, Tarzan is more than a primeval man; he is also Lord Greystoke, although he rejects that title and the effete society which it represents in favor of the beauty and wildness of the unknown interior of Africa. He does so at a time which saw the completion of the evolution from a landed gentry to industrial worker and office clerk in an increasingly urbanized society, both in America and Europe, where so far as the average city-dweller was concerned, the wilderness had, at least, vanished behind farmlands and green parks (the age of mobility had not yet dawned). At the same time, however, the popular audience envied aristocratic wealth—America's 400, for example. Throughout the novels, Burroughs emphasizes that Tarzan is a product of both his environment and his heredity. The third accomplishment needs a specific example. Initially, Tarzan saves Jane from a lioness and then writes a note to her declaring his love, but not until he kills Terkoz after the great ape has seized Jane and carried her into the jungle, do Tarzan and Jane become acquainted:

When the long knife drank deep a dozen times of Terkoz' heart's blood, and the great carcass rolled lifeless upon the ground, it was a primeval woman who sprang forward with outstretched arms toward a primeval man who had fought for her and won her.

And Tarzan?

He did what no red-blooded man needs lessons in doing. He took his woman in his arms and smothered her upturned, panting lips with kisses.

For a moment Jane Porter lay there with half-closed eyes. For a moment—the first in her young life—she knew the meaning of love.

But as suddenly as the veil had been withdrawn, it dropped again and an outraged conscience suffused her face with its scarlet mantle, and a mortified woman thrust Tarzan of the Apes from her and buried her face in her hands.[40]

Tarzan does not understand why she resists him:

Tarzan of the Apes had felt a warm, lithe form close pressed to his. Hot, sweet breath against his cheeks and mouth had fanned a new flame of life within his breast, and perfect lips had clung to his in burning kisses that had seared a deep brand into his soul—a brand which marked a new Tarzan.

Again he laid his hand upon her arm. Again she repulsed him. And then Tarzan of the Apes did just what his first ancestor would have done.

He took his woman in his arms and carried her into the jungle.

Early the following morning . . . (p. 142)

Thus begins one of the immortal love affairs of this century.

In the context of such a passage those critics who have protested that innumerable times Burroughs threatens his heroines with rape but never permits consummation seem incredibly naive. However proper Jane Porter may be, was there a reader at the time of World War I or is there a reader in the 1980s who does not imagine that Tarzan and Jane "made love" during the night? Nor should one forget that they did have a son, Jack—Korak the Killer. Burroughs took advantage of implication and his readers' imaginations to advance the permissible erotic code of popular fiction one step closer to the graphic encounters of the last twenty years. In addition, rape is more violent than seduction, thereby perhaps titillating the members of an industrial society more than did Carrie Meeber and Jennie Gerhardt. They would soon meet Susan Lenox, to say nothing of such former acquaintances as James's governess, among others.

In allowing Tarzan and Jane to become parents, Burroughs made a near fatal mistake, although he allowed the family life to last through eight novels, two of which were spent in rescuing Jane from the Boche. Tarzan grew older and domesticated (see *The Eternal Lover*, 1925) at a time when literary realism became the dominant mode even in popular fiction. Thus even before Burroughs ended the family saga, he fell back on the basic patterns established by Rider Haggard and his imitators. In *Tarzan and the Jewels of Opar* (1916, 1918), he introduces La, the priestess of Opar, the last (and lost) colony of Atlantis. She is the first of many pagan beauties desiring the love of Tarzan. That Tarzan never succumbs is perhaps as much a commentary upon the audience and the times as it is on Burroughs. As a result, Tarzan went from timeless adventure to timeless adventure.

Many have complained that Burroughs was a one-plot writer. He repeated a successful formula; he did not again corner himself as he had in the earlier Tarzan novels. Consequently, he adapted essentially the same pattern to other settings. Beginning with *At the Earth's Core* (1914, 1922) David Innes searches for Dian the Beautiful, Princess of Amoz, throughout the length and breadth of Pellucidar, that prehistoric version of the Symmesian inner world, although as in the John Carter stories, Burroughs focuses primarily on new characters in the later sequels. Three different protagonists find three beauties (one of them the actress, Lys La Rue) in forgotten Caspek near the Antarctic. In addition, there are such individual titles as *The Cave Girl* (1925) and *The Jungle Girl* (1932).

By the time that Burroughs began to write, many of the political and religious issues were dated, while an uncertain mysticism clouded the work of Rider Haggard and his imitators. Essentially, Edgar Rice Burroughs stripped the old themes from the motif. Increasingly, his narratives became a proving ground for his protagonists' masculinity: survival in a hostile world epitomized by a jungle; physical victory in combat over a variety of loathsome creatures, animal or man; and the unquestioning adoration of primitive and sensual women—in short, physical and erotic sensation: adventure. After World War I, although such a writer as George S. Chappell attempted a number of heavy-handed parodies—*The Cruise of Kawa: Wanderings in the South Seas* (1921), *Sarah of the Sahara: A Romance of Nomads Lands* (1923), and *My Northern Exposure: The Kawa at the Pole* (1925) among them—the basic formulas continued to work. Quantitatively, the lost-race novel had never been more popular. Only the primary setting shifted: Asia, the least known area of the world.

Immediately, one thinks of exceptions, in particular, the works of A. Merritt: the South Pacific, *The Moon Pool* (1919); South America, *The Face in the Abyss* (1931); Alaska, *Dwellers in the Mirage* (1932), though that classic fusion of mythologies had ties with Asia, while *The Metal Monster* (1946) involved an encounter with ancient Persians in Central Asia. Merritt continues to rival Burroughs among enthusiasts of the motif, but all of his novels had first been published in the Munsey magazines. Writing as John Taine, Eric Temple Bell sent his explorers to the Antarctic in *The Greatest Adventure* (1929), where they discover artifacts of an ancient race which had discovered the secret of life; like that culture which was destroyed by its knowledge, the protagonists must overcome the threat of uncontrolled growth—monstrosities—which would threaten the world. Bell's fascination with biology continued, for *The Iron Star* (1930), a meteor which fell long ago in Africa, influences the genetic pattern (the "evolution") of those creatures who are affected by its radiation. The former medical missionary, Swain, feeds on the radiation as though it were a drug; he also makes more complex the problem of interpreting Bell's attitude, because Swain originally went to Africa to disprove Darwinian theory. He undertook a personal vendetta against the apes.

Earlier, in *The Gold Tooth* (1927), Bell's protagonist, Jim Blye, had found an elder race in the mountains of Korea while hunting in the area for dinosaur eggs. Strongly attracted to a young woman whom he calls Eve and describes as "almost Caucasian, at least Aryan," he loses her to volcanic action which destroys the valley. In Louis Moresby's *The Glory of Egypt* (1926), Christopher Ross also loses a woman who loves him, Nephthys, "a daughter of the kings of Egypt . . . more beautiful than any dream" (pp. 196, 198). Her suicide is not unexpected, for from the moment Ross sees her in a lost city in Tibet, he realizes that "between [them] was a gulf—of race, of time, of station, of thought—of everything in the world that sets man and woman apart" (p. 196); moreover, although he embraces her as she weeps, he explains to her that "[the] way in which a woman can help a man is obedience. It is but like a child to act hastily and violently. Be patient if you would have my gratitude" (p. 252). She kills herself after saving him from a ruthless companion, but Ross calmly returns to India to his "English girl," Joan Boston. Like so many others, however, he is haunted by the memory of the princess (p. 280).

Of the British writers between the wars, one of the most successful was "Ganpat"—the pseudonym of Martin Louis Alan Gompertz. In *Harilek* (1923) and its sequel, *Wrexham's Romance* (1935), after following clues in a diary dating from 1822, Harry Lake and John Wrexham enter a kingdom in the mountains somewhere north of India, where they find a race blending together pre-Christian Nordics and fifth-century Greeks. Against a background of warfare with a Mongol race, the Shamans, the storylines concentrate on the loves of Harilek and Aryenis and Wrexham and Shaîstra. Their arcadian valley provides a retreat from the restless world of the twentieth century. Something in the tone of Ganpat's novels reminds one of James Hilton's Shangri-la in *Lost Horizon* (1933), although the latter lacks the sense of quiet fulfillment which Ganpat attains.

Among the American writers Harold Lamb sends Captain Robert Gray, the protagonist of *Marching Sands* (1920), into the Gobi Desert to find a legendary white race. He rescues Mary Hastings from the threat of Wu Fang Chien, a warlord who provides, at least by implication, a variant of the Yellow Peril. One element of Norman Springer's *The Dark River* (1928) focuses upon Eric Waithe's reversion to primeval man after he has suffered shell shock on the Western Front during the war and accidentally comes upon a cave once inhabited by Cro-Magnon man. In Borneo, he loves a woman of mixed blood, "a hybrid of the Straits," the golden Mata. In Edison Marshall's *Dian of the Lost Land* (1935), rival scientists find a group of Cro-Magnon people in a hidden valley in Antarctica. One promises to keep the discovery a secret so that civilization will not destroy the tribe, while the other remains as consort to their queen, the blond Dian, daughter of a lost American explorer. When Dian shows her husband a cave filled with paintings, he links her people to those artists who once inhabited the caves at Dordogne, calling them "the last of the Cro-Magnons, aptly called the Greeks of the Old Stone Age, that wonderful race of artists and hunters whose natural gifts were as rich as any civilized race of today" (pp. 93–94).

Still other works can be named. Louis Hermann's "Scientific Fantasy" entitled *In the Sealed Cave* (1935) presents a lost manuscript of Lemuel Gulliver whose premise is that Gulliver encountered a remnant of Neanderthal man and destroyed them by causing an epidemic of the common cold. Rose Macaulay's *Orphan Island* (1925) manages one of the most effective satires of Victorian society when a sociologist from Cambridge sets out to find survivors of a party made up of a governess, a drunken medical doctor, a French nursemaid, and fifty orphans deliberately abandoned on a Pacific Island in 1855. Another variation on the voyage to unknown lands occurred when Ray Cummings either sent his protagonist into a subatomic universe to woo and win *The Girl in the Golden Atom* (1923) or cast him into the future, as in *The Man Who Mastered Time* (1929) or *Tarrano the Conqueror* (1930). Such stories as these may also be described as variants on the "space opera," for they make use of all the conventions of the future-war motif.

In a sense, their very existence underscores the basic problem faced by American science fiction during the 1920s. The lost-race motif was at that time the most popular form of fantasy based on science. Yet one infers that it was caught betwixt and between, so to speak. On the one hand, enthusiasts, like Hugo Gernsback, who preferred the hard sciences and technology, created and contributed to the new specialist magazines from 1926 onward. Ironically, for the first few years those magazines reprinted Poe, O'Brien, Wells, Serviss, Doyle, and Verne—especially praising Verne. On the other hand, the rise of literary realism and naturalism also undercut the motif, as illustrated by Elmer Rice's *A Voyage to Purilia* (1930). At first glance, Rice's novel is a satire of both the imaginary voyage and the portrait of utopian societies. Closer examination reveals that Rice employs these narrative structures as a vehicle for a devastating attack upon the whole of popular literature as well as many aspects of contemporary American society. No summary can do justice to the breadth of its attack.

Its first-person narrator must use the Winstead Gravitator to journey beyond the atmosphere of earth to reach "that fascinatingly mysterious land of whose marvels so many alluring rumors had reached [him]" (p. 6). He centers his attack upon widely accepted attitudes toward sexuality. His guide informs him that the highest caste in the country is that of the Umbilicans, "mothers who have suffered deeply—but since . . . motherhood and suffering are almost synonymous, nearly any mother is eligible (provided she is sufficiently advanced in years and not too tall . . .)" (p. 88). The second caste is that of Pudencians, "young and beautiful girls, ranging in age from eighteen to twenty-two. They are usually blonde, although occasionally one with dark tresses is encountered" (pp. 90–91). He achieves one of his high points when he declares that one of "the most needed reforms in Purilia . . . is the invention of a system which would prevent the Pudencians from falling into the hands of native chieftans" (p. 242). With one thrust he has destroyed the basic plot crisis of most American popular literature of the period.

Appropriately, perhaps, the most original American lost-race novel of the 1930s takes as its setting the Arctic. In *Hawk of the Wilderness* (1936), William L. Chester creates the continent of Nato'wa, home of the American Indian. Originally serialized in *Blue Book*, the novel provides an epic stage for Kioga, the Snow Hawk, actually Lincoln Rand, the orphaned son of medical missionaries. Raised in the wilderness by the she-bear, Yanu, he unites the kindred tribes of the Shoni and loves the young woman, Beth LaSalle, who is shipwrecked in the sub-Arctic wilderness. *Kioga of the Wilderness* (1936), *One Against the Wilderness* (1937), and *Kioga of the Unknown Land* (1938)—in which he finds "the People of the Tusk . . . a mighty culture, the oldest on the earth," beyond the Tamasili Mountains of Nato'wa—bring his saga to an end. The four Kioga stories appear to be the only fiction that Chester wrote, but his accomplishment remains unique. Out of the shopworn conventions inherited from Rider Haggard and Edgar Rice Burroughs he shaped a distinctly American hero. Long neglected, Kioga should join Paul Bunyan, Pecos Bill, and those other popular heroes who raised to mythic levels aspects of the American experience.

In a sense, World War II brought an end to the reign of the lost-race motif. Most simply, after the troops of many nations fought from Africa and the Arctic seas to the South Pacific and Southeast Asia, no one could accept the feasibility of an idyllic society surviving in some forgotten corner of the world. If one sets aside the two stories aimed at a juvenile audience by Ian Cameron, then the last serious attempt to discover a lost race—on a Pacific island—was Jacquetta Hawkes's *Providence Island* (1950). Yet the mystery of prehistory and archaeology has left so deep a literary heritage that William Golding could examine the encounter between the last band of Neanderthal man and *Homo sapiens* in *The Inheritors* (1955). More recently, in one of the finest contemporary science fiction short stories, Gene Wolfe's "The Island of Dr. Death and Other Stories" (1970), Wolfe could rely upon his readers' familiarity with the conventions of the motif in order to build an elaborate symbolic structure by which to measure the anguish of seven-year-old Tackman "Tackie" Babcock as he is unable to distinguish between the imaginary world of Captain Ransom, Dr. Death, and the beautiful Talor of the Long Eyes and the complex horrors of the real world. Wolfe uses the world of the lost-race motif in ironic parallel to the contemporary world.

NOTES

1. Philip Babcock Gove, "Short Title Index to the Imaginary Voyages Arranged Alphabetically by Authors," *The Imaginary Voyage in Prose Fiction* (New York: Columbia University Press, 1940), pp. 190–197. The greater portion of the text (pp. 198–402) is devoted to "An Annotated Checklist," which is more concerned with a description of the books than with an account of their content.

2. J. O. Bailey has been the staunchest advocate of Captain Adam Seaborn as the pseudonym of John Cleves Symme. See, for example, his edition of *Symzonia* (Gainesville, Fla.: Scholars Facsimile Editions, 1965). The Cincinnati and Hamilton County Library complicates the problem by stating that there were two John Cleves Symmes. John Weld Peck identifies them as uncle and nephew.

3. J. O. Bailey, *Symzonia*, [p. iv].

4. J. O. Bailey, *Symzonia*, [p. 2].

5. P. Clark, "The Symmes Theory of the Earth," *The Atlantic Monthly*, 31 (May 1873), 471–480; John Weld Peck, "Symmes' Theory," *Ohio Archaeological and Historical Publications*, 18 (Columbus, Ohio: Fred J. Herr, 1909), 28–42.

6. Edgar Allan Poe, *The Narrative of Arthur Gordon Pym*, introduction by Sidney Kaplan (New York: Hill and Wang, 1960), pp. 88–91. Page references in the text are to this edition.

7. *Selected Writings of Edgar Allan Poe*, edited with an introduction by Edward H. Davidson (Boston: Houghton Mifflin, 1956), p. xxii.

8. Davidson, p. xxiii.

9. E. F. Bleiler, "Edgar Allan Poe," *Science Fiction Writers*, p. 16.

10. While no one can discount those interpretations of *Arthur Gordon Pym* which see in it "an allegorical and didactic damning of the Negro" (Kaplan, p. xxiii, affords one example), one also feels they are in part the product of their period, a natural process. But such interpretations must be made more complex, for at one point Pym remarks of the inhabitants of Tsalal, "There were a great many women and children, the former not altogether wanting in what might be termed personal beauty. They were straight, tall, and well formed, with a grace and freedom of carriage not to be found in civilized society" (p. 154). One must not make too much of such a passage, but it certainly implies a fascination with the non-Caucasian woman which, as noted in the text, characterized the imaginary voyage as it developed in the nineteenth century.

11. E. F. Bleiler, *The Checklist of Science-Fiction & Supernatural Fiction* (Glenrock, N.J.: Firebell Books, 1978), p. 2. I do not recall seeing a copy of this novel.

12. Peter Costello, *Jules Verne: Inventor of Science Fiction* (New York: Charles Scribner's Sons, 1978), p. 83.

13. Mark Hillegas, "An Annotated Checklist of Jules Verne's *Voyages Extraordinaires*," *Extrapolation*, 3 (May 1962), 32–33.

14. Sam Moskowitz, "Around the Worlds with Jules Verne," *Explorers of the Infinite*, p. 79.

15. Frank N. Magill, *Survey of Science Fiction Literature*, 4:1908–1912; Donald L. Lawler, "The She Series," *Survey of Fantasy Literature*, 3:1396–1401.

16. Thomas D. Clareson, "Lost Lands, Lost Races: A Pagan Princess of Their Very Own," in *Many Futures, Many Worlds*, p. 118.

17. Morton N. Cohen, *Rider Haggard: His Life and Works* (New York: Walker and Company, 1961), p. 89.

18. Peter Costello, p. 76.

19. Morton N. Cohen, p. 90.

20. "Modern Marvels," *The Spectator*, 17 (October 1885), 1365–1366. Cohen mentions this review, p. 94.

21. Morton N. Cohen, p. 100.

22. R. Reginald and Douglas Menville add to the number of parodies when, in *They: Three Parodies of H. Rider Haggard's SHE* (New York: Arno Press, 1978), the coeditors include a version of *He* by John De Morgan and a much slighter one also entitled *He* by Andrew Lang and Walter Herries Pollock.

23. Margaret Atwood, "Superwoman Drawn and Quartered: The Early Versions of She," *Alphabet*, no. 10 (July 1965), p. 81. Reprinted in Margaret Atwood, *Second Words: Selected Critical Prose* (Boston: Beacon Press, 1984), pp. 35–54.

24. H. Rider Haggard, *She*, in *Three Adventure Novels of H. Rider Haggard* (New York: Dover Publications, Inc., 1951), pp. 117–118.

25. James Hilton, *Lost Horizon* (New York: William Morrow & Company, 1973), p. 211.

26. H. Rider Haggard, *Allan Quatermain*, in *Three Novels of H. Rider Haggard*, p. 517.

27. Morton N. Cohen, p. 87.

28. So numerous were the lost-race novels that they warrant a booklength study by themselves. For a discussion of some 200 of the most representative and notable titles during the period, see Clareson, *Science Fiction in America, 1870s-1930s*. That selection includes American, British, and Continental titles. Here I have tried to discuss the most significant titles primarily by American authors.

29. Wallace Irwin, "A New Angle on the Old Pole," *Cosmopolitan*, 48 (December 1909), 105–109.

30. As Jimmy is fitting the gown, Bezzanna demands to know the meaning of "hooking up"; Jimmy replies, "It's the chief enemy to domestic peace and happiness. . . . It consists in pouring a woman into a frock one-half size too small for her stays, and trying to keep from swearing in front of the children." When she asks what stays are, he "can't take the responsibility for introducing them," and of course she wants them (pp. 144–145). No phase of American culture is spared. To some extent, in this novel at least, Chester reminds one of Robert W. Chambers.

31. Robert Ames Bennet's *The Bowl of Baal* was originally serialized in *All Around Magazine* (November 1916–February 1917); its only book edition, with an introduction by Stu Teitler, did not appear until 1975 (West Kingston, R.I.: Donald M. Grant, 1975). A thorough examination of the various magazines of the period 1910–1920, especially, should find innumerable stories never published as books, which influenced subsequent writers. The excellent work of such individuals as Sam Moskowitz has merely scratched the surface.

32. See, for example, Betty King, *Women of the Future* (Metuchen, N.J.: Scarecrow Press, Inc., 1984), pp. 5–8. Excerpts from *Mizora* have been included in Carol Farley Kessler, ed., *Daring to Dream: Utopian Stories in the United States by Women: 1836–1919* (Boston: Pandora Press, 1984), pp. 117–137.

33. Thomas D. Clareson, *Science Fiction in America, 1870s-1930s*, p. 164.

34. Articles in American magazines on Atlantis begin at least as early as Edward H. Thompson, "Atlantis Not a Myth," *The Popular Science Monthly*, 16 (October 1879), 759–764. For example, Edward B. Hale, "In Quest of the Lost Continent," *Travel*, 45 (July 1925), 32, reproduces a map showing the position of "Atlantide" as well as an Arctic "Continent Hyperboreen" which serves as a land bridge between America and Europe. This is a review of Louis Spence's *The Problem of Atlantis* (New York: Bretano's, 1925). The most comprehensive work remains L. Sprague de Camp, *Lost Continents: The Atlantis Theme in History, Science, and Literature* (New York: The Gnome Press, 1954).

35. William MacLeod Raines, "The Cave Boy," *Cosmopolitan*, 43 (July 1907), 327–329.

36. See, for example, Betty King, *Women of the Future*, pp. 30–31.

37. Erling B. Holtsmark, *Tarzan and Tradition* (Westport, Conn.: Greenwood Press, 1981).

38. Holtsmark cites Dorothy McGreal, *Tarzan and Tradition*, p. 6.

39. In my class, "Introduction to Popular Culture," at the College of Wooster, in the fall term 1983–1984, some thirty-five students reacted negatively to both *Tarzan and the Jewels of Opar* and *John Carter of Mars*. They objected to his presentation of women, as might be expected, but they also thought that his Africa and Mars were hopelessly dated. On the other hand, they liked such novels as James Hilton's *Lost Horizon*.

40. Edgar Rice Burroughs, *Tarzan of the Apes* (New York: Ballantine Books, 1963), pp. 141–142. Cited in Clareson, "A Pagan Princess of Their Very Own," *Many Futures, Many Worlds*, p. 134.

Journeys to Other Worlds

In England, the vogue for lunar voyages did not begin until after the appearance of Galileo's *Siderius Nuncius* (1610). Francis Hicks published the first English translation of Lucian's *True History* in 1634, the same year in which Johannes Kepler's *Somnium, seu opus posthumum de astronomia lunari* was issued in Frankfurt, although the manuscript of *Somnium* had circulated as early as 1609. The earliest English-language voyage was Francis Godwin's *The Man in the Moone* (1638). Marjorie Nicolson has shown the importance of the cosmic voyage in English literature during the seventeenth and eighteenth centuries[1]; too often, critics who have wanted to trace the historical roots of science fiction have overlooked the single most important fact to emerge from her invaluable study. Although from the first the writers showed their awareness of and fascination with the "new astronomy" of Copernicus and Galileo, they used the voyage to the moon primarily as a narrative structure providing another means to satirize European society. That practice continued into the nineteenth century.

The earliest American contribution, George Tucker's *A Voyage to the Moon* (1827), proved as significant to the development of nineteenth-century science fiction as did Captain Adam Seaborn's *Symzonia*. Probably because he was chairman of the faculty at the University of Virginia, Tucker presented the story as the work of Joseph Atterley, its first-person narrator. Shipwrecked off the Burmese coast and thought to be an English officer of high rank, Atterley is sent to a village in the interior, Mozaun, where he becomes the friend of a hermit, the Brahmin of Benares, who reveals that he has visited the moon three times. When Atterley agrees to join the Brahmin on another trip, he describes their ship:

The machine in which we proposed to embark, was a copper vessel, that would have been an exact cube of six feet, if the corners and edges had not been rounded off. It had an opening large enough to receive our bodies, which was enclosed by sliding pannels [*sic*], with quilted cloth between them. When these were properly adjusted, the machine was perfectly air-tight, and strong enough, by means of iron bars running alternately inside and out, to resist the pressure of the atmosphere, when the machine should be exhausted of its air, as we took the precaution to prove by the aid of an air-pump. On the top of the copper chest and on the outside, we had as much of the lunar metal (which I shall henceforth call *lunarium*) as we found, by calculation and experiment, would overcome the weight of the machine, as well as its contents, and take us to the moon on the third day. As the air which the machine contained, would not be sufficient for our respiration more than about six hours, and the chief part of space we were to pass through was a mere void, we provided ourselves with a sufficient supply, by condensing it in a small globular vessel, made partly of iron and partly of *lunarium*, to take off its weight. (pp. 44–45)

In this way Tucker made use of the idea that "there is a principle of repulsion as well as gravitation in the earth" and that a rare metal, "when separated and purified, has as great a tendency to fly off from the earth, as a piece of gold or lead has to approach it" (p. 35). In short, Tucker introduced the concepts of negative gravity and a super metal, both of which proved essential to the entire field of science fiction until, at least, the first quarter of the twentieth century. In addition, he was, apparently, the first novelist to suggest that space is essentially a vacuum and not ether or some such substance. As the ship ascended from earth, he also referred to a drop in temperature, although the Brahmin introduces "a chemical means" to overcome that change and make the vehicle habitable (p. 49). Tucker concerns himself with other scientific matters. The Brahmin suggests that the moon was once attached to the Pacific basin (pp. 69–72), the travelers experience free fall (pp. 83–84), and Atterley closely examines the polar areas to ascertain whether or not "Captain Symmes's theory" is correct and declares "that that ingenious gentleman is mistaken" (p. 77). Except for the motive power of the ship, none of these topics is necessary to the narrative; Tucker includes the scientific matter for its own sake.

As in the case of his British predecessors, however, he gave most of his attention to philosophical and social issues. The travelers speculate on the futures of the U.S., South America, India, and Africa as they examine those areas through their telescope. Although the Brahmin voices the popular belief that geographical adversity—"frost and snow"—gives "occasion to war and emulation" and thus promotes the growth of "the powers of the human mind" (p. 52), for once the possibility that such areas as the interior of Africa, for example, will one day change the people for the better is deemed possible. Once they reach the moon, the narrative gives way to established convention. The lunar world is very like the earth, complete with oceans, high mountains, and deep forests. Atterley and the Brahmin visit a number of cities and peoples so that various aspects of society, including women's fashions, may be satirized.

In an appended note to "The Unparalleled Adventures of One Hans Pfaall" (June 1835), Poe made explicit reference to *A Voyage to the Moon*, belittling Tucker's use of "a peculiar metal," although he chose not to name title or author.[2] Despite the praise of the accuracy with which Poe handled astronomy and physics in "Hans Pfaall," one cannot overlook the fact that Hans's diary records his sensations in the manner of a *Blackwood's* tale, while even J. O. Bailey acknowledged that the journey was contained within a "facetious envelope."[3] One cannot escape the implication that the story should be read as a satire of lunar voyages, particularly since Poe dismissed the humanoid lunarians as seemingly retarded dwarfs and promised to describe their society in an ensuing narrative, surely a comment upon the efforts of his predecessors. Perhaps the most significant detail of "Hans Pfaall" is that, like Tucker, Poe examined the polar areas to verify the theory of Symmes.

In like manner, because of the search for literary ancestors, one suspects that Richard Adams Locke's "moon hoax"—"Discoveries in the Moon Lately Made at the Cape of Good Hope, by Sir John Herschel," published in the New York *Sun* in five installments, August 25, 26, 27, 28, and 31, 1835—has been praised too highly. Imitatively, it minutely describes the moon as another earth possessing "monstrous amethysts, of a diluted claret color" and a river "abounding with lovely islands, and water-birds of numerous colors" (pp. 25, 27). Poe, of course, called them both "hoaxes," suggesting that Locke's work wanted "a more scrupulous attention to facts and general analogy," and referred specifically to a number of earlier voyages to the moon, calling Bergerac's book "utterly meaningless."[4] Whatever Poe's reaction, however, a generation later, when Edward Everett Hale published "The Brick Moon" in *The Atlantic Monthly* (October-December 1869), Hale felt certain that if his readers had "read Mr. Locke's amusing Moon Hoax as often as [he] ha[d]," they would have details of Lord Rosse's telescope "fresh" in their memories.[5]

Presented as excerpts from "The Papers of Colonel Frederic Ingham" (he was promoted from Captain between the first and second installments), "The Brick Moon" gives a highly personal account of the invention and accidental launching of the first earth satellite. Although one could give a lengthy summary of those events, to celebrate Hale's serial for its scientific content obscures the fact that he uses the device as a point of departure for his sometimes delightfully funny satire. Lamenting that navigators have no natural phenomenon, like the North Star, to help ascertain exact longitude, Ingham, the discursive first-person narrator, explains that among his undergraduate friends at Harvard one man— identified simply as "Q"—suggested "the expedient of the Brick Moon" (24:452). At once, the group agrees that eventually there must be two moons, although Ingham does not recall how they decided that each must have a diameter of 200 feet. Although hollow, they would be made of brick in order to survive the heat of the friction during ascent. To launch the moon, the group sees the need for construction of two large fly-wheels revolving in opposite directions, although their edges must almost touch. They would be powered by some as yet unused waterfall. Once constructed, the moon would be "gently rolled down a gigantic groove . . . till it lighted on the edge of both wheels at the same time" (24:454);

the contact would throw it in a trajectory enabling it to orbit the earth at a distance of 4,000 miles. Once these plans are made, the project is delayed for seventeen years because the bricks alone would cost $60,000.

Only then does George Orcutt, who made his fortune in railroading, announce that he will donate $100,000, but by then the estimated cost has risen to $214,729. The remainder of the first of the three episodes is devoted to an account of the subsequent fund-raising campaign. It falls short. The first suspicion that Hale plans something other than a straightforward account of a scientific achievement occurs when Ingham recapitulates Orcutt's successful career. On his first day running the C. and O., Orcutt advertised: *"Infant children at treble price!"* Ingham praises him:

. . . he was a humane man, who wished to save human life. He would leave these innocents in their cradles, where they belonged. . . . Second, and chiefly, [Orcutt was] a railroad manager caring for the comfort of his passengers. (24:456)

After the failure of the campaign, Halliburton invests all of their money in railroad stocks, while the others return to their jobs. A minister for the Sandemanian church, Ingham lives with his family "for years" in Township No. 9 in the 3rd Range (24:603), which becomes the area where the moon is eventually built, because Halliburton's investments succeed partly as a result of the Civil War. Within the moon are thirteen spheres, each of which provides housing during construction, but before its outer surface is finished, the moon is launched accidentally.

A year passes before Ingham discovers, through such journals as the *Astronomische Nachrichten*, that the Brick Moon—sighted as a new asteroid—has settled into orbit. Ingham and his earthbound companions learn that thirty-seven people survive on the three-acre moon. They establish communication: the inhabitants of the moon jump up and down on its surface, thereby spelling out words in Morse code, while Ingham's group forms giant letters against an appropriate background. Any doubt that Hale's aim was satire ends when Ingham presents the seventeenth message from the Brick Moon: "Write to Darwin that he is all right. We began with lichens and have come as far as palms and hemlocks" (24:685). Its inhabitants also report the secrets of earth's geography: the North Pole is an open ocean; the South Pole, "an island bigger than New Holland"; the Antarctic Continent a cluster of islands; and the Nyanzas only two of a cluster of African lakes (24:688). For the first time, the reader becomes aware that this reflective narrative is a fragment of future history, because the three episodes record the history of the Brick Moon up to April 1871. Hale published "Life in the Brick Moon" in *The Atlantic Monthly* (February 1870), and its major thrust concerns the communication between the two groups of women regarding such matters as fashions, although they reveal that evolution has produced dodos and ostriches thus far.[6] Hale completes his charade by asking:

Can it be possible that our passion for large parties, and large theatres, and large churches, develops no faith nor hope nor love which would not find aliment and exercise in a little "world of our own?" (25:222)

The final result is that Hale achieved what the most ardent science fiction devotees advocate: namely, that an author use an sf storyline to carry a significant theme. In a sense, then, for Hale, the Brick Moon provided the paradise so many authors sought for.

In that "The Brick Moon" appeared in 1869, the same year as the American edition of Jules Verne's *From the Earth to the Moon*, an element of irony occurs early in Hale's narrative when Ingham declares, "but you can build no gun with a bore of two hundred feet now,—far less could you then" (24:454); granted that the size is exaggerated, one must nevertheless infer that he knew Verne's technology. To some degree, at least, one is surprised at the high praise some critics give Verne's lunar voyage. It is, after all, an exploit of The Baltimore Gun Club, and the narrative of the volume is given over to the building of the cannon and the location of its site; the flight provides the climactic incident. Not until *Around the Moon* (1873) did Verne's English-language readers learn that the ship missed the moon, circled it, and returned to the earth. Granted, as noted earlier, that Verne revitalized the imaginary voyage at a crucial time, one nevertheless suspects that this novel measures the limitations of his imagination rather than its strengths. The travelers did not see the unknown far side of the moon because it was invisible to them.

Although the lunar voyage remained a staple component of science fiction, one may argue that few writers in the early decades of the twentieth century turned it into their most innovative stories. H. G. Wells may well prove the exception, although he relied upon such established conventions as negative gravity when Bedford and Cavor became *The First Men in the Moon* (1901). Back on earth, Bedford hopes to return to the moon to obtain more gold, but Cavor's inquiring intellect grows fascinated with the Selenite culture. As noted elsewhere, the confrontation between Cavor and the Grand Lunar certainly was indebted to Swift, for humanity is found wanting in terms of the Grand Lunar's concept of rational norms. But Cavor underscores the horror inherent in the Selenite society, for it has evolved a highly specialized and insectlike social order.[7]

Garrett P. Serviss's "The Moon Maiden" (*Argosy*, May 1915), never published in book form, is little more than a love story in which spiritual force summons the beautiful Vega momentarily from the moon to the earth, while Garret Smith's "The Girl in the Moon" (*Argosy All-Story*, December 1–8, 1928) proves to be another love story, although the action centers on an unsuccessful flight to the moon. Edgar Rice Burroughs's *The Moon Maid* (1926)—made up of three novelettes published in *Argosy All-Story* in 1923 and 1925—may well be his most extravagant narrative. In a narrative frame dated 1967, the protagonist, Air Admiral Julian, recounts three future incarnations. In 2025, the first space flight is sabotaged by the villainous Orthis so that, as Julian V, the Admiral lands on the moon, where he falls in love with Nah-ee-lah, a princess (of course). Her kingdom is conquered by the savage Kalkars, who are communists; in 2050, they invade a helpless earth weakened by universal disarmament and a ban against scientific progress. Generations later, in an America which has reverted to a wilderness whose nomadic society resembles that of the American Indian, Julian 20 marries a descendant of the Or-Tis tribe so that, at last, peace returns to an essentially idyllic, primitive world. The best that can be said of Otis Adelbert Kline's imitative *Maza of the Moon* (1930) is that it transforms the threat of the "Yellow Peril" into a struggle between the P'an-ku of the moon and earthmen who are descendants of white Martians. Ray Cummings's *Brigands of the Moon* (1930) centers upon the efforts of Martian pirates to steal radium mined by earthmen on the moon. Both Kline and Cummings exemplify, though perhaps not in its most elaborate form, what has become known as "space opera."

The clue as to what transformed the interplanetary journey lies in the reference to Martians in Kline and Cummings. What happened in science fiction resulted from a series of discoveries in the field of astronomy which drew the imagination outward from the earth-moon system. In 1846, Johann Gottfried Galle of Berlin found Neptune as a result of the mathematical calculations given him by Urbain-Jean-Joseph Leverrier. The accuracy of this "armchair mathematics" provided a talking point referred to in fiction as late as Paul Kelly's *Prince Izon* (1910). A character remarks that if the geologist leading an expedition into the Grand Canyon does find a lost city of Aztecs, he "will have accomplished a feat as great as the astronomer who in his study, without the aid of the telescopes or other instruments, proved by mathematics the existence of a huge planet unseen by man, and predicted the day and hour when it could be observed" (pp. 34–35).

A second factor involved the great meteoric activity at the turn of the century, culminating in the appearance of Halley's comet in 1909–1911. The works of such writers as George Griffith, Chauncey Tinker, John Mastin, and Philip Wylie come to mind; one cannot recall offhand how many times the earth faced the "world peril" of a collision with a comet, a stray planet plunging toward the sun, or simply space débris (asteroids from the planet existing once upon a time between Mars and Jupiter). In a sense, the climax came in 1877. Asaph Hall reported his observation of the Martian moon Diemos, but more important, Giovanni Schiaparelli announced that he had observed "canali" on Mars.

The simplest translation of "canali," one which appears in the journals of the period, is "channels"; however, Percival Lowell chose to speak of the canals of Mars. Somewhat later William Pickering came out for the existence of Martian oases. A century later one may not realize the full implications of such theories. The idea of canals suggests artifacts rather than accidental geological formations. Undoubtedly, in part because of the date of Schiaparelli's discovery, the idea reinforced the concept of parallel evolution as advanced by John Fiske in *Cosmic Philosophy* (1874). In Herbert Spencer's idea of "necessary progress," Fiske saw scientific proof of the existence of a divine pattern by which the deity governed the entire universe, a pattern which moved inexorably toward a single goal. Culminating in the creation of man, the plan moved toward the eventual perfection of the human soul.

One can infer that the loss of traditional Christian values contributed to the need for a popular belief that the next step in evolution would affect the soul instead of the body. This line of reasoning led to Gustavus W. Pope's statement in his prefatory note to *Journey to Mars* (1894):

It may be assumed, in strict accordance with the spirit of Science, Philosophy, and Religion—as well as analogy—that, Humanity, created in the Image of God, must always and necessarily be the same *in Esse*, in essential Being and Nature, on whatever habitable planet of our Solar System it may find its home, sphere of action and environment, and it is wholly contrary to reason and analogy to assume otherwise. (pp. v-vi)

In an effort to regain orthodoxy in the face of nineteenth-century science, in *Daybreak: The Story of an Old World* (1896), James Cowan allowed the Martian Thorwald to assert that centuries ago Christ had been incarnated on Mars (p. 168). Cowan voiced the sense of despair and cosmic loneliness which resulted in the appearance of Christ on Mars when he wrote in a special postscript to *Daybreak*:

I acquired the belief in the habitability of other worlds when quite young, and it long ago grew to a settled conviction. Firmly held by this idea, what is called the astronomical difficulty in theology gave me great concern. When I considered the vast extent of the universe, and saw, with but little imagination, millions and millions of habitable worlds, I felt the force of the old objection. How could our tiny earth have been chosen for such peculiar and high honor as we read in the gospel story? (p. 396)

The horror of the uniqueness fed the concept of parallel evolution. In *The American Mind*, Henry Steele Commager has emphasized that Spencer—and therefore Fiske—dominated the imagination of the American middle class for at least "the half century after Appomattox" (p. 89).

Such belief was fostered by the astronomers themselves. As early as 1873, Camille Flammarion had hinted that life must exist on Mars,[8] but the theory and the evidence were provided by Fiske and Schiaparelli. (Flammarion's novel *Omega*, published in 1894, not only portrayed the last days of the Earth but also took his surviving man and woman to Jupiter which was at the height of its evolution, ready for mankind.) In the summer of 1892 as the opposition of Mars grew closer, *Nature: A Weekly Illustrated Journal of Science* described the reports made by William Pickering from both Cambridge and Arequipa, Peru, and noted that the United States Naval Observatory invited all observatories having "the necessary equipment" to join in the close examination of Mars between June 20 and September 23; it also announced that by the middle of August the Lick Observatory had mapped "many of the supposed canals" but had found none of them to be double, as Schiaparelli had proposed.[9]

Although Garrett P. Serviss had written about "The Strange Markings on Mars" in 1889, Percival Lowell published the key articles of the period in *The Atlantic Monthly* between May and August 1895; they formed the basis of his first book, *Mars* (1895).[10] His last statement in that four-part article is one of affirmation: from the teachings of astronomy, man "learns that though he will probably never find his double anywhere, he is destined to discover any number of cousins scattered through space" (76:235). So far as Mars was concerned, his theory was a simple one. Mars was a desert world far older than the earth; sometime in the past as its water supply failed, its inhabitants constructed canals with which to irrigate portions of the entire planet. He continued to elaborate on his basic principles after the opposition in 1907. In 1908, David Todd, who had been the first human to sight the Martian moon Phobos, gave an account of the 1907 expedition of the Amherst College Observatory to Alianza, Chile, which he had led and the Lowell Observatory had helped to finance.[11] He supports Lowell's deductions and looks forward to the opposition of 1924 when larger telescopes and "keener" photographic processes would be brought into play to solve the mystery; then he speculates, "and a perfected ethereal telegraphy may, well within reason, permit intelligible speech from planet to planet, across the cosmic void" (44:351). (In this, however, Todd was not original, for in 1899 Nikola Tesla declared that he had discovered electrical disturbances which could have originated only on Mars.) In that same issue of *Cosmopolitan* in 1908, another voice added its authority to that of Todd and Lowell. H. G. Wells described "The Things That Live on Mars," concluding that the "Martians are probably far more intellectual than men and more scientific, and beside their history the civilization of humanity is a thing of yesterday"; he hopes, however, that as the Martians have done, mankind will some day "rule and order and cultivate [the earth] systematically and completely."[12]

As late as 1953 in *The Green and Red Planet*, Hubert Strughold acknowledges that Schiaparelli and Lowell began the modern discussion of the possibility of life on other planets, and he hopes that the first space traveler stepping from his ship to the surface of Mars will not see the "melancholy" spectacle of "a lifeless landscape stretching monotonously to the horizon."[13] Surprisingly, in view of the findings of the *Mariner* space probes that the chance of life on Mars is highly unlikely, the 1981 edition of the *Encyclopaedia Britannica Macropaedia* declares that an "unequivocal answer is not possible" (11:530).

In terms of the history of science fiction, once Schiaparelli made his disclosure, Mars replaced the moon as the favorite destination of interplanetary voyagers. Because of the date of publication, much attention has been given Percy Greg's *Across the Zodiac* (1880). Greg does transform Tucker's *lunarium* into an antigravity force, *apergy*, but otherwise he looks backward, for his principal concern lies in the description and analysis of the 13,000–year-old Martian society, now a monarchy after the failure of communism. Most of the narrative centers around the troubled marital relationships of the narrator with his six wives; much of the difficulty rises from his kindness, for compassion is a quality the Martians do not possess. Although only women may obtain divorces, they are definitely not equal to men. Although Robert Cromie's *A Plunge Through Space* (1890) is dedicated to Verne and has a short introduction by him, the narrative divides its interest among the actual journey to Mars, a guided tour through a utopian civilization, and the love of the Englishman Walter Durand and Mignonette, daughter of the Martian Dr. Profundis. When Durand and his companions leave Mars, Mignonette stows away aboard their ship. Learning that the supply of oxygen is low but that the ship might make it to earth if there were one less person aboard, Mignonette throws herself into space. Her action does not deplete the air supply, but once on earth Durand blows up the ship, its inventor, and himself, thereby preserving the British ambivalence toward the treatment of love stories. After Rider Haggard began to write, most authors seemed to give fuller attention to a love interest, as though they had suddenly discovered it as a means of appealing to an adult audience. George Griffith, for example, gathered together "Stories of Other Worlds," originally published in *Pearson's Weekly* (1900), into the episodic novel *A Honeymoon in Space* (1901). Aboard his ship *Astronef*, the Earl of Redgrave abducts Zadie Rennick from the ocean liner *St. Louis*; as the *Astronef* hovers over the dome of the Capitol in Washington (Redgrave must deliver a copy of an Anglo-American treaty, thereby preventing war with Russia and France), the couple are married before they depart for a sightseeing honeymoon tour of the solar system.

The mood of the American novels dealing with interplanetary travel during the last decade of the nineteenth century differed from the British. Whereas the British seemed more concerned with social matters, the Americans concentrated on philosophy and religion. Thematically, they advanced the concept of progressive and parallel evolution. In the one major novel not concerned with Mars, *A Journey in Other Worlds* (1894), John Jacob Astor reveals his knowledge of Percy Greg's *Across the Zodiac* by making use of *apergy*, but that is the extent of his indebtedness. His narrative divides itself into three distinct books: the first gives a utopian description of earth in the year 2000; the second records an expedition to Jupiter which resolves itself into an exploring and hunting foray; the third records a visit to Saturn, where the travelers meet various disembodied spirits, among them an Anglican bishop, who explain certain of the metaphysical puzzles of the universe in terms of progressive evolution.

Early in the flight, the protagonist, Professor Cortlandt, remarks that he expects to find Jupiter in either its Paleozoic or Mesozoic period. Passing through the asteroid belt, he and his companions discover one—200 miles in diameter—which replicates the earth, even in terms of an ice cap, oceans, continents, mountains, forests, "and green fields" (p. 149). On Jupiter they find an abundance of prehistoric life. The degree to which Jupiter is nothing more than a giant earth may be seen in that Cortlandt explains the mysterious "red spot" in terms of autumnal change in color of foliage caused by a sudden drop in temperature. Similarly analogous is Saturn, although because of its distance from the sun it is frozen in perpetual winter.

Cortlandt projects the concept of parallel evolution outward to the galactic universe when he suggests that the forces which are shaping the earth and solar system "must be at work on 51 M. *Canum Vebaticorum, Andromeda*, and 39 M. *Virginius*, and must inevitably change them to suns, each with doubtless a system of planets" (pp. 259–260). On Saturn the disembodied bishop confirms Cortlandt's speculations. He tells his visitors of Cosmos, the central sun of the entire universe, as well as Cassandra, the Jovian-like ninth planet of the solar system, where all of the damned souls are condemned to exist (p. 390). He echoes Cortlandt:

Far beyond this visible universe, my intuition tells me, are systems more gigantic than this and entirely different in many respects. These systems are but in a later stage of evolution than ours; and in the course of evolution our visible universe will be changed in the same way. (p. 398)

Precisely what transformations will take place, he chooses not to say, but he does describe the wonders of many worlds and many intelligent creatures who populate them. One inconsistency occurs: humanity and the angels are the chosen people, for only they possess immortal souls (pp. 407–408). He reaffirms Astor's basic theme of the perfectability of man when he asserts:

God made man in His own image; does it not stand to reason that He will allow him to continue to become more and more like Himself? Would He grudge him the power to move mountains through the intelligent application of Nature's laws, when He Himself said they might be moved by faith? (p. 317)

One point should be noted. Although many writers probed the future for a possible utopian state while others found an idyllic haven in a bypassed corner of the world, some of them seemed hesitant and desperately hopeful, although uncertain that their envisioned paradises could be achieved. With the exception of James Cowan, who argued defensively that the miracle of Christ must occur throughout the universe, no hesitancy or desperation marred novels like *A Journey in Other Worlds*. Often deeply mystical, the writers were firm in their faith in the doctrine of inevitable, progressive development.

Amid such seriousness, it is pleasant to discover that Astor's travelers are not entirely motivated by interests in science and metaphysics. In discussing one of his young companions, Cortlandt remarks:

"You see, his fiancée is not yet a senior, being in the class of 2001 at Vassar, and so cannot marry him for a year. Not until next June will this sweet girl graduate come forth with her mortar-board and sheepskin to enlighten the world and make him happy. This is, I suspect, one reason he proposed this trip to Jupiter." (p. 94)

In *Journey to Mars* (1894), published as the first of a series of novels dealing with voyages to each of the planets of the solar system, Gustavus W. Pope, as noted, also espouses the theme of parallel evolution. His prefatory note also recommends the "scientific novel" as a literary form worthy of development and of public attention. Pope admonishes prospective writers to avoid "any violations of the laws and principles of Science" (p. vii), thereby demanding the quality called for as early as Poe. One is not certain to whom he next addresses himself, perhaps the advocates of social realism, when he writes:

It has been held by some persons that "scientific romances," the scenes and *dramatis personae* of which are laid on distant spheres, are impractical, owing to certain inherent difficulties of a scientific nature involved in the undertaking, and furthermore, such romances, being outside of, and beyond this mundane sphere, are necessarily beyond the pale of human interest and sympathy. It were needless to add that, the author cannot subscribe to this view. (p. vi)

He then makes his statement about humanity being universally and essentially the same *in Esse*.

Against this doubly serious background, Pope sketches the fabulous adventures of Lt. Frederick Hamilton, U.S.N. After an introductory chapter, in which a sailor delivers Hamilton's manuscript to an unidentified doctor in New York (presumably Pope himself), the narrative opens in a manner that calls up innumerable voyages. In the autumn of 1891, the *Albatross* ventures into Antarctic seas. After it survives a fierce storm, Hamilton and a young Maori named John are among those sent out to take possession of the ocean and ice floe in the name of the United States. The two are separated from the others, and as they find the sea and ice suddenly covered with flame, Hamilton rescues a young man from a shark. The youth's companions are red, yellow, and blue (p. 43). Hypnotized by the youth, Hamilton awakens to find himself in bed cared for by Dr. Hamival, identified as a member of the yellow race, and by Ascopion, identified as a member of the blue race (pp. 57–58). At first he believes that he has encountered "cousins to Bulwer's 'Vril-ya,' or an evolution from Verne's centre earth anthropoid apes," or some such creatures, who have ascended from an inner world through "a great opening at the pole, according to the theory of Captain Symmes" (p. 77). He soon learns that he has rescued Prince Altfoura, but not until they have embarked on an "Ethervolt car" does Hamilton realize that their destination is Mars.

Their ship is powered by antigravity batteries, but it moves swiftly between the worlds because all of the planets are "united in one common bond of brotherhood by Cosmo-magnetic currents . . . generated at the poles of each planet" (p. 90). For almost the next hundred pages, Pope examines various astronomical phenomena during the voyage to Mars. Until the travelers arrive on the red planet, one must praise Pope for his adept use of established conventions. On Mars he makes his innovation. Lt. Frederick Hamilton, U.S.N., falls in love with Altfoura's sister, the Princess Suhlamia, who "quietly" but aggressively returns his affection (p. 252). Much of the remainder of the narrative grows out of his rivalry with the villainous Prince Diavojahr, who for reasons of politics and passion, desires Suhlamia. Pope achieves something of a reversal, although the romance echoes such affairs in Sir Walter Scott. Hamilton is taken prisoner by Diavojahr, but he escapes in time to prevent Suhlamia from signing a marriage contract (p. 449). Quickly, when a meteor shower threatens the destruction of Mars, they flee to the Antarctic region, but when telegraphic contact with Mars informs them that Diavojahr has invaded their country, they prepare to return to Mars. The narrative breaks off as Hamilton leaves his manuscript.

Even before the novel ends, a number of remarks suggest that they should have gone to Venus. They do in *Journey to Venus* (1895). The lovers and their companions enjoy a number of "wonderful adventures" on a prehistoric Venus. Pope obviously wishes to explain away some of the mysteries of earth's pre-history. Thus, the explorers find a subhuman apeman which they consider to be the missing link; they observe over a period of time a giant "anthropopithekos," who will, they believe, evolve into Venus's true man; and they witness the sinking of a great continent. The analogies to earth's prehistory seems obvious. Pope's two novels remain unique among the American novels of the period. He is a master storyteller, and, of course, he is the first to make the love affair between an earthman and a Martian princess a major element of his fiction. At present, one can only wonder whether Edgar Rice Burroughs knew Pope's novels.

In contrast to both Astor and Pope, other Americans who made use of Mars sacrificed both story and a graphic portrayal of the Martian society in favor of a heavy mysticism. James Cowan's *Daybreak* (1896), as noted, was the first to do so. As André Laurie brought the moon close to the earth in *The Conquest of the Moon* (1894), so did Cowan, but for a different purpose. After the moon settles in the Pacific basin, Cowan's protagonist ascends to its surface in a balloon; then suddenly some magnetic phenomenon repels it from the earth, sending it toward Mars so that it provides the means of interplanetary travel. Cowan describes the collision:

The tired and feeble satellite . . . scraped across the continent of South America, received a death blow in collision with the Andes, and fell at last into the South Pacific Ocean. The shock given to the earth was tremendous, but no other result was manifest except that the huge mass displaced water enough to submerge many islands and reconstruct the shore lines of every continent. (pp. 14–15)

Not only is Cowan the most unscientific of these writers, he also gives the most straightforward Christian message: Christ must be incarnated on every world. In contrast, in *The Certainty of a Future Life on Mars* (1903), Louis P. Gratacap provides an abundance of scientific data before he presents one of the fullest theosophic statements in the motif. Of the several novels dealing with some phase of science fiction, this is Gratacap's least realistic, for the narrative concerns itself with the successful effort of the protagonist to communicate with his deceased father who has been reincarnated on Mars. Perhaps Gratacap thought such a point of departure was the most effective way of dealing with the mysticism. He sets two tasks for himself. First, he must convince the reader that the elder Dodd was an accomplished scientist:

He anticipated many advances in electrical science and in mechanical devices, which have made the civilization of our day so remarkable. I recall distinctly as a boy his ingenious approximation of the telephone, and even the recent advances in wireless telegraphy which have been the instrumentality by which my own researches in the field of interplanetary telegraphy have been prosecuted, had been realized by himself. (pp. 10–11)

Second, Dodd must also be a mystic. He believes that the human soul passes through a number of reincarnations on successive spheres, always moving toward perfection, Nirvana. He is certain that one day the human mind will communicate with the universal mind "everywhere in all its specific forms" and that "the abyss of space [will] eventually thrill with the vibrations of conscious communication between remote worlds" (p. 29). Certain that he will be reincarnated on Mars, the elder Dodd gives his belief a bit of help by spending the last months of his life learning the Morse code so thoroughly that it becomes a part of his subconscious mind. After his death he achieves success in this, his greatest experiment. From Mars he communicates with his son at 10 A.M. on September 25, 1893 (how like a certain October morning in 4004 B.C.). In short, Mars is heaven.

It is also, incidentally, a socialistic utopia in which one form of electricity—called "Toto power"—nullifies gravity but is used solely to cast evil souls into the depths of space. All forms of "mechanical invention" are discouraged unless they aid astronomy, "the great profession," for through it the Martians study the relationship of the universe and the soul (p. 109).

Of these novels, Mark Wicks's *To Mars Via the Moon* (1911), is based most solidly on Lowell's theory. Until his voyagers reach the red planet, his novel reads like a textbook on astronomy; then, like Gratacap's *The Certainty of a Future Life on Mars*, it is dominated by mysticism. The journal *Nature* called Verne a new kind of teacher; it might have said the same for Wicks, for in his prefatory note he outlines his plan:

Science readers are already provided for; and it occurred to me that it would be much more useful and appeal to a more numerous class if, instead of writing a book on the usual lines, I wrote a narrative of events which might be supposed to occur in the course of an actual voyage to Mars; and described what might be seen on that planet during a short visit.

Every endeavor has been made to ensure that this scientific information shall be thoroughly accurate so that in this respect the book may be referred to with as much confidence as any ordinary textbook. (pp. ix-x)

He then dedicates the novel to Percival Lowell, "to whose careful and painstaking researches, extending over many years, the world owes so much of its knowledge of the planet Mars" (p. viii).

There is no storyline in the usual sense, although all of the conventions of the motif are employed in the narrative framework. The ship is made from "Martialium," which is "composed of aluminum and two even rarer metals," producing "a substance almost as light as aluminum yet many times harder and tougher than case-hardened steel" (pp. 27–28); "all the machinery was either electric or magnetic" (p. 29); and, of course, the narrative was especially edited and prepared for the public by a companion of the protagonist, Poynders. Yet, except for a discussion of the opposition of Mars on September 18, 1909, at which time the journey supposedly took place (pp. xix-xxi), Wicks does not present any astronomical data until the flight is in progress. Then, developing most of his topics to chapter length, he describes the moon; the sun and galaxy as seen from outer space, with particular emphasis on the solar corona; the size and composition of the sun; the nature and origin of the Milky Way; the nature and origin of both meteors and comets; and the appearance of both the northern and southern hemispheres of Mars, as observed by astronomers. To aid him, he includes a number of plates, all line drawings and diagrams and all, except one, of Mars (the exception pictures the solar system as it was known in 1911). His descriptions of Mars lead him to what he labels "The Martian Controversy"; namely, the question of whether or not life exists on Mars.

Although in his preface Wicks has indicated that Lowell's theories are "not only the most reasonable, but also the most scientific" (p. xi), he recapitulates a history of the debate between 1877 and 1911. After a discussion of the accepted ideas regarding the life cycle of a planet, he concludes:

The inhabitants could not exist without water, and their land would become entirely desert unless supplied with moisture. It will, therefore, be seen that the only thing possible, as a means of self-preservation, would be for them to make channels to carry the water in the most economical way from the poles to the parts where it was needed.

The lines seen show where the canals are, but not the canals themselves, because they are too narrow to be seen. The canals are really broad bands of vegetation irrigated by the canals which run through them, hence the seasonal changes which have been noted in their colour. (pp. 142–143)

Despite his unquestioned support of Lowell, he cites the belief that the markings are natural oases rather than artifacts as well as the conservative guess that they are simply faults in the planet's surface (pp. 139, 144–151). At least half of the first 160 pages are purely expository, a textbook.

That is why the complete change in tone comes so unexpectedly. It occurs as soon as the travelers land. Poynders sees a youth who reminds him of his dead son. When approached, the youth exclaims:

"I am indeed he who in heart and soul is at this moment as truly and affectionately your son, though living in another world, possessing another body, and called by another name. . . .

"Oh, how I have yearned for this meeting, and through what long years have I studied and striven to bring it about." (pp. 168–169)

Thus, once again, Mars is heaven.

The remainder of the narrative advances the established concepts of progressive and parallel evolution as well as successive reincarnations. The only unique feature occurs when the youth explains that the rapid advances during the past generation or so in the areas of electricity, telegraphy, engineering, and astronomy are the result of Martian efforts to transmit some of their knowledge by mental telepathy. Yet, it is Poynders himself who voices what must be regarded as the key belief behind all of the novels as well as the scientific theories. Dated as it may seem seventy years afterward, it nevertheless expresses that affirmation, that optimism, which separated its believers from such individuals as Twain and Howells and such groups as the literary naturalists:

Since the earliest dawn of our creation, the watchword of humanity has been "Onward!" And it is still "Onward," but also "Upward." The possibilities of the development of the human race in the ages yet to come are so vast as to be beyond our conception. This then is the great lesson which Martian civilization teaches us. (p. 301)

Once H. G. Wells had challenged the concept of inevitable human supremacy and had suggested the precariousness of mankind's very existence in such novels and stories as *The Time Machine*, "The Sea Raiders," and *The War of the Worlds*, the single most important British novel at the turn of the century remains Robert William Cole's *The Struggle for Empire* (1900). Not only does Cole's seemingly neglected narrative provide apparently the earliest example of the galactic warfare of the later space operas, but it brings to a climax many of the themes which had shaped British popular fiction since *The Battle of Dorking*. The gospel according to Cole, as expressed in the introduction to his narrative, fulfilled all of Britain's wishful thinking. A megalopolis extending far into the provinces, London of 2236 had become the capital of the world as early as the twentieth century. The first step, suggests his future historian, had come when in the great European war, anticipated and prepared for in the last decades of the nineteenth century, "England, Germany, and the United States stood arrayed against France, Russia, Austria, Turkey, Italy, and a number of minor States" (p. 4); soon after Germany and England divided Europe and much of Asia between them, "the United States were reunited to England," a Teutonic federation was formed, and "finally the Anglo-Saxon race was dominant over all the globe" (pp. 5, 6). Not surprisingly, the "French race gradually died out."

Political triumph simply mirrored scientific progress: "Every day the world was astonished by the news of some marvelous scientific discovery" (p. 7). The lesser achievements included antigravity and the shifting of the axis of the pole so that the British Isles enjoyed an "almost tropical climate" (p. 3). The discovery of three "powerful forces"—"Dynogen, Pralion, and Ednogen"—allowed the Anglo-Saxon race to venture successfully into space, where, often using interstellar ships, individuals or "whole families" sought to obtain worlds of their own.[14] Ironically, an echo from Wells's *The Time Machine* filters through when Cole announces that the "human race had gradually become divided into two parts—those who had great brain power and those who had very little. The former did all the commanding and organizing, the latter did the menial work" (pp. 10–11). This fact lost significance, however, in the face of an encounter with "a race of men," the inhabitants of the Sirian planet Kairet, "who had attained to the same degree of civilization" as humanity, with a resultant "mutual jealousy and dislike" (p. 13). Lieutenant Alec Brandon early acknowledges that the people of Kairet are the "only rival to universal dominion" (p. 35).

One can argue that *The Struggle for Empire* exemplifies a galacticwide adaptation of the future-war motif. In June 2236 in the Sirian system, each of the rivals attempts to colonize the planet Iosia, "particularly rich in mineral wealth and other natural products" (p. 39). Both groups choose the same site for a city. Incidents occur; by May 12, 2237, the opposing fleets assemble. They are described as completely and tenderly as any torpedo boat or ship of the line; indeed, torpedoes are one of their chief weapons (p. 93). The battles are described as though they are naval engagements. Repeatedly, the Anglo-Saxon fleets are defeated until the Sirian fleet bombards London itself; only then does a brilliant scientist, James Tarrant, perfect a force—an Electro-Ednogen machine—which nullifies the "antigravitation apparatus" of the Sirian ships so that they literally fall from the skies. Tarrant's fleet of "torpedo boats" effect the devastation, and the victorious Anglo-Saxons exact a surrender of an additional planet and the payment of an indemnity after the carnage of the six-year war (p. 208).

Almost incidental is a strange love story. At the outset in London, Lieutenant Brandon dines with his fiancée, Flora Houghton, "a beautiful girl, scarcely out of her teens . . . Her features were regular and of the most perfect type, her eyes were of a soft brown colour, and the voluptuous curves of her figure were draped in a light-blue garment" (p. 23). Despite this erotic signal, they are separated by war; Brandon is quite literally rescued from the débris of battle and taken to Neptune, where he becomes enchanted with Celia Eastland, who nurses him after her father, Herbert Eastland, saves him. They are constant companions, usually alone together, so that their flirtation—their "gentle love play" (p. 137) — continues despite the battles around Neptune. Eventually Celia's "great personal attractions" win his heart; he proposes and is accepted. When he returns to London, he writes Flora a letter reporting the change "in his intentions." Although she weeps, she receives him in "calm stateliness" and later finds "consolation for her wounded feelings" in the proposal of James Tarrant, who has always loved her. Heroic inventor and field general that he is, Tarrant asks that he be the Prince of Kairet; "now Flora reigns with him as Princess of Kairet" (pp. 210–213). To dismiss *The Struggle for Empire* as "socially idiotic" naively

ignores the historical context within which it was written.[15] Cole may have
switched protagonists once he had begun the novel, he may have included the
romantic element in an attempt to appeal to more readers, but he alone made
use of a cosmic stage which anticipated the works of the next generation of sf
writers. Only Cole voiced the dream of the Anglo-Saxon race triumphant throughout the galaxy; consequently, one must recognize in his novel the high tide of
a vision that shaped British and American science fiction in the late decades of
the century.

The guise of the future historian permitted Cole and his contemporaries to
rely heavily on exposition and description instead of dramatic scene. A second
convention which identified Cole with his period was the assertion that the citizens
of Kairet were a race of men. Both separate his novel from the dramatic impact
of Wells's *The War of the Worlds*. On the one hand, Wells's first-person narrator's account of the destruction of familiar places—the villages around London—provides his narrative with an immediacy few of his contemporaries
attempted. Some three years after its serialization, with English place-names, in
Cosmopolitan, *The Bookman* emphasized that the realism gave it "the air of
absolute truth, which is the first essential of success for stories of that kind."[16]
That realism also contributed to the effect of horror which he achieved by making
his Martians completely nonhuman—giant octopuses. Yet the principal impact
of *The War of the Worlds* remains thematic. The invasion of the Martians gave
cosmic scope to his warning that the margin by which mankind survives in the
here-and-now is slim, perhaps no more than a matter of chance. Yet the depth
of his pessimism apparently escaped his contemporaries. Within months of the
book publication of *The War of the Worlds*, C. L. Graves and E. V. Lucas issued
The War of the Wenuses (1898), a parody which reduces Wells's concern to
farce, though giving an insight into one of the particular anxieties of British
society: women from Venus invade earth to subjugate men. The coauthors give
their storyline a neat twist in that only the stalwart women of earth can save
their menfolk from succumbing to the brazen "Mash Glance" of the Wenuses.
Graves and Lucas do not need their heavy-handed, explicit references to Wells's
titles, for they effectively capture his style and narrative technique.

In America, Garrett P. Serviss responded as quickly, but he would have no
part of such nonsense. He sought vengeance. Hardly had *The War of the Worlds*
completed its serialization in *Cosmopolitan* (December 1897) before Serviss
invoked the name of America's foremost inventor as he began to run *Edison's
Conquest of Mars* in the New York *Evening Journal* on January 12, 1898. His
initial venture into fiction, it was not issued in book form until 1947.[17] Although
Serviss had established himself as a popularizer of astronomy at least a decade
earlier, his first book being *Astronomy with an Opera Glass* (1888), he surrendered his first novel to the conventions of the day. His first-person narrator opens
the narrative at the moment when the few Martians to survive "earthly diseases"
flee in one of their "projectile cars." To gain the needed escape speed of 7
miles per second, they resort to a mysterious explosive so that their last act

destroys what remains of New York; those not killed by the explosion die in the tidal wave resulting from the collapse of the Palisades into the Hudson. Far worse than the "actual suffering" and physical destruction, asserts the narrator, "was the profound mental and moral depression that followed. . . . All mankind was sunk deep in this universal despair" (p. 4). Within a brief period of time—"suddenly"—Thomas Alva Edison announces first that he has learned how the invaders powered their craft and then that he has successfully "pitted electricity against gravitation" (p. 7) producing, thereby, through antigravity a ship whose test flight takes it to the moon. Immediately, the public hue and cry demands retaliation, the destruction of Mars before "this perpetual threat" again desolates the earth (p. 9).

One cannot be certain, but perhaps writing for a newspaper audience led him to adopt his cavalier attitude toward scientific explanation. His narrator announces:

It would carry me into technical details that would hardly interest the reader to describe the mechanism of Mr. Edison's flying machine. Let it suffice to say that it depended upon the principal [sic] of electrical attraction and repulsion. (p. 7)

When Edison then invents an atomic disintegrator, the narrator declares:

. . . The details of its mechanism could not be easily explained, without the use of tedious technicalities and the employment of terms, diagrams and mathematical statements, all of which would lie outside the scope of this narrative. It was upon the great scientific doctrine, which we have since seen so completely and brilliantly developed, of the law of harmonic vibrations, extending from atoms and molecules at one end of the series up to the worlds and suns at the other end, that Mr. Edison based his invention. (p. 14)

During a Conference of Nations chaired by the American president in Washington—those attending ranged from Queen Victoria, Czar Nicolas, and "Emperor William" to the King of Siam, the Sultan of Zanzibar, and a tribal chieftain from Fiji—the cost of an expeditionary force is quickly underwritten. The "festive mood" and enthusiasm which "now possessed mankind" resulted in a grand ball, during which the Prince of Wales toasts Edison: "I cannot refrain from expressing my happiness in knowing that the champion who is to achieve the salvation of the earth has come forth from the bosom of the Anglo-Saxon race" (p. 30).

Like Napoleon invading Egypt, Edison selected a company of scientists as well as artists and photographers to accompany him (p. 34). Through the future historian who acts as narrator, Serviss gives attention to such phenomena of space flight as free fall. He reaches perhaps his highest point of originality and scientific feasibility when he predicts the use of space suits to permit the men to leave their ships:

Provision had been made to meet the terrific cold which we knew would be encountered the moment we passed beyond the atmosphere—that awful absolute zero which men had measured by anticipation, but never yet experienced—by a simple system of producing within the air-tight suits a temperature sufficiently elevated to counteract the frigidity without. By means of long, flexible tubes, air could be continually supplied to the wearers of the suits, and by an ingenious contrivance a store of compressed air sufficient to last for several hours was provided for each suit. (p. 36)

During the flight he also states most explicitly his central anthropocentric theme:

It was the evolution of the earth against the evolution of Mars. It was a planet in the heyday of its strength matched against an aged and decrepit world which, nevertheless, in consequence of its long ages of existence, had acquired an experience which made it a dangerous foe. (p. 35)

Implicit in this view is the concept of parallel evolution which identified the American interplanetary journey during the period. His major departure from the established conventions occurs when ''a veteran from one of our great observatories'' observes:

. . . ''Mars is red because its soil and vegetation are red.'' . . .
   There were no green trees, and there was no green grass. Both were red, not of a uniform red tint, but presenting an immense variety of shades. . . .
   But what trees! And what grass! And what flowers!
   Our telescopes showed that even the smaller trees must be 200 or 300 feet in height, and there were forests of giants, whose average height was evidently at least 1,000 feet . . . ''I knew it would be so. The trees are big for the same reason that the men are, because the planet is small, and they can grow big without becoming too heavy to stand.'' (p. 106)

The difference in coloration and the phenomenon of giantism—both used, perhaps, to add to the idea of Mars as a threat—mark the highpoints of Serviss's disregard for the theories advanced during the Martian controversy. One detail he does retain; the concept of canals is essential to the outcome of the novel. After portraying a war in which a thousand earthmen fight the Martian fleets of hundreds of ships to a standstill, Serviss permits Edison to learn that he may defeat the Martians by flooding their world. *Syrtis Major* forms a narrow channel through which all of the waters of the oceans must run. During the summer when the southern polar cap melts, this flow is at floodtide; therefore, a system of locks controls the flow of water. Edison destroys these floodgates. Since, conveniently, Mars has no mountains, that world is drowned in a deluge. This action allows Serviss once more to eulogize Edison's genius, for as the foe closes in on his small raiding party, he analyzes the control board of the locks:

It was at this critical moment that the wonderful depth and reach of Mr. Edison's mechanical genius displayed itself. He stepped back, ran his eyes quickly over the whole immense mass of wheels, handles, bolts, bars, and levers, paused for an instant, as if making up his mind, then said decidedly, ''There it is.'' (p. 157)

The few survivors who cling to the tops of such hillocks as exist are forced to surrender and pledge that they never again will attack earth. The narrator emphasizes that the Martian culture has learned to manipulate the growth of the brains of their males; this "brain culture" has produced a brutal and aggressive species despite the resultant knowledge of science. It provides another means of celebrating Edison and the technology of earth. The women, however, never undergo special treatment so that "only female brains upon Mars were entirely well balanced"; Edison's party found that the Martian women were "remarkably charming creatures" (p. 182). As the Martian monarch and his court assemble to receive Edison and his companions, the king strikes down one of the women of his court. Enraged, acting impulsively, one of the earthmen destroys him with the disintegrator. As Edison prepares to reprimand him, the earth girl, Aina, exclaims, "I am glad that it was done . . . for now only can you be safe. That monster was more directly responsible than any other inhabitant of Mars for all the wickedness of which they have been guilty" (p. 184).

The girl Aina is incidental to the plot, but her presence in Serviss's first novel emphasizes the degree to which the mysteries of earth's prehistory—and particularly of ancient Egypt—influenced the popular imagination at the turn of the century. Edison's task force rescues the beautiful Aina, the last survivor of the Aryan race, which had been enslaved and brought to Mars centuries ago after a previous Martian invasion of Earth. She explains that her people had been taken first from their home in Asia to Egypt, where, in imitation of the mountains they had seen for the first time, the Martians built the pyramids "and used them for purposes [her] people did not understand." This revelation causes one of the scientists to exclaim:

"To think that we should have come to the planet Mars to solve one of the standing mysteries of the earth, which had puzzled mankind and defied their efforts at solution for so many centuries! Here, then, was the explanation of how those gigantic rocks that constitute the great Pyramid of Cheops had been swung to their lofty elevation. It was not the work of puny man, as many an engineer had declared that it could not be, but the work of these giants of Mars." (p. 146)

In final estimate, the importance of *Edison's Conquest of Mars* must rest on three features: its relationship to Wells, its adulation of an actual scientist, and its neglect of utopian and mystical materials.

Yet even in Serviss's novels the themes of H. G. Wells did not truly penetrate American science fiction before World War I. Adapting the current themes to their own ends, the American writers maintained their own identity, although in their infatuation with technology they did resemble Verne, particularly in the fiction aimed at a juvenile audience. The writers using the house name Roy Rockwood, for example, took Jack Darrow and Mark Sampson *Through Space to Mars* (1910); the orphans were *Lost on the Moon* (1911); and they were marooned *On a Torn-Away World* (1913). Eventually they journeyed to Venus

(1929) and Saturn (1935). Frances T. Montgomery allowed Harold and Ione to go *On A Lark to the Planets* (1904). Perhaps the most noteworthy of these novels was Weldon J. Cobb's *A Trip to Mars* (1901), which substitutes an attempt to communicate with that planet by means of a "wizard apparatus that will outshine the sun" (p. 33) for an actual journey. Its young protagonist, Frank Edison, "the nephew of a noted scientific savant" (p. 8) becomes the assistant of Nikola Tesla, whose declaration, earlier cited, that he had received signals from Mars appears to have inspired this novel. Although Tesla remains in the background, the awe with which the public regarded him is well reflected in the scene in which young Edison first meets him:

Upon the great wizard of science young Edison fixed his rapt gaze.

He was "next" to the master genius of the twentieth century at last, and Frank felt that he had reached the acme of his ambitions.

He could not speak for awe, and he could not move—for sheer emotion.

The presence of this wonderful man fascinated, numbed Frank for the moment. (p. 107)

Such rapture equals, if not surpasses, anything accorded Edison by Serviss. Like Serviss's novel, Cobb's *A Trip to Mars* contains no mysticism nor social criticism, but relies upon plot action and generalized references to scientific "gadgets" and theories to sustain the readers' interests, a characteristic true of all the fiction intended for a juvenile audience.

Many imitative narratives took their travelers to planets other than Mars. In William Wallace Cook's *Adrift in the Unknown* (1904–1905), Professor Quinn lures four hardened capitalists—Gilholly, Popham, Meigs, and Markham—to his home, which is in reality a spaceship. Denouncing their practices, Quinn launches the house in a flight that ends on Mercury, where social criticism takes second place to a series of captures, and escapes in the kingdoms of Baigadd and Baigol (note the pronunciation) in a Symmesian interior world. When the foursome return to earth, they have, of course, reformed and work only for the good of the people. Professor Quinn remains with the people of Mercury—Mercurials, as the newspaper reporter–narrator calls them—who are small and grotesquely humanoid.

In contrast, an unidentified editor presents the typescript of James Rock, who journeys *Thro' Space* (1909) to Venus. The early portion of the narrative presents a basically tedious account of Rock's growing friendship with Isadore D'Arville, a young Frenchman whose parents have experimented with Radium and Hellium [*sic*], accidentally producing an antigravity force which enables a ship looking like "a submarine boat" to fly (pp. 19, 20). A brief gratuitous trip to the moon reveals that it is inhabited by ungainly quadrupeds some twelve to fourteen meters in length, although the two explorers see no "birds, no foliage, no verdant fields" (p. 52); despite the grandeur of the rugged mountains (there are small pools or lakes), the two almost perish in the thin atmosphere. Only then, as they "chummed together a great deal" through the cities of France, does Isadore remark that although one hears much of Mars and its inhabitants, life on Venus should "be in every way equal to that" on Earth because the planets are so alike (pp. 68–69). The resultant voyage acquaints them with the humanoid Venusians, Um and Ex, who comment at length on both cosmic and mundane matters. The "vastness of the Universe [remains] a mystery" even to them, while they dislike the "unbounded freedom" which allows a "few schemers" to control the government and industries of the United States (pp. 142, 118). Although Rock experiences "joyous rapture" when his hand touches that of a Venusian girl (p.109), once he returns to earth, he dutifully reports his "strange story" to his "dear wife [who] was kind enough to believe the story as here related" (p. 187). James Rock may have been the pseudonym of Clinton A. Patten, who held the copyright to the novel.

The first-person narrator of Garrett P. Serviss's journey to Venus, *A Columbus of Space* (1911), opens his story with the assertion, "I am a hero worshiper; an insatiable devourer of biographies; and I say that no man in all the splendid list ever equaled Edmund Stonewall." As soon as Stonewall acknowledges that he has gained control of "inter-atomic energy" (p. 6), he takes a group of his only intimates, young men who are members of the Olympus Club, into his laboratory and into a "remarkable object" resembling a "boiler" (p. 8). Instead of explaining what he will do with his discovery, Stonewall launches the object into a space flight which ends on the night side of Venus. As in *Edison's Conquest of Mars*, scientific details are dismissed:

"I'm sure you'll excuse me from explaining my method" (there was a little raillery in his manner), "but at least you can understand the plain statement that I've got unlimited power at my command. . . .

"As to the machinery, you'd need a special education in order to understand it. You'd have to study the whole subject from the bottom up, and go through all the experiments that I have tried. I confess that there are some things the fundamental reason of which I don't understand myself. But I know how to apply and control the power." (pp. 9, 21)

One youth is inadvertently left behind (he provides a brief description of the ship's departure and declares that his companions must be dead because they disappeared a year ago), while another accuses Stonewall of kidnapping them. Except for a passage through a meteor shower, such small talk replaces the usual description of astronomical wonders, as in Mark Wicks's *To Mars Via the Moon*, published in the same year. Just before they land on Venus, Stonewall asks if he is not "the Columbus of Space" and they, his lieutenants (p. 40).

Hardly have they touched down on the dark side of the planet before they discover creatures who look "more savage than a gorilla" (p. 47) worshipping the earth, which appears as a bright moon. Aided by the natives, only one of whom survives, they cross icy pinnacles of the "Crystal Mountains" and descend through the cloud cover of the sunny side of Venus. Immediately, they encounter

Ala, the reigning queen, a beautiful woman having chestnut blond hair and sapphire blue eyes (p. 109). With Stonewall especially she communicates telepathically in that *"thought came out of her eyes"* (p. 117). Yet this is no interplanetary love story, for Stonewall and his companions are too busy admiring the wonders of the planet and escaping the traps of Ingra, a jealous noble who desires Ala for himself, to do more than admire the lovely queen. The climax comes abruptly. The *"real human beings"* (p. 107) of Ala's kingdom worship the sun, but when the sunlight breaks through the cloud cover, they are driven mad by the ultraviolet rays, as the sunlight ignites their capital city. Ingra kills Juba, the sole survivor from the night side who has become a faithful servant. The earthmen flee, although Stonewall admits that he would stay if he thought there were the slightest chance that Ala had lived through the inferno (p. 283). They bury Juba in high ceremony before leaving for earth. Appropriately, this extraordinary voyage is dedicated to Verne, but at its very end one thinks of Wells's *The Time Machine* in that, like the Traveller, Stonewall disappears, perhaps undertaking another journey by himself.

Such was the state of the American interplanetary voyage when Edgar Rice Burroughs entered the field with *Under the Moons of Mars*, first serialized in *All-Story* (1912) and then published as *A Princess of Mars* (1917). He has been damned critically for his creation of Lowellian Mars as well as for his reliance, once again, on the threat of "the fate worse than death" to move his storylines (of necessity, then, one must condemn many of his contemporaries, whether fantasists or realists).[18] Richard Lupoff has inferred that somehow Burroughs obtained and was deeply influenced by Edwin Lester Arnold's last novel, *Lieut. Gullivar Jones; His Vacation* (1905).[19] The title itself implies a spoof on the imaginary voyage. Alone in New York and discouraged by naval bureaucracy and his sweetheart, Gullivar Jones, the first-person narrator, gains possession of a Turkish rug (p. 5) which transports him to Mars when he impulsively wishes himself "out of this red-tape-ridden world" (p. 9). Accepted by a gentle, primitive tribe, he falls in love with the charming, flirtatious Princess Heru (pp. 103–104), whom he must save repeatedly. Much of the narrative recounts his odyssey across an exotic Martian landscape as he sets out to rescue Princess Heru from the tyrannical Ar-hap, who has claimed her as part of his annual tribute. Although Jones returns her to her people, when Ar-hap and his warriors attack the village, Jones seeks desperately to escape and wishes himself in New York. The rug returns him to a faithful sweetheart and a naval promotion. Gullivar Jones cannot be described as heroic.

As Lupoff acknowledges, one cannot be sure how or *if* Burroughs actually knew *Lieut. Gullivar Jones*; seemingly, no direct evidence survives among Burroughs' papers. Thus, one can argue as easily for the influence of Gustavus W. Pope's *Journey to Mars* (something Sam Moskowitz has been reluctant to do[20]), for Pope first transformed Rider Haggard's influential formula into the love of a naval lieutenant for a princess of Mars. While one readily acknowledges that

Burroughs gave a new appeal to established conventions primarily by discarding outworn social criticism and mysticism in favor of high adventure, one cannot easily tie him to a single source.

In a "Foreword" to *A Princess of Mars*, Burroughs presents himself both as the editor of the "strange manuscript" left by Captain Carter of Virginia and as the executor of Carter's estate. He first knew Carter, apparently an uncle, on the eve of the Civil War, saw him some fifteen or sixteen years later after Carter had supposedly been prospecting, and finally arranged his funeral on May 4, 1886. Carter's body lies in a tomb which can only be opened from the inside. Such stage-setting is elaborate but essentially conventional.

As the first-person narrator, John Carter explains that in 1866, after being trapped in a cave by Apaches, he became aware that his soul had separated from his "lifeless clay"; seeing the planet of Mars, he "stretched out [his] arms to the god of [his] vocation." Following an instant of bitter cold he looks upon the landscape of Mars (Barsoom), where he almost immediately becomes the prisoner of a band of savage green Tharks led by Tars Tarkas. Thus begin his epic adventures, most of them involving the rescue of Dejah Thoris, Princess of Helium, for John Carter is a superb swordsman and his human musculature gives him a physical prowess on Mars which more than compensates for the giantism of so many of the Martians. Late in the novel he marries Dejah Thoris; as her prince consort, the Jeddak of Helium, he lives happily with her for nine years until the atmosphere machine supplying all of Barsoom stops. In an attempt to start it, he falls unconscious, awakening at the Arizona cave. But Burroughs' opening note implies that John Carter has returned to Mars. In the second and third volumes of the original trilogy, *The Gods of Mars* (1913, 1918) and *The Warlord of Mars* (1913–1914, 1919), he is reunited—at intervals—with Dejah Thoris, joins together most of the known city-states into the empire of Helium, and fights his way upward to become the Jeddak of Jeddaks, the Warlord of Barsoom. Although Carter himself is the protagonist of such later tales as *Swords of Mars* (1934–1935, 1936) and "Skeleton Men of Jupiter" (1943, 1946), as well as several times the narrator, for the most part he and Dejah Thoris remain in the background, while "other protagonists rescue the women they love."[21] Their son Cathoris saves *Thuvia, Maid of Mars* (1920); Prince Gahan of Gathol searches for their daughter, Tara of Helium, in *The Chessmen of Mars* (1922); while *Llana of Gathol* (1948) is their granddaughter. Thus the John Carter series becomes more than the story of a solitary hero; it becomes something of a family saga.

He had his imitators here as with Tarzan. Once again, the writer most often compared with him is Otis Adelbert Kline, whose earthman Robert Ellsmore Grandon loves the blond Vernia, ruler of the kingdom of Reabon on the planet Zorovia (Venus).[22] Despite such hardware as a spaceship, Burroughs' own Carson Napier reverts to the primitive on Venus, where, of course, he loves Princess Duare. However scornful some critics may be of Edgar Rice Burroughs, there can be no doubt whatsoever that contemporary heroic fantasy—"sword and sorcery"—has descended through him and the barbarians of Robert E. Howard.[23]

Those readers who wanted more scientific accounts of interplanetary voyages had to wait for the sf specialist magazines, as the proposed name "space fiction" of the 1930s suggests, although Gernsback in particular reissued many of the earlier works. *Amazing Stories*, for example, serialized Serviss's *A Columbus of Space* in 1926.

Among the American titles, Jack London's "The Red One" (1918) remains the classic of the period.[24] Comparison to Joseph Conrad's *Heart of Darkness* may help some readers, but London's narrative does not really need the assist.[25] Bassett's encounter with "The Star-Born" deep in the brutal jungles of Guadalcanal blends one element of fantasy into a story whose entire fabric is naturalistic. London structures the story in terms of one of naturalism's basic motifs; he follows Bassett's degeneration from the effects of malaria from the early stages of the disease until, "realizing that he is near death, Bassett deliberately chooses to see 'the messenger between the worlds' a second time and die at the hand of Ngurn," the headhunter.[26] As far as motivation is concerned, the instincts of survival and sexuality shape the action. London adds an innovation, a purely intellectual drive which unites the scientist Bassett and the savage Ngurn. Their rapport reveals itself when Bassett asks that Ngurn allow him to hear the "wonder voice" of the Red One as Ngurn beheads him, and the old witch doctor promises him, "Your head shall be my greatest piece of work in the curing of heads" (p. 86). They are intellectuals from disparate cultures thrown together by circumstance. London makes much of their relationship, for Ngurn, like Bassett, is "a scientist first, a humanist afterward" (p. 76).

Throughout the imaginary voyages, innumerable of London's predecessors and contemporaries had chosen the South Seas as a backdrop, returning modern man to an unspoiled and often idyllic setting. In "The Red One" London will have none of this. "From the beheading of Sagawa and the pursuit of Bassett through the 'dank and noisome jungle,' he divorces the island and its 'bushmen' from any idealizing primitivism. The separation shows itself from the first in the images that Bassett recalls from his nightmare flight" into the interior (p. 88). London's break with convention shows itself most vividly in his substitution of the "wizened," apelike Balatta, the native woman Bassett uses sexually, for those incomparable pagans, ranging from Ayesha, "She-Who-Must-Be-Obeyed," to Dejah Thoris. Aware of the débris of living sacrifices made for unnumbered generations to "The Star-Born," which serves as god to twelve villages, Bassett survives amid the violence and savagery of a stone-age world. Nothing could provide more effective irony, for he has encountered the vision which haunts mankind. The Red One is a spaceship—"a creation of artifice and mind . . . [a] colossal portent of higher life within the distances of the sidereal universe" (pp. 78, 79)—which has fallen among savages who cannot imagine the dream of communication between the interstellar worlds.

Yet London probes beneath this surface irony. Bassett "cannot remember whether he shot the hanging girl, he may have burned the old bushman to death, and he stomped to death the wounded bushman lying at his feet in the jungle. Yet he dreams of communicating to civilization the secrets of the 'Red One,' secrets which 'would make each man's life on earth, individual and collective, spring up from its present mire to inconceivable heights of purity and power' '' (p. 89). To achieve his end, Bassett imagines escaping and returning to the island to steal the "prodigy," extracting its secrets, " 'although the entire population of Guadalcanal be destroyed.' '' For all his dreams, for all his intelligence and science, Bassett is as brutal as the island world, which thus becomes symbolic of earth (p. 89).

In a sense, written only months before his death, "The Red One" becomes London's *cri de coeur*. Appalled by a mechanistic universe governed by determinism, he asserts that in the "cosmic ferment . . . all must be comparatively alike" and asks whether or not aliens have achieved "Brotherhood" and whether or not "strife [is] life." Thus, "London remains a product of his milieu, tortured by the dream of what man might be, the reality of what he is" (p. 90). To some extent at least, in "The Red One" the reader gains a sense of that cosmic loneliness which haunts Arthur C. Clarke's "The Sentinel" a generation later. Within London, too, one perceives another haunting question: if paradise cannot exist on earth, perhaps somewhere out there among the stars . . . perhaps beyond far Centaurus. . . .

NOTES

1. Marjorie Hope Nicolson, *Voyages to the Moon* (New York and London: Macmillan, 1948). For a briefer discussion of the early period, see Thomas D. Clareson, "The Emergence of Science Fiction," *The Anatomy of Wonder* (1981), pp. 3–87.

2. "New Appendix II: Edgar Allan Poe's Comment on *The Moon Hoax*," in Richard Adams Locke, *The Moon Hoax*, introduction by Ormond Seavey (Boston: Gregg Press, 1975), pp. 69–74. Apparently, the June issue of the *Southern Literary Messenger*, in which Poe's "Hans Pfaall" first appeared, was not published until a few weeks before Locke's article in the *Sun*.

3. J. O. Bailey, *Pilgrims Through Space and Time*, p. 46.

4. "Edgar Allan Poe's Comment on *The Moon Hoax*," pp. 69–74.

5. [Edward Everett Hale], "The Brick Moon," *The Atlantic Monthly*, 24 (October 1869), 451–460; (November 1869), 603–611; (December 1869), 679–688. This specific reference is to 24:682.

6. [Edward Everett Hale], "Life in the Brick Moon," *The Atlantic Monthly*, 25 (February 1870), 215–222.

7. Clareson, *Anatomy of Wonder*, p. 85.

8. For an annotated bibliography of articles concerned with "The Martian Controversy," see William B. Johnson, "A Checklist to Articles on the Martian 'Canal' Controversy," *Extrapolation*, 5 (May 1964), 40–48. Flammarion's article, "Mars, by the Latest Observations," was published in *The Popular Science Monthly*, 4 (December 1873), 187–193.

9. "Our Astronomical Column," *Nature*, June 23, 1892, p. 179; July 14, 1892, p. 258; August 25, 1892, p. 400.

10. Garrett P. Serviss, "The Strange Markings on Mars," *The Popular Science Monthly*, 35 (May 1889), 41–56.

11. David Todd, "Professor Todd's Own Story of the Mars Expedition," *Cosmopolitan*, 44 (March 1908), 343–350.

12. H. G. Wells, "The Things That Live on Mars," *Cosmopolitan*, 44 (March 1908), 338–342. The quotations are from pp. 340 and 342.

13. Hubertus Strughold, *The Green and Red Planet: A Physiological Study of the Possibility of Life on MARS* (Albuquerque, N.Mex.: The University of New Mexico Press, 1953), pp. 3, 97.

14. Although Cole seems to approve a blatant imperialism as much as, if not more than, any of his contemporaries, there is a note of ambivalence even in the following passage:

Exulting in their might, the gray-haired scientists steered their vessels through the dark depths of space, while they ransacked worlds for treasures and luxuries; some even towed great masses of valuable rock or precious metal behind their ships. Rare and beautiful plants were uprooted, and strange animals were captured and stowed away in the interior of the ships, and finally deposited in London or the other great cities of the world. Whole families would band together and buy an interstellar ship, and rush out into space to seek for themselves a new country and more splendid fortunes.

There were many deeds of darkness done in those distant regions which no one ever heard of. (p. 19)

As Cole's historian prepares to describe the initial battle, he enunciates his greatest reservation: "Many secretly wished that the national ambition had been more restrained, and that they had been contented with their own planet, and not crossed the oceans of space in search of fresh lands and fresh enemies" (p. 62). For a recent treatment of the same theme which indicates the change in attitude toward imperialism, see Robert Silverberg's *Nightwings* (1969).

15. Darko Suvin, *Victorian Science Fiction in the UK: The Discourses of Knowledge and of Power* (Boston: G.K. Hall, 1983), p. 79.

16. "Chronicle and Comment," *The Bookman*, 7 (March 1900), 4.

17. Garrett P. Serviss, *Edison's Conquest of Mars*, introduction by A. Langley Searles (Los Angeles: Carcosa House, 1947).

18. R.D. Mullen, "Edgar Rice Burroughs and the Fate Worse Than Death," *Riverside Quarterly*, 4 (June 1970), 186–191; "The Undisciplined Imagination: Edgar Rice Burroughs and Lowellian Mars," in Thomas D. Clareson, ed., *SF: The Other Side of Realism*, pp. 229–247.

19. Richard A. Lupoff, "A Phoenician on Mars," *Edgar Rice Burroughs: Master of Adventure* (New York: Canaveral Press, 1965), pp. 18–33.

20. Gustavus W. Pope, *Journey to Mars*, introduction by Sam Moskowitz (Westport, Conn.: Hyperion Press, 1974), [pp. ii-iii].

21. Thomas D. Clareson, *Science Fiction in America, 1870s-1930s, An Annotated Bibliography of Primary Sources* (Westport, Conn.: Greenwood Press, 1984), p. 8.

22. Sam Moskowitz has provided the best account of the feud in which Burroughs and Kline "stole" each other's planet in their novels first published in the pulps. See "To Barsoom and Back with Edgar Rice Burroughs," *Explorers of the Infinite*, pp. 185–187.

23. For the best appraisals of Howard, see L. Sprague de Camp, Catherine Crook de Camp, and Jane Whittington Griffin, *Dark Valley Destiny: The Life of Robert E. Howard, The Creator of Conan* (New York: Bluejay Books, 1983) and Don Herron, ed., *The Dark Barbarian: The Writings of Robert E. Howard, A Critical Anthology* (Westport, Conn.: Greenwood Press, 1984).

24. London wrote "The Red One" in 1916 a short time before his death; it was published in book form in 1918.

25. See Gordon Beauchamp, *Jack London* (Mercer Island, Wash.: Starmont House, 1984). Beauchamp's study includes a bibliography citing several appropriate articles from the 1970s. I believe that the first passing reference, in recent years, linking "The Red One" and Conrad occurred in my anthology, *A Spectrum of Worlds* (1972), p. 88.

26. See Thomas D. Clareson, "Notes to Jack London's 'The Red One,' " *A Spectrum of Worlds*, p. 87. Pagination in the text both to my notes and to the story itself are from this volume.

Bibliography

The following titles represent a selected bibliography of secondary studies which emphasize, to some degree at least, the development of science fiction (and fantasy) before the appearance of the specialist magazines in the 1920s and 1930s. For special editions of the works of an individual writer, as well as important articles in the general magazines—especially those in the nineteenth and early twentieth centuries—please consult the end notes to the appropriate chapters.

Aldiss, Brian W. *Billion Year Spree: The True History of Science Fiction*. Garden City, N.Y.: Doubleday and Company, Inc., 1973.

Amis, Kingsley. *New Maps of Hell*. New York: Harcourt, Brace and Company, 1960.

Armytage, W.H.G. *Yesterday's Tomorrows: A Historical View of Tomorrow's Societies*. Toronto: University of Toronto Press, 1968.

Attebery, Brian. *The Fantasy Tradition in American Literature from Irving to Le Guin*. Bloomington, Ind.: Indiana University Press, 1980.

Bailey, J. O. *Pilgrims Through Space and Time*. New York: Argus Books, 1947; 2d ed., Westport, Conn.: Greenwood Press, 1972.

Barron, Neil, ed. *Anatomy of Wonder: A Critical Guide to Science Fiction*. New York and London: R.R. Bowker, 1976; 2d ed., 1981.

Beauchamp, Gordon. *Jack London*. Mercer Island, Wash.: Starmont House, 1984.

Birkhead, Edith. *The Tale of Terror: A Study of the Gothic Romance*. London: Constable and Company, 1921.

Bleiler, Everett F., ed. *The Checklist of Fantastic Literature*. Chicago, Ill.: Shasta Publishers, 1948.

———. *The Checklist of Science-Fiction and Supernatural Fiction*. 2d ed. Glen Rock, N.J.: Firebell Books, 1978.

———, ed. *The Frank Reade Library*. 2 vols. New York and London: Garland Publishing, Inc., 1979.

———. *The Guide to Supernatural Literature*. Kent, Ohio: Kent State University Press, 1983.

———, ed. *Science Fiction Writers: Critical Studies of the Major Authors from the Early Nineteenth Century to the Present Day*. New York: Charles Scribner's Sons, 1982.

————, ed. *Supernatural and Horror Writers*. New York: Charles Scribner's Sons, 1985.

Borello, Alfred. *H. G. Wells: Author in Agony*. Carbondale and Edwardsville: Southern Illinois University Press, 1972.

Clareson, Thomas D. *Science Fiction Criticism: An Annotated Checklist*. Kent, Ohio: Kent State University Press, 1972.

————. *Science Fiction in America, 1870s-1930s: An Annotated Bibliography of Primary Sources*. Westport, Conn.: Greenwood Press, 1984.

————, ed. *A Spectrum of Worlds*. Garden City, N.Y.: Doubleday and Company, 1972.

————, ed. *Many Futures, Many Worlds: Theme and Form in Science Fiction*. Kent, Ohio: Kent State University Press, 1977.

————, ed. *SF: The Other Side of Realism*. Bowling Green, Ohio: Bowling Green University Popular Press, 1971.

Clarke, I.F. *The Pattern of Expectation: 1644–2001*. New York: Basic Books, Inc., 1979.

————. *The Tale of the Future*. 2d ed. London: The Library Association, 1972.

————. *Voices Prophesying War: 1736–1984*. London, New York, and Toronto: Oxford University Press, 1966.

Cohen, Morton N. *Rider Haggard*. New York: Walker and Company, 1960.

Costello, Peter. *Jules Verne: Inventor of Science Fiction*. New York: Charles Scribner's Sons, 1978.

Cowart, David, and Thomas L. Wymer, eds. *Dictionary of Literary Biography. Vol. 8: Twentieth Century American Science Fiction Writers*. 2 vols. Detroit, Mich.: Gale Research Company, 1981.

de Camp, L. Sprague. *Literary Swordsmen and Sorcerers: The Makers of Heroic Fantasy*. Sauk City, Wis.: Arkham House, 1976.

————. *Lost Continents: The Atlantis Theme in History, Science and Literature*. New York: The Gnome Press, Inc., 1954.

Dizer, John T., Jr. *Tom Swift & Company: "Boys Books" by Stratemeyer and Others*. Jefferson and London: McFarland, 1982.

Eichner, Henry M. *Atlantean Chronicles*. Alhambra, Calif.: Fantasy Publishing Company, 1971.

Ellis, Peter Berresford. *H. Rider Haggard: A Voice from the Infinite*. London and Henley: Routledge & Kegan Paul, 1978.

Frank, Frederick S. *Guide to the Gothic: An Annotated Bibliography of Criticism*. Metuchen, N.J.: The Scarecrow Press, Inc., 1984.

Gove, Philip Babcock. *The Imaginary Voyage in Prose Fiction*. New York: Columbia University Press, 1941; reprint ed., Arno Press, 1975.

Gunn, James. *Alternate Worlds: The Illustrated History of Science Fiction*. Englewood Cliffs, N.J.: Prentice-Hall, Inc., 1975.

Hillegas, Mark R. *The Future as Nightmare: H.G. Wells and the Anti-Utopians*. New York: Oxford University Press, 1967.

Holtsmark, Erling B. *Tarzan and Tradition: Classical Myth in Popular Literature*. Westport, Conn.: Greenwood Press, 1981.

Johannsen, Albert. *The House of Beadle and Adams*. Norman, Okla.: The University of Oklahoma Press, 1950.

Kagarlitski, Julius. *The Life and Thought of H.G. Wells*. London: Sidgwick and Jackson, 1966.

Kerr, Howard, John W. Crowley, and Charles L. Crow. *The Haunted Dusk: American Supernatural Fiction, 1820–1920*. Athens: University of Georgia Press, 1981.

Kessler, Carol Farley, ed. *Daring to Dream: Utopian Stories by United States Women: 1836–1919*. Boston: Pandora Press, 1984.

Ketterer, David. *New Worlds for Old: The Apocalyptic Imagination, Science Fiction, and American Literature*. Bloomington and London: Indiana University Press, 1974.

King, Betty. *Women of the Future: The Female Main Character in Science Fiction*. Metuchen, N.J.: The Scarecrow Press, Inc., 1984.

Lewis, Arthur O. *Utopian Literature in the Pennsylvania State University Libraries: A Selected Bibliography*. University Park, Pa.: Pennsylvania State University Libraries, 1984.

Lovecraft, Howard Phillips. *Supernatural Horror in Fiction*. New York: Ben Abramson, 1945; reprint ed., New York: Dover Books, 1975.

Magill, Frank N., ed. *Survey of Modern Fantasy Literature*. 5 vols. Englewood Cliffs, N.J.: Salem Press, 1983.

————, ed. *Survey of Science Fiction Literature*. 5 vols. Englewood Cliffs, N.J.: Salem Press, 1979.

Moskowitz, Sam, ed. *The Crystal Man: Stories by Edward Page Mitchell*. Garden City, N.Y.: Doubleday and Company, Inc., 1973.

————. *Explorers of the Infinite: Shapers of Science Fiction*. Cleveland and New York: The World Publishing Company, 1963.

————, ed. *Science Fiction by Gaslight; A History and Anthology of Science Fiction in the Popular Magazines, 1891–1911*. Cleveland and New York: The World Publishing Company, 1968.

————. *Science Fiction in Old San Francisco*. 2 vols. West Kingston, R.I.: Donald M. Grant, 1980.

————, ed. *Under the Moons of Mars: A History and Anthology of "The Scientific Romance" in the Munsey Magazines, 1912–1920*. New York: Holt, Rinehart and Winston, 1970.

Nicholls, Peter, ed. *The Science Fiction Encyclopedia*. Garden City, N.Y.: Doubleday and Company, Inc., 1979.

Nicolson, Marjorie Hope. *Voyages to the Moon*. New York: The Macmillan Company, 1948; paperback ed., 1960.

Parrington, Vernon Louis, Jr. *American Dreams: A Study of American Utopias*. 2d ed. New York: Russell and Russell, 1964.

Pattee, Frederick Lewis. *The Development of the American Short Story*. New York and London: Harper and Bros., 1923.

Philmus, Robert M. *Into the Unknown: The Evolution of Science Fiction from Francis Godwin to H.G. Wells*. Berkeley and Los Angeles: University of California Press, 1970.

Porges, Irwin. *Edgar Rice Burroughs: The Man Who Created Tarzan*. Provo, Utah: Brigham Young University Press, 1975.

Reginald, R. *Science Fiction and Fantasy Literature: A Checklist, 1700–1974*. 2 vols. Detroit, Mich.: Gale Research Company, 1979.

Roemer, Kenneth M., ed. *America as Utopia*. New York: Burt Franklin and Company, 1981.

————. *The Obsolete Necessity: America in Utopian Writings, 1888–1900*. Kent, Ohio: Kent State University Press, 1976.

Sargent, Lyman Tower. *British and American Utopian Literature 1516–1975: An Annotated Bibliography*. Boston: G.K. Hall, 1979.

Scarborough, Dorothy. *The Supernatural in Modern English Fiction*. New York and London: G.P. Putnam's Sons, 1917.

Silverberg, Robert, ed. *The Mirror of Infinity*. New York: Harper and Row, 1970.

Spector, Robert Donald. *The English Gothic: A Bibliographic Guide to Writers from Horace Walpole to Mary Shelley*. Westport, Conn.: Greenwood Press, 1984.

Stevenson, Lionel. *Yesterday and After, 11, The History of the English Novel*. N.Y.: Barnes and Noble, 1967.

Suvin, Darko. *Victorian Science Fiction in the UK*. Boston: G.K. Hall, 1983.

Tymn, Marshall B., ed. *Horror Literature: An Historical Survey and Critical Guide to the Best of Horror*. New York and London: R.R. Bowker, 1981.

Walsh, Chad. *From Utopia to Nightmare*. New York and Evanston: Harper and Row, 1962.

Williamson, Jack. *H.G. Wells: Critic of Progress*. Baltimore, Md.: The Mirage Press, 1973.

Wu, William F. *The Yellow Peril: Chinese Americans in American Fiction, 1850–1940*. Hamden, Conn.: The Shoe String Press, Inc., 1982.

Index

Absurd, 5, 16
Aces, 77
Achievements of Luther Trant, The, 42
Across the Zodiac, 204–205
Adams, Frederick U., 106, 133
Adams, Henry, 5
Adams, Samuel Hopkins, 98, 136
Adam's First Wife, 184
Adhemar, Joseph Alphonse, 175
A.D. 2000, 112, 125
Adrift in the Unknown, 217
advanced weaponry, 51–65, 72–75, 131, 212
"Adventures of the German Student, The," 20–21, 84
Adventurer, The, 178
Adventures of Jones, The, 95, 109–110
aerial warfare, 51, 53, 60, 62, 63, 68, 72, 73, 110
Africa, 11, 62, 74, 75, 108, 136, 161, 164–165, 168, 180, 191, 198, 200
Afterglow, The, 127
After London, 103
After the Cataclysm, 117–118
After Worlds Collide, 132
Agassiz, Louis, 4, 10
Agrippa, Cornelius, 16
Aimard, Gustave, 162–163

Alaska, 190
Albertus, Magnus, 16
alchemy, 16, 17, 81, 82, 88, 99, 107
Alchohuans, The, 184
Aldiss, Brian, 3
Aldrich, Thomas Bailey, 39
Alger, Horatio, 92
aliens (extraterrestrial), 211–217
Allan Quatermain, 165, 167
Allen, Frederick Lewis, 7, 105, 106
All for His Country, 72
All-Story Magazine, 188, 219
Alta, 185
"Altar of the Dead, The," 108
Amazing Stories, 221
American Civil War, 6, 24, 26, 60, 71, 73, 200
American Communist Party, 175
American Labor Movement, 57, 105
American Mind, The, 203
American Psychical Society, 24
American Transcendentalism, 4, 65
American West, 6, 60, 92, 107, 111, 161, 162
Amerinds, 33, 44–45, 74, 75, 82, 132, 162–63, 170, 171, 178, 185, 193, 202
Andrée, Falomon August, 174
"Angel in the House, An," 32
Angel Island, 181–182

Angel of the Revolution, The, 137
Anglo-American, 61, 141, 205. *See also* Anglo-Saxons
Anglo-American Alliance, An, 61
Anglo-Saxons (race), 53, 60–62, 104, 131, 211–214
Anglo-Saxons, Onward!, 61
Antarctic, 10, 86, 117, 158–162, 169, 173–174, 176–177, 190–192, 200, 207, 208
Antarctic Mystery, An, 161
antigravity, 62, 72, 82, 99, 204, 205, 207, 209, 211, 212
anti-Semitism, 73–74, 142
Appleton, Victor, 93
Arcadia, 103, 106, 108, 132, 191
Arcadia, 168
archaeology, 164, 184, 193
Arctic, 10, 17, 133, 174–176, 178, 193, 200
Argosy, 77, 111, 201
Argosy All-Story, 201
Armageddon, 60
armaments race, 50
Arnold, Edwin Lester, 35, 36, 219
Around the Moon, 201
Around the World in Eighty Days, 163, 165
Arthur, Chester A., 8
Arthur Mervyn, 3
Artificial Mother, 147
Aryan race, 27, 49, 74, 104, 180, 191, 216
Asia, 27, 49, 53, 54, 59, 62, 69, 73–78, 132, 135–136, 140, 164, 180, 184, 190–192, 197, 198
Asimov, Isaac, 15
"Assignation, The," 22
Astayanax, 185
Astor, John Jacob, 205–206
Astronomy with an Opera Glass, 213
Atavar: The Dream Dancer, 43
atavism, 43, 186, 187, 192
Atherton, Gertrude, 143
Atlantic Monthly, The, 4, 10, 22, 24, 25, 83, 159, 199, 200, 204

Atlantis, 36, 115, 157, 163–164, 178–179, 185–186
Atlantis: The Antedeluvian World, 185
Atman: The Documents in a Strange Case, 39
atomic energy, 53, 57, 58, 65, 66, 128–130, 214, 218
Atterley, Joseph (pseud. George Tucker), 197–198
At the Earth's Core, 190
At the Queen's Mercy, 180
Atwood, Margaret, 166, 167
Aubrey, Frank, 179, 187
Aurifodina, 162
Austin, F. Britten, 33–34, 73
Austin, William, 20
Australia, 95, 119
Avenging Ray, The, 51, 53, 68, 72, 93–94, 124
Awakening of Noahville, The, 110
"Ayesha, She-Who-Must-Be-Obeyed," 164–168, 176, 221
Ayesha: The Return of She, 165
Aztec Treasure House, The, 177

Bachellor, Irving, 40–41
Bachelor Girl, The, 142
Bacillus of Beauty, The, 142–143
Bacon, Sir Francis, 3
Bailey, J.O., 104, 132, 157, 158
Balch, Frank, 178
Ball, Sir Robert, 10
Ballantine Books, 188
Ballou, William Hosea, 142
Balmer, Edwin, 42, 132
Banzai!, 72
barbarism, 113, 120–122, 126–127, 130, 221
"Bard, The," 15
Barnes, James, 57
Barney, J. Stewart, 62–63
Barr, Robert, 118
Barton, Samuel, 55
Bashore, Harvey B., 10
Battle for the Pacific, The, 72
Battle of Dorking, The, 49, 50, 56, 211

Battle of the Swash, The, 55
Beadle and Adams, 91
"Beast in the Jungle, The," 29
Beatty, John, 184
Beeding, Francis, 73
Before Adam, 186
Before the Dawn, 187
Behaviorists, 16
Bell, Alexander Graham, 7
Bell, Eric Temple, 129, 187, 191
Bellamy, Edward, 40, 69, 103, 105, 169
Benet, Stephen Vincent, 132
Benjamin, Park, 58, 59
Bennet, Robert Ames, 175, 180–181
Beowulf, 52
Beresford, J.D., 35, 140
Beresford, Leslie, 138
Bergerac, Cyrano de, 199
Besant, Walter, 136–137
Bess, 165
Bessemer, Henry, 111–112
Bessemer steel, 7, 8, 111–112
Between the Dark and the Daylight, 32
Beyond the Great Oblivion, 126–127
Beyond the Great South Wall, 170–171
Big Change, The, 7, 106
Bigly, Cantell A., 162
Bierbower, Austin, 185–186
Bierce, Ambrose, 24, 25–28, 32–33, 38–39, 82–83, 98, 186
"Bietigham", 67–68
Billion Year Spree, 3
Bingham, Hiram, 10
Birkhead, Edith, 3
Biron, H.C., 165
"Birthmark, The," 22–23
"Black Cat, The," 22
Black Cat, The, 22
"Black Dog, A Night of Spectral Terror," 33
Black Oxen, 143
blacks, 42, 55, 77, 105, 141, 179, 180
Blackwood, John, 50, 136

Blackwood's Magazine, 3, 16, 20, 21, 22, 25, 50, 71, 199
Blake of the "Rattlesnake", 50
Blanchard, H. Percy, 117–118
Blavatsky, Madame, 109
Bleiler, E.F., 90–92, 164
Bleuler, Eugen, 44
Blithedale Romance, The, 23
Blodgett, Mabel Fuller, 180
Blot, Thomas, 109
Blue Book, 188, 193
"Boarded Window, The," 25
Boer War, 51
Bohr, Neils, 5
"Bolted Door, The," 34
Bolton, Charles E., 111–112
Bond, James (Agent 007), 77
Bonner, Richard, 93
Bonwill, W.G.A., 4
Book of Algoonah, The, 184
Boston, 7, 67, 76
Boucicault, Dion, 138
Bouve, Edward T., 173
Bowl of Baal, The, 180–181
"Bowman, The," 52
Boy Inventors and the Diving Torpedo Boat, The, 93
Boy Inventors' Flying Ship, 93–94
Boy Inventors' Vanishing Gun, The, 93
Boy Inventors' Wireless Triumph, The, 93
boys series books, 67, 91–101, 216–217
Bradford, Columbus, 151
Bradshaw, William, 168, 171–173
Brasil, 157
Brave New World, 104, 106, 129, 131
"Brick Moon, The," 199–201
Bridge of Time, The, 184
Brigands of the Moon, 202
Brinsmade, Herman Hines, 108
Brooks, Byron, 108
Brown, Charles Brockden, 3, 16, 18–20, 38, 81
Brown, Joseph M., 185
Bruere, Martha Bensley, 148–149

Brush, Charles F., 8
Bryce, Lloyd, 69
Buffon, Count George, 157
Burdick, Eugene, 68
Burgoyne, Alan H., 50
Burland, Harris, 175
burlesque, 22
Burroughs, Edgar Rice, 36, 188–
    190, 193, 200, 208, 219, 220.
    See also specific titles
"By the Water of Babylon," 132
Bywater, Hector, 73, 76

Caesar's Column, 105
Cairnes, Captain, 50–51
Camberwell Miracle, The, 35
Campbell, John, 15
Camperdown, 141
Canada, 50, 55–57, 70, 75–76, 108,
    144, 181
Candide, 157
Can Such Things Be?, 25
capitalism, 56, 74, 105, 107, 111–
    112, 120–122, 127, 134, 217
Captain Jinks: Hero, 55
Captain of the "Mary Rose," The,
    50
Captain Singleton, 157
Carnegie, Andrew, 7, 57
Carruth, Hayden, 95, 109
Carter, Everett, 81
"Case of Metaphantasmia, A," 32
Case of Summerfield, The, 84–85,
    113
Casey, Patrick and Terence, 180
"Cask of Amontillado, The," 22
Casparian, Gregory, 61
Cast Away at the Pole, 176
Castaways of the Year 2000, 111
Castle of Otranto, The, 16
Cat and the Curate, The, 150–151
catastrophe motif, 33, 72, 84, 85,
    89–90, 112–132, 191
Catt, Mrs. Carrie Chapman, 151
Caucasian (race), 113, 132, 191. *See
    also* Aryan race
"Cave Boy, The," 186
Cave Girl, The, 190

cavemen, 181, 185–188
Caxton's Book, 84
Centaurus, 222
Central America, 55, 75, 119, 177
Centuries Apart, 173–174
*Certainty of a Future Life on Mars,
    The*, 208–209
Chalk Face, 44
Chambers, Julius, 179
Chambers, Robert W., 41, 144–148,
    153
Chapman, S.E., 95
Chappell, George S., 190
Chappelle, Abbe de la, 19
Charcot, J.M., 34
Chase, Herbert E., 35
Chavannes, Albert, 108
Chesney, Sir George Tomkyns, 45,
    56, 78
Chessmen of Mars, The, 220
Chester, George Randolph, 110,
    176–177
Chester, William L., 193
Chesterton, G.K., 103
Chicago, 8, 11, 92, 103, 125, 126,
    136
Chicago *Tribune*, 76
Chicago World's Columbian Exposi-
    tion, 6, 8, 9
Childers, Erskine, 77
"Children of Tomorrow," 77
China, 49, 69–75
Christ-figure, 40, 41, 74, 107, 128–
    129
Christianity, 5, 15, 18, 24, 37, 39–
    41, 107–108, 115, 118, 128–129,
    132, 177–178, 203, 206–208
Christian Science, 35
Clark, P., 159
Clarke, Arthur C., 222
Clarke, I.F., 4, 49, 51, 52, 54, 59,
    103, 127, 132
Cleveland, Grover, 8
"Cliffs at Rugen, The," 15
Climbing Doom, The, 179
Clowes, Sir William Laird, 50
Cobb, Weldon, J., 92, 217
Coffin, Charles A., 9

Cohen, Morton, 164, 167
Colburn, Frona Eunice Wait, 184
Cole, Robert William, 113, 211–213
Colerdige, Samuel Taylor, 158
Collier, John, 72, 150
Collier's Weekly, 56
Collins, Wilkie, 24, 38, 98
Colomb, Admiral Philip, 50
Columbus of Space, A, 218–219, 221
comet, 52, 113, 152, 210
Coming of the Amazons, The, 151–152
Coming Waterloo, The, 50
Commager, Henry Steele, 4, 6, 7, 9, 203
communism, 75, 132, 136, 169, 204
Connecticut Yankee in King Arthur's Court, A, 110
Connington, J.J. (pseud. Alfred Walter Stewart), 127–128
Conquest of America, The, 67–68
Conquest of the Moon, The, 208
coquette, 138, 179
Conrad, Joseph, 221
Converse, Frank H., 178
Cook, Dr. Frederick A., 10
Cook, William Wallace, 95, 110, 176, 217
Copernicus, 197
Copley, Frank Barkley, 133
Corelli, Marie, 143
corporations. *See* trusts
Cory, Charles B., 33
Cosmic Philosophy, 5, 202
cosmic voyage, 36, 121, 197
Cosmopolitan, 22, 42, 43, 71, 96, 110, 144–145, 176, 188, 204, 213
Costello, Peter, 163–165
Coverdale, Henry Standish, 55, 105
Cowan, Frank, 169–170
Cox, Erle, 185
Crane, Stephen, 11, 33
Crane, William Ward, 49, 58
Creationism, 5
Crittenden, Marriott, 179
"Crocodile Island," 21, 22
Cromie, Robert, 50, 51, 178, 205

Crosby, Ernest, 55
Cross, Victoria, 136, 138–139
Cruger, Mary, 39
Cruise of the Kawa, 190
Cruso, Solomon, 73–74
Crystal Age, A, 103
Crystal Button, The, 107–108
Cummings, Ray, 84, 130, 192, 202
Cummins, Harle Owen, 33
Curie, Marie and Pierre, 5, 88
Czar Nicolas, 124, 214

Dail, C.C., 184
Dake, Charles Romyn, 161
"Damned Thing, The," 83
"Danger," 51
Dark River, The, 192
"Darkest Africa," 11
Darkness and Dawn, 125–127
"Dark Thing at Hatchet Lake, The," 33
Darwin, Charles, 5, 128, 200
Darwin, Erasmus, 3, 19
Darwinian theory, 4, 16, 97, 173, 191
"Darwinism and Divinity," 4
Dash at the Pole, A, 176
Davidson, Edward H., 159, 160
Davis, Richard Harding, 37
Day of the Brown Horde, The, 186–187
Day of the Triffids, The, 127
Daybreak, 203, 208
Death Maker, The, 90
Debs, Eugene V., 106
"Debt, The," 97–98
DeCamp, Etta, 37
Decimon Huydas, 109
Defoe, Daniel, 157
DeForest, John, 81
"DeGrey: A Romance," 25
Delaney, Samuel R., 106–107
DeMille, James, 171–172
DeMorgan, John, 165
DeQuatrefages, A., 4
"Devil and Tom Walker, The," 20
Devil's Dictionary, The, 27
Devil Tree of El Dorado, The, 187

"Diamond Lens, The," 83–84
Dian of the Lost Land, 192
Dibdin, Charles, 157
Discoveries of . . . Guiana, The, 178
"Discoveries in the Moon . . . Herschel," 199
Dixon, Thomas, 67
Doc Savage, 185
Dr. Heidenhoff's Process, 40
Doctor Huguet, 42
Doctor Jones' Picnic, 95
Dr. Thorne's Idea, 114
"Dolbaden Castle, North Wales," 15
"Dolph Heyliger," 20
Donnelly, Ignatius, 42, 55, 105, 108, 169, 185
"Doom of London, The," 118
Doomsman, The, 115–117
Dooner, Pierton W., 69
doppelgänger, 16, 22
Dorrington, Albert, 96
Double Life, A, 35
Doyle, Sir Arthur Conan, 10, 24, 34, 51, 127, 185, 187, 192
Drayton, Henry S., 177
dream, 6, 17, 26, 36, 40, 42–43, 69, 70, 82, 99, 103, 107, 109, 110, 132, 133, 221
Dream Doctor, The, 42–43
Dream of Conquest, A, 69
Dream of John Ball, The, 103
Dreiser, Theodore, 4, 11, 105
Drowsy, 115
drugs, 36, 38, 135, 165, 185
dual personality. *See* multiple personality
Dunn, Waldo Hilary, 184
Dusty Ayres and His Battle Birds, 77
Dwellers in the Mirage, 190
Dwyer, James Francis, 180
Dynamite Ship, The, 55
dynamo, 9, 117
dystopia, 69, 104, 106, 128–129, 185

Eads, Captain James Buchanan, 7–8
Earth Revisited, 108

earth satellite, 199
"Earth's Hot Center, The," 84
Earth-Tube, The, 75
Easter Island, 180
Edison, Thomas A., 8, 9, 58, 59, 68, 96, 118, 123, 213–216, 217
Edison's Conquest of Mars, 213–216, 218
Edson, Milan C., 108
Egbert, H.M. (pseud. Victor Rousseau Emanuel), 129
Egypt, 124, 137, 165, 191, 216
Egyptology, 124, 137, 184, 216
Eighth Wonder, The, 95
Einstein, Albert, 5
El Dorado, 157, 164, 168, 184
El Dorado, 178
electricity, 6, 8, 9, 17, 23, 35, 40, 41, 55, 58, 62–64, 71, 72, 83, 86, 88, 89, 92, 95–96, 98, 112, 117, 172, 209, 210, 211, 214
Elizabethan age, 16, 36
Ellis, Edward S., 91
Ellis, Peter Berresford, 167
Ellsburg, Commander Edward, 130
Elsie Venner, 24, 33
Emerson, Ralph Waldo, 177
Emperor Jones, The, 27
Empire of the World, 50
Encyclopedia Britannica Macropaedia, 204
"End of New York, The," 49, 58
England, George Allan, 63, 105, 122, 125
Enlightenment, 4, 15
Enton, Harry, 91, 92
"Epidemic Delusions," 5
erotic, 180, 181, 190, 212, 218. *See also* sexuality
Eternal Lover, The, 36, 290
Etidorhpa, 177, 178
eugenics, 130, 147, 148
Eureka, 159
Evacuation of England, The, 119
L'Eve Future, 8
evolution, 4, 97, 177–178, 200, 203, 207, 215
existential confrontation, 5

"Eyes, The," 34
"Eyes of the Panther, The," 26

Fabian Socialists, 105
Face in the Abyss, The, 190
"Facts in the Case of M. Valdemar,
    The," 23, 81
Fail-Safe, 68
Fairman, Henry Clay, 174
Fall of the Nation, The, 22
"Fanciful Predictions of War," 49
fantasy, 38, 39, 44, 77, 82, 83,
    115, 141–142, 160, 164, 192, 221
fascism, 74, 76, 136
Faustus, 16, 17, 19, 85
Fawcett, Colonel P.H., 178
Fawcett, E. Douglas, 51
Fawcett, Edgar, 36
fear (as motivation), 27, 32, 33, 45,
    132
femme fatale, 137
Fezandie, Clement, 95
Fiction Magazine, 58
Field, Marshall, 8
Final War, The, 51, 53
First American King, The, 108
"First Days of the World, The," 10
First International Congress of Mon-
    ists, 4
First Men in the Moon, The, 201
Fiske, John, 4, 5, 10, 202, 203
*Five Hundred Million of the Begum,
    The*, 92
Five Weeks in a Balloon, 163
Flame, The, 52
Flammarion, Camille, 203
Flying Aces, 77
Flying Dutchman, 159
"Flying Machine, The," 10
Food of the Gods, The, 104
"Fool and His Joke, The," 33
Forbes, Allan B., 6
Ford, Henry, 9, 65
For England's Sake, 50
Forever War, The, 113
Foul Play, 138
France, 50, 51, 53, 55 63, 131,
    135, 205, 211

Franco-Prussian War, 50
Frank, Frederick S., 16
Frank Merriwell, 92
*Frank Reade, Jr.'s Great Electric
    Tricycle*, 92
Frank Reade Library, The, 91–92
Frank, Waldo, 44
Frankenstein, 3, 16–18, 81
Frankenstein motif, 37, 45, 85, 137,
    143
Franklin, Edgar, 95
Franklin, Sir John, 174
Freeland, 103
Freud, Sigmund, 16, 24, 30, 42–44
Freudian theory, 30, 42–45
Friedrich, Caspar David, 15
From Monkey to Man, 185–186
From the Earth to the Moon, 201
frontier. *See* American west
Full Circle, 72
Fuller, Alvarado M., 112, 125
Fuller, Sam, 152
Future as History, The, 104, 129
future history, 54, 61, 68, 69, 74,
    77, 108, 114–118, 141, 200, 213
future war motif, 49–80, 108, 113–
    114, 192, 205, 212

Gabriel over the White House, 135
gadgets, 82–100, 217. *See also*
    technology
Galatea, 143
Galaxy, 25
Galileo, 197
Galle, Johann Gottfried, 202
gangsters, 130, 134–135
Gann, W.D., 73
Ganpat (pseud. Martin Louis Alan
    Gompertz), 191
Garland, Hamlin, 24, 34
Garnett, David, 150
Gary, Judge Elbert H., 9
Gawain, Edward (pseud. Edward
    Penray), 74
Gay Rebellion, The, 147–148
G-8 and His Battle Aces, 77, 90
General Electric, 8, 9
genetics, 5, 129, 181, 185, 191

genocide, 73–74
geology, 119, 125, 132, 163, 164, 169
Germany, 50–58, 60, 67, 72, 73, 133
germ warfare, 70
Gernsback, Hugo, 7, 82, 100–101, 192
Geyserland, 175
Ghost of Guy Thyrle, The, 36–37
ghost story, 21, 24–33, 82
"Ghostly Rental, The," 25
G.H.P. (pseud. George Haven Putnam), 142
Gibbons, Floyd, 75
Giesy, J.U., 72
Gilded Age, The, 81
Gilded Man, The, 179
Gillmore, Inez Haynes, 181–183, 184
Gilman, Charlotte Perkins, 181, 183, 184
Gilson, Charles, 150
Girl Aviators and the Phantom Airship, The, 94–95
Girl Aviators' series, 94
Girl in the Golden Atom, The, 192
"Girl in the Moon, The," 201
Givins, Robert C., 95
"Glamour of the Arctic, The," 10
Gleig, Charles, 51
Glory of Egypt, The, 191
Glossop, Captain (pseud.), 72
Goddess of Atvatabar, The, 168, 171–173
Godfrey, Hollis, 63, 90
Gods of Mars, The, 220
Godwin, Francis, 3, 197
Golden Age of Patents, The, 109
Golden Blight, The, 105
Golden Bottle, The, 105, 108
Golding, William, 193
Goldsmith, John F., 136
Gold Tooth, The, 191
Golem, 82
Gompertz, Martin Louis Alan, 191
Goslings, The, 140–141
Gothic, 3, 15–25, 83

Gothic novel, 3, 15, 34, 107
Gove, Philip Babcock, 157
Graham, Tom (pseud. Sinclair Lewis), 95
Grant, James Augustus, 164
Grant, Robert, 55
Grant, Ulysses S., 54
Gratacap, Louis, 119, 175, 186, 208–209
Graves, C.L., 213
Grautoff, Ferdinand Heinrich, 72
Gray, Asa, 10
Great Britain, 50–63, 73, 103, 119, 135, 136, 164
Great Depression, 106, 134
Greatest Adventure, The, 191
Great Exhibition of 1851, 6
"Great Good Place, The," 29
Great Naval War of 1887, The, 50
Great Pacific War, The, 73
Great Stone of Sardis, The, 96–97
"Great War, The." *See* World War I
Great War of 189-, The, 50
Great War Syndicate, The, 56–57, 97
Great War with England on 1897, The, 50
Great Weather Syndicate, The, 53–57, 137–138
Great White Way, The, 175
Green and Red Planet, The, 204
Green Fire, 129–130
Green Mouse, The, 145–146
"Green Tea," 24
Greer, Tom, 51
Greg, Percy, 168, 204–205
Griffith, George, 52, 53, 137, 202, 205
Griffith, Mary, 141
Grosset & Dunlap, 93
Guadalcanal, 221–222
Gulliver, Lemuel, 192
Gulliver's Travels, 4

Hackett, General John, 78
Haeckel, Ernst, 5
Haggard, Sir H. Rider, 161, 164–

169, 176, 180, 184, 187, 190,
    193, 205, 219
Haldeman, Joe, 113
Hale, Everett Edward, 199–201
Hall, Asaph, 202
Halley's Comet, 89, 202
hallucination, 18–19, 23–29, 34, 38,
    44
Hamilton, John B., 81
Hampden Magazine, 147
Hancock, H. Irving, 67
Hannah Hewit, 157
Hannibal's Man, 35
Harilek, 191
Harper, Vincent, 41
Harper's Monthly Magazine, 10
Harris-Ingram Experiment, The,
    111–112
Hartmann the Anarchist, 51
Hastings, George Gordon, 108
Hatfield, Richard, 175
Hatton, Joseph, 178
Hawaii, 59, 64, 73
Hawk of the Wilderness, 193
Hawkes, Jacquetta, 193
Hawthorne, Julian, 110, 167–168
Hawthorne, Nathaniel, 16, 21, 22–
    23, 25, 84
Hay, William Delisle, 104
Hayes, Rutherford B., 54
He: A Companion to She, 165
Heart of Darkness, 221
Heinlein, Robert A., 15
Herland, 181
Hermann, Louis, 192
Herodotus, 157
Heroic fantasy, 221
Herrick, Robert, 132
Hertzka, Theodor, 103
Hicks, Francis, 197
Hidden Kingdom, The, 73
Hidden Valley, The, 184
Hike and the Aeroplane, 95
Hillegas, Mark, 92, 103, 109, 129
Hilliers, Ashton, 187
Hilton, James, 166, 191
Hilzinger, J.G., 184
His First Million Women, 152

His Monkey Wife, 150
His Wisdom, the Defender, 61–62,
    68
Hitler, Adolph, 77
Hobson, Captain Richard Pearson,
    71
Hodge, Charles, 4
Hogg, James, 21
Holberg, Ludwig, 3
"Hollow of the Three Hills, The,"
    23
Holmes, Oliver Wendell, 24, 33
Holt-White, W., 51, 54
"Holy Terror, A," 25
Home Efficiency, 149
Honeymoon in Space, A, 205
"Horla, Le," 83
horror, 16, 20–21, 29, 77, 90, 194,
    203, 213
Hothouse World, The, 130
House, Edward, M., 133
House of Beadle and Adams, 91
House of the Seven Gables, The, 23,
    25
Howard, Robert E., 185, 221
Howells, William Dean, 5, 32, 33,
    39, 148, 211
"How I Found Dr. Livingstone," 11
"How I Overcame My Gravity," 82
Hudson, W.H., 103, 112
Huge Hunter, The, 91
humor, 20, 95. *See also* parody
Huxley, Aldous, 104, 129, 131, 185
Hyne, Cutcliffe, 50, 185
Hyperaesthesia, 39–40
hypnotism, 23, 36–37, 40–42, 82,
    107, 131, 207

"If War Should Come," 71, 72
Ilian: A Psychological Tale . . ., 32
imaginary kingdoms, 157, 178
imaginary presidents, 61, 106, 120,
    133–136
*Imaginary Voyage in Prose Fiction,
    The*, 157
imaginary voyage motif, 113, 153,
    157–222

imaginary wars. *See* future war
  motif
immigration, 11, 105
Immortal Girl, The, 143
*Impeachment of President Israels,
  The*, 133
imperialism, 55, 67, 78, 171–172
In Brighter Climes, 108
Incubated Girl, The, 137
Indian Scout, The, 162
industrialization, 6, 7, 9, 11, 81,
  103, 105, 106
"Infernal Machine, The," 33
Inheritors, The, 193
inner world, 3, 161, 163, 171–173,
  190, 217
In Oudemon, 177
In Search of an Unknown Race, 178
In Search of the Unknown, 144–145
INTELSTAT, 4
interplanetary voyage motif, 197–
  224
In the Beginning, 187
"In the China Sea," 73
In the Days of the Comet, 73
In the Dwellings of the Wilderness,
  184
In the Midst of Life, 25
In the Morning of Time, 186
In the Sealed Cave, 192
Invasion, 76
Invasion of New York, The, 59
"Invasion of the United States,
  The," (juvenile series), 67
Invisible Man, The, 86
Ireland, 51, 55, 57, 108
Iron Heel, The, 63, 120–121
"Iron Shroud, The," 22
Iron Star, The, 191
Irving, Washington, 20, 84
Irwin, Wallace, 176
"Is Electricity Life?," 4
"Is the Airship Coming?," 10
Island of Doctor Death, 193–194
Island of Dr. Moreau, 86
Isle of Dead Ships, The, 179
Isle of Virgins, The, 179
It, 165

It Can't Happen Here, 76, 134
It Never Could Happen, 134

Jacobean age, 16
James, G.P.R., 116
James, Henry, 24–25, 28–34, 38–
  39, 148
James, Henry, Sr., 10, 24
James, William, 24, 33, 34
Jameson, Dr. L.S., 53
Jane, Fred T., 50, 137
Janvier, Thomas A., 177
Japan, 49, 59, 60, 64, 70–75, 78,
  95, 135
Jeannette, 174
Jeffries, Richard, 103, 112
Jenney, William Le Baron, 8
Jews, 73–74, 82
Jingo, The, 176–177
"John Inglesant," 168
Johnson, George L., 34
Johnson, Owen, 151–152
Journey in Other Worlds, A, 205–
  206
Journey to Mars, 203, 206–208, 219
*Journey to the Center of the Earth,
  A*, 163
*Journey to the World Under-
  Ground, A*, 3
Journey to Venus, 208
"June 1993," 110
Jung, Carl, 24, 43, 44
Jungle Girl, The, 190
Jupiter, 205

Kaiser Wilhelm, 52–54, 62–65, 124,
  137, 214
Kaloolah, 161–162, 165, 169
Kane, Chaplain James J., 38
Kelly, Paul, 202
Kennedy, J.P., 21
Kenton, Edna, 30
Kepler, Johannes, 4, 197
King Arthur, 52
Kingdom of Prester John, 157, 164
King in Yellow, The, 144
Kinglake, A.W., 50
King's Men, The, 55

King of Kor, The, 165
King Solomon's Mines, 164–167
King Solomon's Treasures, 165
King Solomon's Wives, 165
Kioga of the Unknown Land, 193
Kioga of the Wilderness, 193
Kip, Leonard, 35
Kipling, Rudyard, 168, 180
Kirk, Hyland C., 109
Kline, Otis Adelbert, 202, 220
Knights of Labor, 105
Knowlton, J.A., 184
Knox, Ronald A., 141
Kontrol, 90
Krupp, Frederick, 111

labor movement, 105, 111–112,
    117, 122
Labour Party, 105
Lady into Fox, 150
Lake, Henry, 4
Lake of Gold, The, 54
Lamarre, Joseph, 150
Lamb, Harold, 191
Land of Flies, 106
Landis, S.M., 108
Land of the Mist, The, 35
Lane, Mary E. Bradley, 181
Lang, Andrew, 165
Langley, Samuel P., 10
Last American, The, 114–115
Last Days of the Republic, 69
Last Man, The, 3, 112
Last of the Incas, 163
Last of the Japs and the Jews, The,
    73–74
"Last of the Valerii, The," 28–29
Laurie, Andre, 208
Leakey, Mary and Louis, 185
Leeuwenhoek, Anton van, 83
LeFanu, Joseph Sheridan, 24
"Legend of Sleepy Hollow, The,"
    20
Leinster, Murray, 77
Lemuria, 151
Lentala of the South Seas, 183–184
Le Plongeon, Augustus, 177
LeQueux, William, 50, 137

Leverrier, Urbain-Jean-Joseph, 202
Lewis, Sinclair, 79, 95, 134
Lewis, W.G., "Monk," 16
Lick Observatory, 123, 203
Lieut. Gullivar Jones, 219
"Life in Death," 22
"Life in the Brick Moon," 200–201
"Ligeia," 22
Lilith, 184
Lippincott's Magazine, 10, 37, 49
literary naturalism, 5, 115, 144,
    167, 168, 190, 211
literary realism, 5, 25, 144, 167,
    168, 190, 192
Livingstone, David, 11, 164
Llana of Gathol, 220
Lloyd, John Uri, 177–178
Locke, John, 15
Locke, Richard Adams, 199
Loeb, Jacques, 4
London, 50–55, 118, 127, 137, 163,
    165, 211–213
London *Evening News*, 52
London, Jack, 11, 36, 50, 70, 98,
    105, 113, 119–122, 132, 144,
    186, 221–222
London Magazine, 120
Lone Eagle, The, 77
Looking Backward, 69, 103, 105
Looking Further Backward, 69
"Loss of Breath," 21
Lost Canyon of the Toltecs, The,
    177
Lost Continent, The, 185
Lost Horizon, 166, 191
lost race motif, 110, 157–194
"Lost Room, The," 83
Lost World, The, 187
Lovell, Ernest J., 15
love story (as plotline), 71–72, 100–
    101, 111–113, 116–117, 126–127,
    130, 146–147, 163, 170–174,
    176–178, 183–184, 201
Lowell, Percival, 10, 204, 209–210
L.P.M.: The End of the Great War,
    62–63
Lucas, Anthony F., 9
Lucas, E.V., 213

Lucian, 3, 197
Lupoff, Richard, 219
Lyell, Sir Charles, 5
Lysistrata, 148, 151, 152
Lytton, Lord Edward Bulwer, 50, 168, 207

Ma, 165
Mabbott, Thomas, O., 21
Macaulay, Rose, 192
McAllister, Ward, 108
McBride, James, 158
McClure's Magazine, 10, 67, 118
MacDonald, Raymond, 87–88
MacHarg, William, 42
Machen, Arthur, 52
Machu Picchu, 10
MacIsaac, Fred, 130
Mackay, Donald, 55
McKesson, Charles L., 179
McMasters, William H., 133
Madden, Samuel, 4
mad scientist, 63, 73, 81–90
Mad Scientist, The, 87–88
madness, 17, 19–22, 25–26, 33–34, 39, 43–44, 152
Magill, Frank, 163
Maker of Moons, The, 144
Making the Stand for Old Glory, 67
"Man and the Snake, The," 26–27, 186
Manatitlans, The, 169
Man from Mars, The, 109
Manifest Destiny, 55
Man in the Moone, The, 3, 197
Manless World, A, 141–142
mannikin. *See* robot
Manson, Marsden, 71
Man Who Ended War, The, 63–64, 90
Man Who Mastered Time, The, 192
Man Who Rocked the Earth, The, 65
Man Who Stole the Earth, The, 51–52, 54
"Man Who Was Not Afraid, The," 33
"MS Found in a Bottle," 159
Maracot Deep, The, 185

Marble Faun, The, 25
Marching Sands, 192
Marconi, Marchese Gugliemo, 9
Marie Celeste, 98
Mariner space probes, 204
marriage, 54, 138, 147, 162, 179, 204–205
Mars, 10, 84, 168, 202–205, 209–211, 215, 218, 219
Mars, 204
Marshall, Edison, 187, 192
Marshall, S.J., 165
Martha Brown, M.P., 136, 138–140
Martian controversy, 202, 210, 215
Martin, John, 15
Marx, Karl, 128
Marxism, 106
Master-Girl, The, 187
Master-Knot of Human Fate, The, 115
Master of Silence, The, 40
Mastin, John, 202
Maturin, Charles, 16
"Maud Evelyn," 29–30
Maupassant, Guy de, 83
Maupertis, Pierre Louis Moreau de, 157
Maxim, Hudson, 11
Mayo, W.S., 161, 169
Maza of the Moon, 202
medical doctor, 19, 24, 27–28, 34, 39, 40, 95, 142–143
medieval, 25, 26, 103, 110
Melmoth the Wanderer, 16
Melville, Herman, 162, 165
Memoirs of the Twentieth Century, 4
Memories of the Future, 141
Mendel, Gregor Johann, 128
Menlo Park, 8
Mercury, 217
Meredith, Ellis, 115
Merritt, A., 82, 190–191
mesmerism. *See* hypnotism
Messiah of the Cylinder, The, 128–129, 131
Metal Monster, The, 190
"Metzengerstein," 22
Mexico, 72, 76

"Middle Toe of the Right Foot,
  The," 26
Mildred Carver, U.S.A., 148–149
Minor, John W. (pseud.), 67, 68
miscegenation, 69, 76, 188
Missing: A Romance, 179
*Mr. Hawkins' Humorous Adven-
  tures*, 95
"Mr. X" (pseud.), 133
Mitchell, J.A., 114–115
Mitchell, J. Leslie, 185
Mizora: A Prophecy, 181
Modern Daedalus, A, 51
Modern Utopia, A, 103
Moffett, Cleveland, 10, 44, 67–68,
  149–150
Moncrief, George, 50
Monroe Doctrine, 67, 72
Montezuma's Castle, 33
Montgomery, Frances T., 217
"Moonlit Road, The," 28
Moon Maid, The, 201–202
"Moon Maiden, The," 21
Moon Metal, The, 85–87
Moon Pool, The, 190
More, Sir Thomas, 3, 104
Moresby, Louis, 191
Morgan, J. Pierpont, 106
Morrell, Ed, 36
Morris, Charles, 10
Morris, Gouverneur, 187
Morris, William, 103
Morrow, William C., 183–184
Mortgage on the Brain, The, 41
Moskowitz, Sam, 82, 91, 163, 219
Motor Maids' School Days, The, 94
"Motor Maids' Series," 94
Mott, Laurence, 33
Mound builders, 184, 185
Mudford, William, 22
Mullen, Richard D., 128, 129
multiple personality, 22, 24, 38, 39,
  41–44, 152
Mundo, Otto, 69
Munsey magazines, 188, 191
Mussolini, 74
My Northern Exposure, 190
"Mysterious Bride, The," 21

Mysterious Island, The, 163
Mystery, The, 89, 98–100
Mystery of Evelin Delorme, 41
mysticism. *See* Christianity;
  Theosophy
myth, 17, 18, 52, 59, 60, 106, 107,
  112, 123–125, 127, 150, 162,
  184, 193
mythic heroes, 16, 52, 77, 143,
  162, 193
mythic kingdoms, 157, 211

Napoleon of Notting Hill, The, 103
*Narrative of Arthur Gordon Pym,
  The*, 159–161
Nation, The, 24
nationalism, 50–59, 68, 125
National Sunday Magazine, 67
Natty Bumppo, 162
Nature, 203, 209
naval warfare, 58, 63, 69, 73, 76
Neanderthal man, 126, 164, 192,
  193
negative gravity. *See* Antigravity
Nelson, Arthur A., 180
neoprimitivism, 125, 144, 168
neurology, 35
"New Angle on the Old Pole, A,"
  176
New Atlantis, The, 3
Newcomb, Cyrus, 184
Newcomb, Simon, 10, 61
New Crusade, The, 50–51
New Jerusalem, 106
New Northland, The, 175
"New Theory of the Universe, A,"
  10
New York City, 7, 8, 28, 58, 59,
  67, 72, 78, 83, 85, 88, 92, 95,
  108, 116, 123, 125–127, 132,
  136, 142, 207, 214, 219
New York *Evening Journal*, 213
New York *Herald*, 10, 11
New York *Sun*, 199
New York Times, 10, 115
Next War, The, 54–55
Nicolson, Marjorie, 157, 197
Nihilism. *See* revolution

Nineteen Eighty-Four, 104
1943, 133–134
"Noname" (pseud. Luis P.
    Senarens), 91–92
"Nona Vincent," 29
Nordenholt's Millions, 127–128
Norris, Frank, 11
North, Franklin, 110
Norton, Roy, 52, 54, 64, 71, 113,
    180
"Novel Writing and Novel Read-
    ing," 5
Noyes, Pierrepont B., 131–132

"O" (pseud.), 71
O'Brien, Fitzjames, 24, 82–84, 192
occult, 33, 35, 40, 81
oceanography, 163
Odysseus, 188
Odyssey, The, 157
Ogden's Strange Story, 187
Ohio Archaeological and Historical
    Society Publications, 159
Olga Romanoff, 137
Omega, 203
On a Lark to the Planets, 217
On a Torn-Away World, 216
One Against the Wilderness, 193
O'Neill, Eugene, 27
"One of the Missing," 26
Operator #5, 17
Oriental tale, 16
Orphan Island, 192
Orphan of Space, The, 72
Orwell, George, 104, 129, 185
Osborne, Duffield, 179
Osbourne, Lloyd, 178
O'Sheel, Shaemus, 134
Out of the Silence, 185
"Oval Portrait, The," 22
Owen, Robert Dale, 10

Pa, 165
Pacific, 59, 73, 98, 180, 190, 193,
    198, 208, 221
Pacifico, 73
pagan princesses. *See* women: beau-
    tiful princesses, queens

Pagan's Progress, The, 187
Paine, Albert Bigelow, 41, 175
paleontology, 164
Pallid Giant, The, 131–132
Palmer, John H., 59
Parabellum (pseud. Ferdinand Hein-
    rich Grautoff), 72
Paracelsus, 16
parallel evolution, 202–206, 211,
    215
Paris, 50, 52, 64, 66, 109–110, 213
parody, 21, 41, 51, 52, 87, 176,
    190
Parrish, Randall, 185
Parry, David, 185
Parry, William, 176
Partisan Leader, The, 54
Passion Island, 138
Passion of the Beast, The, 150
pastoral society, 108, 117, 127
Patmore, Coventry, 182
Pattee, Frederick Lewis, 30, 83
Patten, Clinton A., 218
Paul Bunyan, 193
Pearson's Weekly, 205
Peasants' Revolt, 103
Peck, Wallace, 109
Pecos Bill, 193
Penray, Edward, 74
People of the Ruins, The, 72
"Peter Rugg, the Missing Man," 20
Pettersen, Rene Oldsfield, 150
Pfaelser, Jean, 105
Phantom President, The, 134
Pharaoh's Treasure, 184
"Phases in the Life of John
    Pollexfen," 84
Phelps, William Lyon, 176
Philip Dru: Administrator, 133
photography, 11, 84, 94, 96
Phra the Phoenician, 36
Pickering, William, 202–203
Pier, Garrett Chatfield, 184
"Pit and the Pendulum, The," 22
Pithecanthropus, 126, 184
Planck, Max, 5
"Planet Mars, The," 10
Plato, 3, 104, 168

Pliocene. *See* prehistory
Plunge Through Space, A, 205
Poe, Edgar Allan, 15, 20, 21–23, 25, 81, 83, 144, 158–161, 192, 198–199
Poison Belt, The, 127
Police!, 145
Pollock, W.H., 165
Pope, Gustavus W., 203, 206–208, 219
Popular Science Monthly, The, 4, 5
Populist Movement, 57, 105
Possessed, 44, 149–150
"Possibility of Life on Other Worlds, The," 10
"Pot of Tulips, The," 82
"Predicament, A," 21
prehistory, 10, 36, 131, 141, 144, 184–188, 192, 193, 205
Prelude to Prague, 73
President John Smith, 105, 133
President Randolph as I Knew Him, 136
President Vanishes, The, 135
Prince Izon, 202
Princess of Mars, A, 219, 220
Princess Thora, The, 175
Prisoners of Chance, 185
"Professor Hiram Bingham's Report . . . ," 10
prostitution, 139, 140, 151–152
"Psychanalysis, The," 42–43
"Psyche Zenobia, The," 21
psychical research, 24, 34, 36, 37
psychic influence, 145–147, 175
psychoanalysis, 42–43
psychological empiricists, 5, 15, 32
psychology, 16, 18–34, 37, 39, 40, 42, 44, 81, 82, 83
pulp fiction, 77, 128, 131. *See specific titles*
Purple Cloud, The, 112
Putnam, George Haven, 142
Pygmalion, 143

Queen of Atlantis, A, 179
"Queen of Sheba, The," 39

Queen Victoria, 53, 55, 214
Questionable Shapes, 32

race memory, 36, 186
"Race to the North Pole," 10
racism, 42, 54–55, 63, 68, 78, 104, 105, 141, 183–184, 191
Radcliffe, Mrs. Ann, 16, 22, 24
"Radio Detectives," 95
radioactivity, 63–65, 96, 98–100, 179, 202, 217
radium. *See* radioactivity
Radium Terrors, The, 96
railroads, 6, 8, 127, 200
Raines, William MacLeod, 186
Raleigh, Sir Walter, 178
Ralph 124C41 +, 100–101
rape, 152, 189
Reade, Charles, 91, 138
"Real Right Thing, The," 29
Reciprocity, 108
Recovered Continent, The, 69–70
Red Napoleon, The, 75–76
"Red One, The," 120, 221–222
Rees, Arthur R., 44
Reeve, Arthur B., 42, 96
Reign of George VI 1900–1925, The, 4
reincarnation, 35, 36, 184, 186, 201–202, 209, 211
"Relic of the Pliocene, A," 144
Remington, Frederic, 6
Remington Arms Company, 7
Renaissance, 157
Republic, The, 104, 168
Republic Without a President, 133
retribution, 16, 19, 25
Return of Frank Stockton, The, 37
Revi-Lona, 169–170
Revolt, 133
Revolt of Man, The, 136, 137
revolution, 54, 72, 105, 106, 128, 130, 134
Revolution and Other Essays, 70
Reynolds, Jeremiah N., 158, 160
Rhodes, Cecil, 180
Rhodes, William H., 84, 113
Rice, Elmer, 192

Riddle of the Sands, The, 113
"Rime of the Ancient Mariner,
    The," 159
"Rip Van Winkle," 20
Roberts, Charles G.D., 186
Robinsonade, 138, 163
Robinson Crusoe, 157
robots, 82, 110–111, 142
Rock, James, 217
Rockefeller, John D., 7, 8
Rockwood, Roy (pseud.), 216
Roebling, John, 8
Roemer, Kenneth, 107
"Romance of Certain Old Clothes,
    A," 25
romantic love, 41–42, 71, 130–131,
    144–148, 171, 174, 182
Romanticism, 7, 15, 115, 117, 161,
    168
Roosevelt, Theodore, 58
Rose, William Gannon, 92
Round Trip to the Year 2000, A,
    110–111
Rousseau, Victor (pseud. Victor
    Rousseau Emanuel), 128, 130,
    131
Royal, Matthew J., 179
Royce, Josiah, 33
Ruck, Amy Roberta, 143
Rush, Benjamin, 61
Russia, 50–61, 71–73, 75, 205, 211
Rutherford, Ernest, 66

Sacramento *Union,* 84
St. Brendan's Isle, 211
St. Louis World's Fair, 6
Saki (pseud. H.H. Munro), 52
Samurai, 104
San Francisco, 7, 27, 59, 72, 85,
    119, 121, 138
San Francisco *Examiner,* 25
Sarah of the Sahara, 190
Sargasso Sea, 179, 185
Saturday Evening Post, 65
Saturn, 205, 206, 217
Savage, Juanita, 138
Savile, Frank, 170–171
Scarlet Empire, The, 185

Scarlet Letter, The, 23, 25
Scarlet Plague, The, 50, 113, 120–
    122, 132
Schiaparelli, Giovanni, 202, 203
"scientific detective," 42–43
"Scientific Fantasy," 192
"scientific novel," 207
"scientific romance," 119, 163, 207
scientist (as hero), 42–43, 52, 55,
    58, 60–64, 72, 81, 84, 89–90,
    97–101, 120–127, 129, 212–215
Scott, Sir Walter, 174, 208
"Scythe of Time, The," 21
Seaborn, Captain Adam (pseud.
    John Cleves Symmes), 157–158,
    197
Sea Demons, The, 129–130
Sea Girl, The, 130
Seagoing Tank, The, 73
"Sea Raiders, The," 113, 211
"Search for the Last Inca Capital,
    A," 10
Second Deluge, The, 123–125, 132
Secret of the Crater, The, 179–180
"Secret of Macgarger's Gulch,
    The," 26–27
Sedberry, J. Hamilton, 71
seduction, 19, 38, 40, 189
Seekers, The, 35
Senarens, Luis P., 91–92
"Sentinel, The," 222
Seola, 184
Serviss, Garrett P., 86, 122–125,
    132, 192, 201, 204, 213, 218,
    221
Seven Cities of Cibola, 211
sex change, 61
sex roles, 136, 138–139, 151–152,
    179–183, 187
sexuality, 30–32, 34, 38, 43, 44,
    61, 68, 105, 107, 119, 128–129,
    132, 138–139, 140–141, 149–153,
    164–170, 172, 177, 179–182,
    188, 189, 193, 213, 221
Shadow, The, 77
Shadow World, The, 24, 34
Shaler, Nathaniel, 33
Shangri-la, 166, 191

Shanks, Edward, 72
She: A History of Adventure, 164–168
She and Allan, 165
Shearer, W.B., 73
Shelley, Mary, 3, 16–17, 20, 81, 112
Shelley Circle, 17
Sherlock Holmes, 42
Shiel, M.P., 70, 112
Sholes, C. Latham, 7
Short and Truthful History . . . , A, 69
Sibson, Francis H., 72–73, 130–131
Siderius Nuncius, 197
Sidney, Sir Philip, 168
Sign at Six, The, 89–90, 113
Silverberg, Robert, 131
Simak, Clifford D., 109
Sinclair, Upton, 105
"Sir Edmund Orme," 28–29
Sir Galahad, 52
"Skeleton Men of Jupiter," 220
Sky Fighters, 77
Slayer of Souls, The, 145
"Sleep and a Forgetting, A," 39
Small, Austin J., 90
Smile, R. Elton, 169
Smith, Garret, 201
Smith, Mrs. J. Gregory, 184–185
Smith, Titus, 108
Smyth, Clifford, 179
Snell, Edmund, 90
Snell, Roy, 73
social reform, 54, 75, 103–109, 127–128, 133–136, 141
Social War of the Year 1900, The, 108
socialism, 57, 74, 103–109, 127–129, 134, 140–141, 177, 185, 209
Socratic dialogue, 107, 113
"Solarion," 37
Solaris Farm, 108
Some Ladies in Haste, 41–42, 145
Sometime, 132
"Some Unsolved Problems of Astronomy," 10
Somnium, 4, 197

"Sorakachi-Prometheus," 72
"Soul Analysis, The," 43
South America, 44, 61, 75, 82, 93, 119, 138, 164, 169, 177–180, 187, 190, 198, 208
Southern Literary Review, The, 158
"space fiction," 221
space opera, 192, 202, 211
spaceship, 62, 197–198, 211–213, 221
space suit, 214–215
Spain, 55, 58, 59, 61, 71
Spanish-American War, 49, 55
Spanish Civil War, 73, 132
Spectator, The, 15
Spector, Robert Donald, 15
Speke, John Hanning, 164
Speller, Robert and Jane, 184
Spencer, Herbert, 4, 202, 203
Spider, The, 77
spiritualism, 10, 34–35
"Spiritualism New and Old," 10
Spotted Panther, The, 180
Sprague, Frank, 8
Springer, Norman, 192
"Staley Fleming's Hallucination," 26
Stanley, H. M., 11, 164
"Star, The," 73, 113
Stark, Harriet, 142–143
Star Rover, The, 36, 121
Star Wars, 113
Statler, Ellsworth M., 9
Stead, William T., 37
Stephens, John Lloyd, 177
Stevens, Rowan, 72
Stevenson, Lionel, 38
Stevenson, Robert Louis, 38, 164–165, 168
Stockton, Frank, 56–57, 96–97
Stolen Continent, The, 130–131
Stories by American Authors, 58
"Stories of Other Worlds," 205
Stories Revived, 25
Story of Ab, The, 186
Stout, Rex, 135
Strand Magazine, 51

Strange Case of Dr. Jekyll and Mr Hyde, The, 38–39
Strange Case of William Hyde, The, 180
Strange Discovery, A, 161
Strange Manuscript Found in a Copper Cylinder, A, 171
"Strange Markings on Mars, The," 204
Struggle for Empire, The, 113, 211–213
Strughold, Hubert, 204
subatomic universe, 83–84, 192
subconscious, 28, 43, 45, 146
submarine, 51, 56, 58, 63, 92, 124, 163, 172
Submarine Tour, A, 178
"Suitable Surroundings, The," 27
Sullivan, Alan, 187
Sullivan, Mark, 6
supernatural, 3, 21–27, 82
Survivors, The, 130
suspended animation, 36, 72, 100–101, 107, 109, 128–130, 133, 179
Sutphen, Van Tassel, 115–117
Swoop, The, 52
"sword and sorcery," 221
Swords of Mars, 220
Symmes, John Clever, 157–158
Symmes' theory, 159, 198, 199, 207
Symmes' Theory of Concentric Spheres, 158
"Symmes' Theory of the Earth, The," 159
Symzonia: A Voyage of Discovery, 157–159, 197

Tahiti, 157
Taine, John (pseud. Eric Temple Bell), 129, 187, 191
Tale of Terror, The, 3
Tales of a Traveller, 20
Tales of Men and Ghosts, 34, 97
Tales of Soldiers and Civilians, 25
Tales of the Folio Club, The, 21
Tarrano the Conqueror, 192
Tarzan and the Jewels of Opar, 190

Tarzan, Lord Greystoke, 36, 188–190
Tarzan of the Apes, 188–189
Taylor, C. Bryson, 184
technology, 6, 7, 9, 51, 60, 79, 81–101, 104, 109, 181, 185, 201, 208–209, 216
telegraphy (interplanetary), 208–209, 211
telepathy, 40, 98, 127, 211, 219
"Telescopic Eye, The," 84
television, 135, 188
"Tell-Tale Heart, The," 22
terra australis incognita, 157, 211
Terrania, 151
"Terrible Night, A," 82
Terror, The, 52
Tesla, Nikola, 204, 217
Test Tube Baby, 152
Theosophy, 24, 41, 109, 171–172, 208
"Things That Live on Mars, The," 204
Third World, The, 174
Third World War, The, 78
Thirteen, 33
Thirty-nine Articles, 4
Thomas Houston Company, 9
"Though One Rose from the Dead," 32
Thousand Miles an Hour, A, 95
Three Go Back, 185
Three Hundred Years Hence, 141
Threshold of Fear, The, 44–45
Thro' Space, 217
Through Space to Mars, 216
Through the Earth, 95
Thuvia, Maid of Mars, 220
Thyra, 175
Time Machine, The, 104, 211, 212, 219
time travel, 110–111, 130, 136, 185, 192
Tinker, Chauncey, 107–108, 202
Todd, David, 204
Toll of the Sea, The, 180
Tolstoi, Count, 168

To Mars Via the Moon, 209–211, 218
"Tomorrow," 77–78
Tom's A-Cold, 72
Tom Swift, 92–93
Tooker, Richard, 186
"Tough Tussle, A," 27
Tousey, Frank, 91
Tracy, Louis, 51, 53, 60
Train, Arthur, 65
transmigration, 35, 42, 109, 145, 188, 220
Treasure Island, 164
Treasure Train, The, 43
Treasure Vault of Atlantis, The, 185
Trip to Mars, A, 92, 217
True History, 197
trusts, 11, 63, 133, 136, 148
Tucker, Beverly, 54
Tucker, George, 197–199, 204
Tunnel Thru the Air, 73
Turner, J.M.W., 15
"Turn of the Screw, The," 29–32
Twain, Mark, 5, 110, 184, 211
Tweed, Thomas F., 135
Twenty-Fifth Man, The, 36
Twenty Thousand Leagues Under the Sea, 92, 163
Twice Told Tales, 21
"Two Thousand Miles in the Antarctic Ice," 10
Typee, 162

ultimate energy, 89–90, 98–100, 112, 212
ultimated metal, 75, 86, 123, 173, 198, 210
ultimate weapon, 56–57, 73–74
Under Pike's Peak, 179
"Under the Lens," 33–34
Under the Moons of Mars, 188, 219
Under the Sign of the Cross, 71
United States Steel, 9
"Unparalleled Adventures of One Hans Pfaall, The," 198–199
"Uparalleled Invasion, The," 70
Unpardonable War, The, 57–58
Unthinkable, 72–73

urbanization, 6, 9, 103–109, 189
utopia, 62, 69, 103–112, 127, 139, 169–172, 181, 192, 205, 209
Utopia, 3

Vacant World, The, 126
Vanishing Fleets, The, 54, 64–65, 71, 113
Van Loon, Hendrik, 76, 134
Venus, 138, 150, 208, 216, 218, 220
Venus, 150
Venus Girl, The, 138
Vera the Medium, 38
Verne, Jules, 84, 90–92, 161, 163, 178, 180, 192, 201, 209, 219
Verrill, A. Hyatt, 95
Villiers de l'Isle-Adam, Jean, 8
Vinland, 157
Vinton, Arthur Dudley, 69
Voltaire, 157
Voyage to Purilia, A, 192–193
Voyage to the Moon, A, 197–198

Wallace, King, 54–55
Walpole, Horace, 16
Wandering Jew, 16
Ward, Herbert D., 133
War God Walks Again, The, 73
War in the Air, The, 51, 53, 104
Warlord of Mars, The, 220
Warner, William Henry, 184
War of 1938, The, 73
"War of the Purple Gas," 77
War of the Wenuses, The, 213
War of the Worlds, The, 49, 113, 121, 211, 213
Washington, D.C., 119, 134
"Watcher by the Dead, A," 27
Waterloo, Stanley, 35, 36, 60–61, 186
Watson, John B., 16, 24
We, 104, 131
Wells, H.G., 49, 51, 53, 73, 85, 86, 91, 103, 104, 107, 109, 113, 121, 122, 141, 192, 201, 204, 211, 213, 216, 219

*Weird Adventures of Professor De-
    lapine . . . , The*, 34
Weiss, Sara, 109
Welsh Rarebit Tales, 33
Western Front, 52, 66, 77, 90
western frontier. *See* American West
Westinghouse, 9
Weston, George, 152
Wharton, Edith, 34, 97
*What May Happen in the Next
    Ninety Days*, 54
"What Was It?", 83
Wheeler, Harvey, 68
When All Men Starve, 51
When the Sleeper Wakes, 104
When the World Grows Young, 109
When William Came, 52
When Worlds Collide, 132
Whilomville Stories, 33
White, Stewart Edward, 89–90, 98,
    113
White Darkness, The, 33
White King of Manoa, The, 178
"White Tanks, The," 33
White, Thomas W., 21
"Why I Deny Evolution," 4
Wicks, Mark, 209–211, 218
Wieland, 18–20, 23, 81
Wilcox, Ella Wheeler, 68
Wilkes, Lieutenant Charles, 162
William, Francis Howard, 39
"William Wilson," 22
Wilson, Edmund, 30
Wilson, Woodrow, 65, 106
Wings, 77
Wings of Danger, 180
Wisdom's Daughter, 165
Wister, Owen, 6
witchcraft, 6
"Within an Ace of the End of the
    World," 118
Wodehouse, P.G., 52
Wolfe, Gene, 193–194
Wolton, Robert, 69
Woman in White, The, 24
Woman of the Ice Age, A, 186
women: beautiful princesses, queens,
    123–124, 129–130, 137, 138,

    161, 165–166, 171–180, 184,
    185, 190, 191, 201, 207–208,
    212, 219, 220; non–Caucasian,
    161–162, 166, 179, 180–181,
    183–184, 187–188, 191, 192,
    207–208; role in society, 124,
    133, 136–153, 181–182
Wonder, William, 108
"Wondersmith, The," 82
Wood, Robert William, 65
Woolworth, F.W., 7
World Goes Smash, The, 136
World of Women, A, 140–141
world peace, 54, 57, 60, 71
World Peril of 1910, The, 52
World Set Free, The, 5, 104
world state, 62, 70, 74, 105, 128–
    129, 135, 211
World War I, 9, 35, 53, 58–59, 60,
    67–69, 72, 77, 103, 106, 107,
    109, 114, 115, 129, 132, 134,
    144, 145, 148, 177, 184, 216
World War II, 77, 78, 88, 94, 106,
    112, 113
Worts, George F., 134
Wrexham's Romance, 191
Wright, Orville and Wilbur, 9
Wright, S. Fowler, 73
Wylie, Philip, 132, 202
Wyndham, John, 127

Yellow Danger, The, 70
yellow peril, 70–73, 77, 192, 202
Yellow Peril in Action, The, 71
Yellow War, The, 71
Young, Laurence D., 179
Young Diana, The, 143
Yourell, Agnes Bond, 141–142
Yukon, 187

Zagat, Arthur Leo, 77–78
Zalea: A Psychological Episode . . . ,
    34, 37–38
Zamiatin, E., 104, 129, 131, 185
Zeppelin, Count Frederick von, 9
Zola, Emile, 168
Zoonomia, 19
Zoraida, 137

About the Author

THOMAS D. CLARESON, Chairman of the Department of English at the College of Wooster (Ohio), has edited *Extrapolation: A Journal of Science Fiction and Fantasy* since 1959. One of the founders of the Modern Language Association (MLA) Seminar on Science Fiction in 1958, he was also the first president of the Science Fiction Research Association (SFRA) from 1970 to 1976. He is the author of *SF: The Other Side of Realism*, *A Spectrum of Worlds*, *SF Criticism: An Annotated Checklist*, *Robert Silverberg*, and *Robert Silverberg: A Primary and Secondary Bibliography*. He is the editor of *Science Fiction Periodicals, 1926-1978* (Greenwood Press, 1975, 1978), a collection of 20 magazines and one critical journal on microfilm. He has brought together almost 100 important novels to be microformed by Greenwood Press in conjunction with *Science Fiction in America, 1870s-1930s*.